Governing Science and Technology under the International Economic Order

Governing Science and Technology under the International Economic Order

Regulatory Divergence and Convergence in the Age of Megaregionals

Edited by

Shin-yi Peng

Professor of Law, National Tsing Hua University, Taiwan

Han-Wei Liu

Assistant Professor of Law, National Tsing Hua University, Taiwan

Ching-Fu Lin

Assistant Professor of Law, National Tsing Hua University, Taiwan

Edward Elgar
PUBLISHING

Cheltenham, UK • Northampton, MA, USA

Published by
Edward Elgar Publishing Limited
The Lypiatts
15 Lansdown Road
Cheltenham
Glos GL50 2JA
UK

Edward Elgar Publishing, Inc.
William Pratt House
9 Dewey Court
Northampton
Massachusetts 01060
USA

A catalogue record for this book
is available from the British Library

Library of Congress Control Number: 2018931713

This book is available electronically in the **Elgar**online
Law subject collection
DOI 10.4337/9781788115568

MIX
Paper from
responsible sources
FSC® C013056
FSC www.fsc.org

ISBN 978 1 78811 555 1 (cased)
ISBN 978 1 78811 556 8 (eBook)

Typeset by Servis Filmsetting Ltd, Stockport, Cheshire
Printed and bound in Great Britain by TJ International Ltd, Padstow

Contents

PART III ENVIRONMENTAL AND ENERGY POLICY

PART IV FOOD SAFETY AND PUBLIC HEALTH

PART V INTELLECTUAL PROPERTY RIGHTS

Contributors

Won-Mog Choi is a professor of Ewha Law School, Ewha Women's University in Seoul and director of the WTO Law Center, Seoul, South Korea. He was the President of the Korea Society of International Economic Law and is the editor-in-chief of the *Korean Journal of International and Comparative Law* (Brill). Professor Choi is a member of the Editorial Board of many journals including the *Journal of International Economic Law* (Oxford), the *Law and Development Review*, *Indian Journal of International Economic Law*, *Journal of Korea Trade*, and the *Beijing Law Review*. He was a visiting professor or professorial fellow to National University of Singapore, Hong Kong University, University of New South Wales in Sydney, Australia and Southwest University of Political Science and Law, China. He received his legal education in South Korea (Seoul National University, LLB and MPA) and the United States (Georgetown Law, LLM and SJD). Prior to joining the faculty of Ewha, he worked for the Foreign Ministry of South Korea as a diplomat and legal officer in charge of numerous trade issues. After joining academia, Won-Mog has provided law and policy advice to most of the trade negotiations in which South Korea has participated so far. He is also the president of Korea ABS forum. He is widely recognized as a renowned columnist in South Korea, regularly contributing columns on the topics of trade and foreign affairs in major newspapers in South Korea. Among his numerous academic writings, his work on the topics of products in WTO Agreement and his research on FTA issues are widely recognized as authoritative, and the outcome of these researches was recently collected in the *Max Planck Encyclopedia of Public International Law*.

Shujie Feng is Associate Professor at Tsinghua University (Beijing), School of Law and Director of Innovation and Competition Law Center. He is a council member of the China Intellectual Property Research Association, Member of the Editorial Board of French Review of Intellectual Property (RFPI), Chair of the IP working group of French commercial chamber (Beijing and Shanghai). He is Vice-president of the trademark and unfair competition committee of the IP case law center (Beijing) of Chinese National Supreme People's Court. He was Visiting Professor at the University of Milan, Italy; and University of Toulouse I, University

Paris I and University Paris XI, France. He received his SJD and LLM from University Paris I – Panthéon Sorbonne, LLM from Renmin University of China, and LLB from Shandong University (China). He researches, teaches and practices in the areas of trademark, copyright, patent, industrial design, domain name and unfair competition law. He has published more than 50 research articles on intellectual property issues in English, French and Chinese. He is author of the textbook *Trademark Law: Theory and Practice* published in 2017 and is co-author of two textbooks: one on e-commerce law and the other on private international law. He has frequently participated in conferences and been interviewed by CCTV, China Radio International, among others, on intellectual property issues. He is also an invited expert for consultancy of government and courts. He is one of the 50 representative persons for the 50th Anniversary of the Sino-French diplomatic relationship.

Anton Ming-Zhi Gao is Associate Professor at the Institute of Law for Science and Technology at National Tsing Hua University (NTHU). He received a master's degree from the National Taiwan University, where he wrote a thesis on electricity liberalization. In July 2005, he received another master's degree in energy and environmental law (LLM) from the Institute of Environmental and Energy Law of KU Leuven, Belgium. In October 2005 he began a PhD program at KU Leuven, and received his PhD in Law in December 2009. He currently teaches several courses, including energy law and policy and European environmental law. He is the Taiwanese scholar with the greatest number of articles published in international energy and environmental law journals. In recent years, he has been very active in international publications concerning investigations into the legal issues of international, European, Asian, and Taiwanese energy laws.

Branislav Hazucha is Associate Professor at Hokkaido University Graduate School of Law, Japan. His research interests focus on various impacts of intellectual property protection on the development of new information and communication technologies. He has published widely in English and Japanese in leading academic journals (including *Law Quarterly Review* and *Copyright Law Journal*) and edited volumes published by Cambridge University Press, Edward Elgar Publishing, Springer, Routledge and Intersentia. At the moment he publishes a commentary on new Slovak Copyright Law with C.H. Beck. He has previously taught at Kyushu University and Nagoya University, Japan and National Tsing Hua University, Taiwan. Before entering into academia, he practiced law in a top law firm in Slovakia (Cechová & Partners) and worked at the Institute for Approximation of Law at the Office of the Government of the Slovak Republic. He obtained his law degrees in Slovakia (Comenius University and Trnava University), United Kingdom (Oxford University) and Japan (Kyushu University).

Ching-Fu Lin is Assistant Professor of Law at National Tsing Hua University (NTHU), Taiwan, where he teaches international health law, food law and policy, and international law and global governance. Professor Lin received his LLM and SJD from Harvard Law School, USA, with the honor of receiving the John Gallup Laylin Memorial Prize (for best paper in public international law) and Yong K. Kim Memorial Prize (for best paper in East Asian legal studies). He also holds a double degree in law (LLB) and chemical engineering (BS) from National Taiwan University. Before joining NTHU in 2015, Professor Lin served as Visiting Fellow at Graduate Institute of International and Development Studies in Geneva, Switzerland. He was also Peter Barton Hutt Student Fellow at Petrie-Flom Center for Health Law Policy, Biotechnology, and Bioethics as well as Visiting Scholar Coordinator at East Asian Legal Studies Program at Harvard Law School, USA. Active in legal academia, Professor Lin has been invited to lecture in many academic settings, such as Summer Academy in Global Food Law and Policy in Spain, Brescia University School of Law in Italy, and World Food Law Program and the United Nations Food and Agriculture Organization in the United States. His legal scholarship has appeared in numerous journals and edited collections, including *Virginia Journal of International Law*, *Columbia Science and Technology Law Review*, *Food and Drug Law Journal*, and *Journal of World Trade*.

Han-Wei Liu joined the Institute of Law for Science and Technology at National Tsing Hua University, Taiwan, as an Assistant Professor of Law in 2015. He works in the areas of international economic law, international law, global governance, and cyber-law. Prior to entering academia, he practiced with Baker & McKenzie and Russin & Vecchi. Han-Wei earned his PhD, summa cum laude, from the Graduate Institute, Geneva (IHEID)/University of Geneva, Switzerland, where he was awarded full scholarship by the Kathryn Davis Foundation, and his master's degrees from Columbia Law School, USA and Oxford University, UK on a Taiwan Government Scholarship and British Chevening Scholarship, respectively. He also received his LLM and LLB degrees from National Chengchi University, Taiwan. His publications appear in leading international law journals, such as *Journal of International Economic Law* (Oxford University Press), *Journal of World Trade* (Kluwer International), *U.C. Davis Journal of International Law & Policy*, and *Columbia Journal of European Law*. Han-Wei has also presented his works in conferences held by Cambridge University, UK; Duke University, USA; the Graduate

Institute, Geneva, Switzerland; University of Luxembourg; Academia Sinica, Taiwan; and Groningen University, the Netherlands, among others. Han-Wei was formerly a visiting researcher/scholar at Harvard Law School and Columbia Law School, USA and served as a staff editor at *Columbia Journal of European Law*.

Chang-Fa Lo has been Justice of the Constitutional Court of the ROC (Taiwan) since October 2011. Prior to his current judicial position, he was University Chair Professor and Lifetime Distinguished Professor at National Taiwan University (NTU); Dean of NTU College of Law; Director of the Asian Center for WTO and International Health Law and Policy of NTU College of Law (ACWH); Director of Center for Ethics, Law and Society in Biomedicine and Technology of NTU; Commissioner of Taiwan's Fair Trade Commission (in charge of the competition law in Taiwan); Commissioner of Taiwan's International Trade Commission; and legal advisor for Taiwan's GATT/WTO accession negotiations. In his capacity as the Director of ACWH, Professor Lo launched two English-language journals, *Asian Journal of WTO and International Health Law and Policy* and *Contemporary Asia Arbitration Journal* (CAAJ) in 2006 and 2008, respectively. In his capacity as Dean of NTU College of Law, he also launched an English-language journal, *NTU Law Review*. Prior to his teaching career, he practiced law in Taipei. He received his SJD degree from Harvard Law School in 1989. He was appointed by the WTO as a panelist for DS332 *Brazil — Measures Affecting Imports of Retreaded Tyre* in 2006 and for DS468 *Ukraine — Definitive Safeguard Measures on Certain Passenger Cars* in 2014, and as a member of the Permanent Group of Experts under the ASCM in 2008. Since 2013, he has been chairman of the Asia WTO Research Network (AWRN). He received an Outstanding Scholarship Chair Professorship Award (2006.08–2011.07, by Foundation for the Advancement of Outstanding Scholarship) and a National Chair Professorship Award (2001.8–2004.7, by the Ministry of Education, Taiwan) in recognition of his scholarly achievements.

Petros C. Mavroidis is Edwin B. Parker Professor of Law at Columbia Law School in New York City, USA. He has acted as the Chief Reporter for the American Law Institute Study 'Principles of International Trade: the WTO' (2013). His latest major publication is *Regulation of International Trade*, published by the MIT Press in 2016.

Bryan Mercurio is Professor, Associate Dean (Research) and Vice Chancellor's Outstanding Fellow of the Faculty of Law at the Chinese University of Hong Kong (CUHK). Specializing in international economic law, Professor Mercurio is a leading expert in the intersection between trade law and intellectual property rights. His work also frequently deals with free trade agreements, dispute settlement and increasingly international investment law. Professor Mercurio is the author of one of the most widely used casebooks on WTO law (Hart Publishing, 2018, 3rd edn, with S. Lester and A. Davies) and the editor of the leading collection on bilateral and regional trade agreements (Cambridge University Press, 2nd edn, 2016, with S. Lester and L. Bartels). Prior to relocating to Hong Kong in 2007, Professor Mercurio taught in the faculty of law at the University of New South Wales and as visitor at universities in Australia and North America. He has held visiting positions at a number of institutions in Asia, Europe and North America and is currently a Senior Fellow at the Melbourne Law School.

Yoshiko Naiki is Associate Professor at Osaka University, Graduate School of International Public Policy, Japan. She holds a PhD in public policy from Osaka University. Before coming to Osaka University, she worked as research associate at the Fletcher School, Tufts University, USA and as deputy director at the WTO dispute settlement section in the Ministry of Economy, Trade and Industry, Government of Japan. Her work focuses on domestic regulations and WTO law, in particular, regulations and standards concerning food safety and the environment. Her research interests also include a wide range of regulation and governance, such as private standards/certification systems or public–private partnerships. She has published articles on these topics in the *Journal of Environmental Law*, *Journal of World Trade*, *International and Comparative Law Quarterly*, and *European Journal of International Law*.

Shin-yi Peng is a Professor of Law at National Tsing Hua University (NTHU), Taiwan, and the Associate Dean of NTHU's College of Technology Management. Prior to her current position, she was on secondment as Commissioner at the National Communications Commission (2012–2016) and was Director of the Institute of Law for Science and Technology at NTHU (2007–2012). Before joining NTHU, Professor Peng taught the course 'Legal Aspects of Doing Business with Greater China' on the JD program at University of Wisconsin Law School, USA, where she received her SJD degree. A member of the New York Bar, she was an intern at George, Hull, Porter & Kohli in Seattle, Washington. Her research focuses on international economic law, with a particular emphasis on trade in services. She was a Visiting Fellow at Georgetown Law's Institute of International Economic Law (IIEL), USA, and a Visiting Professor at the Faculty of Law of Maastricht University, the Netherlands. Professor Peng has published in leading IEL journals, including *Journal of International Economic Law*, *Journal of World Trade* and *Cornell International Law Journal*. She has spoken at the WTO Headquarters in Geneva and has been a frequent speaker at international conferences in Europe, America and Asia. She is the Case Author of the 6th European Law Students' Association (ELSA) Moot Court Competition on WTO Law. Professor Peng has received a number of awards including Outstanding Research Award from the National Science Council of Taiwan. She frequently serves in an advisory and consultative capacity to the Ministry of Economic Affairs, advising the government on trade law and policy issues. She is a member of the Indicative List of Governmental and Non-Governmental Panelists for resolving WTO disputes. She was an Executive Council member (2012–2016) and is Co-Executive Vice President of the Society of International Economic Law (SIEL).

Sherzod Shadikhodjaev is a professor at the Korea Development Institute (KDI) School of Public Policy and Management, one of the largest public policy schools in the Republic of Korea and Asia. He obtained his LLB (with honors) from the University of World Economy and Diplomacy (Uzbekistan), and LLM and PhD in Law from the Korea University (Republic of Korea). Previously, he worked for the Korea Institute for International Economic Policy – one of the biggest think tanks under the Primer-Minister's Office consulting the Korean government – as a research fellow. In addition to the policy analytical work, he has carried out extensive academic research in the areas of trade and international economic law. His book *Retaliation in the WTO Dispute Settlement System* was published by Kluwer Law International in 2009. His articles were published in globally-recognized journals including, but not limited to, *American Journal of International Law* (American Society of International Law), *Journal of International Economic Law* (Oxford University Press), *Chinese Journal of International Law* (Oxford University Press), *World Trade Review* (Cambridge University Press) and *Journal of World Trade* (Kluwer). He has also been a frequent speaker in international conferences in and out of the Republic of Korea.

Rolf H. Weber is a Professor Emeritus for International Business Law at the University of Zurich and a practicing attorney-at-law in Zurich, Switzerland. From 2000 to 2015 he was a Visiting Professor at the University of Hong Kong. His main fields of research are Internet and Information Technology Law, International Business Law, Telecommunications and Media Law, Competition Law and International Financial Law. He is director of the European Law Institute and the Center for Information and Communication Law at the University of Zurich. Since 2008 he has been a member of the Steering Committee of the Global Internet Governance Academic Network (GigaNet) and of the European Dialogue on Internet

Governance (EuroDIG) and since 2009 he has been a member of the High-level Panel of Advisers of the Global Alliance for Information and Communication Technologies and Development (GAID). In addition, he is engaged as an attorney-at-law and as a member of the editorial board of several Swiss and international legal periodicals and serves as expert for several international and national organizations in his wide-spread fields of research. Professor Weber has intensively published both books and peer-reviewed articles on matters of Internet Governance, the Internet of Things, international financial law and generally on global governance. His research focus lies on the legal problems related to his research topics, in particular the strengths and weaknesses of possible regulatory regimes. In October 2017, Professor Weber received the Hou-De Honorary Chair of the National Tsing Hua University, Taiwan.

Mark Wu is an Assistant Professor at Harvard Law School, USA. His research focuses on international trade law, including issues concerning emerging economies, digital trade, intellectual property, trade remedies, environment, and investment. At Harvard, Wu is a Faculty Director of the Berkman Klein Center for Internet and Society. He serves as a member of the Faculty Advisory Committees of the East Asian Legal Studies Program and the Fairbank Center for Chinese Studies. He is also a Faculty Associate of Harvard University's Center for the Environment. In 2016, he was appointed by the World Trade Organization to serve on the Advisory Board for the WTO Chairs Programme. Wu also serves on the World Economic Forum's Global Future Council on Trade and Foreign Direct Investment. In addition, he works with the World Bank on assessing trade agreements and serves on multiple expert groups convened by the International Centre for Trade and Sustainable Development. He is an Editorial Board member of the *World Trade Review* and of the World Intellectual Property Organization's series on intellectual property, innovation and economic development. Prior to academia, Wu served as the Director for Intellectual Property in the Office of the US Trade Representative. He was the lead US negotiator for the IP chapters of several free trade agreements. He continues to serve as a principal liaison to the Trade and Environment Policy Advisory Committee. Before government service, Wu worked as a management consultant at McKinsey & Co. where he led engagements in technology sectors. He began his career as an economist and operations officer with the World Bank in China, working on environmental, urban development, health and rural poverty issues. He also worked briefly as an economist for the United Nations Development Programme in Namibia.

Peter K. Yu is Professor of Law, Professor of Communication, and Director of the Center for Law and Intellectual Property at Texas A&M

University, USA. He previously held the Kern Family Chair in Intellectual Property Law and was the founding director of the Intellectual Property Law Center at Drake University Law School. He was Wenlan Scholar Chair Professor at Zhongnan University of Economics and Law, China and a Visiting Professor of Law at Hanken School of Economics, Finland; the University of Haifa, Israel; the University of Helsinki, Finland; the University of Hong Kong, China; and the University of Strasbourg, France. He has served as the general editor of the *WIPO Journal* published by the World Intellectual Property Organization (WIPO) and is currently the Co-Director of Studies of the American Branch of the International Law Association.

Abbreviations

ACTA	Anti-Counterfeiting Trade Agreement
AD	anti-dumping
AI	artificial intelligence
ALOP	appropriate level of protection
AMCA	Australian Communications and Media Authority
ANDA	Abbreviated New Drug Application
APEC	Asia-Pacific Economic Cooperation
AQSIQ	Administration for Quality Supervision Inspection and Quarantine
ASEAN	Association of Southeast Asian Nations
BCR	binding corporate rules
BIT	Bilateral Investment Treaty
BWIPS	China Broadband Wireless Internet Protocol Standard Working Group
CBD	Convention on Biological Diversity
CETA	Comprehensive Economic and Trade and Agreement
CFIUS	Committee on Foreign Investment in the United States
CGP	Code of Good Practice
CJEU	Court of Justice of the European Union
CMA	critical mass agreement
CTC	cooperative technical consultations
EAC	East African Community
ECHR	European Convention on Human Rights
EEA	European Economic Area
EEG	Renewable Energy Act (Germany)
EGA	Environmental Goods Agreement
EG&S	environmental goods and services
EPA	Economic Partnership Agreement
EU	European Union
FAO	Food and Agriculture Organization of the United Nations
FDA	Food and Drug Administration
FIT	feed-in tariff
FSANZ	Food Standards Australia/New Zealand
FSCF	Food Safety Cooperation Forum (APEC)

FSMA	Food Safety Modernization Act (US)
FTA	Free Trade Agreement
FTAAP	Free Trade Area of the Asia-Pacific
GATS	General Agreement on Trade in Services
GATT	General Agreement on Tariffs and Trade
GDP	gross domestic product
GDPR	General Data Protection Regulation
GMF	genetically modified food
GMO	genetically modified organism
GPA	Agreement on Government Procurement
GVC	global value chain
HACCP	Hazards Analysis and Critical Control Points
HS	Harmonized System
HSA	Health Sciences Authority (Singapore)
ICT	information and communications technology
IEEE	Institute of Electronical and Electronics Engineers
IEL	international economic law
IP	intellectual property
IPPC	International Plant Protection Convention
IPR	intellectual property right
ISO	International Organization for Standardization
ISP	Internet Service Provider
IT	information technology
ITO	International Trade Organization
JCCT	United States–China Joint Commission on Commerce and Trade
LCR	local content requirement
MFN	most-favored nation
MII	Ministry of Information Industry (China)
MLP	National Mid-Term and Long-Term Science and Technology Development Plan (China)
MLPS	Multi-Level Protection Scheme (China)
MNE	multinational enterprise
MRA	mutual recognition agreement
NAFTA	North American Free Trade Agreement
NCC	National Communications Commission (Taiwan)
NIEO	New International Economic Order
NTB	non-tariff barrier
OAS	Organization of American States
OECD	Organisation for Economic Co-operation and Development
OIE	International Office of Epizootics
OIRA	Office of Information and Regulatory Affairs

PCT	Patent Cooperation Treaty
PRC	People's Republic of China
PRM	package-related measure
PTA	Preferential Trade Agreement
PV	photovoltaic
R&D	research and development
RAPEX	China-EU Rapid Alert System for Nonfood Dangerous Products
RCC	Canada–United States Regulatory Council
RCEP	Regional Comprehensive Economic Partnership
RIA	regulatory impact analysis
RTA	regional trade agreement
SAC	Standardization Administration of China
SADC	Southern African Development Community
SCM	Subsidies and Countervailing Measures
SME	small and medium-sized enterprise
SOE	state-owned enterprise
SPS	sanitary and phytosanitary
STC	specific trade concern
TABD	Transatlantic Business Dialogue
TACD	Transatlantic Consumer Dialogue
TBT	Technical Barrier to Trade
TFDA	Taiwan Food and Drug Agency
TGA	Therapeutic Goods Administration (Australia)
TiSA	Trade in Services Agreement
TPA	Trade Promotion Agreement
TPP	Trans-Pacific Partnership
TRIMS	Trade-Related Investment Measures
TRIPS	Trade-Related Aspects of Intellectual Property Rights
TTIP	Transatlantic Trade and Investment Partnership
UN	United Nations
UNCTAD	United Nations Conference on Trade and Development
UNDP	United Nations Development Programme
UNFCCC	United Nations Framework Convention on Climate Change
USTR	United States Trade Representative
VAT	value-added tax
VCLT	Vienna Convention on the Law of Treaties
WAPI	WLAN Authentication and Privacy Infrastructure
WIPO	World Intellectual Property Organization
WTO	World Trade Organization

Acknowledgements

This book is a product of collective efforts of its authors. The editors are grateful to each contributor's patience in responding to our remarks on their submissions. Along the way we have also incurred numerous debts. We thank the Ministry of Science and Technology of Taiwan and the Research Center for Humanities and Social Sciences of the National Tsing Hua University (NTHU) for funding a workshop in Taipei in November 2016 where contributors to this volume discussed the draft chapters. Thanks also go to Petros Mavroidis for agreeing to review and comment on the design of the collection. Last but not least, we gratefully acknowledge the excellent editing assistance by Hsien Wu and Li-Ying Lin, and the support of our assistants at NTHU's Institute of Law for Science and Technology, Rebecca Yu, Chen-Ning Wang, Roger Kai, and Hua-Chuan Sun.

PART I

Introduction

1. Governing science and technology in the era of megaregionals

Shin-yi Peng, Han-Wei Liu, and Ching-Fu Lin

I. INTRODUCTION

We live in one of the golden ages of scientific and technological advances. Neoliberalism in the post-World War II era has geared up the pace of globalization.[1] Under the banner of deregulation and privatization, globalization has contributed to a set of economically driven rules and processes under the auspices of the World Trade Organization (WTO). The goal of globalization is to increase market efficiency by minimizing political interference. This ideology is evidenced by the important proxies (e.g., nondiscrimination, necessity test, international standard, and scientific evidence) embedded in the WTO that address behind-the-border measures and their ramifications.

Taken together, the neoliberal governance has facilitated cross-border movements of capital, people, and trade, fueling breakthroughs in fields such as information and communications technology (ICT), genetic engineering and bioscience, and renewable energy and environmental mechanics. On the one hand, such innovations have contributed significantly to individual lives and society, as their application has increased productivity and efficiency. On the other hand, new technologies have posed potential risks to safety, health, and the environment.[2] Characterized by its very nature—complex, uncertain, and constantly evolving—technological innovation is challenging for any regulator to keep up with. In an interdependent world, such challenges go beyond geographic boundaries and call for rigorous transnational

---

1 See e.g., Stephen Gill, *Globalisation, Market Civilisation, and Disciplinary Neoliberalism*, 24 MILLENNIUM J. INT'L STUD. 399 (1995); Elaine Hartwick and Richard Peet, *Neoliberalism and Nature: The Case of the WTO*, 590 ANNALS AM. ACAD. POL. & SOC. SCI. 188 (2003).

2 See JACQUELINE PEEL, SCIENCE AND RISK REGULATION IN INTERNATIONAL LAW (Cambridge University Press, 2013).

coordination, yet regulatory cooperation can be equally, if not more, problematic.[3]

The diversity of regulatory approaches reflects different cultural, economic, social, and political underpinnings. In addition, harnessing new technologies can deter or promote specific segments of an industry, which not only matters for market competition, but for a nation's prosperity and long-term development. Regulatory interventions have emerged as a mixture of public interests and national economic and political strategies. Time and again, the jurisprudence of, and many specific trade concerns raised before, the WTO have underscored the difficulty of drawing a clear-cut distinction between disguised protectionism and legitimate protection of public goods.[4] To complicate the matter, governments have initiated diverse, and sometimes conflicting, regulatory responses to limit those ramifications, exacerbating tensions between international cooperation and regulatory autonomy, and undermining the multilateral framework.

II. INTERNATIONAL ECONOMIC ORDER: IMPLICATIONS OF MEGAREGIONALS

Governments around the globe have thus been compelled to reconfigure the default rules and locate an optimal institutional design for concerted actions. While the WTO has been struggling to keep pace with the scientific and technological developments and the resulting ramifications, several governance models have emerged as possible alternatives to multilateralism. The Trans-Pacific Partnership (TPP)—rebranded as the Comprehensive and Progressive Agreement for Trans-Pacific Partnership (CPTPP) after the United States' withdrawal and subsequent renegotiations among the other eleven parties)—lays down a set of ground-rules for present and even future challenges. In the ICT sector, the TPP/CPTPP addresses not only topical issues in the online setting, such as cross-border

---

[3] See e.g., MARA BURRI AND THOMAS COTTIER (EDS.), TRADE GOVERNANCE IN THE DIGITAL AGE (Cambridge University Press, 2012); ANNETTE KUR AND MARIANNE LEVIN (EDS.), INTELLECTUAL PROPERTY RIGHTS IN A FAIR WORLD TRADE SYSTEM (Edward Elgar Publishing, 2011); BRYAN MERCURIO AND KUEI-JUNG NI (EDS.), SCIENCE AND TECHNOLOGY IN INTERNATIONAL ECONOMIC LAW: BALANCING COMPETING INTERESTS (Routledge, 2014); YULIA SELIVANOVA (EDS.), REGULATION OF ENERGY IN INTERNATIONAL TRADE LAW: WTO, NAFTA AND ENERGY CHARTER (Wolters Kluwer, 2011).

[4] See MEREDITH KOLSKY LEWIS AND SUSY FRANKEL (EDS.), INTERNATIONAL ECONOMIC LAW AND NATIONAL AUTONOMY (Cambridge University Press, 2010).

data flows and data localization, source code, and anti-spam, but the ICT standard-setting process, a source of controversy in the offline world. The TPP/CPTPP's new institutional designs include extending intellectual property rights (IPRs) holders' rights by introducing patent linkage, incorporating SPS-Plus arrangements to strengthen the importance of scientific evidence in setting public health and food safety measures, and setting forth cross-cutting rules to promote renewable energy, environmental protection policy, and sustainable trade. Despite the United States' withdrawal, these gold standards enshrined in the TPP/CPTPP may find their way through other channels and continue to exert considerable influence in current and future negotiations.[5] Beyond the TPP/CPTPP, the Transatlantic Trade and Investment Partnership (TTIP) and the Regional Comprehensive Economic Partnership (RCEP), two other pillars of megaregionalism, promise to respond to those governance challenges in one way or another.

As promising as these megaregional initiatives may look, there has been no empirical evidence of their efficacy as regulatory uncertainty remains omnipresent. An immediate hurdle is the political climate on both sides of the Atlantic, which makes it problematic to conclude, ratify, and implement these new rules.[6] Moreover, addressing these issues through different trading blocs in a piecemeal fashion may fail to stand as a valid alternative to multilateralism.[7] What has been proposed are noteworthy efforts by the United States, the European Union, and China behind these megaregional blocs to manage ramifications. All these issues cast doubt on the

---

[5] See e.g., Valerie Volcovici, *Trump Adviser: TPP 'Dead', Will Move Quickly on Bilateral Trade Deals*, Reuters (January 13, 2017), available at www.reuters.com/article/us-usa-trump-trade-adviser-idUSKBN14X1X8 (last visited 21 August 2017); Alex Capri, *The TPP Moves Forward without Trump's America*, Forbes (22 May 2017), available at www.forbes.com/sites/alexcapri/2017/05/22/the-tpp-moves-forward-without-trumps-america/#668bfd234fed (last visited 21 August 2017).

[6] See e.g., Sean O'Grady, *By Scrapping TPP and TTIP, Trump has Boosted American Jobs in the Short Term—and Destroyed them in the Long Term*, Independent (24 January 2017), available at www.independent.co.uk/voices/donald-trump-trade-deals-tpp-ttip-american-business-workers-boost-short-term-destroy-long-term-a7543706.html (last visited 21 August 2017); *Europe Gets Ready for Donald Trump*, The Economist (19 January 2017), available at www.economist.com/news/europe/21714998-next-american-president-seems-view-eu-indifference-or-contempt-europe-gets-ready (last visited 21 August 2017).

[7] See e.g., Cédric Dupont, *ASEAN+, RCEP and TPP: A Clash of Integration Concepts*, *in* The Future of the World Trading System: Asian Perspectives 109 (Richard Baldwin et al. eds., 2013); Chad P. Brown, *Mega-Regional Trade Agreements and the Future of the WTO*, 8(1) Global Pol'y 107 (2017).

megaregional governance model and its prospects for forging regulatory convergence among governments.

Such a sea change and emerging challenges lead us to ask the following analytical questions. First, what, if any, are the scientific and technological advancements that have triggered, or are likely to trigger government interference, a new battleground in the international economic law community? Second, in what way have (or will) regulators step in? Do countries have different solutions to the same problem, and if so, why? What are the rationales for regulatory intervention? What are their implications for international economic order? Third, how can the WTO framework accommodate such challenges? This raises a more crucial issue: what mechanisms, if any, will the multilateral, plurilateral, or bilateral economic integration arrangements design to address the resulting ramifications? Will the emerging megaregional agreements help promote regulatory cooperation/coherence? If so, how? This phenomenon has raised more questions than it has answered in terms of regulatory divergence.

III. REGULATORY DIVERGENCE AND CONVERGENCE: THE ARGUMENT IN BRIEF

International economic law (IEL) and technology interact when trade rules encourage or interfere with the development of technology. IEL and technology also interact when international society decides that technology produces undesirable results and must use global norms to modify those results. This book reflects the editors' understanding of the interplay between IEL and technology, and how that interplay can be improved. The chapters of this volume offer a framework for deeper forays into the issues raised in this chapter. The contributions featured here are organized into five Parts and sixteen chapters, covering the most critical challenges: trade in ICT goods and services, environmental and energy policy, food safety and public health, and intellectual property rights.

In Chapter 2, Petros Mavroidis reminds us of the role of the WTO in managing international trade relations. By outlining the changing landscape of non-tariff barriers (NTBs) and trade liberalization through the lens of the global value chains (GVCs), Mavroidis draws our attention to 'New WTO Think': an integration strategy rooted in the General Agreement on Tariffs and Trade (GATT) premise but is more inclusive of regulators and non-state actors and more flexible and positive. Mavroidis calls upon governments to maintain the policy-relevance of the WTO by embracing the confluence of shared social preferences and trade as a motivation for advancing international regulatory cooperation.

Part II focuses on emerging challenges facing trade policy-makers in the ICT industry. In Chapter 3, Rolf Weber takes up the nexus between cross-border data flows and digital trade from a European perspective. By examining recent developments along the lines of the Digital Single Market Strategy for Europe and the General Data Protection Regulation (GDPR), Weber underscores the challenges and opportunities facing the European Union policy-makers while negotiating new disciplines under the aegis of the Trade in Services Agreement (TiSA), TTIP, and Comprehensive Economic and Trade Agreement (CETA). Using unsolicited commercial electronic messages as a case study, in Chapter 4, Shin-yi Peng points out the limits of regulatory coherence under Chapter 25 of the TPP/CPTPP to address recurring problems in the context of electronic commerce. As Peng remarks, while, in theory, regulatory coherence seems a promising way to reconcile divergent regulatory approaches, its efficacy would rest upon how governments read and apply it. Chapter 5, by Mark Wu, explains how governments leverage export policies, technology controls, and investment reviews to shape the market competition for the technology-related GVCs. Wu offers a nuanced appraisal of the development of new disciplines on the use of these strategic instruments amid the trend of megaregionalism and underscores the role of the US-Sino relationship. In Chapter 6, Han-Wei Liu picks up another interesting yet less explored issue in the digital trade literature by offering a detailed account of China's indigenous standards and innovation policy in the ICT industry and their implications for trade. While many see China's 'techno-nationalism' as a credible threat to the global trading system, Liu argues that techno-nationalism may be less serious than it appears because of the internal and external constraints that may place limits on home-grown initiatives in megaregionalism.

Part III studies the importance of environmental governance and renewable energy promotion in megaregional trade negotiations. In Chapter 7, Won-Mog Choi deciphers the relationship between trade and biodiversity in addition to the philosophical tension between Bretton Woods trade liberalism and the New International Economic Order. Building upon an analysis of relevant TPP/CPTPP texts, Choi discusses how countries may promote sustainable use of biological diversity and respect knowledge and practices of indigenous and local communities relating to sustainable use of biodiversity. He suggests that the TPP/CPTPP has taken a mega-step for the prevention of global clashes between trade and environment regimes toward mutually reinforcing governance in the twenty-first century. In Chapter 8, Sherzod Shadikhodjaev points out that the ongoing talks on the Environmental Goods Agreement that focus on tariff removal (reduction) are unlikely to cover regulatory issues of renewable energy.

He notes that some megaregional agreements, such as the TPP/CPTPP and TTIP, incorporate (or will incorporate) specific provisions dedicated to issues of renewable energy regulation. Shadikhodjaev examines multilateral and regional trade rules with reference to localization measures, government support, infrastructural facilities, technical standards, and services, and suggests adopting a more renewables-oriented regulatory approach. In Chapter 9, Ming-Zhi Gao evaluates the potential implications of promoting renewable electricity technology in megaregional agreements for regulatory convergence and divergence. Gao analyzes the dynamic interactions between the regimes of international economic law and international climate/environmental law, and explores possible ways to strike a balance.

Part IV turns to food safety and public health, one of the most controversial areas of scholarly attention due to its multifaceted normative implications. In Chapter 10, Yoshiko Naiki analyzes food and product safety issues in the TPP/CPTPP, and examines whether its rules require countries to relax their criteria in their national laws, standards, or labelling requirements. Naiki highlights the TPP/CPTPP's unique practice of including product-specific provisions relating to genetically modified organisms (GMOs), used and remanufactured goods, motor vehicles, cosmetics, organic products, and food additives, and argues that it reflects the trade interests and concerns of individual exporting parties. She concludes that such provisions do not have a substantial impact on national safety standards, but may promote cooperation, the exchange of information, and transparency of national measures. In Chapter 11, Ching-Fu Lin uses the TPP/CPTPP sanitary and phytosanitary (SPS) Chapter as a vantage point for exploring the transformation of food safety governance in the era of megaregionals. By referencing the WTO SPS Agreement and other essential legal instruments, Lin carefully articulates the normative meanings of the SPS-Plus institutional designs, and discusses their interactions with cross-cutting regulatory coherence requirements, and more broadly, the multilateral trading system. He argues that the SPS-Plus designs in the TPP/CPTPP SPS Chapter, which incorporates a few regulatory practices of the United States, a strengthened dispute prevention and settlement mechanism, and more importantly, a multilateral anchor tied to the WTO regime, may transform the way food safety issues are governed in the future. Chapter 12, written by Chang-fa Lo, takes up the challenge of packaging-related food safety issues and offers a detailed analysis on whether they have been properly addressed in the recent megaregional agreements. According to Lo, when comparing the SPS and TBT Agreements under the WTO, the TPP/CPTPP does not offer much progress with respect to the protection of food safety. He therefore offers an interpretative view to avoid the result of interpretations of the SPS and TBT provisions becoming absurd.

Part V considers IPRs, an overarching issue that affects almost every scientific and technological activity. Chapter 13, by Peter Yu, offers a high-level overview of the most recent developments of IPR-related disciplines in the age of megaregionalism. By considering other norm-setting initiatives, including the TPP/CPTPP, Yu evaluates whether the proposed RCEP norms would lead to more regulatory convergence, divergence, or what commentators have now advanced as 'crossvergence', while identifying issues that domestic policy-makers and international negotiators should consider in reconfiguring their future norms. Branislav Hazucha, in Chapter 14, engages in a similar pursuit by revisiting the trend of harmonization of IPRs. Built upon his studies of the practices of regional trade agreements, he clearly illustrates, despite the increased harmonization, a considerable divergence in the application of international standards of IPR protection amongst countries. In Chapter 15, Bryan Mercurio addresses the linkage between patent, public health, and international trade by exploring the purpose and effect of the common pharmaceutical patent law provisions in recent free trade agreements. While harmonization of patent laws would yield benefits and efficiency, Mercurio's analysis underscores its undesired consequences in terms of pharmaceutical patents. He suggests that any normative standards should be tailored to the context of the country at issue; the harmonization of practical standards could reduce costs and increase efficiency in the public health system. Chapter 16, by Shujie Feng, concludes Part V by focusing on the interaction between IPRs and fair competition. Using high-profile cases in Mainland China as examples, Feng describes the concerns about unfair competition that emerge from the way in which some leading high-tech companies in China leverage their technologies to attract consumers in the online environment. Feng offers a thorough analysis of the role of international and regional agreements in addressing unfair competition and indicates the possible convergence and its limits by taking into account the variations in local contexts.

IV. GOVERNING SCIENCE AND TECHNOLOGY: TODAY AND TOMORROW

Working in the field of international economic law, we were naturally interested in questions about megaregionals. We took notice of the proliferation of research on global governance in science and technology. We believe that it would be useful for scholars and practitioners in IEL to have a book that explores different aspects of regulatory convergence between international trade and technological development, that reflects theoretical diversity, and thereby contributes to the organically evolving norms regarding the global governance of science and technology. This scholarly endeavor brings together contributions from experts who reflect upon and approach these intellectual and practical inquiries in an exceptionally informed, insightful, and invigorating fashion. We hope that the contributions in this edited collection offer responses to the new challenges in specific fields, sectors, or industries.

To conclude, this book identifies key areas that have been theoretically and practically demonstrated as carrying the most significance for generations to come: digital trade, climate change and environment, food safety and public health, and IPRs. In terms of digital trade, this collection picks up what others have left out by addressing the timeliest issues: data localization and cross-border information flow, anti-spam, and the Sino-US laws and politics in addressing ICT-related trade and investment conflicts. On climate change and environment, the Paris Agreement is a promising milestone in multilateral efforts to address global climate change and environmental justice, yet how its bottom-up approach based on state pledges will play out remains to be seen. Emerging technologies such as carbon removal and solar geoengineering initiatives and their interactions with the megaregional trading systems merit a serious survey of normative implications. In addition, food safety and public health are among the most controversial areas of scholarly attention, as their regulatory consequences are not limited to trade or public health. Rather, the interactions between megaregional regimes, national regulatory sovereignty (with vastly diverse political, social, cultural, and ideological underpinnings), and the background rules under the WTO pose crucial inquiries to configuring and reconfiguring global trade governance. Finally, our attention turns to IPRs by placing an old debate in a new context, discussing how megaregionals approach and harmonize IPR rules while taking into account public health, local values, and market competition. While these issues are valid in their own right, concentrating on them risks losing sight of the whole picture. This leads us to revisit the implications of the overarching notions of regulatory coherence and cooperation, and more crucially, the relevance of the decade-long WTO negotiations, which have the potential to forge a common governance infrastructure to promote regulatory harmonization and consistency among diverse institutions, processes, and interests.

In short, given the rapidly evolving landscape of digital technology, e-commerce, climate change, as well as food safety and public health, how best to govern their ramifications has become a daunting task for both practitioners and academics. While the rising megaregional agreements have taken on these challenges innovatively, their approaches involve uncertainty and fragmentation that may present obstacles rather than solutions. None of these issues, however, have been adequately addressed. Previous attempts to produce surveys of this kind are outdated. Therefore, this is a good time to map out the new dynamic challenges posed by scientific and technological advances and corresponding regulatory approaches, and capture, more broadly, the emerging contour of global trade governance in the age of megaregionals. This volume would therefore be a valuable research reference and a useful text for courses on, for instance, international economic law, technology law, political science, political economy, administrative law, international business, and global governance.

Taken as a whole, the viewpoints in this volume reflect the status of regulatory response to technological innovations at this unsettling time. The chapters may only begin to answer these questions while identifying the direction of evolving norms. This reality explains the book's subtitle. Some of these propositions leave crucial questions unanswered, especially from the viewpoint of a sectoral policy-maker struggling to respond to IEL development while sensibly balancing regulatory objectives. Nonetheless, covering all the issues related to science and technology governance in the mega-regional era with comprehensiveness is impossible. Should we have addressed the problems of nanotechnologies? Or should we have prioritized the debates over emerging threats of robots and artificial intelligence (AI)? Should we have continued to add to the voluminous literature on megaregional trade agreements in Trump's world? Likewise, there is an avalanche of writing on China-led regional initiatives. Choices had to be made and we tended to venture into areas which are important but have to date been underexplored. Having said that, this book represents not only a valuable and necessary addition to the literature but also a point of departure that invites further research, exploring the way to rise to the challenges ahead.

2. Regulatory cooperation in the WTO: Why it matters now? How could it be achieved?

Petros C. Mavroidis

I. INTRODUCTORY REMARKS

Governments were unable through proclamations and solo measures to arrest the cycle of retaliation that followed the US Smoot-Hawley Tariff Act of 1930, resulting in tariff levels of nearly 50 percent among the major powers. That experience led to the negotiation of the General Agreement on Tariffs and Trade (GATT). The GATT-think was that reciprocal liberalization would curb unilateral protection and the negative externalities that result from uncoordinated and nontransparent actions in a trading system with many partners.[1] It succeeded beyond any reasonable expectation. This rules-based global trading system helped reduce tariffs and other border restraints and institutionalized global economic integration as a force for peace and prosperity. The average level of tariffs for Organisation for Economic Co-operation and Development (OECD) member countries fell to 3 percent.[2] Membership in the GATT and its successor institution, the World Trade Organization (WTO), grew from twenty-three countries in 1947 to 164 nations today.[3] It would not be far-fetched to argue that the GATT has contributed to fewer wars and improved living standards in most nations of the world.[4]

---

[1] Kyle Bagwell and Robert W. Staiger, *Economic Theory and the Interpretation of GATT/WTO*, 46(2) Am. Econ. 3 (2002).

[2] WTO, World Trade Report 2014, Trade and Development: Recent Trends and the Role of the WTO 69 (2014).

[3] WTO, *Accessions: Afghanistan to Become 164th WTO Member on 29 July 2016*, WTO News, 29 June 2016, available at www.wto.org/english/news_e/news16_e/acc_afg_29jun16_e.htm (last visited 1 August 2017).

[4] Steven Radelet, The Great Surge: The Ascent of the Developing World 258–9 (2015); Steven Pinker, The Better Angels of Our Nature: Why Violence Has Declined 284–90, 341–2, 682–4 (2011); Douglas A. Irwin et al.,

Greater global economic integration, democratization, rising living standards, and increased awareness of risks have increased the demand for more regulations and rules, as means of preserving and advancing social preferences on matters such as worker, environmental, and public health protection.[5] More trade occurs now via global value chains (GVCs), which rely on consistent, efficient, and adequate regulatory oversight to function.[6] The challenge of organizing consistent regulations is likely to grow with more products integrating value-added services and cross-border data flows—areas in which the WTO trade disciplines are few.

The WTO still hews to the negative integration strategy of the GATT on regulations and social preferences, geared toward preventing domestic policies from being used to erode tariff concessions. This approach helped reduce explicitly protectionist regulations, but has done little to improve the international regulatory cooperation that is increasingly critical to freer trade. Without that progress, countries are turning to bilateral and regional preferential trade agreements (PTAs) to deepen their integration on regulatory matters. Businesses and consumers are relying on private or nonprofit organization standards and third-party certifications to enforce social preferences and quality requirements. The resulting cacophony of rules and private standards has increased compliance costs and undermined effective international regulatory oversight.

More international cooperation would improve the consistency, efficiency, and adequacy of regulations, which is in the mutual interest of trade officials and regulators alike. This, however, does not mean more international regulatory cooperation will spontaneously occur. Here, the

---

The Genesis of the GATT (2008); Cordell Hull, one of the architects of the GATT trading regime, was awarded the Nobel Prize for Peace for his contributions, see Gunnar Jahn, Chairman of the Nobel Committee, Award Ceremony Speech, The Nobel Peace Prize 1945: Cordell Hull (10 December 1945), available at www.nobelprize.org/nobel_prizes/peace/laureates/1945/press.html (last visited 1 August 2017).

[5] In this chapter, we define social preferences as fundamental interests that are not necessarily limited to a particular state. That definition distinguishes social preferences, which may transcend national boundaries, from the domestic policies of nation-states or the transient negotiating demands, foreign policy goals, or bargaining positions that those states use to conduct foreign affairs. This definition draws loosely from the notion of preferences in Andrew Moravcsik, *Taking Preferences Seriously: A Liberal Theory of International Politics*, 51 Int'l Org. 513, 519 (1997).

[6] Michael Porter popularized the value chain concept. His underlying notion was that a firm should focus on the stages and support functions in which that firm has a comparative advantage and outsource the rest. Michael E. Porter, *Technology and Competitive Advantage*, 5(3) J. Bus. Strategy 60 (1985).

WTO has an important role to play. Pursuing regulatory cooperation on a multilateral basis and within the WTO avoids the need for multiple, parallel cooperation initiatives between the various sets of regulatory agency counterparts and trading partners involved in a GVC. It also takes advantage of the emphasis on rules-based, nondiscriminatory trade and process for regulatory convergence, albeit rudimentary, that already exist at the WTO. To do this, we advocate that the WTO should embrace the confluence of shared social preferences and trade, where it exists, as a motivation for advancing international regulatory cooperation. We also recommend that the WTO rethink its corporate governance along the lines of variable geometry, an idea outlined in Lawrence (2006) and Hoekman and Mavroidis (2015).[7] Building on that work, we develop a workable mechanism for multilateralizing the progress being made on regulatory cooperation initiatives at the sub-WTO level.

II. THE WAY WE WERE

There are sizable benefits to eliminating protectionist policies, irrespective of whether other nations do the same. For this reason, some economists have characterized the multilateral trade system as enlightened mercantilism, a framework of rules and reciprocal liberalization to create political trade-offs and domestic lobbies for making the tariff reductions that governments should already do for economic reasons.[8] There are of course, good arguments why some nations protect.[9] Proponents of the terms of trade theory would suggest that those who have the bargaining power profit from imposing tariffs that reduce the world price to their

---

[7] Robert Z. Lawrence, *Rulemaking Amidst Growing Diversity: A Club-of-Clubs Approach to WTO Reform and New Issue Selection*, 9(4) J. INT'L ECON. L. 823 (2006); BERNARD M. HOEKMAN AND PETROS C. MAVROIDIS, WORLD TRADE ORGANIZATION (WTO): LAW, ECONOMICS, AND POLITICS (2015).

[8] In other words, the prospect of tariff reductions in other nations helps generate enough support from domestic export-minded interests to overcome the domestic opposition to lower tariffs and the possibility of increased imports. See Paul R. Krugman, *The Move Toward Free Trade Zones*, 76(6) ECON. REV.—FED. RES. BANK KAN. CITY 5 (1991); Paul R. Krugman, *What Should Trade Negotiators Negotiate About?*, 35 J. ECON. LITERATURE 113 (1997).

[9] See Donald H. Regan, *What Are Trade Agreements For? Two Conflicting Stories Told by Economists with a Lesson for Lawyers*, 9(4) J. INT'L ECON. L. 951 (2006) (citing revenue-raising, socially valued redistribution, and correcting externalities, including those affecting infant industries, as among the 'perfectly proper' goals for protection).

advantage.[10] Economic history is full of examples of tariff impositions for various reasons.[11] Absent international agreement, (some) nations might have little incentive to eliminate protection. By drawing more countries into a rules-based system, multilateral trade agreements create static and dynamic efficiencies of scale. The genius of the GATT lies with its approach to disciplining protection. Instead of seeking to define and prohibit protectionism in all its potential forms, the GATT channels protectionism from outright import quotas (which it outlaws *per se*) toward a less pernicious and more transparent form of protection (tariffs) and requiring that it be nondiscriminatory and negotiable.[12] Once bound, tariff levels may only decrease. Having the outcome of tariff negotiation extend to all GATT members on a nondiscriminatory basis created a powerful incentive for other nations to participate in the system. Enforceable dispute resolution kept them following the rules. So if negotiations persisted and succeeded, protection would gradually become extinct. Or, at least, this was the idea.[13] The negotiators were determined to avoid a repeat of the escalating tariffs and trade wars that had characterized the interwar period.[14] The framers were well aware of the risk of policy substitution in this arrangement, for some of the brightest minds of that generation participated in the negotiation of the GATT.[15] What does it mean to bind customs duties, if domestic

---

[10] Harry G. Johnson, *Optimum Tariffs and Retaliation*, 21 REV. ECON. STUD. 142 (1953–54); see also Bagwell and Staiger (n. 1 above).

[11] An extreme example is the US Morrill Tariff (1861), which raised revenue for the upcoming war in the United States. See Morrill Act (Tariff), 12 Stat. 178 (1861).

[12] There remains no operational definition of protectionism in international law.

[13] The GATT discipline is discussed in detail in JOHN H. JACKSON, WORLD TRADE AND THE LAW OF GATT (1969); Robert E. Baldwin, *Determinants of the Commodity Structure of U.S. Trade*, 61(1) AM. ECON. REV. 126 (1971). Mavroidis (2016) adds the case law during the GATT and the WTO years. The GATT-think did not totally solve the problem of defining 'protection'. It requested from judges (panels) to come up with a workable definition every time they would be asked to pronounce whether domestic policies had been applied in nondiscriminatory (e.g., nonprotectionist) manner. Alas, this is an area where panels did not manage to rise to the challenge. PETROS C. MAVROIDIS, THE REGULATION OF INTERNATIONAL TRADE: GATT (2016).

[14] Tariffs levels had receded some by the time that GATT negotiations began, but the average tariff was still 22 percent in 1947. Chad P. Bown and Douglas A. Irwin, *The GATT's Starting Point: Tariff Levels circa 1947*, *in* ASSESSING THE WORLD TRADE ORGANIZATION: FIT FOR PURPOSE? 45 (Manfred Elsig et al. eds., 2016). See also IRWIN ET AL. (n. 4 above) (explaining that the fight against the UK imperial preferences was a major target of the US negotiators).

[15] See IRWIN ET AL. (n. 4 above).

taxes (to consumers) and subsidies (to producers) are left unconstrained? The discipline on domestic policies, however, was softer. Those adhering to the GATT had to promise to place domestic and imported competing goods on an equal footing. Nondiscrimination was thought to be an adequate insurance policy against erosion of the value of tariff bindings.[16] Tariffs, a negotiable instrument, remained as the only permitted means to protect domestic producers.

1. Tariff Classifications

To facilitate the tariff negotiation, a common description of goods for tariffs had to be invented, which became the current Harmonized Commodity Description and Coding System ('Harmonized System' or 'HS') classification.[17] This taxonomy provides a uniform classification of goods with numerical codes. A two-digit number refers to the family of goods (e.g., textiles), whereas a six-digit number, the maximum number of digits permitted in the HS system, identifies the species of that good (e.g., shirts with polyester). The HS system classifies products according to their characteristics and properties, and they do not reflect social preferences (e.g., produced consistent with environmentally-sustainable or labor-friendly standards), but rather product characteristics (e.g., cotton or polyester).

Article 3.3 of the International Convention on the Harmonized Commodity Description and Coding System ('HS Convention') allows for national sub-classifications. The European Union, and the United States and others negotiate at the eight-, ten- and higher digit level classifications. These remain, however, national idiosyncratic classifications. The first attempt to design a multilateral tariff classification that includes social preferences—the WTO Environmental Goods Agreement (EGA)—is under way at the moment of writing, although the December 2016 meeting did not prove to be a success. Eventually, that classification will

---

[16] The negotiating record is clear. See *ibid.* The WTO Appellate Body accepted as much in the WTO. See Appellate Body Report, *Japan–Taxes on Alcoholic Beverages*, WTO Doc. WT/DS8/AB/R, WT/DS10/AB/R, WT/DS11/AB/R (adopted 1 November 1996).

[17] The HS is governed by the International Convention on the Harmonized Commodity Description and Coding System, 14 June 1983, 1503 UNTS 167, and maintained by the World Customs Organization. More than 200 countries use the HS, which covers 5,000 commodity groups and more than 98 percent of the world's trade, World Customs Organization, What is the Harmonized System (HS)?, available at www.wcoomd.org/en/topics/nomenclature/overview/what-is-the-harmonized-system.aspx (last visited 1 August 2017).

provide the basis for negotiating tariff reductions for products involving clean energy, energy efficiency, air pollution control, and environmental monitoring and analysis.

2. Disciplines on Non-tariff Barriers

A GATT member that wishes to restrict import of goods or services inconsistent with its environmental, labor, and food safety preferences has two options. The government may block the imports at the border and, if challenged by another member, try to justify its action through recourse to general exceptions to the GATT (Article XX). Or, the regulating government could impose a regulatory measure, such as a sales ban, and, if challenged, explain why that regulatory action is nondiscriminatory. The first option has no advantages at all under the GATT. The burden of proof stays with the regulating state, and it still has to meet the nondiscrimination-test embedded in the chapeau of Article XX of the GATT. In the second case, the complainants carry the associated burden of proof and persuasion.[18] Unsurprisingly, GATT members prefer to impose regulatory measures that ban sales instead of banning imports. The burden then falls to the GATT (and later the WTO) judge to determine whether the measure is nondiscriminatory. The purpose of this chapter is not to debate the quality of case law in this context, beyond noting that the exercise has been fraught.[19] Defining 'protection', especially in the regulatory context, is difficult and dependent on the activity and regulatory context. Trade effects could be the necessary and unintended by-product of pursuing a legitimate social objective.

Protectionist intent is difficult to reveal since, as in the prisoner's dilemma, the regulator, the possessor of the private information, has little or no incentive to reveal the true intent of its actions.[20] Without a demonstrated intent to protect (and/or protectionist effect), many regulatory measures can be interpreted in multiple ways.

---

[18] Viewed this way, it is remarkable that the United States defended its measures in *US-Shrimp* under Art. XX rather than Art. III of GATT, by adopting a sales ban on shrimps that were fished in a manner that prejudiced the life of sea turtles. Appellate Body Report, *United States—Import Prohibition of Certain Shrimp and Shrimp Products*, WTO Doc. WT/DS58/AB/R (adopted 6 November 1998).

[19] 2 Mavroidis (n. 13 above) 447–53.

[20] See Bagwell and Staiger (n. 1 above).

3. The Consequence

The GATT framers devoted several provisions to the treatment of tariffs (Articles II, XXVIII, XXVIII*bis*, and indirectly VI, VII, VIII of GATT), but only one provision on the treatment of non-tariff measures, namely, the non-discrimination requirements in Article III. The agreement is largely unconcerned whether domestic policies and their underlying social preferences are pursued unilaterally. It also does not address the negative externalities that may result from uncoordinated regulatory action. The nondiscrimination requirement on domestic policies in the GATT exhibits a binary function. Even excessive legislation passes muster provided that it is nondiscriminatory. The GATT does not attempt to rationalize domestic policies or facilitate their efficiency and effectiveness. As long as the same burden is imposed on domestic and foreign goods, measures satisfy the nondiscrimination requirement.[21]

Baldwin (1971) has persuasively argued that tariffs were high and regulation mostly nondiscriminatory in 1947 and, thus, it is understandable that domestic policies were not the focus of GATT framers.[22] Participating governments had little interest in limiting their freedom in areas like product safety for the sake of 'a mere trade agreement'.[23] Social preferences and regulations did not fit easily with the notion of reciprocal negotiations central to the GATT. Workers' rights, competition policy, and other economic and social regulations were to be taken up later in the International Trade Organization (ITO), of which the GATT was meant to be a part.[24] As Horn et al. (2011) show, when returns become diminishing, trade negotiators are apt to call it a day and leave it to subsequent negotiation(s) and/or adjudicators to 'complete' the contract.[25] Even with this limited mandate, the GATT produced important benefits. These include binding negotiated tariff reductions, establishing the principle of

---

[21] See Gene M. Grossman and Hendrik H. Horn, *Why the WTO? An Introduction to the Economics of Trade Agreements*, *in* Legal and Economic Principles of World Trade Law 9–66 (Hendrik H. Horn and Petros C. Mavroidis eds., 2013) (explaining this point in detail).

[22] See Baldwin (n. 13 above).

[23] Jagdish Bhagwati and Robert E. Hudec, Aggressive Unilateralism: America's 301 Trade Policy and the World Trading System (1990).

[24] Anne Marie Slaughter, *Regulating the World: Multilateralism, International Law, and the Projection of the New Deal Regulatory State*, *in* Multilateralism Matters: The Theory and Praxis of an Institutional Form 125–56 (John Ruggie ed., 1992).

[25] Henrik Horn et al., *Trade Agreements as Endogenously Incomplete Contracts*, 100(1) Am. Econ. Rev. 394 (2010).

nondiscrimination in international trade, improving the transparency and predictability of many trade policy measures, and providing a forum for future negotiations and the peaceful resolution of bilateral disputes.[26]

III. MANAGING GATT'S SUCCESS

By the 1970s, tariffs had declined dramatically, at least on the industrial goods on which higher-income countries were willing to negotiate. With lower tariffs, the role of regulations and standards as potential barriers to trade became more apparent.[27] New regulatory institutions arose and social preferences evolved, expanded, and were embedded in government policies in the decades following the post-war era.[28] Economic growth expanded the middle class in many higher-income nations and spurred a greater interest in quality of life concerns.[29]

Unsurprisingly, the multilateral trade agenda shifted tentatively in the direction of addressing non-tariff measures in the Tokyo Round of the GATT (1973–1979) and the negotiation of 'codes',[30] that is, plurilateral agreements negotiated and voluntarily adopted by only some GATT members on non-tariff issues, including subsidies, government procurement, bovine meat, dairy, and technical barriers to the trade in goods (i.e., labeling, packaging, production, and product regulations and standards). With the start of the Uruguay Round in 1986, higher income countries, which had already significantly reduced tariffs in their sectors of greatest interest, pushed for disciplines on the emerging priorities of their exporters, such as intellectual property rights and trade in services. The results were mixed. More than seventy low- and middle-income countries have joined the GATT/WTO since the start of the Uruguay Round. The goods sectors that remained stubbornly outside of the GATT were tamed with the signing of the Agreement on Agriculture, and the Agreement on Textiles and Clothing. With tariffs on their way out of most other sectors, the focus of the WTO shifted to non-tariff measures and barriers, but its

---

[26] See Bown and Irwin (n. 14 above).

[27] See Baldwin (n. 13 above).

[28] David Levi-Faur, *The Global Diffusion of Regulatory Capitalism*, 598 ANNALS AM. ACAD. POL. & SOC. SCI. 12 (2005).

[29] Robert Inglehart, *Globalization and Postmodern Values*, 23(1) WASH. Q. 215 (2000).

[30] A more limited use of plurilateral codes began in the Kennedy Round of negotiations of the GATT in the 1960s, which, for example, produced a plurilateral code on anti-dumping.

approach remained largely one of negative integration. Multilateral trade liberalization largely ground to a halt after the Uruguay Round; the current Doha Round has stalled since 2001.

The question that WTO framers needed to ask was whether the approach to disciplining non-tariff measures should change from GATT-think. Was the priority for disciplines on non-tariff measures still ensuring against erosion of tariff concessions once global tariffs levels were relatively low and countries began unilaterally reducing tariff levels well beyond their bound levels? With the expansion of the GATT/WTO membership, should there be more positive integration of countries' regulatory objectives and social preferences into multilateral trade cooperation? WTO framers responded with the German word '*jein*', something between '*ja*' and '*nein*', as we explain in what follows.

1. Tariff Classifications in the WTO Era

Originally, only the EU and United States had elaborate tariff classifications. Now, other WTO members are doing the same. Expanded tariff classifications allow countries to target narrower classes of goods for preferential treatment, including those that reflect important social values. But with more elaborate tariff classifications, WTO members may advance demanding regulatory standards, which can reduce their possible sources of those goods to a handful of developed nations. The obligation to extend concessions on these regulation-informed tariff lines to other WTO member states on a nondiscriminatory (most-favored nation) basis may not mean much without a corresponding effort to improve their technical capacity to meet its requirements. National tariff classifications do not benefit from an irrefutable presumption of legality. They are WTO-compliant only if the classification meets the standard embedded in Article 3.3 of HS, which is that they are sub-classifications of HS classifications at the six-digit level. Case law suggests that it may be permissible to include, *inter alia*, end uses and consumer preferences in those sub-classifications.[31] Surprisingly, there have been no disputes on this score yet, even though consumers and governments may have different preferences (otherwise there is no need to preempt consumers' choice through elaborate classifications).

---

[31] 1 Mavroidis (n. 13 above) 137 ff.

2. Non-tariff Barriers

The Agreement on Technical Barriers to Trade (TBT) is an update of the Tokyo Round agreement on the same subject, whereas the Agreement on Sanitary and Phytosanitary (SPS) measures is new and covers measures protecting human and animal health, and the environment from pests and diseases. The GATT also remained in place and covers transactions that do not fall under the SPS and the TBT Agreements. The TBT and SPS Agreements mostly function as an insurance policy to preserve the value of tariff concessions. This is particularly true for the SPS Agreement, which was included to guard against the EU reintroducing its common agricultural policy (CAP) through regulation.[32] Parts of the TBT and SPS Agreements, however, do more than protect against erosion of tariff concessions. Both Agreements include provisions that promote consideration of the negative impact that unilateral or excessive exercise of regulatory authority might entail, but do not go so far as to oblige WTO members to adopt a particular standard of protection or most efficient measure to achieve the stated social preference.

Performance over process (technology)-based measures are recommended, because there may be gains from having different approaches to meet regulatory objectives.[33] TBT requires governments to base their interventions on international standards, if they exist and are appropriate to the social preferences pursued.[34] It mandates that regulatory measures be necessary to achieve their objective and applied in a nondiscriminatory manner.[35] 'Necessary' means that WTO members must, when faced with equally effective regulatory alternatives to achieve the stated social preferences, choose the measure that has less impact on the global volume of goods traded.[36] Both the TBT and SPS Agreements urge WTO members to contemplate the necessity to intervene with their own regulatory measure in the first place.[37] International standards are presumed necessary under the TBT Agreement.[38] Finally, the TBT includes a mix of legally binding

---

[32] *Ibid.* at 2:455 ff.

[33] Agreement on Technical Barriers to Trade, Art. 2.8, 15 April 1994, Marrakesh Agreement Establishing the World Trade Organization ('WTO Agreement'), Annex 1A, 1868 UNTS 120 ('TBT Agreement').

[34] TBT Agreement, Art. 2.4.

[35] *Ibid.* Arts. 2.1, 2.2.

[36] 2 Mavroidis (n. 13 above) 493–4.

[37] Appellate Body Report, *United States—Measures Concerning the Importation, Marketing and Sale of Tuna and Tuna Products*, WTO Doc. WT/DS381/R (adopted 13 June 2012), paras. 321–2.

[38] TBT Agreement, Art. 2.5.

obligations (like obligations to notify and explain national regulations) and a best efforts requirement to pursue mutual recognition, equivalency, and harmonization initiatives with other WTO members.[39]

Besides fulfilling all the same requirements that are in the TBT Agreement, WTO members must, by virtue of the SPS Agreement, also adopt science-based measures and be consistent in formulating their policies.[40] A basis is, of course, another indicator that a measure has not been enacted with protectionist intent. The consistency-requirement reinforces that requirement, since it requires WTO members to treat risks in a comparable manner.[41] The provisions on necessity, science, consistency, and international standards in the TBT and SPS Agreements serve as additional proxies (besides the nondiscriminatory application of measures) for suppressing protectionist behavior, but seek to do more. These rules are also meant to discourage measures that have no disparate impact on imports, but are still excessive in achieving their intended regulatory objective.[42] The WTO is still largely in a negative integration mode on regulatory measures and social preferences.[43] The WTO has only now started to take the first steps towards regulatory cooperation.

3. Regulatory Cooperation in the WTO

The term 'regulatory cooperation' is like an accordion. It has been used to mean as little as dialogue and an agreement to notify and consult on a new or proposed regulatory measure, or as much as to refer to an obligation to adopt international standards or to recognize or harmonize with another nation's laws.[44] Unlike tariffs, one cannot (and should not) eliminate

---

39 *Ibid.* Arts. 2.5–2.7.

40 Agreement on Application of Sanitary and Phytosanitary Measures, Art. 2.2, 15 April 1994, Marrakesh Agreement Establishing the World Trade Organization, Annex 1A, 1868 UNTS 493 ('SPS Agreement').

41 SPS Agreement, Art. 2.3.

42 See Regan (n. 9 above) (describing the purpose of the TBT and SPS Agreements as restraining 'domestically irrational' policies).

43 Liberalization of investment is, of course, a mitigating factor, since foreign investors will lobby host governments and press for adoption of measures consistent with their regulatory interests. But it is only a mitigating factor.

44 The Organisation for Economic Co-operation and Development (OECD) categorizes international regulatory cooperation into eleven different types. These include: informal regulatory dialogue; nonbinding guidelines or principles; incorporation of international standards codes; transgovernmental networks of regulators; mutual recognition agreements; regional trade agreements with regulatory integration provisions; membership in intergovernmental organizations; formal regulatory cooperation agreements; and harmonization through supranational or joint

regulation. Regulations are essential tools for promoting public health and safety, safeguarding the environment and rights of citizens, and ensuring the proper functioning of markets.[45] Prohibiting discriminatory non-tariff barriers to trade ('negative integration') has helped open markets, but not yielded consistent, efficient, and effective oversight. The OECD (2013) has identified three categories of costs from international regulatory incoherence: (1) informational costs of identifying and understanding different regulations; (2) specification costs of complying with divergent and duplicative regulatory standards; and (3) conformity assessment costs of demonstrating compliance with standards.[46] Absent cooperation or the ability to pay these adjustment costs, foreign producers and suppliers, especially small and medium-sized enterprises, face market exclusion.[47]

International regulatory incoherence, even when not directed against foreign producers, may occur and not be effectively restrained by the provisions in the SPS and TBT Agreements. First, regulatory authorities may impose duplicative rules and conformity assessment procedures. Second, regulatory authorities may impose divergent but similarly stringent rules. This scenario is most likely to occur among states at similar levels of economic development.[48] Third, regulatory authorities may impose divergent rules and conformity assessment procedures with different levels of stringency. This scenario is most likely to occur with states at different levels of economic development. At low levels of income, citizens and their governments tend to prioritize economic growth and efficiency over stringent domestic regulatory oversight.[49] As personal incomes increase, many lower-income nations are raising regulatory standards and improving oversight, especially over goods and services destined for export, but face capacity, resource, and governance challenges in doing so.[50] The regulatory incoherence in each of these scenarios does not run

---

institutions. OECD, International Regulatory Co-operation: Addressing Global Challenges (2013).

[45] Alan O. Sykes, *The (Limited) Role of Regulatory Harmonization in International Goods and Services Markets*, 2(1) J. Int'l Econ. L. 49 (1999).

[46] See OECD (n. 44 above).

[47] Keith E. Maskus et al., *The Cost of Compliance with Product Standards for Firms in Developing Countries: An Econometric Study* (World Bank Pol'y Res. Working Paper No. 3590, 2005).

[48] Daniel W. Drezner, All Politics is Global: Explaining International Regulatory Regimes (2008).

[49] *Ibid.* (comparing stringent regulation to a luxury good with high-income elasticities of demand).

[50] Institute of Medicine (IoM), Ensuring Safe Foods and Medical Products Through Stronger Regulatory Systems Abroad (2012). See also

afoul of WTO restrictions on discriminatory measures or the provisions in the TBT and SPS Agreements on using necessary, science-based, and consistent regulatory measures and international standards where appropriate. The TBT and SPS Agreements include mutual recognition and equivalence provisions to help address the problem, but they are limited to best endeavors.[51]

Dialogues and cooperation agreements, for instance, can help improve transparency, sensitize trading nations to others' needs and costs, and advance coordination among regulators and between regulators, businesses, and trade officials.[52] Peer-to-peer regulatory networks, consensus best practice guidelines and principles, and intergovernmental organizations promote work sharing and build regulatory and enforcement capacity, making it cheaper for nations to adopt policy reforms and maintain consistent regulatory oversight.[53] At the same time, mutual recognition agreements and regional trade deals can help increase the benefits of adopting convergent, adequate, and efficient regulations and conformity assessment by reinforcing their link to market access.[54]

Cornelius van der Meer, China's Compliance with Food Safety Requirements for Fruits and Vegetables: Promoting Food Safety, Competitiveness and Poverty Reduction (2006) (describing a two-tier regulatory model in which products for export are fairly well regulated, but those for domestic consumption are not).

[51] TBT Agreement, Art. 2.7; SPS Agreement, Art. 4.

[52] Examples of dialogues include the Transatlantic Business Dialogue (TABD) and the Transtlantic Consumer Dialogue (TACD). Examples of cooperation agreements include the Canada-United States Regulatory Council (RCC) and the Rapid Alert System for Nonfood Dangerous Products (RAPEX), established pursuant to the EU-China Regulatory Cooperation Framework.

[53] Examples of peer-to-peer regulatory networks include the Basel Committee on Banking Supervision and the Africa Medicines Regulatory Harmonization initiative. The APEC and the OECD put forward a frequently cited voluntary checklist to promote regulatory quality and efficiency. See APEC-OECD, APEC-OECD Integrated Checklist on Regulatory Reform (2005). Other institutions besides APEC and OECD involved in promoting regulatory cooperation and common standards include the International Organization for Standardization (ISO).

[54] Examples of mutual recognition agreements include the Trans-Tasman Mutual Recognition Arrangement (see Trans-Tasman Mutual Recognition Act 1997 (NZ)), which has had the notable output of the Food Standards Australia/New Zealand (FSANZ, see Food Standards Australia New Zealand Act 1991 (Austl.)), an effort to cooperate on the development of food standards before the adoption of national standards. Examples of regional trade agreements include the Comprehensive Economic and Trade Agreement (CETA), a deal between Canada

(1) Cooperation in the WTO on non-tariff barriers

Both the TBT and SPS Agreements[55] include measures to promote regulatory transparency and adoption of international standards, which facilitate trade and regulatory objectives by providing predictability for exporters and investors and simplifying regulatory compliance.[56] Both agreements also provide a procedure for raising specific trade concerns (STCs), a more intensive avenue for engagement on non-tariff measures that stops short of formal dispute settlement. STCs are formal requests for clarification by a WTO member regarding another member state's TBT- or SPS-related measure. STCs could lead to informal settlement or provide the basis for a formal dispute.[57] STCs represent a modest form of cooperation that could lead to more common rules. Since the advent of the WTO, there has been an upward trend in the STCs filed annually, from four in 1995 to eighty-five in 2014.[58]

Annex 3 of the TBT Agreement includes the Code of Good Practice (CGP) for the Preparation, Adoption and Application of Standards, which encourages transparent standard setting and nondiscriminatory, performance-based, and nonduplicative standards. In 2000, the WTO Committee on Technical Barriers to Trade ('TBT Committee') agreed to additional principles for international standard setting bodies, which include an open, impartial, and consensus-driven approach that promotes effective standards and incorporates the concerns of developing countries.[59] The TBT Committee has also promoted the use of

---

and the EU with extensive provisions on product standards, mutual recognition, and regulatory cooperation.

55 This issue is discussed in detail in Petros C. Mavroidis and Robert Wolfe, *From Sunshine to a Common Agent: The Evolving Understanding of Transparency in the WTO*, 21 Brown J. World Aff. 117 (2015).

56 SPS Agreement, Arts. 2.3, 3, 5.4; TBT Agreement, Arts. 2.2s, 2.4, 2.8; General Agreement on Trade in Services, Arts. 2.2, 2.3, 5.6, 15 April 1994, Marrakesh Agreement Establishing the World Trade Organization, Annex 1B, 1869 UNTS 183 (GATS).

57 Once aware of a challenge against its measure, a WTO member might drop its original complaint. It could also,take the view that it has a strong case before a WTO panel.

58 Erik N. Wijkström, *The Third Pillar: Behind the Scenes, WTO Committee Work Delivers* (E15 Task Force on Reg. Systems Coherence Think Piece, August 2015).

59 Committee on Technical Barriers to Trade, Decisions and Recommendations adopted by the WTO Committee on Technical Barriers to Trade since 1 January 1995, Note by the Secretariat, Revision 47, WTO Doc. G/ TBT/1/Rev.12 (21 January 2015).

good regulatory practices.[60] These practices promote the exchange of information and more coordination among regulators, standard setting bodies, and trade officials. In 2014, the WTO Committee on Sanitary and Phytosanitary Measures ('SPS Committee') launched a mechanism to mediate rising trade tensions over food safety and animal-plant health measures.[61]

(2) Tariffs

Although not formally under the auspices of the WTO, for the time being at least, negotiations of the Environmental Goods Agreement (EGA) were launched in July 2014.[62] The purpose of this negotiation is to agree on preferential tariffs for goods that protect the environment. To do this, negotiators have to agree on classifications that reflect regulatory processes that protect the environment and provide tariff advantages to those goods that conform to the agreed process.

IV. CHANGE KNOCKING ON THE WTO'S DOOR

GVCs started in the 1960s when international companies took advantage of lower tariffs, the containerization of shipping, and better information and communication technologies to slice up and outsource parts of their manufacturing supply chains to lower-cost, specialist suppliers abroad. In the 1990s and 2000s, the shift to GVCs expanded to services and to sectors ranging from food production to medical research and development (R&D). With the 2008 global economic crisis, GVCs evolved again, becoming more regional and reorienting around

---

[60] See e.g., Committee on Technical Barriers to Trade, Summary Report of the TBT Workshop on Good Regulatory Practice 18–19 March 2008, Note by the Secretariat, WTO Doc. G/TBT/W/287 (6 June 2008); Committee on Technical Barriers to Trade, Fifth Triennial Review of the Operation and Implementation of the Agreement on Technical Barriers to Trade under Article 15.4, 5–6, WTO Doc. G/TBT/26 (13 November 2009).

[61] For more details, see WTO, *Steps Officially Agreed for Mediating Food Safety, Animal-plant Health Friction*, WTO News (10 September 2014), available at www.wto.org/english/news_e/news14_e/sps_10sep14_e.htm (last visited 1 August 2017).

[62] Eighteen countries are participating in the negotiation: Australia; Canada; China; Chinese Taipei (Taiwan); Costa Rica; the EU; Hong Kong, China; Iceland; Israel; Japan; Korea; New Zealand; Norway; Singapore; Switzerland; Liechtenstein; Turkey; United States, available at www.wto.org/english/tratop_e/envir_e/ega_e.htm (last visited 1 August 2017).

large emerging economies with rising production capabilities and more domestic consumer demand.[63] The inputs and components in GVCs comprise 56 percent of the global goods trade and 73 percent of the services trade.[64]

The rise of GVCs has had significant benefits.[65] Unbundling affords businesses the opportunity to scale economies, implement just-in-time production, and greater flexibility in meeting consumer demand. Consumers gain more affordable goods and services. GVCs have contributed to the shift of employment in labor-intensive sectors away from higher-income nations—a painful and unsettling process for the workers and communities affected—but also created specialized, higher-wage jobs in those nations coordinating production networks and in product design, branding, and other large-margin activities. Sustaining and expanding these benefits of GVCs requires consistent, adequate, and efficient regulation. GVCs involve the cross-border movement of capital, knowledge, and intermediate services and parts. As the number of countries and cross-border transactions in GVCs multiply, so do the economic costs of inefficient, duplicative, and divergent regulations. The proliferation of uncoordinated regulations challenges even sophisticated multinationals. The high costs of regulatory compliance can keep small and medium-sized businesses out of GVCs altogether. Divergent rules on data storage and analysis and product testing can act as localization requirements, making production in other jurisdictions infeasible.[66] According to the WTO *World Trade Report* (2009), one-third of the global trade in goods (estimated US$15.8 trillion in 2008) was affected by standards that differ across jurisdictions.[67]

Inability to comply reliably with food safety rules, labor standards, or environmental requirements can lead to border detentions and import bans, liability and reputational damage, and contractual penalties for

---

[63] Gary Gereffi, *A Global Value Chain Perspective on Industrial Policy and Development in Emerging Markets*, 24 DUKE J. COMP. & INT'L L. 433 (2014).

[64] WTO, WORLD TRADE REPORT 2011, THE WTO AND PREFERENTIAL TRADE AGREEMENTS: FROM CO-EXISTENCE TO COHERENCE (2011).

[65] See the excellent analysis of this issue in Bernard M. Hoekman, *Supply Chains, Mega-Regionals and Multilateralism: A Road Map for the WTO* (EUI Working Paper RSCAS 2014/27, 2014), available at http://cadmus.eui.eu/bitstream/handle/1814/30198/RSCAS_2014_27_Rev2.pdf (last visited 1 August 2017).

[66] OECD and World Bank, *Inclusive Global Value Chains: Policy Options in Trade and Complementary Areas for GVC Integration by Small and Medium Enterprises and Low-Income Developing Countries*, available at www.oecd.org/trade/OECD-WBG-g20-gvc-report-2015.pdf (last visited 1 August 2017).

[67] WTO, WORLD TRADE REPORT 2009, TRADE POLICY COMMITMENTS AND CONTINGENCY MEASURES (2009).

manufacturers and suppliers. It can deter foreign direct investment in countries. Particularly in export driven lower-income economies, the costs of regulatory noncompliance can be significant. In the context of GVCs, adequate, consistent regulatory oversight no longer just ensures social preferences; it is an investment in economic development and trade facilitation.[68] Health, labor, financial and environmental policymakers likewise have an interest in adequate, consistent, and collaborative international regulation. In the GVC context, regulatory agencies cannot do their jobs without the help of their counterparts. Imports that the US Food and Drug Administration (FDA) regulates, for example, have grown nearly six-fold (from 6 million to 35 million shipments) over the twelve years and now involve more than 300,000 facilities in more than 150 different countries.[69] There are legal and practical limits on inspecting such a multitude of producers and suppliers. Border and port surveillance can supplement but not replace oversight, control, and surveillance by local regulators and industry. In sectors involving global public goods, such as stemming climate change, financial contagion, or pollution, regulatory objectives cannot be met without international coordination. International collaboration helps regulators gather information and share best regulatory practices and tools, building their knowledge base for effective regulation.[70] For all these reasons, and in many sectors, regulatory oversight in one country increasingly depends on the adequacy and consistency of regulatory oversight in other countries.[71]

---

[68] IoM (n. 50 above). See also Miet Maertens and Jo Swinnen, *Food Standards, Trade, and Development, Review of Business and Economics*, 54(3) Rev. Bus. & Econ. 313 (2009); World Bank, *Food Safety and Agricultural Health Standards: Challenges and Opportunities for Developing Country Exports* (World Bank Pol'y Res. Working Paper No. 31207, 2005); Spencer Henson, *Food Safety Issues in International Trade, in* Food Safety in Food Security and Food Trade Brief 5 (Laurian J. Unnevehr ed., 2003).

[69] US Food and Drug Administration, Global Engagement Report 3 (2012), available at www.fda.gov/downloads/AboutFDA/ReportsManualsForms/Reports/UCM298578.pdf (last visited 1 August 2017).

[70] Gráinne De Búrca et al., *Global Experimentalist Governance*, 44 Brit. J. Pol. Sci. 477 (2014); Charles F. Sabel and David G. Victor, *Governing Global Problems under Uncertainty: Making Bottom-Up Climate Policy Work*, 136 Climatic Change 1 (2015).

[71] Thomas J. Bollyky, *Global Health Interventions for Food and Drug Safety* (CSIS Global Health Pol'y Ctr. Report, November 2009); Thomas J. Bollyky, *Regulatory Coherence in the Trans-Pacific Partnership Talks, in* The Trans-Pacific Partnership: A Quest for a Twenty-First Century Trade Agreement 171–86 (C.L. Lim et al. eds., 2012); Thomas J. Bollyky, *A Role for the WTO on*

1. A Positive Integration Strategy

Why don't governments undertake the necessary regulatory reforms unilaterally? Here, a partial analogy to GATT-think helps demonstrate the need for international regulatory cooperation and the reasons why negotiators and regulators need to pursue that objective together. There are regulatory reforms that government may undertake unilaterally that benefit trade. Countries may increase their export competitiveness by unilaterally adopting good regulatory practices.[72] Improving the quality, transparency, and predictability of regulatory measures helps domestic actors and importers alike.[73] Over time, adoption of administrative law practices like regulatory impact assessment might also assist exporters if it brings the trade and regulatory communities closer and sensitizes both sides to each other's concerns.[74]

Structured international regulatory cooperation provides benefits that may not be easily achieved unilaterally: predictability, accountability for backsliding, iterative engagement on deepening integration, and gains in efficiencies from increased scale.[75] Regulations are also not like tariffs, which emerging economies have effectively liberalized unilaterally in order to attract GVC-related investment.[76] Regulations are dynamic, with rules and their enforcement changing in response to emerging political and market demands, past performance, and new scientific developments.[77]

Regulatory Coherence (E15 Task Force on Reg. Systems Coherence Think Piece, August 2015).

72 OECD, OECD Guiding Principles of Regulatory Quality and Performance (2005), available at www.oecd.org/regreform/sectors/37318586.pdf (last visited 1 August 2017). See also Jose Guilherme Reis and Thomas Farole, Trade Competitiveness Diagnostic Toolkit 94–5 (2012); OECD, Regulatory Policies in OECD Countries: From Interventionism to Regulatory Governance (2002).

73 Scott Jacobs and Peter Ladegaard, Regulatory Governance in Developing Countries (2010).

74 Cary Coglianese, *Measuring Regulatory Excellence*, *in* Achieving Regulatory Excellence 291–308 (Cary Coglianese ed., 2016).

75 Douglas A. Irwin, Free Trade Under Fire (4th ed., 2015).

76 Richard Baldwin, *Unilateral Tariff Liberalization* (NBER Working Paper No. 16600, 2010), available at www.nber.org/papers/w16600.pdf (last visited 1 August 2017).

77 This is particularly true for experimentalist regulatory or adaptive regimes that rely on continous monitoring and assessment of performance in ways designed to induce continuous learning and revision of standards. See Charles F. Sabel and William H. Simon, *Minimalism and Experimentalism in the Administrative State*, 100 Geo. L.J. 53, 82–3 (2011) (citing the Hazards Analysis and Critical Control Points (HACCP), the international risk management methodology, and

Unilateral adoption of good regulatory practices can only do so much to spur freer trade and more effective oversight if nations are not regularly engaged with each another on adopting and maintaining internationally consistent, adequate measures and shared conformity assessments.[78]

International, rules-based cooperation has an important role in improving domestic-decision making. Even in democratic governments, domestic interests may subvert good regulatory practices, such as the obligation to provide notice and comment and assess the cost-benefits of proposed rules. The accountability and transparency that comes with iterative international regulatory engagement on shared goals provides an important restraint on that occurring.

Trade negotiators are unlikely to advance their priorities on improved international regulatory coherence without the support and active participation of regulatory officials. The reasons are two-fold. First, consistent, efficient regulatory oversight depends as much on how rules are interpreted and enforced as the rules themselves. Even with the support of a country's leadership, it is difficult in a top-down approach to mandate and maintain iterative, cooperative behavior. Meaningful, sustained progress is more likely if the objective is addressing transnational regulatory priorities as well as facilitating international commerce. Second, without the engagement of regulatory authorities, concerns about diminishing cherished social preferences would make the already difficult politics of trade liberalization unworkable. Fears over food safety and genetically modified organisms have driven a fierce backlash in the EU against the Trans-Atlantic Trade and Investment Partnership (TTIP) negotiations. Popular support for greater global economic integration is more likely to occur in a regulator-supported effort to ensure that freer trade also results in safer goods, a more protected environment, and more assured public health and welfare.

Regulatory cooperation initiatives have better prospects if pursued in partnership with trade officials and aligned with the needs of exporters and their governments. Here too, the reasons are two-fold. First, regulatory agencies are chronically underfunded and domestic in their orientation. Few of these agencies have the resources, staff, and mandate to pursue international cooperation and capacity building. Trade talks provide the structure, resources, and high-level political commitment that international regulatory dialogues often lack. Second, advancing international cooperation in regulatory dialogues alone is unlikely to exploit the opportunity

---

equivalence assessment and acceptance, as international examples of approaches that incorporate an experimentalist approach).

78 Bollyky (2012) (n. 71 above).

that the rise of GVCs presents. The challenge of achieving international cooperation is greatest in areas where (1) regulatory regimes are mature, and (2) the responsible agencies in large consumer-markets disagree.[79] Even non-substantive changes, such as adoption of common forms or sharing of inspection reports, impose adjustment costs on regulatory agencies with well-established systems. The adoption of international standards in many heavily regulated sectors has been slow, and in high-income countries, such as the United States, poor.[80] Regulator-to-regulator dialogues such as the International Conference on Harmonization of Technical Requirements for Registration of Pharmaceuticals for Human Use can make progress, but often require decades to do so.[81]

The rise of GVCs provides a powerful, but time-limited, incentive for regulatory agencies to incur adjustment costs in order to engage with each other and spread common norms and standards to the many other countries involved in producing goods and services for import in their markets. The incentive exists because engagement on the adoption of common rules and certification regimes among large consumer markets makes it easier for exporters and investors in other countries to achieve economies of scale by participating in the process and complying with the common regulations that result from that engagement.[82] That incentive is time-limited because it may become harder to drive adoption of international norms as emerging economies grow and their consumer markets become a bigger target for exporters. Further growth and a shift to more domestic consumption in emerging economies are positive trends, but adding more large-consumer markets will make reaching agreement on regulatory standards harder, especially in the absence of an effective multilateral institutional support. The emerging trends of large multinational companies localizing production in big end-use markets[83]

---

[79] Drezner (n. 48 above).

[80] See e.g., Donna Roberts and Tim Josling, *Tracking the Implementation of Internationally Agreed Standards in Food and Agricultural Production* (Int'l Food & Agric. Trade Pol'y Council Pol'y Brief, 2011).

[81] IoM, International Regulatory Harmonization Amid Globalization of Drug Development: Workshop Summary (2013).

[82] David Vogel, Trading Up: Consumer and Environmental Regulation in a Global Economy (1995); Miet Maertens and Johan F.M. Swinnen, *Trade, Standards, and Poverty: Evidence from Senegal*, 34 World Dev. 161 (2009); Brian Greenhill et al., *Trade-based Diffusion of Labor Rights: A Panel Study, 1986–2002*, 103 Am. Pol. Sci. Rev. 669 (2009).

[83] Jeffrey Immelt, CEO, General Electrics, Commencement Address to New York University Stern School of Business (2016), available at http://fortune.com/2016/05/20/ge-immelt-globalization/ (last visited 1 August 2017).

and the increasing reliance of these companies on private standards, third-party certifications and proprietary quality management systems only compound that challenge.

2. Bilateral and Regional Initiatives

In 1990, there were approximately seventy active PTAs; today there are more than 500.[84] The explosive growth of PTAs began with the end of the Uruguay Round and the increased relative importance of non-tariff measures as potential restraints on trade.[85] Roughly sixty PTAs have terms that go beyond the WTO TBT commitments; fifty have SPS commitments that exceed those in WTO Agreements.[86] Countries with greater participation in GVCs are more likely to enter into these 'deep integration' PTAs and more likely to reap the benefits of doing so.[87] The four major PTAs under negotiation at the time of writing—the Regional Comprehensive Economic Partnership (RCEP), the Trans-Pacific Partnership (TPP), the Trade in Services Agreement (TiSA) and the TTIP—all include efforts to advance regulatory cooperation beyond disciplines on nondiscrimination. Serious regulatory cooperation also occurs in the International Organization for Standardization (ISO) and other standard-setting institutions that include trade facilitation and promoting common standards in their mandate.

The most ambitious regulatory cooperation efforts have occurred in PTAs among like-minded nations with regional ties. The EU has pursued regulatory integration among its 28 Member States through a wide variety of means, including mutual recognition, harmonization, and cooperative approaches such as joint reviews. The United States has launched regulatory cooperation councils with Canada and Mexico.[88] More of the Comprehensive Economic and Trade Agreement (CETA), the deal between Canada and the EU, is devoted to product regulation, mutual recognition, and regulatory cooperation than to reducing tariffs and other border restraints.[89]

Developing countries have agreed to environmental commitments in

---

[84] Nuno Limão, *Preferential Trade Agreements*, *in* HANDBOOK OF COMMERCIAL POLICY 279–367 (Kyle Bagwell and Robert W. Staiger eds., 2016).

[85] Petros C. Mavroidis and André Sapir, *Dial PTAs for Peace: The Influence of Preferential Trade Agreements on Litigation Between Trading Partners*, 49 J. WORLD TRADE 351 (2015).

[86] WTO (n. 64 above).

[87] Gianluca Orefice and Nadia Rocha, *Deep Integration and Production Networks: An Empirical Analysis* (WTO Staff Working Paper ERSD-2011-11, 2011).

[88] Debra P. Steger, *Institutions for Regulatory Cooperation in 'New Generation' Economic and Trade Agreements*, 39 LEGAL ISSUES ECON. INTEGRATION 109 (2012).

[89] CETA entered into force provisionally on 21 September 2017.

PTAs, when those states have not exhibited similar eagerness to do so at the multilateral level.[90] One reason might be the additional trade gains afforded in a PTA. The intensity of cooperation may differ, however, among heterogeneous trade partners. Like-minded trading partners have proven more willing to agree to binding disciplines than unlike-minded players.[91] Still, nonbinding commitments may help sensitize trading partners to the worries of their counterparts, encourage information exchange on the rationale for a regulatory intervention, and to set the stage for more rigorous cooperation in the future.

Policy independence and regulatory sovereignty were among the reasons (along with anti-immigration) cited in the United Kingdom's June 2016 vote to exit the EU.[92] The 2007 initiative by Australia and New Zealand to create a joint regulatory agency for medicines and medical devices failed.[93] Previous initiatives to improve EU-US regulatory cooperation made little progress.[94] The near-term prospects for a successful conclusion of the TTIP talks do not look good at the time of writing.

Association of Southeast Asian Nations (ASEAN) countries have used mutual recognition agreements (MRAs) and cooperation on standards, technical regulations, and conformity assessment to promote themselves successfully as a GVC hub.[95] Transatlantic cooperation initiatives may have led to few regulatory changes, but they have helped reduce trade friction.[96] The China-EU Rapid Alert System for Nonfood Dangerous

---

90 See e.g.,the United States-Peru Trade Promotion Agreement, chapter 18, 12 April 2006, available at https://ustr.gov/sites/default/files/uploads/agreements/fta/peru/asset_upload_file953_9541.pdf (last visited 1 August 2017) (as an illustration of this effect).

91 See Henrik Horn et al., *Beyond the WTO? An Anatomy of the US and EU Preferential Trade Agreements*, 33 World Econ. 1565 (2010) (offering some examples to this effect).

92 Brexit Brief, *Dreaming of Sovereignty*, The Economist (10 March 2016), available at www.economist.com/news/britain/21695056-talk-taking-back-power-may-be-delusional-more-democracy-not-dreaming-sovereignty (last visited 1 August 2017).

93 Australian Government Department of Health, Therapeutic Goods Administration (TGA), *Australia New Zealand Therapeutic Products Authority (ANZTPA) postponed*, TGA Media Releases and Statements (16 July 2007), available at www.tga.gov.au/media-release/australia-new-zealand-therapeutic-products-authority-anztpa-postponed (last visited 1 August 2017).

94 Shayerah Ilias Akhtar and Vivian C. Jones, *Transatlantic Trade and Investment Partnership (TTIP) Negotiations* (Congressional Research Service Report, February 2014).

95 WTO (n. 64 above).

96 Raymond J. Ahearn, *Transatlantic Regulatory Cooperation: Background and Analysis* 16–17 (Congressional Research Service Report, August 2009).

Products (RAPEX), initially spurred by trade concerns, has investigated and helped constructively resolve thousands of product safety concerns. The US FDA recently established a trade office to take a more 'comprehensive and proactive' role in the regulatory cooperation discussions occurring as part of the TPP and TTIP negotiations, in contrast to the more defensive posture that the Agency had previously taken.[97]

3. PTAs, a Second Best

PTAs are a second-best solution to the problem of achieving freer trade and better regulation because these agreements do not encompass the range of countries in global commerce.[98] The organization of production and trade into GVCs means that products are affected by many regulatory jurisdictions. Those jurisdictions are diverse, including nations at different stages of economic development and some with relatively nascent regulatory agencies.[99] Agreements that do not span all these economies cannot effectively advance global integration and efficiency, particularly in sectors dominated by GVCs and dependent on cross-border data flows and digital commerce.

Pursuing international regulatory cooperation on a multilateral basis avoids the need to introduce multiple parallel discussions among regulatory and trading partner counterparts. It also leverages the process for regulatory convergence, albeit rudimentary, that is already in place at the WTO. Many developing countries, especially the lowest-income nations, are not included in RCEP, TPP, or the other PTAs with ambitious commitments on regulatory cooperation and coordination. The EU has agreements that include regulatory cooperation with African countries, but those are generally not binding.[100] The PTAs that involve low- and middle-income countries do not include particularly 'deep' or enforceable

---

[97] *FDA Takes More Active Role In TTIP, TPP Talks; Establishes Trade Team*, Inside U.S. Trade (3 September 2013), available at http://insidetrade.com/daily-news/fda-takes-more-active-role-ttip-tpp-talks-establishes-trade-team (last visited 1 August 2017). More recently, the FDA has pushed for the regulatory cooperation inititiates with the EU, started as part of the TTIP talks, to occur in parallel, but separate from those negotiations.

[98] PTAs with countries at different stages of economic development tend to have less integration on TBT and SPS regulation. WTO (n. 64 above) 141–2.

[99] Richard Baldwin, *Global Supply Chains: Why They Emerged, Why They Matter, and Where They are Going* (CTEI Working Paper 2012-13, 2012) (demonstrating the range and diversity of countries in GVCs and their degree of engagement).

[100] See Horn et al. (n. 91 above).

regulatory commitments that go beyond those in WTO agreements.[101] There has been some targeted engagement between the trade and regulatory agencies of varying levels of economic development, especially on food safety and in the Asia-Pacific Economic Cooperation (APEC) Forum, but progress has been slow.[102]

V. WTO 2.0

The original precepts of GATT-think—reducing the negative externalities that result from uncoordinated and non-transparent actions in a trading system with many partners—remains as relevant as ever. But, the corporate governance of the GATT/WTO must change to reflect the decline in tariffs and the other traditional barriers to commerce and the emerging challenges of advancing trade, regulation cooperation, and social preferences in a global economy dominated by GVCs. We refer to this integration strategy as the 'new WTO-think'. The remainder of this chapter explores the parameters of that concept, and provides our 'nudge' for a serious discussion on WTO institutional reform.

1. Change the Corporate Governance of the WTO

The WTO was designed for a different global economy in which mostly finished goods moved across national borders. With the rise of GVCs, tariffs and other border restraints matter less and the protection of investments and intellectual property, and free flow of components, services, and people, matters more. As a result, the rules and the institutions that support that trade must also evolve. A focus on market access, simple and broadly applied rules, and dispute resolution will not advance the deeper integration that is increasingly required in the world economy. Nondiscrimination and reciprocity cannot assure market access when it is conditioned upon satisfying country-specific regulatory standards and social preferences.[103] The availability of binding dispute resolution will do little to attract the active engagement of regulatory authorities in international cooperation, when those

---

[101] See *ibid.*; WTO (n. 64 above).

[102] FSANZ, APEC, avaiable at http://www.foodstandards.gov.au/science/international/apec/Pages/default.aspx (last visited 1 August 2017) (introducing the APEC Food Safety Cooperation Forum (FSCF)).

[103] Pol Antràs and Robert W. Staiger, *Offshoring and the Role of Trade Agreements*, 102(7) Am. Econ. Rev. 3140 (2012).

regulatory authorities have bitterly resented past WTO reviews of their choices.

2. A Strategy for WTO 2.0

The challenge is doing so at a time when global economic power is increasingly diffuse and there is little appetite for empowering a supranational institution to reduce the market segmenting effects of regulatory policies and social preferences.[104] This will require supplementing the traditional approach of the GATT/WTO—fixed, universal rules subject to binding dispute resolution—with the opportunities for interested members to pursue shared social preferences, plurilateral agreements, and outside partnerships, and to multilaterize the regulatory cooperation occurring via PTAs and regional economic communities.

(1) Social preferences advance cooperation

Advancing international trade liberalization has emerged as an important way to pursue social preferences. The reverse is also becoming true.[105] The WTO should embrace and reinforce this positive link between trade and social preferences, wherever it exists, to advance multilateral agreements on regulatory cooperation. An increasing number of PTAs, particularly those involving the United States and EU, advance social preferences such as labor and environmental protections, human rights, rule of law, and other aspects of public governance.[106] The trend began with the North American Free Trade Agreement as a way to resolve political differences in the United States over trade. In the most recent iteration, the TPP, many of the labor and environmental measures are enforceable and subject to dispute resolution. Promoting social preferences as part of PTAs spreads the benefits of trade liberalization, discourages the worst mistreatment of workers and the environment, and builds public support for trade deals.[107]

---

[104] Bernard M. Hoekman, *'Behind the Border' Policies: Regulatory Cooperation and Trade Agreements*, *in* Future of the Global Trade Order 69–96 (Bernard M. Hoekman and Carlos A. Primo Braga eds., 2016).

[105] See Benjamin M. Friedman, The Moral Consequences of Economic Growth (2005) (on bidirectional link between economic growth and advancing moral benefits such as improving the environment, reducing poverty, promoting democracy, and making for a more open and tolerant society).

[106] We reference here PTAs that the EU has entered with other nations, not the EU integration process itself.

[107] Kimberly A. Elliott, *Labor Standards and the TPP*, *in* The Trans-Pacific Partnership: A Quest for a Twenty-First Century Trade Agreement 200–10 (C.L. Lim et al. eds., 2012).

Conversely, the desire to advance shared social preferences has also spurred interested states to pursue trade initiatives in sectors of concern. The EU, for example, established a Forest Law Enforcement Governance and Trade Initiative to engage lower-income nations in promoting trade in legal timber, to increase the market demand for sustainable forestry, and to reduce the supply of illegally harvested timber.[108]

Social preferences are particularly important to trade initiatives on regulatory cooperation. Shared preferences provide the basis for establishing a framework of shared goals that may attract the active support and participation of regulators.[109] These regulators, in turn, have the sector-specific understanding and mandate to implement, monitor, and maintain meaningful cooperation.[110] Trade disciplines, like most laws and regulations, are generally less effective when they require taking iterative, positive action instead of barring unwanted behavior. Compliance with the notification or technical transfer requirements in trade agreements, for example, has been poor.[111] Mandating that regulators cooperate or consider the trade impact of their proposed rules is likely to be less effective than providing a workable framework for interested states to advance shared social preferences and consistent, effective, and efficient oversight in commercially important sectors.

The WTO has taken a tentative step in this direction with the EGA.[112] In addition to embracing the social preferences of interested members to advance trade and regulatory goals, the EGA negotiation sets two other precedents that should be more widely embraced: the renewed use of WTO plurilateral agreements and the effort to multilateralize progress that occurred first on a bilateral or regional basis.

---

[108] Gregory Shaffer, *How the World Trade Organization Shapes Regulatory Governance*, 9 Reg. & Governance 1 (2015).

[109] In this sense, social preferences may play an analogous role in advancing international regultory cooperation in a trade context as framework goals do in experimentalist regulatory regimes. See Sabel and Simon (n. 77 above) 79; Christine Overdevest and Jonathan Zeitlin, *Assembling an Experimentalist Regime: Transnational Governance Interactions in the Forest Sector* 7 (Comparative Res. in L. & Pol. Econ. Res. Paper No. 16/2012, 2012), available at http://digitalcommons.osgoode.yorku.ca/clpe/18 (last visited 1 August 2017).

[110] See De Búrca et al. (n. 70 above).

[111] Keith E. Maskus, Private Rights and Public Problems: The Global Economics of Intellectual Property in the 21st Century (2012).

[112] 2012 APEC Leaders Declaration, Annex C, 8 September 2012, available at http://apec.org/~/media/Files/LeadersDeclarations/2012/2012_AELM_Declaration_AnnexC.pdf (last visited 1 August 2017).

(2) Variable geometry

The WTO has 164 very heterogeneous members, ranging from Switzerland, Norway, and Liechtenstein to the least developed countries in the sub-Saharan Africa. The social preferences of each member are of course, defined endogenously and depend, in part, on the capacity of each member to finance the necessary regulatory policies to give effect to those preferences. Preferences also reflect culture, religion, the particulars of the legal system, and the relative homogeneity of that society. Whereas some social concerns are almost universal (climate change), others are quite local (pollution of a lake shared between two WTO members). Under these circumstances, it is highly unlikely that regulatory cooperation will involve all its members.

With the exception of the Agreement on Government Procurement (GPA), the WTO has largely moved away from the Tokyo Round model of plurilateral integration. Some criticized this Tokyo Round model of integration as increasing transaction costs for WTO members. But the advantage of that approach was the increased legitimacy. Each trading nation agreed to the commitments with which it could live. What we recommend here is, in a nutshell, a return to that approach, at least on the issue of regulatory cooperation.

The WTO should encourage the formation of plurilateral agreements, a design that, unlike free trade areas, keeps the umbilical cord between international regulatory cooperation and the multilateral trading regime tight. Intense regulatory cooperation is occurring within free trade areas, especially among like-minded partners. In light of this, it appears that trading nations gave up on the Tokyo Round approach of Codes too soon. Those Codes evolved at a moment when WTO agreements on non-tariff barriers became a pressing issue, and when agreement across all GATT members would have been impossible. That same dynamic is even more pronounced today.

The advantages of WTO plurilateral agreements over PTAs are that the former provide greater transparency, input, and an explicit path to accession to non-party WTO members in the future. They are also less likely than PTAs to impose negative externalities on third countries.[113] There are two ways in which a subset of WTO members may currently undertake additional commitments and trade liberalization: critical mass agreements

---

[113] Bernard M. Hoekman and Petros C. Mavroidis, *Embracing Diversity: Plurilateral Agreements and the Trading System*, 14(1) World Trade Rev. 101 (2015); Bernard M. Hoekman and Petros C. Mavroidis, *WTO 'à la carte' or 'menu du jour'? Assessing the Case for More Plurilateral Agreements*, 26(2) Eur. J. Int'l L. 319 (2015).

(CMAs) and plurilateral agreements (PAs). A CMA is an agreement in which negotiated disciplines apply only to a subset of WTO members, but its benefits are implemented on a most-favored nation (MFN) basis and, thus, must apply to all WTO members. The significant advantage of CMAs is that these agreements do not require unanimous approval of the full WTO membership. The disadvantage of CMAs is that they allow free-riders and MFN disciplines are an uneasy fit with forms of cooperation that depend on like-minded regulatory agencies with similar capacities.[114]

In contrast, neither the benefits nor the commitments undertaken in PAs extend to non-signatories. The major other advantage of PAs is, unlike CMAs, clear legal authority exists to extend and deepen WTO commitments on regulatory matters in areas other than services. The major disadvantage of PAs, however, is that their incorporation into the WTO must occur 'exclusively by consensus' of the full membership, which greatly undermines the value of proceeding on a plurilateral basis. For PAs to become a feasible approach for advancing deeper regulatory cooperation at the WTO, Article X:9 of the WTO Agreement must be amended to no longer require approval of PAs by the full membership. In order to secure the necessary support for that amendment, WTO members should also agree to binding principles limiting the use of PAs. These principles should include assurances that non-signatories will not be compelled to adopt PAs at a later date. The principles should also provide that members may join PAs later with the same conditions that applied to the original signatories and require implementation support to be provided for least developed member countries.[115] Requiring the creation of an observer status for non-participating WTO members would also ensure that non-participating WTO members have full transparency and can raise concerns.

The subject matter for PAs should be member state driven and reflect the need for interested governments to advance shared social preferences and efficient and effective regulatory oversight as part of global economic integration. This is most likely to occur in GVC-dominated sectors that raise important social welfare issues and depend on internationally consistent, adequate, and efficient standards for both freer trade and more effective regulatory oversight.[116] One promising area is digital trade in goods and services, where regulatory paradigms are less entrenched in many countries and the adequacy and effective oversight of

---

[114] See Bollyky (2015) (n. 71 above).
[115] See Lawrence (n. 7 above).
[116] See Bollyky (2015) (n. 71 above).

privacy, security, consumer protection, and contract enforcement depends on international cooperation and consistency.[117] Other potential areas include global food and drug safety[118] and trade-related measures to mitigate harmful emissions and adapt to the changing environment of climate change, such as climate smart agriculture.[119] The design of PAs should, of course, depend on the sector and the objectives for trade and regulatory cooperation. The WTO General Agreement on Trade in Services (GATS) provides a potentially useful model for a rolling process of rule-making in a still novel area. The contribution of the GATS was to expand the coverage of services in the multilateral trading system but to do so in a way that afforded flexibility to countries undertaking new commitments.

In the regulatory cooperation context, this approach might involve a baseline set of rules and goals and a venue for engaging on regulatory transparency, information sharing, and monitoring progress. The agreement should establish priorities, transparent procedures, and a mechanism for monitoring and reporting progress but otherwise be left broad, allowing member countries the flexibility to collaborate on emerging challenges. It might operate in a hub-and-spoke model and include voluntary, topic-specific, regulator-led working groups for interested members to negotiate deeper forms of regulatory cooperation.[120] The hub, perhaps a committee of participating member states with observer member states present, should: prepare common technical regulations and standards; recommend adoption of international standards; and promote the sharing of surveillance data and inspection reports through the development of confidentiality arrangements. The substance of these recommendations and proposals should be generated through ad hoc, regulator-led working groups. These groups should be open to consultation with non-state actors and experts. The recommendations and proposals of the Committee should be made public, allow expert consultation, and be subject to notice and comment.[121]

---

[117] See James Manyika et al., *Digital Globalization: The New Era of Global Flows* (McKinsey Global Institute Report, 2016); Joshua P. Metzler, *A New Digital Trade Agenda* (E15 Expert Group on the Digital Econ. Overview Paper, August 2015).

[118] IoM (n. 50 above); Bollyky (2009) (n. 71 above).

[119] See Climate Change and Food Systems: Global Assessments and Implications for Food Security and Trade (Aziz Elbehri ed., 2015), available at www.fao.org/3/a-i4332e.pdf (last visited 1 August 2017).

[120] See Richard B. Stewart, *State Regulatory Capacity and Administrative Law and Governance under Globalization* (Inst. for Int'l L. & Just. Working Paper 2016/1, 2016) (making a similar suggestion).

[121] Bollyky (2012) (n. 71 above) (makes similar recommendations with regard

Maintaining the sovereignty and local accountability of national regulatory authorities will be essential to the success. Agreed upon regulatory cooperation measures should not have binding domestic legal effect. Thereby, where new legislation is required to implement such measures, opportunity for parliamentary scrutiny is assured. Participating member states should, however, commit to decide on whether to adopt these joint recommendations within a fixed period of time and to provide a written, detailed explanation when deciding not to do so. Given the relative novelty of regulatory cooperation and sensitivities around policy independence, subjecting the agreement to WTO dispute resolution would discourage participation and inclusion of strong provisions in this area.

(3) Expanding partnerships

Public-private partnerships are now common in GVCs. The WTO needs to play a larger role in working with partners to create the broadly-supported governance frameworks that can advance international regulatory cooperation in the areas that most affect trade and investment.[122] Regulatory cooperation is not the exclusive mandate of the WTO. Many other institutions, including the OECD, Food and Agriculture Organization of the United Nations (FAO), World Economic Forum, World Health Organization, and the International Centre for Trade and Sustainable Development, are in this space and can take the lead in setting substantive norms. The World Bank, regional development banks, and donors such as the Bill and Melinda Gates Foundation are all supporting regulatory cooperation initiatives and might offer financial resources for capacity-building, policy dialogue, and monitoring.

Firms participate in and manage GVCs, engage in private and nongovernmental international standard setting initiatives, and support corporate social responsibility and capacity building programs. Civil society, nongovernmental institutions, and academic institutions have expertise and the deep understanding of local circumstances to contribute agenda setting and ongoing problem solving.

(4) Multilateralizing progress in PTAs

The WTO needs a mechanism to 'multilateralize' the important regulatory cooperation that will inevitably happen in smaller clubs of

---

to what would have been a '21st century approach' to regulatory coherence in the TPP).

[122] See Hoekman and Mavroidis (n. 7 above).

like-minded countries, such as PTAs or regional economic communities.[123] Multilateralizing that progress would reduce business costs, expand regulatory cooperation and fulfillment of shared social preferences, and unlock the welfare benefits of trade liberalization in both the WTO and the PTAs.[124]

One idea could be to initiate automatic negotiations any time a fixed number of countries belonging to the three distinct WTO groups (developed, developing, and least developed countries) entered into comparable arrangements on regulatory cooperation in separate agreements. Another idea would be to tie those automatic negotiations to the adoption of regulatory cooperation in a PTA covering a high percentage (such as 85 percent or more) of global trade in a goods or services sector.

VI. CONCLUSION

Can the WTO evolve? The institution remains a product of the post-World War II, Bretton Woods era, created by a coalition of powerful states, and vested with their authority to act as their agent in addressing well-defined coordination and governance problems emerging from their interdependence. Like many of its sister institutions from this era, such as the World Bank, the International Monetary Fund, the United Nations and its agencies such as the World Health Organization, the WTO has struggled as power dispersed to a greater number of states and non-state interests and broad-based consensus became harder to reach. It is no answer to state that the WTO will evolve because it must to survive. This has been true for many post-World War II era intergovernmental institutions for decades. Many have not and may never evolve.

The emergence of GVCs, however, provides the WTO with an

---

123 For similar suggestions see Richard Baldwin et al., *Beyond Tariffs: Multilateralising Non-tariff RTA Commitments*, *in* MULTILATERALISING REGIONALISM: CHALLENGES FOR THE GLOBAL TRADING SYSTEM 79–141 (Richard Baldwin and Patrick Low eds., 2009); Joel P. Trachtman, *International Trade: Regionalism*, *in* RESEARCH HANDBOOK IN INTERNATIONAL ECONOMIC LAW 151–76 (Andrew T. Guzman and Alan O. Sykes eds., 2007).

124 Baldwin et al. (n. 123 above) (notes that the EU has a similar 'clubs within the club' approach with its Closer Cooperations, or Enhanced Cooperations). See also Robert Wolfe, *The OECD Contribution to the Evolution of 21st Century Trade Law*, 43 GEO. WASH. INT'L L. REV. 277 (2011) (expressing a similar view regarding the role of OECD, as an institution that shapes but, unlike the WTO, does not codify trade law. PTAs codify trade law, of course, but may also be able to shape the multilateral process as well).

opportunity. In the sectors where this production model dominates, GVCs create a potential alignment of the interests of a wide diversity of states and non-state actors interested in freer trade, better regulation, and broader economic development. PTAs, standard setting organizations, and regulator-to-regulator initiatives are making important progress in advancing the international regulatory cooperation needed in the GVC era. That progress is limited, however, because these arrangements do not encompass the full range of countries in global commerce.

This chapter advocates changes in the corporate governance of the GATT/WTO to reflect the decline in tariffs and border restraints to commerce and the emerging challenges of advancing trade, regulation cooperation, and social preferences in a global economy dominated by GVCs. Together, these changes form a positive integration strategy that we refer to as the new WTO-think. This strategy remains rooted in the original rationale of the GATT (or GATT-think) of reducing the negative externalities of unilateral action and solving important international coordination challenges, but is more inclusive of regulators and non-state actors and more flexible and positive in its means. In particular, the WTO should embrace the confluence of shared social preferences and trade, where it exists, as a motivation for advancing international regulatory cooperation. It should multilateralize the important regulatory cooperation occurring in smaller clubs of like-minded countries and adopt changes to facilitate the use of PAs where agreement across all WTO members is not yet possible.

PART II

Trade in ICT goods and services

3. Free flow of data and digital trade from an EU perspective

Rolf H. Weber*

I. INTRODUCTION

The creation of a Digital Single Market (DSM) has been acknowledged by its institutions as a pivotal objective of the European Union (EU). The foundational document is the Commission's Communication for a DSM Strategy for Europe, presented on 6 May 2015.[1] The main aim of the DSM Strategy is to put more emphasis on the free flow of information and data, thereby removing cross-border restrictions of international data transfers.

This Communication is based on the assumption that the EU needs liberalized digital facilities encompassing better online access for consumers and businesses to infrastructures, and outlining cross-border e-commerce rules that are trustworthy.[2] The chosen approach also impacts the international trade relations of the EU; the broad understanding of the thirty concerned countries (including the European Economic Area (EEA)) influences megaregional agreements such as the negotiated Transatlantic Trade and Investment Partnership Agreement (TTIP) between the EU and the United States.

The main objective of the DSM Strategy consists in the attempt to strengthen the digital ecosystem and overcome market fragmentation. Furthermore, the Commission proposes to create the right conditions and a level playing field for advanced digital networks and innovative services. Thereby, a data economy should be built (Big Data, Cloud services, Internet of Things) which is likely to increase the competitiveness of the EU industry; in addition, wealth maximization should be

* Valuable support given by Dr.iur. Dominic J. Staiger is highly appreciated.

1 European Commission, *A Digital Single Market Strategy for Europe*, COM(2015)192 final (6 May 2015).

2 For an overview, see Rolf H. Weber, *Competitiveness and Innovation in the Digital Single Market*, 2 Eur. Cybersecurity J. 72 (2016).

boosted through standardization and interoperability based on innovative technologies.[3]

For obvious reasons a stable and foreseeable legal framework for digital services needs to be implemented as a cornerstone of the single market concept.[4] Since data privacy rules have an impact on the cross-border data flow, the new General Data Protection Regulation (GDPR), adopted in April 2016, is another important pillar of the legal framework.[5] Therefore, data protection should no longer be viewed as a negative factor but as an 'essential competitive advantage' in the DSM, i.e., data protection principles need to be embedded into the corresponding strategy for the data economy.

II. FREE DATA FLOW AND THE MAJOR COLLIDING OBJECTIVES: DATA PRIVACY AND SECURITY

Taken literally, the principle of free cross-border flow of data should remove all restrictions related to data transfers. However, other interests in the society, particularly data privacy, can eventually collide with such an objective.

1. The Ends: Data Protection

In the case of personal data, specific protection objectives are given and justify certain restrictions of data transfers. As a consequence, the respective tensions must be addressed in order to overcome (potential) collisions. In the Digital Market Strategy, the Commission did not clearly address these tensions between the free movement of data and the protection of personal data but the most recent Communication of January 2017 on Building a European Data Economy more intensely addresses the respective issues.[6]

The problem with the tensions already starts at the level of the

---

[3] See European Commission (n. 1 above) 4–9.

[4] See European Commission, *Building a European Data Economy*, COM(2017)9 final (10 January 2017) at 4.

[5] Regulation (EU) 2016/679 of the European Parliament and of the Council of 27 April 2016 on the protection of natural persons with regard to the processing of personal data and on the free movement of such data, and repealing Directive 95/46/EC (General Data Protection Regulation) [2016] OJ L119/1–88.

[6] European Commission (n. 4 above) 5.

applicable international human rights instruments: For example, the European Convention on Human Rights (ECHR) guarantees the freedom of expression and the freedom of information (Article 10 ECHR), as well as the fundamental right to privacy (Article 8 ECHR) equally. Many cases help to assess the borderlines between these two human rights but legal uncertainties in the interest balance tests still exist.[7] In addition, even in the privacy field, a parallel notion of the mentioned fundamental right to privacy and the specific data protection regulations does not prevail.[8] Concretely, the question can be asked whether the right to be forgotten as created and acknowledged by the Court of Justice of the European Union (CJEU) in the *Google* v. *Spain* case is identical to the specific condition on the deletion of data contained in Article 17 GDPR.[9]

In parallel to the Digital Market Strategy, the Commission also launched a European Cloud Initiative that encompasses topics such as services notification, cloud contracts, switching of providers, and open research facilities.[10] This initiative attempts to bring the public and private sectors together with the objective of creating an EU-wide Cloud market. Specific considerations to data protection are missing but the corresponding activities show that the free flow of data cannot be perceived only as an expression of fundamental rights but must also be understood as a 'network' of legal relations that are influencing and channeling information distribution.[11]

In general, the legal uncertainties in respect of potential collisions between the free flow of information and data protection in the case of cross-border data transfers show a certain lack of trust in the respective services on the part of both the consumers as well as businesses. In particular, the exact scope of the fundamental rights remains unclear even if the CJEU has rendered some basic decisions (mainly related to the right to be forgotten in the *Google* v. *Spain* case).[12]

Transparency is another core issue that has gained importance in various

---

[7] See Rolf H. Weber, *The Right to be Forgotten: More Than a Pandora's Box?*, 2 J. Intell. Prop. Info. Tech. & Electronic Com. L. 120, 120–30.

[8] Philippe Boillat and Morten Kjaerum, Handbook on European Data Protection Law 21 (2014).

[9] For further details, see Rolf H. Weber, *On the Search for an Adequate Scope of the Right to be Forgotten*, 6 J. Intell. Prop. Info. Tech. & Electronic Com. L. 2, 2–8.

[10] European Commission, *European Cloud Initiative: Building a Competitive Data and Knowledge Economy in Europe*, COM(2016)178 final (19 April 2016).

[11] *Ibid.* at 3 ff.

[12] C-131/12 *Google Spain SL, Google Inc.* v. *Agencia Española de Protección de Datos (es), Mario Costeja González*, ECLI:EU:C:2014:317.

contexts over the last few years. On the one hand, public access rules have been expanded and procedures developed for sharing information in the hands of public agencies; however, on the other hand, the private sector impacting private life in an equally relevant way through the control of electronic communications has been touched on much less in the respective discussions.[13] At least, the GDPR will soon require a minimum level of disclosure to the data subject in case of a data security breach (so-called 'data breach notification'). However, the way in which data transfers are (not) restricted should become more transparent.

The core challenges for enterprises in this respect consist in the lack of a digital contract network which reflects their own sub-processor contracting, as well as of any further parties down the supply chain. Mostly, such information is only given in the form of paper contracts which are time intensive and costly to manage and do not allow for the timely vendor management necessary under the GDPR. Such a software-based solution would allow for a more transparent and real-time management of data protection risks arising in the processor chain.

2. The Means: Data Localization

During the last few years, a new issue has emerged that could jeopardize the free movement of data in the EU, particularly the cross-border transfer of data, namely, the imposition of unjustified data localization requirements by public authorities since these measures effectively reintroduce digital 'border controls'.[14] Examples are requirements to store certain data locally, process local data in the respective country, and have local archives.

Data location requirements can be based on legal rules or administrative guidelines or practices requiring the processing or storage of data in an electronic format to be limited to a particular geographical area of jurisdiction (often on the assumption that local authorities are able to more easily scrutinize locally stored data).[15] Theoretically, localization can be used as a proxy for assurances in terms of privacy or data security, however, in practice these measures rarely contribute to the objectives they are intended to achieve but—to the contrary—cause a potential loss of cost savings and efficiency gains.[16]

---

[13] See e.g., Association for Progressive Communications, *Freedom of Expression and the Private Sector in the Digital Age*, available at www.ohchr.org/Documents/Issues/Expression/PrivateSector/APC.pdf (last visited 10 July 2017).

[14] European Commission (n. 4 above) 6.

[15] *Ibid.*

[16] See Matthias Bauer et al., *Unleashing Internal Data Flows in the EU: An*

Recently, the trend, both in Europe and elsewhere, goes towards more data localization, partly based on the misconception that localized services are safer than cross-border services. Data localization also negatively influences the wider adoption of Cloud computing and storage, and results in higher costs.[17]

III. NEW DATA PROTECTION FRAMEWORK IN THE EUROPEAN UNION

1. General Background

At a very early stage, namely, in the 1970s, the Council of Europe had started to draft a document intended to harmonize data protection levels throughout Europe. The Council of Europe has forty-seven member states more or less covering the whole Continent of Europe and some countries in Asia being geographically close to Europe.

The respective Convention No. 108 was released in 1980 and subsequently adopted by most Member States of the Council of Europe.[18] Notwithstanding the fact that this Convention encompasses most of the basic substantive principles of data protection, the wording is relatively vague and enforcement is not easily possible. In addition, the EU rules have partly superseded Convention No. 108.

Due to rapid technological advances, it has recently become unavoidable to amend Convention No. 108. The respective revised wording is nearly completed,[19] however, the European Commission insisted on having the EU Regulation implemented at first stage. Nevertheless, an adoption and ratification of the revised Convention No. 108 can be expected soon.

Economic Assessment of Data Localisation Measures in the EU Member States, Eur. Ctr. Int'l Pol. Econ. (December 2016), available at http://ecipe.org/app/uploads/2016/12/Unleashing-Internal-Data-Flows-in-the-EU.pdf (last visited 10 July 2016).

[17] European Commission (n. 4 above) 6.

[18] Convention for the Protection of Individuals with regard to Automatic Processing of Personal Data, 10 October 1985, ETS No. 108.

[19] Draft Modernised Convention for the Protection of Individuals with regard to the Processing of Personal Data (September 2016), available at https://rm.coe.int/CoERMPublicCommonSearchServices/DisplayDCTMContent?documentId=09000016806a616c (last visited 10 July 2017).

2. General Data Protection Regulation as Distillation of Experience

In October 1995, the EU released Directive 95/46 on the Processing of Personal Data.[20] Contrary to a Regulation, the contents of a Directive must be transformed into national law. This normative situation does not only cause an eventual legal fragmentation between different countries but also a substantial time delay in the implementation; this fact is particularly cumbersome in view of the fast-occurring technological advances.

Apart from the mentioned technological developments, data protection has also become more frequently an issue in court practice based on applicable fundamental rights. In two landmark decisions, the CJEU has acknowledged a specific right to be forgotten (*Google* v. *Spain*)[21] as a new human right, and has also invalidated the Safe Harbour Agreement between the EU and the United States (*Schrems* v. *Ireland*).[22] Even before this, the CJEU critically assessed the previous Data Retention Directive.[23] On the one hand, the increased importance of the EU fundamental rights approach complements the data protection framework, on the other hand, it can also cause tensions and conflicts if the concepts are not more or less identical.[24] Therefore, new data protection rules have become imperative.

In April 2016, as mentioned, the new General Data Protection Regulation ('the Regulation') has been adopted;[25] this Regulation will come into force in late May 2018. The new Regulation contains more than double the number of provisions compared to the previous Directive. Its provisions are directly applicable in the EU Member States; some reservations are carved-out in order to allow nation-states to adopt specific rules.

3. Main Principles of the New Regulation

The new Regulation reiterates the existing principles for data protection, namely, the correctness of the data; the proportionality between the data processing and the actual need to have data available for the concerned

---

20 Directive 95/46/EC of the European Parliament and of the Council of 24 October 1995 on the protection of individuals with regard to the processing of personal data and on the free movement of such data [1995] OJ L281/31, 31–50.

21 *Google Spain* (n. 12 above) paras. 89–99.

22 C-362/14 *Maximillian Schrems* v. *Data Protection Commissioner, Joined Party Digital Rights Ireland Ltd.*, ECLI:EU:C:2015:650.

23 C-293/12 and C594/12 *Digital Rights Ireland and Seitlinger and others*, ECLI:EU:C:2014:238.

24 See Part II.1.

25 See n. 5 above.

enterprise; the data minimization principle; and the good faith processing requirement.[26] Generally, the processing of personal data under the GDPR is only allowed if either (i) the data is being processed for the performance of a contract; (ii) the data subject has given his or her consent to the processing; (iii) the controller of the data can demonstrate the legitimate interest and compliance with the fundamental rights of the data subject.[27]

The key persons in the data protection framework are the controller and the processor of data. The controller determines the purpose and means of processing of personal data; in comparison with the former Directive, the controller definition in the GDPR also includes the element that the controller must not only determine the means but also the purpose of the processing.[28] Data controllers may only appoint data processors who provide sufficient guarantees to implement appropriate technical and organizational measures, thereby ensuring the proper data processing. Since the data controller must exercise surveillance functions, the conclusion of a binding contract with the data processor is imperative.[29] Data processors are under an obligation to maintain a record of all categories of processing activities and to implement appropriate security measures.[30]

In principle, the GDPR is designed in a technology-neutral way.[31] This approach is appropriate since technology plays a major role in the new regulatory setting. Notions like privacy by design and privacy by default (article 25) are included in the new Regulation. Such measures should also improve data security (article 32). Bigger enterprises will be obliged to conduct data protection impact assessments (article 35) and have implemented data protection management programs on a rolling or at least yearly basis, thereby analyzing whether or to what extent data protection principles are complied with.

The new Regulation also extends the transparency elements. Information requirements are substantially enlarged: when the data is not obtained from the data subject directly but comes from a third-party source, the controller is obliged to inform the data subject of the relevant facts, as well as the recipients or categories of recipients of personal data, where applicable.[32] When a problem in data processing or data storage occurs,

---

26 GDPR, art. 5.
27 *Ibid.* art. 6.
28 *Ibid.* art. 5(7).
29 See e.g., *ibid.* art. 46(2)(e).
30 *Ibid.* art. 30.
31 *Ibid.* recital 15.
32 *Ibid.* art. 13.

the controller is responsible for sending a data breach notification to the concerned person and to the competent authorities.[33]

A highly-contested part of the new Regulation concerns the fines and penalties. Similarly to antitrust law, fines are to be determined on the basis of the yearly turnover of the failing data controller or data processor, respectively. The maximum 4 percent level can lead to fines of several millions.[34] Therefore, the responsibility of ensuring compliance with the obligations of the GDPR is vested in the management of the concerned company. Potential criminal liability for substantial violations of the data protection laws further create heavy pressure on the management of a company to ensure a basic level of compliance.[35]

From a surveillance practice, the functions of the supervisory authorities in data protection matters have been enlarged; in addition, the harmonization of the substantive rules will most likely help in better coordinating the cross-border activities of the supervisory authorities.[36]

4. Transborder Data Flow

(1) Problem of legal fragmentation

In view of the globalization of information and communications networks, different national regulations can lead to the lack of legal interoperability or to legal fragmentation, respectively. Deviating regulatory regimes make information and communications exchanges more difficult and jeopardize cross-border trade. Therefore, the achievement of legal interoperability has become an increasingly discussed topic.[37]

In many fields, the strengths and weaknesses of legal interoperability can be assessed. A particularly good example is the data protection framework.[38] As far as data privacy regulations are concerned, not only legal but also technical interoperability (for example, through a standardization of encryption technologies) is of importance: The optimal degree of technical interoperability should be developed by information technology (IT) engineers implementing the designs of the interoperability criteria.[39]

---

33 *Ibid.* art. 33.

34 *Ibid.* art. 83.

35 *Ibid.* recital 149.

36 *Ibid.* art. 57.

37 See Rolf H. Weber, *Legal Interoperability as a Tool for Combatting Fragmentation* (Global Commission on Internet Governance Paper Series No. 4, 2014).

38 John Palfrey and Urs Gasser, Interop: The Promise and Perils of Highly Interconnected Systems 77 ff. (2012).

39 Weber (n. 37 above) 11.

In respect of legal interoperability, in theory global privacy rules should be available in order to avoid any kind of data transfer restrictions. In practice, however, data protection laws are very different in the various regions of the world and a harmonization of these rules is not to be expected in the near future. But a certain pressure to harmonize data protection standards can be seen on a regional level (not only in the European Union but also in the Asia-Pacific Economic Cooperation (APEC))[40] and reflects the requirements of international trade law: different levels of protection jeopardize the cross-border rendering of services, particularly IT and electronic commerce services.

Due to the complexity of technology, such as Cloud computing, regulations are often difficult to implement. But transparency could facilitate the decision-making processes for businesses considering how to handle transborder data flows. Instead of the 'traditional' geographical approach of looking at the risks caused by the country or location to which the data are to be transferred on the basis of the notion of adequate level of protection, an organizational model should rather be implemented that examines the risks caused by the holder (controller) of the data that are being transferred.[41] This model would substantially rely on an accountability concept allocating the responsibility for the proper treatment of data when shipped abroad to the data controller. Thereby, an appropriate level of protection can be contractually designed by the parties involved.[42]

However, the boundaries of such an approach are reached once the national law of the country in question overrides the contractual provisions that are implemented in order to enable a required level of data protection. Thus, some personal data transfers will remain to bebarred despite all commercial parties seeking to adhere to all data protection requirements. In addition to the application of the national law, the question of effective control and enforcement remains to be assessed. Whether the third party outside the EU adheres to the EU data protection requirements cannot be ascertained by the EU business. It relies heavily on certifications and contractual provisions without any technical hard evidence or control over the use and transfer of the data.

---

40 Asia-Pacific Economic Cooperation (APEC), Privacy Framework (2015), available at www.apec.org/Publications/2017/08/APEC-Privacy-Framework-(2015) (last visited 1 March 2018).

41 Weber (n. 37 above) 12.

42 *Ibid.*

(2) EU framework

In respect of the transborder data flow, the new GDPR in the EU does not deviate significantly from the previous Directive in substance. In principle, data transfers outside the EU are only permissible if certain conditions are fulfilled:[43] the three justification concepts are (i) a determination by the European Commission that a third countries' data protection law provides sufficient safeguards; (ii) the establishment of appropriate binding corporate rules (BCR) by the concerned controller; or (iii) the implementation of contractual arrangements which are securing an adequate data protection. Apart from these conditions stated in the GDPR, bilateral agreements between the EU and third countries could provide for an adequate level of protection, such as in the case of the EU-United States Privacy Shield Agreement (previously the invalidated Safe Harbour Agreement).[44] In practice, the standard contractual clauses offer the most sufficient and reliable way in which businesses can transfer personal data to and from countries outside the EU. Even if the flexibility might be restricted in case of application of this regime, political issues of interpretation problems are less likely to occur than in the case of other approaches.[45]

(3) International cooperation and collision

As mentioned, legal fragmentation leads to tensions between different regulatory regimes. This problem mainly occurs in the Cloud environment, being a highly complex structure if multiple cloud providers are offering their services. In practice, a data controller placing data into the Cloud through a multilayered system must be careful in assessing the involved legal orders.[46]

Data protection regulations can become a trade barrier for international cooperation.[47] However, the view on this topic, as well as its effects, differ, as the United States, for example, is a data importing country which benefits greatly from the flow of data to its online service economy. Thus, any impediment to this data flow in the form of data protection laws is viewed as a barrier to trade in services. The EU does not share this view, as

---

43 GDPR, art. 44.

44 *Ibid.* art. 45.

45 *Ibid.* art. 46(2)(c), (d).

46 Rolf H. Weber and Dominic N. Staiger, Transatlantic Data Protection in Practice 3 ff. (2017).

47 However, this view is not shared by the EU despite the efforts made by the United States to push this issue. See *FOIA Request Confirms Data Protection is Not a Barrier to Trade*, EDRi (2 December 2015), available at https://edri.org/foia-request-confirms-data-protection-is-not-a-barrier-to-trade/ (last visited 10 July 2017).

it only seeks to ensure the protection of its citizens' personal data. If other countries adhere to the same standard as the EU they can freely transfer data based on an adequacy decision of the EU Commission.

Furthermore, contrary to other markets (for example, financial markets), the cooperation between the data protection supervisory authorities is not very well developed. Nevertheless, the exchange of information through administrative assistance is becoming increasingly important. At least within regional areas such as the EU, new provisions of the GDPR are facilitating cooperation between the national supervisory authorities.[48]

5. Law Enforcement

The enforcement of data protection obligations is key for the effectiveness of the regulatory framework. Therefore, the enforcement provisions of the GDPR now provide for a wide range of new instruments; supervisory authorities particularly have the discretion to impose fines and other sanctions. From a procedural perspective, it is important that non-profit organizations and associations can become involved in the exercise of individual rights under the GDPR.[49] As a consequence, it is anticipated that a growth in the number of complaints will be seen in the future.

Of importance is also the fact that interest groups are entitled to bring 'class actions' before courts in Europe, being a measure not traditionally applied outside of the United States. This field is particularly suitable for associations interested in supporting individuals having suffered from a violation of data protection laws.[50]

Associations approved by national law can also bring claims without complaint by the concerned data subject and thus are in a position to act as a compliance monitoring body with a market regulatory function in such cases in which the supervisory authorities have not been able to take measures due to their limited resources.[51] As a consequence, the number of judicial proceedings is likely to increase; thereby, law enforcement will not only be strengthened but legal certainty in the interpretation of GDPR provisions also improved.

---

48 GDPR, recital 139.
49 *Ibid.* recital 142.
50 *Ibid.* art. 80.
51 *Ibid.* art. 80(2).

IV. DIGITAL TRADE

1. EU Data Economy

As mentioned, the European Commission published a Communication with the title Building a European Data Economy in January 2017, mainly dealing with the possibilities of addressing the issue of access to data. The details of a regulatory framework facilitating data access could constitute a building block for a future legal framework designing the proper functioning of the data economy.[52]

The mentioned Communication takes into account the applicable data protection framework[53] but rather concentrates on non-personal data.[54] In particular, machine-generated data being created without direct intervention by computer processes, applications or services, or by sensors processing information received from equipment or machinery, whether virtual or real, gain importance.

As pillars for the future digital economy the following issues are mentioned:[55]

- data producers' rights and rules on access, partly including a monetary remuneration as compensation;
- default contract rules that can be combined with an unfairness control in business to business contractual relationships.

The elaboration on the rights to data requires a clear delineation between rights to exclusive use, rights to non-exclusive use, and integrity protection.[56] In the light of the growing interconnectedness of data-driven economies, clear rules as to the use and right to data need to be established. Often three main areas of law affect this notion. These areas encompass intellectual property rights, data protection rights (mainly access and deletion rights of the data subject), as well as property rights as far as the data is part of a physical device.[57] The complex interaction of these legal frameworks must be harmonized to allow a truly open EU data economy which can benefit from the vast range of new technologies and services.

---

52 European Commission (n. 4 above) 8 ff.

53 *Ibid.* 5 ff.

54 *Ibid.* 9.

55 *Ibid.* 11–12.

56 *Ibid.* 12.

57 See Gabriella Cattaneo et al., *Data Ownership and Access to Data: Key Emerging Issues* 10 ff. (Eur. Data Mkt. SMART 2013/0063 D 3.6 & D 3.7, 2016).

2. Supply of Digital Content

The European Commission adopted the DSM Strategy of the European Union in May 2015. The most important legal instrument presented subsequently to the publication of the DSM Strategy is the draft for a Directive on certain aspects concerning contracts for the supply of digital content (Digital Content Directive, September 2015).[58] The proposed Directive attempts to overcome the existing differences between the offline and the online regulatory environment and to avoid unjustified impediments for online transactions. The Commission proposes to have implemented so-called fully harmonizing rules. In addition and in parallel, a second draft for a Directive on contracts for the online and other distance sales of goods has been presented by the Commission.[59]

The scope of application of the proposed Digital Content Directive is quite broad insofar as the term 'digital content' encompasses a wide variety of data being produced and supplied in digital form and of services allowing the creation, processing, or storage of data in digital form. This definition shows that all data content which potentially plays a role in connection with digital transactions, particularly databases, social networks, electronic auctions and trading platforms, blogging environments or even streaming services, will be covered by the new legal instrument.[60]

An important novelty consists in the provision that the new Directive shall apply to any contract where the supplier delivers digital content to the consumer or undertakes to do so and, in exchange, a price is to be paid or the consumer actively provides counter-performance other than money in the form of personal data or any other data (article 3). Consequently, the European Commission acknowledges that information about persons or market participants do have a comparable value to traditional money.[61] This acknowledgement is probably the most important element in the digital contract legislation since data is accepted as a tradeable commodity.

---

58 European Commission, *Proposal for a Directive on Certain Aspects Concerning Contracts for the Supply of Digital Content*, COM(2015)634 final (9 December 2015).

59 European Commission, *Proposal for a Directive on Certain Aspects Concerning Contracts for the Online and Other Distance Sales of Goods*, COM(2015)635 final (9 December 2015).

60 For more details, see Rolf H. Weber and Dominic Oertly, *E-Commerce und Sharing Economy in der Europäischen Union: Ein vertragsrechtlicher Überblick*, JUSLETTER IT 28 (2016).

61 European Parliament Briefing, *Contracts for Supply of Digital Content to Consumers* (February 2018), available at www.europarl.europa.eu/RegData/etudes/BRIE/2018/614707/EPRS_BRI(2018)614707_EN.pdf (last visited 1 March 2018).

In case of cancellation of the contract and reimbursement of already executed 'compensation', the supplier is obliged in case of a previous payment for data to retransfer the data to the customer in a technologically acceptable format without charging the customer for this service (article 12).[62]

3. Sharing Economy

So far, the European Commission has not presented a legal instrument that would fully encompass all aspects of the sharing economy. A reason for this fact can be seen in the allocation of competences; due to the subsidiarity principle, the Commission only has limited competences in certain respects.

Sharing economy can be defined as 'an economic system in which assets or services are shared between private individuals either for free or for a fee, typically by means of the Internet'.[63] If the sharing takes place on an online platform, the legal relationship probably falls into the scope of the application of the new (above mentioned) Digital Content Directive. However, other facets of daily life are not covered by this Directive; a more overarching approach could help to encompass a wide range of new online business models.

Particularly, questions arise as to the treatment of new services such as Airbnb and Uber. These services are no longer caught by the traditional notion of 'consumer' since the individuals are using and offering these services at the same time; in other words, the previous consumer can easily also become a trader (so-called 'prosumer').[64]

In order to overcome this lack of a comprehensive regulatory framework, the European Commission has published a European Action Plan for a Collaborative Economy in June 2016 inviting EU Member States to coordinate their national laws with the EU legislative initiatives. Substantive issues are:[65]

- improvement of market access;
- more legal clarity in labor relationships and taxes;
- concretization of liability issues and consumer protection.

---

[62] For further details, see Rolf H. Weber, *Data Protection in the Termination of Contract*, *in* CONTRACTS FOR THE SUPPLY OF DIGITAL CONTENT: REGULATORY CHALLENGES AND GAPS 189, 201–2 (Reiner Schulze et al. eds., 2017).

[63] See https://en.oxforddictionaries.com/definition/sharing_economy.

[64] Rolf H. Weber, *Share Economy in the EU and the Law of Contracts*, GEO. WASH. L.REV. 85 (2017), 1777, 1794–1801.

[65] European Commission, *A European Agenda for the Collaborative Economy*, COM(2016)356 final (2 June 2016).

From a general viewpoint, it can be assumed that the market access regulations will become more flexible as this is in the interest of online businesses. However, based on the complexity of some of the above-mentioned areas of law and their differences in the EU Member States, these adjustments will most likely be implemented only with slow speed.

4. Regulatory Convergence?

Over the last two decades, digital trade has grown to be a substantial part of any industrialized economy. Enabling open data flow and trade in data through cross-border regulatory convergence supports the competitive environment. Therefore, the relevant factors, including data protection and privacy rights, must be balanced against each other and harmonized on the international level. The WTO and its active support in the negotiations conducted within the WTO Working Group on E-Commerce are essential in reaching the goal of a compatible international digital trade framework. This not only includes personal but also non-personal data.

However, in this field, there are currently no obligations to guarantee even a minimum level of data portability. This is partly due to the requirements for implementing data portability that can be technically demanding and costly, as manifold providers of the same services may store data differently.[66]

Recently the first steps for a closer Northern American cooperation was reached through the conclusion of a regional Preferential Trade Agreement, namely, with Canada (Comprehensive Economic and Trade Agreement (CETA)). However, the CETA does not allow the suspension of the transfer of data from one country to the other. Thus, even if Canada violated citizens' rights to privacy and personal data protection, the EU would be prevented from ensuring Canada grant an adequate level of protection. Although the CETA provides some safeguards and exceptions that could allow the parties to adopt rules protecting privacy and personal data, these clauses can only be activated if they are not inconsistent with other provisions of the CETA. In essence, this leads to the Charter of Fundamental Rights of the European Union being placed on a lower level than the CETA.

Additionally, the parties must adhere to the standards of international organizations in which both parties are a member. As Canada is not a member of the Council of Europe's Convention on the Protection of Personal Data, the only standards that Canada can be held to are much

---

[66] European Commission (n. 4 above) 15.

lower than the ones currently applicable in Europe. More concerning is the Regulatory Cooperation Forum created by the CETA, in which companies are able to lobby legislators when laws are being drafted.[67]

Similar to the CETA the EU sought to enter into a trade agreement with the United States. This Transatlantic Trade and Investment Partnership (TTIP) has been suspended by President Trump, as it is being viewed by the current administration as potentially harming US interests. Although the EU would have greatly benefitted from easier access to the US market, the United States would also gain an advantage through easier data transfers. During the initial TTIP negotiations, many commentators viewed the trade agreement as a tool to undermine the GDPR, since large US-based IT companies had heavily lobbied against this new data protection instrument. Thus, the TTIP was viewed as a chance to 'combat' the otherwise strong EU data protection framework. The withdrawal of the United States from the TTIP negotiations has positive effects with regard to data protection as this second avenue of potentially creating loopholes through a wide interpretation of 'interoperability' provisions is no longer available.[68]

V. OUTLOOK

The future of free data flow and trade in services will strongly depend on international agreements which set the boundaries and standards for data usage. However, as there is no global agreement on privacy and data protection in sight due to the large differences in the national data protection frameworks, many challenges will remain over the next decade. Nevertheless, as experience has shown, open data flow and trade in data have increasingly become a regulatory topic of megaregional agreements such as the TTIP and the Trans-Pacific Partnership (TPP) Agreement. This trend is likely to grow over the next years.

To some extent, technology will probably also resolve several of the issues relating to the protection and portability of data. For example, ledger technology (e.g., BlockChain) can be used to identify the rights associated with a certain data-set and can manage the processing according

---

[67] Maryant Fernández Pérez, *CETA Puts the Protection of Our Privacy and Personal Data at Risk*, EDRi (5 October 2016), available at https://edri.org/ceta-puts-protection-privacy-and-personal-data-at-risk/ (last visited 10 July 2017).

[68] Keno Franke, *TTIP and the Right to Protect Personal Data*, open Democracy (30 November 2015), available at www.opendemocracy.net/can-europe-make-it/keno-franke/ttip-and-right-to-protect-personal-data (last visited 10 July 2017).

to the variables included in the chain.[69] Thus, despite large differences in the legal protection of personal data on the national level, technology may be an important factor in bridging the legal gap between jurisdictions.

Finally, data governance by authorities and businesses has become more important. Compliance with data protection standards is a part of the overall governance regime in large organizations. Due to the increased attention to accountability issues, the cross-border privacy standards to be embedded in megaregional agreements might play a bigger role in the future.

69 For further details, see Rolf H. Weber, *Regulatory Environment of the Ledger Technology*, 18(1) COMPUTER L. REV. INT'L 1 (2017).

4. Lessons from the TPP Regulatory Coherence Chapter: The laws governing unsolicited commercial electronic messages as a case study

Shin-yi Peng

I. INTRODUCTION

Traditionally, regulations are designed by governments which seek to contend with perceived market failures.[1] Regulatory interference with the market may be motivated by the need to accomplish economic objectives such as market competition, or non-economic social goals such as consumer protection.[2] To illustrate, in an unregulated market, the competitive mechanism may not always assure socially desirable levels of availability of a service, e.g., universal telecommunications services. Regulation is then justified as a means of generating socially desirable results.[3] In short, domestic regulation is essential to achieve legitimate policy objectives intertwined with trade in services, as the markets do not always work perfectly and cannot always bring the desired results by themselves.[4]

However, regulatory protectionism may impose disadvantages on services in a manner that is not necessary for the fulfilment of a genuine public policy objective.[5] Arbitrary qualification requirements or unclear licensing procedures may limit service trade, just as tariffs, quotas, or other protectionist measures do.[6] Excessive standards or conformity assessment

---

[1] Panagiotis Delimatsis, International Trade in Services and Domestic Regulations: Necessity, Transparency and Regulatory Diversity 87–91 (2007).

[2] *Ibid.* at 91.

[3] *Ibid.* at 87–8. See also Robert Baldwin et al., Understanding Regulation: Theory, Strategy and Practice 2–3 (2012).

[4] Delimatsis (n. 1 above) 87.

[5] Alan Sykes, *Regulatory Protectionism and the Law of International Trade*, 66 U. Chi. L. Rev. 1, 1–3 (1999).

[6] Thomas Bollyky, *Regulatory Coherence in the TPP Talks*, *in* The Trans-

procedures may seriously prevent service suppliers from competing on a level playing field.[7] Domestic regulation adopted and applied without adequate prior notification also disadvantages foreign service suppliers who relatively lack inside information on their domestic competitors.[8] That said, further development of domestic regulation disciplines should be politically popular. Such disciplines will safeguard the effectiveness of market access commitments and therefore ensure that domestic regulations do not render any market access commitments meaningless.[9] Where such disciplines exist, the likelihood of disguised or unnecessary restrictive impediments to service trade may be significantly lower.[10] In this context, the ambition of the international 'good regulatory practice' agenda is aimed at fostering regulatory cooperation by offering a systemic response to the inherent potential problem of regulation that may impose costs but add little overall benefits.[11]

In addition to the problem of regulatory protectionism, another driving force for regulatory coherence is the phenomenon of regulatory fragmentation. As the numbers of countries involved in the supply chains increase, differences in service requirements and standards become more significant as trade obstacles.[12] From the perspective of compliance, service suppliers often confront significant challenges when attempting to comply with diverse national 'behind-the-border measures'.[13] The lack of regulatory consistency among countries creates a costly and burdensome task for service suppliers as they must meet different standards or seek multiple approvals. In short, regulatory fragmentation directs resources away from more effective mechanisms.[14]

To summarize, there are several 'drivers' for regulatory coherence of

---

Pacific Partnership: A quest for a Twenty-first Century Trade Agreement 172 (C.L. Lim et al. eds., 2012).

[7] *Ibid.* at 172–3.

[8] *Ibid.* at 172.

[9] Markus Krajewski, National Regulation and Trade Liberalization in Services 140 (2003).

[10] Pierre Sauvé, Trade Rules Behind Borders: Essays on Services, Investment and the New Trade Agenda 113–15 (2003).

[11] Martin Lodge and Kai Wegrich, Managing Regulation: Regulatory Analysis Politics and Policy 211 (2012).

[12] Bollyky (n. 6 above) 172.

[13] Sauvé (n. 10 above) 113–15.

[14] Bollyky (n. 6 above) 172. See also Shin-yi Peng, *The Soft Law Approach to Regulatory Harmonization: Are We Trading Away Privacy for Economic Integration?*, *in* A 'Liber Amicorum': Mitsuo Matsushita, A Critical Assessment of the International Economic Law and Governance 335 (Julien Chaisse et al., 2016).

the service trade. The General Agreement on Trade in Services (GATS) has recognized that effective implementation of good regulatory practices is critical in minimizing unnecessary trade barriers.[15] However, the GATS contains too few obligations of a truly general nature.[16] In fact, arguably, Article VI of the GATS remains provisional.[17] In this context, the Regulatory Coherence Chapter of the Trans-Pacific Partnership (TPP) addresses the overall system through which TPP members develop regulations,[18] which, as had been advocated by the United States Trade Representative (USTR) of the Obama administration, is 'critical to creating open, fair and predictable environments for businesses operating in Asia-Pacific markets' as supply chains across borders become more integrated.[19] While the United States' trading partners are greatly disappointed by the Trump administration's decision to withdraw from the TPP, the eleven remaining signatory countries ('TPP-11') contend that the deal is far from dead and will move ahead without the United States.[20] In July 2017, the TPP-11 agreed to continue their pursuit of the Agreement and decided to move forward with 'minimal tweaks'.[21] Among the TPP-11, Japan, Australia, and New Zealand expressed the position to quickly put the pact into force 'as is'.[22] In any event, the Regulatory Coherence Chapter of the TPP will serve as a useful reference for future trade negotiations. Section II of this chapter reviews the notion of regulatory coherence and discusses the core elements of regulatory impact analysis (RIA).[23] Section III of this chapter conducts a critical examination of the Regulatory Coherence Chapter. Such an examination focuses on the question of whether RIA can serve as an effective tool to promote regulatory coherence. The main body of this chapter highlights the challenges of the Regulatory Coherence Chapter by using anti-spam legislation as an example. In the final part of this chapter, the main findings are summarized.

---

15 Sykes (n. 5 above) 1.

16 Sauvé (n. 10 above) 34–44.

17 *Ibid.* at 21–8.

18 USTR, *Regulatory Coherence*, available at https://ustr.gov/sites/default/files/TPP-Chapter-Summary-Regulatory-Coherence.pdf (last visited 22 August 2017).

19 *Ibid.*

20 Tomohiro Ebuchit et al., *The TPP 11 Agree to Move Forward with Minimal Tweaks*, Nikkei Asian Review (20 July 2017).

21 *Ibid.*

22 *Ibid.*

23 For simplicity, this article uses the terms 'regulatory impact analysis' and 'regulatory impact assessment' interchangeably.

II. REGULATORY COHERENCE IN THE TPP

1. Regulatory Coherence Chapter

Historically speaking, the origin of regulatory reform was primarily domestic, which focused on improving regulatory quality and streamlining administrative procedures.[24] The US Office of Information and Regulatory Affairs (OIRA), as an example, represents an early movement aimed at facilitating coordination of regulatory decision-making and promoting regulatory harmonization.[25] These domestic deregulatory initiatives evolved over time into a broader political agenda of good regulatory practices that emphasize transparency and efficiency, which has subsequently been embraced across countries.[26] Prior to the launch of the TPP, international-level efforts to promote regulatory reforms and to better harmonize regulatory and trade objectives had primarily evolved through the efforts of the Organisation for Economic Co-operation and Development (OECD) and the Asia-Pacific Economic Cooperation (APEC).[27]

To illustrate, the notion of regulatory coherence has emerged in conjunction with the initiatives of the OECD, which have subsequently converged into the agenda of the APEC.[28] The OECD's 'Recommendation of the Council on Improving the Quality of Government Regulation' ('1995 OECD Report') was the first-ever international statement of regulatory principles common to its members.[29] In addition to the 1995 OECD Report, the Competition Committee adopted a series of Recommendations on regulatory reform,[30] with a view to providing updated responses to

---

[24] Bollyky (n. 6 above) 174. See also Rodrigo Polanco, *The Trans-Pacific Partnership Agreement and Regulatory Coherence*, *in* TRADE LIBERALIZATION AND INTERNATIONAL COOPERATION: A LEGAL ANALYSIS OF THE TRANS-PACIFIC PARTNERSHIP AGREEMENT 232–8 (Tania Voon ed., 2013).

[25] Bollyky (n. 6 above) 174–8.

[26] Polanco (n. 24 above) 235.

[27] Bollyky (n. 6 above) 178.

[28] Polanco (n. 24 above) 231.

[29] See generally OECD, Recommendation of the Council on Improving the Quality of Government Regulation, OECD Doc. C(95)21/FINAL (1995).

[30] See e.g., OECD, REPORT ON REGULATORY REFORM, OECD Doc. C/MIN(97)10 (1997); OECD, *The OECD Guiding Principles for Regulatory Quality and Performance* (2005), available at www.oecd.org/fr/reformereg/34976533.pdf (last visited 22 August 2017); OECD, *The Competition Assessment Toolkit*, available at www.oecd.org/competition/assessment-toolkit.htm (last visited 22 August 2017); OECD, *A Recommendation on Competition Assessment*, OECD Doc. C(2009)130 (2009); OECD, REGULATORY POLICY AND GOVERNANCE: SUPPORTING ECONOMIC GROWTH AND SERVING THE PUBLIC INTEREST (2011).

the challenges of regulatory policy.[31] Those Recommendations set out the importance of political commitment to regulatory reform and 'good regulation' and established links with the elimination of trade barriers.[32] In 2005, the OECD and the APEC launched an Integrated Checklist on Regulatory Reform, which sought to 'improve regulatory quality to enhance the economic performance, cost-effectiveness, or legal quality of regulations and related government formalities'.[33] The checklist is voluntary in nature. Nevertheless, it provides guidance which member economies may use to evaluate their respective regulatory reform efforts during the process of development and implementation of domestic regulation.[34]

As had been stressed by the USTR of the Obama administration, the inclusion of a Chapter on regulatory coherence in the TPP reflects 'a growing appreciation of the relevance of this issue to international trade and investment'.[35] TPP parties' commitments to regulatory coherence are expected to promote good regulatory practice principles in the regulatory development process, which include, for example, coordination among regulators of the TPP parties, opportunities for stakeholder input, and fact-based regulatory decisions.[36] In light of the fact that the legal and regulatory environment in TPP parties is diverse, the USTR had repeatedly advocated for the incorporation of regulatory coherence into the TPP, which will serve to eliminate the problem of 'overlapping and inconsistent regulatory requirements or regulations being developed unfairly and without a sound basis'.[37] Thus, the Chapter will play an important role in 'enhancing the benefits of the TPP Agreement and promoting regional trade and investment'.[38]

In fact, the Chapter on Regulatory Coherence is brief, and the key goal of the Chapter is to 'encourage' TPP parties to strive for widely accepted good regulatory practices in the development of their domestic

---

31 OECD, *Recommendation of the Council on Regulatory Policy and Governance* 20 (2012), available at www.oecd.org/governance/regulatory-policy/2012-recommendation.htm (last visited 22 August 2017).

32 *Ibid.*

33 APEC and OECD, *The APEC-OECD Integrated Checklist on Regulatory Reform*, available at www.oecd.org/regreform/34989455.pdf (last visited 22 August 2017).

34 *Ibid.*

35 USTR (n. 18 above).

36 *Ibid.*

37 *Ibid.*

38 *Ibid.* See also generally the Text of the TPP, available at https://ustr.gov/trade-agreements/free-trade-agreements/trans-pacific-partnership/tpp-full-text (last visited 22 August 2017).

regulatory environment, especially in conducting RIAs when developing regulatory measures, which involve assessing the need for a regulatory proposal, examining feasible alternatives, explaining the grounds for concluding that the selected alternative achieves the policy objectives in an efficient manner, and relying on the best reasonably obtainable existing information.[39]

2. Regulatory Impact Analysis

RIA has been defined as a systemic approach to critically identifying and assessing the effects of proposed and existing regulations and non-regulatory alternatives.[40] RIA strives to be an analytical tool for informing political decision-makers on whether and how to regulate to achieve public objectives.[41] Governments are now facing challenges to design regulatory frameworks, and a major component of such challenges is to ensure that regulations are implemented in an efficient and effective manner.[42] Policy decisions require a careful balance of the public interests, which is not easy to determine.

Arguably, 'better' decision-making processes should result in 'better' policy decisions.[43] At the core of RIAs is an important element of evidence-based approaches to rule-making.[44] Subject to the principle of proportionality, a RIA will generally: (1) identify the problem; (2) identify alternative regulatory options; (3) assess alternative options; and (4) identify the preferred policy option.[45] In the first stage, administrative agencies wishing to propose a new regulation are asked to identify and describe the problem and its drivers.[46] In the second stage, the need for intervention

---

[39] TPP Agreement, Art. 25.5(2), available at https://ustr.gov/sites/default/files/TPP-Final-Text-Regulatory-Coherence.pdf (last visited 22 August 2017).

[40] Polanco (n. 24 above) 250; OECD, Regulatory Impact Analysis: A Tool for Policy Coherence 185 (2009).

[41] *Ibid.* at 12.

[42] *Ibid.* at 9.

[43] *Ibid.* at 12–15.

[44] *Ibid.* at 185.

[45] Office of Communication (OFCOM), Better Policy Making: Ofcom's Approach to Impact Assessment 6–8 (2005), available at www.ofcom.org.uk/__data/assets/pdf_file/0026/57194/better_policy_making.pdf (last visited 22 August 2017).

[46] International Telecommunication Union (ITU), Using Regulatory Impact Analysis to Improve Decision Making in the ICT Sector 9–15 (2014), available at www.itu.int/dms_pub/itu-d/opb/pref/D-PREF-BB.RPT5-2014-PDF-E.pdf (last visited 22 August 2017).

must be translated into concrete policy options, and regulatory officials should be able to identify underlying rationale for any particular regulatory proposal.[47] Stage three is a crucial element of the RIA, as it helps to ensure an integrated discussion of the characteristics of different policy interventions.[48] The assessment of this stage can be qualitative or quantitative and can also be accomplished using different techniques, e.g., cost-benefit analysis, which leads to the final stage of identifying the most preferred policy option.[49]

The OECD reports demonstrate that RIAs can underpin the capacity of governments to ensure that regulations are efficient and effective in a complex world.[50] However, the implementation of RIAs presents complex challenges.[51] Many countries have failed to date in their attempt to mainstream the RIA mechanism in their policy cycle,[52] primarily because it not only requires changes in the institutional setting but also demands adjustments in the behavior and mindset of civil servants.[53] In addition, according to the OECD studies, an overall review of the effectiveness of RIA implementation experiences also suggests mixed success.[54] To conclude, implementing RIAs is challenging from both procedural and methodological perspectives.[55] How, then, can RIA serve as an effective tool to promote regulatory coherence in the TPP?

III. CAN RIA SERVE AS AN EFFECTIVE TOOL?

1. Uncertain Coverage: Self-determined Scope of Application

Article 25.1 of the TPP Agreement explicitly stipulates that the 'covered regulatory measure' under the Regulatory Coherence Chapter refers to 'the regulatory measure determined by each Party'.[56] According to Article 25.3 (Scope of Covered Regulatory Measures), each TPP party shall promptly, and no later than one year after the date of entry into force of

---

47 *Ibid.* at 6.

48 OECD (n. 40 above) 116.

49 ITU (n. 46 above) 17–25. OECD (n. 45 above) 116.

50 See generally *Ibid.* at 185. See also LODGE AND WEGRICH (n. 11 above) 194; BALDWIN (n. 3 above) 315–19.

51 OFCOM (n. 45 above) 6–8.

52 ITU (n. 46 above) 9.

53 *Ibid.* at 8.

54 OECD (n. 40 above) 3.

55 *Ibid.*

56 TPP Agreement, Art. 25.1.

the TPP Agreement for that party, determine and make publicly available the scope of its covered regulatory measures. Article 25.3 further requires that 'in determining the scope of covered regulatory measures, each Party should aim *to achieve significant coverage*' (emphasis added).[57]

In other words, although the definition of 'regulatory measure' is rather broad, referring to any 'measure of general application related to any matter covered by this Agreement adopted by regulatory agencies with which compliance is mandatory',[58] the exact scope of the 'covered regulatory measures' lacks a legally binding commitment. Each party has the right to decide to what extent its domestic regulation should be subject to TPP regulatory coherence obligations. The applicable coverage of the Regulatory Coherence Chapter, as a result, is entirely uncertain.

In short, the scope of measures that will be subject to the regulatory coherence obligation is flexible, as it will be chosen by each TPP party. The loose requirements that 'the coverage is expected to be significant' and that 'the choosing criteria for determining the scope of coverage must be made public' cannot change the voluntary nature of the Chapter, under which governments have the discretionary power regarding what 'measures' or 'agencies' are not covered.[59] Based on Article 25.3, TPP parties are entitled to choose whether to make RIA compulsory for all regulatory acts, or only for certain types of regulation.[60] Considering that the RIA process generally takes time and resources to complete, governments may tend to set a minimum threshold for the obligation to perform RIA.[61]

---

[57] *Ibid.* Art. 25.3.

[58] *Ibid.* Art. 25.1.

[59] See generally Elizabeth Sheargold and Andrew Mitchell, *The TPP Good Regulatory Practices: An Opportunity for Regulatory Coherence to Promote Regulatory Autonomy?*, 15(4) World Trade Rev. 587 (2016). See also Jane Kelsey, *A Preliminary Analysis of the Draft TPP Chapter on Regulatory Coherence* (2011), available at https://Itsourfuture.Org.Nz/Wp-Content/Uploads/2013/09/JK-Memo-On-Reg-Coh.Pdf.

[60] ITU (n. 46 above) 17–18.

[61] *Ibid.* It should also be noted that, according to Art. 25.11 of the TPP Agreement, the obligations of regulatory coherence and the requirements relating to RIA would not be subject to dispute settlement under the TPP. Such an exemption is considered necessary to encourage TPP parties to include a broad range of domestic regulatory measures within the scope of the Regulatory Coherence Chapter. Sheargold and Mitchell (n. 59 above) 599. Therefore, as Elizabeth Sheargold and Andrew Mitchell pointed out, failure to comply with good regulatory practices would not necessarily have any negative consequences for a TPP party.

2. Vague Requirements: Primary v. Secondary Legislation

Unlike the Transatlantic Trade and Investment Partnership (TTIP),[62] the definitions of 'regulatory acts' and 'regulatory authorities' are ambiguous in the TPP. If we take a closer look at the provisions regarding the reach of the 'covered regulatory measure', clearly there is one fundamental question left unanswered, which is, whether the application of the Chapter is only limited to TPP parties' secondary legislation, e.g., rules and regulations, or whether the Chapter is also applicable to parties' primary legislation, e.g., laws and acts proposed by the administration, or, even further, if regulatory coherence obligations should be introduced in Congresses and Parliaments.[63]

The plain text of Article 1.3 of the TPP Agreement,[64] which defines 'measure' as 'any law, regulation, procedure, requirement or practice',[65] seems to suggest that both primary and secondary legislation can fall into the ambit of 'measure of general application' as defined in Article 25.1. However, the main interpretative difficulty in the term 'covered regulatory measure' is the meaning of the word 'regulatory'. The connection of the term 'measure' with the adjective 'regulatory' suggests that the reach of the phrase 'regulatory measure' is not as broad as that of 'measure'. The ordinary meaning of 'regulation' is 'a rule of order issued by a government agency',[66] which is defined as 'not laws but having the force of law since they are issued by governmental agencies at all levels'.[67] Those who take

---

[62] The leaked texts of the TTIP show that 'regulatory acts' and 'regulatory authorities' have been carefully defined by the EU and the United States, respectively. See European Communities, *In Focus: TTIP*, available at http://ec.europa.eu/trade/policy/in-focus/ttip/ (last visited 22 August 2017).

[63] ITU (n. 46 above) 17–18.

[64] Vienna Convention on the Law of Treaties (VCLT), Arts. 31 and 32 have effectively become a fundamental part of WTO law. See e.g., DAVID PALMETER AND PETROS C. MAVRVOIDIS, DISPUTE SETTLEMENT IN THE WORLD TRADE ORGANIZATION 80–84 (2nd ed., 2004). VCLT, Art. 31 stipulates that a treaty shall be interpreted in accordance with the ordinary meaning of its terms in their context and in light of the object and purpose of the treaty. Article 32 deals with supplemental means of interpretation including the preparatory work of the treaty and the circumstances of its conclusion.

[65] TPP Agreement, Art. 1.3, available at https://ustr.gov/sites/default/files/TPP-Final-Text-Initial-Provisions-and-General-Definitions.pdf (last visited 22 August 2017).

[66] FINDLAW LEGAL DICTIONARY, *Regulation* ('An agency is often delegated the power to issue regulations by the legislation that created it. Regulations must be made in accordance with prescribed procedures'), http://dictionary.findlaw.com/definition/regulation.html (last visited 22 August 2017).

[67] LAW.COM—SEARCH LEGAL TERMS AND DEFINITIONS, *Regulation*, available at

a textual approach may suggest that the application of the Regulatory Coherence Chapter is limited to TPP parties' secondary legislation, namely, the implementing regulation authorized by law.

When interpreting 'covered regulatory measure' in context, it appears that the TPP negotiators intended to impose a broad obligation. Article 25.2 stipulates that regulatory coherence refers to the use of good regulatory practices in the process of 'planning, designing, issuing, implementing and reviewing' regulatory measures. In this context, RIA should at least be carried out by the ministries preparing the legislation. However, the term 'relevant regulatory agencies' is repeatedly stressed in Article 25.5 (Implementation of Core Good Regulatory Practices), which again creates confusion.[68] The contextual approach therefore is of little help in interpreting the vague requirements of the 'covered regulatory measure'.

It is also important to verify whether the interpretations of 'covered regulatory measure' are consistent with the object and purpose of the TPP Agreement.[69] The stated goal of the inclusion of the Regulatory Coherence Chapter in the TPP Agreement is to eliminate unnecessary regulatory barriers.[70] If RIAs are introduced as primary legislation in national Congresses/Parliaments, legal trade barriers would be directly engaged.[71] On the other hand, if RIAs are adopted only by the executive branch, the RIAs would at most be carried out by ministries/agencies preparing to draft primary legislation and would be performed to improve the quality of secondary legislation at the stage of implementation.[72] Apparently, the trade implication of the former is substantially greater than that of the latter. In the case of the information and communications technology

---

http://dictionary.law.com/Default.aspx?typed=regulation&type=1 (last visited 22 August 2017).

[68] TPP Agreement, Art. 25.5(1), (b).

[69] Although the 'object and purpose' of the TPP is critically relevant here, the 'object and purpose' of the Regulatory Coherence Chapter itself is also a central consideration. See e.g., WTO Panel Report, *European Communities—Conditions for the Granting of Tariff Preferences to Developing Countries* ('*EC—Tariff Preferences*'), WTO Doc. WT/DS246/R (adopted 20 April 2004), para. 7.40; Appellate Body Report, *European Communities—Customs Classification of Frozen Boneless Chicken Cuts* ('*EC—Chicken Cuts*'), WTO Doc. WT/DS269/AB/R (adopted 27 September 2005), paras. 238–9.

[70] Polanco (n. 24 above) 231.

[71] See Cass Sunstein, *The Office of Information and Regulatory Affairs: Myths and Realities*, 126 HARV. L. REV. 1838 (2013).

[72] *Ibid.* at 1838–9; see Bojan Bugarič, *Openness and Transparency in Public Administration: Challenges for Public Law*, 22 WIS. INT'L L.J. 483 (2004).

(ICT) sector, for example, the former refers to the general legal framework, including a country's telecommunications law, while the latter only covers the implementing secondary legislation (if the telecommunications law gives the administrative agency discretion), such as the auction rules of spectrum allocation.[73] That said, a broader interpretation of 'covered regulatory measure' may find support in the 'object and purpose' of the TPP Agreement.

Finally, I am of the view that the fact that the United States has withdrawn from the TPP will not affect the legal interpretation when considering 'the preparatory work of the treaty'. Nevertheless, the preparatory work made during the TPP negotiations is of little help in interpreting the extent of 'covered regulatory measure'. As previously mentioned, the notion of regulatory coherence has primarily emerged from the OECD and APEC, and the TPP negotiations on regulatory coherence were built on the efforts of the OECD/APEC and the United States' OIRA experiences. In this context, the term 'regulation' is defined broadly in the OECD/APEC documents as 'laws, formal and informal orders and subordinate rules issued by all levels of government, and rules issued by non-governmental or self-regulatory bodies to which governments have delegated regulatory powers'.[74] On the other hand, although it is true that regulations are relatively highly centralized in the federal government in the United States,[75] RIA applies only to federal regulatory measures under the US OIRA scheme.[76] In other words, unlike the practices in the EU, where RIA is applied to all primary legislation,[77] RIA does not apply at all to US congressional legislation.[78]

To conclude, leaving this key question regarding the application of

---

[73] ITU (n. 46 above) 18.

[74] OECD (n. 31 above).

[75] Administrative agencies play a major role in regulatory decision-making in the United States. Reeve T. Bull et al., *New Approaches to International Regulatory Cooperation: The Challenge of TTIP, TPP, and Mega-Regional Trade Agreements*, 78 L. & Contemp. Probs. 1, 10 (2015).

[76] *Ibid.*

[77] John Graham, *Saving Lives Through Administrative Law and Economics*, 57 U. Pa. L. Rev. 395 (2008) (in the article the author stressed that the EU applies RIA to all primary legislation and argued that the United States could do something similar by making better use of the Congressional Budget Office). See also Susan Dudley, *Prospects for Regulatory Reform in 2011*, 11(1) Engage 7, 7–9 (2011) (in the article the author indicated that the EU has relied on an Impact Assessment Board to evaluate new legislation before it is implemented since 2006, and in January 2009 the EU updated its guidance on analyzing RIA).

[78] See generally ITU (n. 46 above) 18; USTR (n. 18 above); Sunstein (n. 71 above).

the Regulatory Coherence Chapter unanswered would certainly lead to controversy. Arguably, Article 25.1 was politically motivated by the desire to have a vaguely drafted requirement and to leave plenty of room for individual interpretation given the highly divergent political and institutional structures of the TPP parties.[79]

3. Divergent Methodologies: RIA Itself Needs to be Coherent

The Regulatory Coherence Chapter also falls short of a clearly defined threshold for how a RIA operates. Article 25.5(2) establishes the 'concept' of how RIA should be conducted by highlighting four elements:

> Recognizing that differences in the Parties' institutional, social, cultural, legal and developmental circumstances may result in specific regulatory approaches, regulatory impact assessments conducted by a Party should, among other things:
>
> (a) *assess the need for a regulatory proposal*, including a description of the nature and significance of the problem;
> (b) *examine feasible alternatives*, including, to the extent feasible and consistent with laws and regulations, their costs and benefits, such as risks involved as well as distributive impacts, recognizing that some costs and benefits are difficult to quantify and monetize;
> (c) *explain the grounds for concluding that the selected alternative achieves the policy objectives in an efficient manner*, including, if appropriate, reference to the costs and benefits and the potential for managing risks; and
> (d) *rely on the best reasonably obtainable existing information,* including relevant scientific, technical, economic or other information, within the boundaries of the authorities, mandates and resources of the particular regulatory agency. (Emphasis added)

TPP parties' understanding of RIAs, however, can be divergent, ranging from substantive regulatory harmonization to mutual recognition in the application of domestic laws.[80] The reality is that the adoption of RIAs is now widespread, but it is organized differently within governments.[81] According to the OECD studies on RIA practices within various jurisdictions, while the use of RIAs is relatively popular, their

---

[79] In the United States, RIAs are primarily used as a tool to control delegated rule-making of regulatory agencies. In contrast, across European parliamentary democracies and the EU commission, RIAs are used in the preparation of laws and policies by ministerial departments. LODGE AND WEGRICH (n. 11 above) 202.

[80] OECD (n. 40 above) 15.

[81] *Ibid.*

design and application vary significantly.[82] Often, RIA is equated with the practice of a cost-benefit analysis. Such an understanding, however, is wrong.[83] Methodologically speaking, a RIA can host a variety of methodologies, which can be designed based on the nature of analysis to be performed.[84] Depending on the extent of impacts to be assessed and the likelihood that the regulatory proposal generates substantial indirect costs and benefits, various RIA methodologies can be chosen,[85] including but not limited to 'least-cost analysis', 'cost-effectiveness analysis', and 'cost-benefit analysis'.[86]

Given that the RIA has been widely adopted but uniquely practiced, a somewhat deeper and more concrete view of methodologies employed in the incorporation of RIA is necessary.[87] After all, the success of a RIA process relies on its systematic incorporation in the development of policy that leads to regulation,[88] and such a process can only be ascertained by examining the detailed component elements of the RIA.[89] Without a clearly defined threshold for how these processes operate, concerns such as 'whether there is a requirement to demonstrate that the benefits of regulation justify the costs' will repeatedly arise.[90] In this regard, the TPP text is less ambitious than it should be.[91] As commentators have criticized, it would be premature to celebrate a new era of regulatory coherence as a dominant feature of the TPP Agreement, because the concept of 'regulatory coherence' means different things to different TPP parties.[92] Critical methodological questions must be answered in Article 25.5(2).

4. Self-centered Regulatory Agencies: Trade v. Nontrade Concerns

The required RIA process under the TPP is also weakened by the lack of a clear and enforceable mechanism to ensure that the trade impact will

---

82 *Ibid.*
83 ITU (n. 46 above) 18–19.
84 *Ibid.* at 18.
85 See generally OECD (n. 40 above) 23–58.
86 ITU (n. 46 above) 19–24.
87 OECD (n. 40 above) 17.
88 *Ibid.* at 15–17.
89 *Ibid.*
90 *Ibid.*
91 Polanco (n. 24 above) 255.
92 Theodore R. Posner and D.J. Wolff, *Making 'Regulatory Coherence' Coherent*, LAW 360, 25 April 2011, available at www.crowell.com/files/Making-Regulatory-Coherence-Coherent-International-Trade-Law360.pdf (last visited 22 August 2017).

be properly taken into account by all regulatory agencies. Indeed, one of the primary procedural challenges in the introduction of RIA is the need for increased cooperation between national regulatory agencies.[93] For a long time, sectoral regulators and trade officials have taken care of their respective businesses in cautious, if not hostile, parallel.[94] Trade negotiators generally do not consider themselves adequate to domestic regulation, while sectoral regulators in most cases focus on implementing the most effective regulation without paying attention to its trade impact.[95] The OECD studies have consistently pointed to a tendency among government officials to perform an 'incomplete' analysis of the economic costs and benefits of regulatory proposals.[96] Very often, civil servants fail to generate a full evaluation of the possible impacts of regulation, resulting in a 'silo effect' or 'stove-piped' internal decisions that lead to conflicting regulatory approaches by different agencies responsible for related issues.[97]

Lack of collaboration and integration between/among regulatory agencies probably also explains why many social policies that have been the subject of trade disputes are measures that were implemented following a RIA process.[98] With a full evaluation of the possible impact of regulation, regulators may more easily distinguish between a regulation affecting trade which benefits producers at the expense of consumers in their country, and a regulation that generally promotes trade and only restricts trade in situations where the benefits outweigh the costs.[99] However, as argued by Sheargold and Mitchell, the language of the RIA process in the TPP Regulatory Coherence Chapter does not explicitly require the TPP parties to consider the impact of each alternative on foreign traders or investors. It therefore raises the question of how RIAs can contribute to ensuring

---

93 Polanco (n. 24 above) 253.

94 Bollyky (n. 6 above) 178–9.

95 *Ibid.* See also ITU (n. 46 above) 16–17.

96 OECD (n. 40 above) 17.

97 USTR (n. 18 above).

98 Sheargold and Mitchell (n. 59 above) 600.

99 Office of Management and Budget and the Secretariat General of the European Commission, Review of the Application of EU and US Regulatory Impact Assessment Guidelines on the Analysis of Impacts on International Trade and Investment 12–15 (2008), available at www.whitehouse.gov/sites/default/files/omb/assets/regulatory_matters_pdf/sg-omb_final.pdf. In this context, an analysis of the direct costs on foreign firms is a useful proxy of the costs on the domestic economy. As pointed out by the report, if a regulation raises the cost of the imports, and therefore raises domestic prices, the costs to domestic consumers should be considered in the impact analysis.

that a measure is consistent with trade obligations if the trade impact is not required as a key element of the impact analysis.[100]

At the core of the issue is how to better incorporate international trade impact into the analysis of regulation. This chapter argues that the implementation of RIA requires adequate governance arrangements, i.e., a regulatory oversight body that is in charge of coordinating the diverse perspectives of across-regulatory agencies, guiding administrations in the drafting of RIA, and scrutinizing the quality of the RIA results.[101] After all, the executive branch as a whole itself is a 'they' not an 'it'.[102] Without the oversight of good governance arrangements, sectoral regulators may fail to consider the trade effects of their regulation. The primary organizational challenges in the introduction of RIAs, therefore, is the need for a regulatory oversight body under which trade liberalization and regulatory objectives can be pursued in an integrated manner, trade and nontrade concerns can be balance through increased cooperation between national regulatory agencies, and an orderly planning of legislative or regulatory activities can be guaranteed. Here again, the TPP text is far less ambitious than it should be. Article 25.4 merely 'encourages' parties to have 'mechanisms' (subject to each party's political and institutional structures) to facilitate effective inter-agency coordination among domestic agencies.[103]

5. Inevitable Regulatory Capture: Public-Private 'Partnership'

An additional issue worth noting is the inevitable risk of regulatory capture. Article 25.2 correctly stresses the importance of considering input from interested persons in the development of regulatory measures. Moreover, Article 25.5(2) further indicates that regulatory agencies should rely on 'the best reasonably obtainable existing information', which includes relevant 'scientific, technical, economic or other information' when conducting a RIA. Indeed, stakeholder involvement is the central support of smart regulation. Public consultation, which is driven by a search for consensus, can in some respects be viewed as negotiation and bargaining with stakeholders.[104]

---

100 Sheargold and Mitchell (n. 59 above) 600.

101 ITU (n. 46 above) 16–17.

102 Kenneth A. Shepsle, *Congress Is a 'They', Not an 'It': Legislative Intent as Oxymoron*, 12 INT'L REV. L. & ECON. 239, 254 (1992). Adrian Vermeule, *The Judiciary Is a They, Not an It: Interpretive Theory and the Fallacy of Division*, 14 J. CONTEMP. LEGAL ISSUES 549, 550 (2005).

103 TPP Agreement, Art. 25.4(1).

104 EUROPEAN COMMISSION, STAKEHOLDER CONSULTATION ON SMART REGULATION

In practice, RIA is conducted by regulators, who arguably face strong pro-regulatory incentives due to their specific regulatory responsibilities.[105] To some extent, a degree of systematic bias in favor of regulation in their RIA is expected.[106] That said, allowing stakeholders to jointly shape the policy may serve to counter-balance an 'inherently pro-regulatory bias', through either an overestimation of benefits or an underestimation of costs, held by regulatory agencies.[107] In addition, governments need informational resources provided by private actors.[108] As Shaffer argued, neither public nor private entities possess all of the knowledge and information required to solve complex and dynamic problems.[109] The networks of regulatory agencies and stakeholders must be established primarily because they depend on each other's resources.[110] In this increasingly complex world, government officials do not possess the resources to effectively implement public policy without the assistance of private parties.[111] Stakeholders in the supply chain will seek access to the regulatory process in any way possible.[112] Therefore, it is of practical importance to establish efficient forms of participation to incorporate RIA as a tool, promoting transparency and advancing interaction among interested groups.

At the core of the issue is the fact that regulators may be vulnerable to regulatory capture. As Shaffer argued, not all members of the private sector enjoy equal opportunities to participate in and influence the policy-making process.[113] The consultation mechanism in many situations represents an effective vehicle for big firms or lobbying groups to press their case for future regulation or deregulation. In reality, industry associations repeatedly become active players in the process of regulation design, raising the risk that regulators might respond to one-sided

---

IN THE EU: FOLLOW UP TO THE 2010 COMMUNICATION ON SMART REGULATION (2012), available at http://ec.europa.eu/smart-regulation/consultation_2012/docs/consultation_en.pdf (last visited 22 August 2017); OECD, BETTER REGULATION IN EUROPE: GERMANY 2010 (2010), available at www.oecd.org/gov/regulatory-policy/betterregulationineuropegermany.htm (last visited 22 August 2017).

105 OECD (n. 40 above) 94.

106 *Ibid.*

107 BRONWEN MORGAN AND KAREN YEUNG, AN INTRODUCTION TO LAW AND REGULATION: TEXT AND MATERIAL 61–2 (2007).

108 *Ibid.* at 61.

109 GREGORY SHAFFER, DEFENDING INTERESTS: PUBLIC-PRIVATE PARTNERSHIPS IN WTO LITIGATION 14 (2003).

110 *Ibid.*

111 *Ibid.* See also Henry Gao, *Public-Private Partnership: The Chinese Dilemma*, 48(5) J. WORLD 983, 990 (2014).

112 Polanco (n. 24 above) 243.

113 SHAFFER (n. 109 above) 15.

demands of interested groups.[114] Therefore, on the one hand, transparency and participation are associated with the consultation process of RIA, which at the same time allows for input from stakeholders and thus enables regulators to have vital empirical data to incorporate into the RIA.[115] On the other hand, regulators may fail to do their job because they have become too close to interested groups.[116] In short, interested groups are an important source of relevant information on the effects of regulation, but they have incentives to engage in rent-seeking behavior for their own economic returns.[117]

Wide and equal access among stakeholders is a crucial element in realizing the full benefits of RIA. A balanced representation of interests should be guaranteed.[118] Moreover, RIA requires adequate professionals to counteract such influence. A regulatory agency, as a gatekeeper, must have some ability to hold a quality assurance role in relation to RIA.[119] After all, all RIAs involve some sort of trade-off—certain interested groups gain from the new regulation, but other groups lose. There are always some stakeholders who demand new regulation, while others advocate deregulation.[120] Overreliance on information provided by stakeholders under the 'public-private partnership' may lead to asymmetric influence, and RIAs cannot function well if the problem of regulatory capture emerges.

IV. TOWARDS COHERENCE? ANTI-SPAM LAWS OF TPP PARTIES AS A CASE STUDY

The boom in online transactions led the TPP parties to go beyond traditional market access in services by establishing ground rules on electronic commerce in Chapter 14.[121] The TPP Agreement is labeled as 'the most

---

114 *Ibid.* at 144; OECD (n. 40 above) 14.

115 Polanco (n. 24 above) 253.

116 See generally Lodge and Wegrich (n. 11 above) 29, 123, 169.

117 Edward J. Balleisen and David A. Moss, Government and Markets: Toward a New Theory of Regulation 230–31(2010).

118 European Commission (n. 104 above); OECD (n. 104 above).

119 OECD (n. 40 above) 94.

120 *Ibid.* at 14; Balleisen and Moss (n. 117 above) 230.

121 See Shin-yi Peng and Han-wei Liu, *The Legality of the Data Residency Requirements: How Can the TPP Help?*, 51(2) J. World Trade 183 (2017). See also Shamel Azmeh and Christopher Foster, *The TPP and the Digital Trade Agenda: Digital Industrial Policy and Silicon Valley's Influence on New Trade Agreements* (Int'l Dev. Working Paper Series No. 16-175, 2016), available at www.lse.ac.uk/

ambitious and visionary Internet trade agreement ever attempted'. Among other goals, the parties attempted to regulate the 'unsolicited commercial electronic message' (which is defined as 'an electronic message which is sent for commercial or marketing purposes to an electronic address, without the consent of the recipient or despite the explicit rejection of the recipient, through an Internet access service supplier') in Article 14.14 (Unsolicited Commercial Electronic Messages) as follows:[122]

> 1. Each Party shall adopt or maintain measures regarding unsolicited commercial electronic messages that:
>
> (a) require suppliers of unsolicited commercial electronic messages to facilitate the ability of recipients to prevent ongoing reception of those messages;
> (b) require the consent, as specified according to the laws and regulations of each Party, of recipients to receive commercial electronic messages; or
> (c) otherwise provide for the minimisation of unsolicited commercial electronic messages.
>
> 2. Each Party shall provide recourse against suppliers of unsolicited commercial electronic messages that do not comply with the measures adopted or maintained pursuant to paragraph 1.
>
> 3. The Parties shall endeavour to cooperate in appropriate cases of mutual concern regarding the regulation of unsolicited commercial electronic messages.

As previously indicated, according to Article 25.3, each TPP party is to determine and make publicly available the scope of its 'covered regulatory measures'.[123] The scope of measures that will be subject to the regulatory coherence obligation is flexible, as it will be chosen by each TPP party. Thus, the discussion below will be based on the assumption that most of the TPP parties, pursuant to the requirement that each party should aim to achieve significant coverage in determining the scope of covered

---

internationalDevelopment/publications/Working-Papers/WP175-ShamelAzmeh.aspx (last visited 22 August 2017).

[122] For the definition of 'unsolicited commercial electronic message', see TPP Agreement, Art. 14.1, available at https://ustr.gov/sites/default/files/TPP-Final-Text-Electronic-Commerce.pdf (last visited 22 August 2017) ('Unsolicited commercial electronic message means an electronic message which is sent for commercial or marketing purposes to an electronic address, without the consent of the recipient or despite the explicit rejection of the recipient, through an Internet access service supplier or, to the extent provided for under the laws and regulations of each Party, other telecommunications service').

[123] See III:1 above.

regulatory measures, will decide whether their anti-spam laws and regulations will be subject to the TPP regulatory coherence obligations.

1. Regulatory Objectives: Economic v. Non-economic Interests

The primary problem of spam is that telecommunications and Internet Service Providers (ISPs) are forced to carry these unwanted messages when spam e-mails are traveling from the sender to the recipient, which generally consumes massive amounts of network bandwidth, storage space and other resources.[124] While those in-between systems are piggybacked to deliver these e-mails, their resources are not being used to process other 'legitimate' information.[125] In this context, spam may have a harsh effect on developing countries that are still building their telecommunications and Internet infrastructure if relatively scarce bandwidth is clogged with spam.[126] Another equally serious problem related to spam is that it externalizes costs to millions of users. In other words, it is profitable largely because its costs are shifted from the spammers to the end-users.[127] Evidence suggests that spam has been placing the economic burden on end-users, as individually deleting each piece of spam can be translated from a time cost to a financial cost.[128] In short, while it is relatively inexpensive to send spam, it is costly in terms of time for those who receive it.[129]

However, spam governance touches upon a sensitive issue: the constitutional restrictions against regulating 'speech'.[130] Indeed, the informational value of spam depends upon the recipient.[131] Essentially, spam is a part of the marketplace of ideas, containing innovations, even unwanted, in speech. Thus, the regulatory agency for communications (e.g., the Australian Communications and Media Authority (AMCA)) must narrowly regulate spam.[132] Any anti-spam legislation or regulation involves complex policy

---

[124] See generally Rebecca Bolin, *Opting Out of Spam: A Domain Level Do-Not-Spam Registry*, 24 YALE L. & POL'Y REV. 399, 403 (2006).

[125] Jay Reyero, *The Can-Spam Act of 2003: A False Hope*, 11 SMU SCI. & TECH. L. REV. 195, 199 (2007).

[126] Meyer Potashman, *International Spam Regulation and Enforcement: Recommendations Following the World Summit on the Information Society*, 29 B.C. INT'L & COMP. L. REV. 323, 325 (2006).

[127] Bolin (n. 124 above) 400–401. Potashman (n. 126 above) 326.

[128] David E. Sorkin, *Technical and Legal Approaches to Unsolicited Electronic Mail*, 35 U.S.F. L. REV. 325 (2001). See also Reyero (n. 125 above) 200.

[129] Reyero (n. 125 above) 199–200.

[130] Potashman (n. 126 above) 338.

[131] Bolin (n. 124 above) 404.

[132] See Potashman (n. 126 above) 338–43.

questions about how much 'commercial speech' is appropriate and to what extent it intrudes on the rights/interests of others.[133] In many jurisdictions, if the commercial speech meets certain criteria, then any law/regulation of it must directly advance a 'substantial governmental interest' and must not be 'more extensive than necessary' to meet that objective.[134]

Rationales for and against regulatory involvement in spam messages will be even more complex when introduced into a RIA mechanism. As previously discussed, without the oversight of good governance arrangements, the communications regulator may fail to consider the effects of regulation on another part of government. In addition, considering that RIAs are uniquely organized within governments, in the case of anti-spam regulations where economic and non-economic interests are competing, a somewhat concrete view of the methodologies employed in the incorporation of RIA is necessary so as to facilitate regulatory coherence.

2. Feasible Alternatives: Opt-in v. Opt-out

In fact, most TPP parties have already implemented spam legislation.[135] Among these jurisdictions, there are two primary alternative models for securing recipient consent, under which recipients either 'opt-in' to receiving spam e-mails or 'opt-out' from receiving spam e-mails.[136] Under an opt-in regulatory scheme, a party interested in sending an e-mail must obtain consent prior to initiating e-mail messages to consumers. In other words, an e-marketer is prohibited from such marketing unless it has first secured consent from its intended recipients.[137] The Spam Act 2003 of Australia, for example, prohibits the sending of spam without prior consent of the recipients, and adherence to the express consent requirement is mandatory.[138] 'Consent' can be satisfied under various circumstances, as long as recipients are aware they may receive commercial messages.[139] In any event, the opt-in approach requires an e-marketer to make efforts

---

133 Bolin (n. 124 above) 403–5.

134 *Ibid.* at 414–19.

135 See ITU, *Anti-Spam Laws and Authorities Worldwide*, available at www.itu.int/osg/spu/spam/law.html (last visited 22 August 2017).

136 See e.g., Karen Ng, *Spam Legislation in Canada: Federalism, Freedom of Expression and the Regulation of the Internet*, 2 U. OTTAWA L. & TECH. J. 447, 466 (2005).

137 *Ibid.*

138 Australian Communications and Media Authority (AMCA), *Anti Spam*, available at www.acma.gov.au/Home/Industry/Marketers/Anti%20Spam (last visited 22 August 2017) (Austl.).

139 *Ibid.*

to secure a recipient's consent before sending any e-mail,[140] which is obviously the preferred model advocated by anti-spam groups.

On the other hand, the alternative to an opt-in approach is an opt-out system, wherein spammers are free to target any recipients until told to stop.[141] Under this model, spam messages commonly include opt-out instructions, e.g., an e-mail address or webpage for submitting such requests,[142] and the message itself must contain a notice indicating that the recipient is given an opportunity to refuse further commercial e-mail messages from the sender.[143] The fundamental problem with this narrowly tailored approach is the difficulty in actually preventing spam,[144] simply because senders may communicate with everyone except those who have explicitly opted out.[145]

The 'opt-in v. opt-out' debate presents two approaches, both of which result in a problem in efforts to create any enforceable international/regional anti-spam regime. An e-marketer doing business around the world must comply with myriad spam regulations, which are conflicting in terms of the opt-in and opt-out consent methods. In the context of international trade, the 'regulatory jungle' of spam laws is represented by trade barriers. E-marketers confront significant challenges when attempting to comply with often conflicting requirements, and such regulatory fragmentation makes compliance more and more challenging. That said, a less fragmented and more coherent anti-spam regulatory framework would bridge the differences among jurisdictions, increase compliance, and provide benefits to both e-marketers and end-users, thereby contributing to global economic growth.

This raises the question of how the TPP Regulatory Coherence Chapter can help harmonize the two models.[146] Can RIAs, subject to

---

140 Ng (n. 136 above) 466–8.

141 *Ibid.* at 466.

142 Sorkin (n. 128 above) 329.

143 Ng (n. 136 above) 466. See also David Lorentz, *The Effectiveness of Litigation under the Can-Spam Act*, 30 Rev. Litig. 559 (2011).

144 See Reyero (n. 125 above) 195–6. See also generally Edwin Lavergne, *FCC Gives Teeth to the Can-Spam Act of 2003*, 1 N.Y.U. J.L. & Bus. 861 (2004).

145 Empirical evidence suggested that the opt-out model is rarely effective. Ironically, most spammers reportedly collect and sell e-mail addresses of those who have submitted such opt-out requests. Sorkin (n. 128 above) 353.

146 It should be noted that TPP Agreement, Art. 25.5(8) stipulates that 'to the extent appropriate and consistent with its law, each Party should encourage its relevant regulatory agencies to consider regulatory measures in other Parties, as well as relevant developments in international, regional and other fora when planning covered regulatory measures'.

the principle of proportionality, serve as an effective tool to ensure that spam regulations are implemented in an efficient and effective manner? Can the anti-spam legislation become more uniform under the TPP? Would Japan align itself with the opt in anti-spam approach? Or will TPP parties that have enacted sophisticated anti-spam laws transform to incorporate the narrowly tailored 'opt-out' model, which is the 'lowest common denominator' of the existing domestic regulation of TPP parties?

3. Cost/Benefit Analysis: To Regulate or Not to Regulate

Spam governance becomes extremely complicated when considering how different societies value the freedom of commercial speech, as well as the factors and criteria that must be evaluated by policy-makers in different countries when balancing competing economic and non-economic interests. Currently, anti-spam regimes vary among the TPP parties, and the relevant laws/regulations also differ, spanning from the opt-in approach (Australia, Canada, New Zealand, Singapore)[147] to the opt-out approach (Chile, Japan, Mexico, Peru, Vietnam),[148] to the non-existent (Brunei and Malaysia).[149] The question of 'to regulate or not to regulate' remains.

One key element of the RIA is to identify and access alternative options. In the case of anti-spam regulations, 'the need for intervention' has been established and translated into concrete policy options in most jurisdictions. Alternatives to 'heavy-handed' regulation, such as light-touch regulation, and to intervention, such as self-regulation, should be duly taken into account.[150] At the crux of the matter is how the communications authority of each TPP party will assess the characteristics of different policy interventions through myriad techniques, including cost-benefit analysis. More important is how to take into account input from interested persons in the development of the regulatory measures while at the same time refraining from overreliance on relevant scientific, technical, economic, or other information provided by stakeholders.

In this context, Taiwan's efforts to combat spam provide an interesting case study, as Taiwan failed to regulate spam when there was a clear need.

---

147 *See* ITU (n. 135 above).

148 *Ibid.*

149 *Ibid.* Malaysia does not have a specific anti-spam law or regulation. The country relies on the Telecommunications Law to promote self-regulation of spam.

150 ITU (n. 46 above) 6.

The National Communications Commission (NCC) of Taiwan issued a draft Anti-spam Law in 2005.[151] Pursuant to articles 155 and 156 of the Administrative Procedure Law, which establishes uniform and clear obligations pertaining to consultation procedures for all regulation at the central government level, the NCC began public consultation under the framework of transparency, allowing foreign and domestic service suppliers equal opportunity to participate in consultation. Stakeholders primarily include sectoral experts, consumer protection unions, and ISPs. During the consultation stage, most participating experts and representatives of consumer protection groups expressed concern about how to improve enforcement of the proposed anti-spam law. The overwhelming opinion was that the ISPs should to some degree be held accountable for the transmission of spam originating on their networks.[152] Sectoral experts seemed to share the viewpoint that technically speaking, the most effective way to stop spam would be to require the ISPs to place filters on the source.[153] Consumer protection unions therefore proposed that the draft law should impose obligations on ISPs to block spam at its source as they are in the best position to do so. However, the NCC faced strong pressure from the ICT industry, which stressed that the ISPs are innocent bystanders, if not victims, of spam problems.[154] They argued that the ISPs are not in any position to control the transmission of spam messages. Any legal obligations imposed on them would be more burdensome than necessary on their technical and administrative systems.[155] They also stressed that holding ISPs liable for spamming would also substantially increase the risk of deleting 'legitimate' (wanted) e-mails, which would pose a significant threat to the Internet economy.[156] After several rounds of consultation, the NCC, based on the results of stakeholder participation, decided not to hold ISPs responsible for e-mail transmitted via their services.[157]

In reality, communications agencies seem to be vulnerable to regulatory

---

[151] NCC, *Prevention of Spam Mails*, available at www.ncc.gov.tw/chinese/news.aspx.

[152] *Ibid.*

[153] *Ibid.*

[154] In fact, the question of whether to impose liability on the ISPs has been discussed in many jurisdictions. See e.g., John Soma et al., *Spam Still Pays: The Failure of the Can-Spam Act of 2003 and Proposed Legal Solutions*, 45 HARV. J. ON LEGIS. 165, 185 (2008). Potashman (n. 126 above) 329.

[155] NCC (n. 151 above).

[156] For more discussion of ISP responsibility, see generally Potashman (n. 126 above) 329–36; Soma et al. (n. 154 above) 186–92.

[157] NCC (n. 151 above).

capture, as ICT industry associations are becoming more and more active in every rule-making process. Political lobbying expenditures by ICT firms have increased substantially in recent years.[158] ICT companies are now playing an increasingly significant political role, and this is particularly true in many TPP parties.[159] When lobby interests dominate, regulation will not represent public interest, but will instead be designed and operated primarily for the benefit of the dominant industry.[160] As shown in the legislative anti-spam history of the NCC, the ICT associations became key political lobbying forces in the process of the legislation's design.[161] The RIA process suffered from bias towards cost overestimation and benefit underestimation. After all, consultation is a policy tool, not a substitute for political judgment.[162] Regulatory agencies are always the primary actors, with full discretion as to which scientific or economic evidence should be recognized and which information should be dismissed.[163]

To conclude, there is a risk that consultation procedures in particular will weight the costs and benefits, which in many cases is transformed into an arena for political wrestling.[164] The key methodological problem of the RIA is the imbalance in terms of measuring costs and benefits,[165] but

---

158 Kelsey (n. 59 above). Azmeh and Foster (n. 121 above).

159 OECD (n. 40 above) 14 (ICT companies are becoming key political lobbying forces in both domestic policy-making process and trade negotiations). See also ITU (n. 46 above) 16–17.

160 Baldwin et al. (n. 3 above) 47–8.

161 *Ibid.* at 48.

162 Shin-yi Peng, Transparency and Public Consultation Mechanisms in the Regulatory Processes: Experience in the Separate Customs Territory of Taiwan, Penghu, Kinmen, and Matsu, Chairman's Report (annex presentations), Thematic Session on Good Regulatory Practice, Committee on Technical Barriers to Trade, World Trade Organization, 18–19 March 2014 (transcript on file with the author).

163 Shin-yi Peng, 4G Licensing in Chinese Taipei: Re-farming GSM Spectrum? APEC Workshop: Development and Implementation of Methodologies to Improve the Quality of Regulations, 11–12 April 2013 (transcript on file with the author).

164 See Lodge and Wegrich (n. 11 above) 192–5, who pointed out that those who see the purpose of consultation as a means to ensure that further evidence is generated may see little value in supporting extensive citizen participation. In that case, civil servants may wonder why they should listen to 'ignorant laypeople'. In any event, RIAs are unable to remove politics and discretion from the regulatory process.

165 Empirical evidence show that the interested groups have come increasingly involved in discussion regarding the criteria relevant for cost-benefits analysis. They see such process as critical in advancing their agenda, making the RIA process itself a key battleground. *Ibid.* at 199–205.

Article 25.5(2) of the TPP Agreement does not provide any guidance as to how to address this problem.

V. CONCLUDING REMARKS

I raised the question at the outset of this chapter of whether, and if so, how, the RIA can serve as an effective tool to promote regulatory coherence in the TPP. The laws governing unsolicited commercial electronic messages provide an interesting case study on challenges to the Regulatory Coherence Chapter.

First, whether governments will decide that their anti-spam laws and regulations are going to be subject to the TPP Regulatory Coherence Chapter is entirely uncertain. Second, an examination of the relevant provisions of the Chapter, in accordance with Articles 31 and 32 of the Vienna Convention on the Law of Treaties (VCLT), confirms that the Chapter was politically motivated by the desire to have ambiguously drafted provisions and to leave plenty of room for individual interpretation as to 'who' is required to apply RIAs to their decision-making processes. In the case of the anti-spam laws, if RIAs are introduced to primary legislation in national Congresses/Parliaments, legal problems would be engaged directly. Third, RIA methodologies must be harmonized. In the case of anti-spam regulations where economic and non-economic interests are in competition, a somewhat concrete view of the methodologies for the incorporation of RIA is necessary to facilitate regulatory coherence. Fourth, this chapter argues that the implementation of RIA requires adequate governance arrangements, i.e., a regulatory oversight body. In the case of anti-spam legislation, rationales for and against regulatory involvement in spam messages are particularly complex because they touch upon a sensitive issue: the constitutional restrictions against regulating 'speech'. Without the oversight of good governance arrangements, communications regulators may fail to consider the effects of their regulation on another part of government. Finally, as shown in the NCC experience in drafting the anti-spam law, an effective RIA requires adequate professionals within the regulatory agency to counteract such influence. Without sufficient quality assurance mechanisms, the cost-benefit analysis may not be properly applied.

It remains to be seen how the TPP-11 continue to salvage the agreement without excessive revisions. In any event, the Regulatory Coherence Chapter of the TPP will serve as a useful reference for future trade negotiations. As evidenced by the regulatory cooperation chapter of the Comprehensive and Economic Trade Agreement (CETA) and the draft regulatory cooperation/coherence chapters of the TTIP,[166] trade negotiators simply can't stop dancing to the rhythm of the TPP.

[166] See CETA, Chapter 21 (Regulatory Cooperation), available at http://ec.europa.eu/trade/policy/in-focus/ceta/ceta-chapter-by-chapter/ (last visited 22 August 2017). See also Corporate Europe Observatory, *TTIP: Cross-cutting Disciplines and Institutional Provisions, Position Paper, Chapter on Regulatory Coherence*, available at https://corporateeurope.org/sites/default/files/ttip-regulatory-coherence-2-12-2013.pdf (last visited 22 August 2017).

5. Export policies, technology transfer policies, and investment reviews: How states compete in the era of global high-tech value chains

Mark Wu

I. INTRODUCTION

In the past quarter century, international trade has undergone a remarkable transformation, driven in part by rapid advances in information and communication technology (ICT).[1] Much of the world's production of higher value-added goods, as well as an increasing share of services, is no longer done by a single firm in a single country. Instead, production is increasingly organized across multiple firms and across multiple sites, tied together through global value chains (GVCs).[2] The nature of these arrangements may vary across firms and across industries; various terms cover different aspects of this phenomenon including offshoring, outsourcing, vertical integration, supply chain integration, value-added production, etc. But this phenomenon has certainly upended trade. Nowhere is this more true than in the Pacific Basin, home to the largest and most rapidly growing trading area. Since 2000, trade in intermediate goods has constituted over 50 percent of exports and over 60 percent of imports in East Asia.[3]

[1] For an excellent overview of this phenomenon and its impact on trade flows, in general, see RICHARD BALDWIN, THE GREAT CONVERGENCE (2016).

[2] See Christophe Degain et al., *Recent Trends in Global Trade and Global Value Chains*, *in* MEASURING AND ANALYZING THE IMPACT OF GVCS ON ECONOMIC DEVELOPMENT 37 (Global Value Chain Development Report 2017, 2017); Organisation for Economic Co-operation and Development (OECD), *Trade Policy Implications of Global Value Chains* (November 2015), available at www.oecd.org/tad/trade-policy-implications-gvc.pdf (last visited 10 September 2017).

[3] Victor K. Fung, *Governance Through Partnership in a Changing World*, *in* GLOBAL VALUE CHAINS IN A CHANGING WORLD xix (Deborah K. Elms and Patrick Low eds., 2013).

This change has dramatically altered the nature of competition between states when it comes to international trade and high-tech sectors. No longer are states aiming exclusively to create a 'national champion' to out-compete foreign competitors in order to grab a greater share of the domestic, and eventually global, market for a given good. Instead, states now increasingly aim to find ways to aid domestic firms to grab a slice of the GVC and then, over time, move up the value chain and capture the higher value-added portions of the chain.[4] States with large numbers of incumbent firms, on the other hand, seek to protect these valuable portions of the GVC for their firms.

Alongside this change has been the remarkable development of international trade law curtailing the ability of governments to use outright protectionist measures to assist firms through a mercantilist industrial policy. Much of this is a result of the Uruguay Round itself. Some are the result of the jurisprudence that has developed through subsequent litigation of the Uruguay Round agreements at the World Trade Organization (WTO). Consequently, traditional tools such as local content requirements, discriminatory standards, and subsidies with adverse trade effects have been rendered illegal.

This does not mean, however, that trade takes place unencumbered across borders. This chapter argues that the contours of competition between states in technology sectors have simply shifted. A new set of policy instruments now take on increasing importance. They are: (1) export-oriented policies, (2) technology transfer policies, and (3) investment reviews. Each can be deployed on its own, but their use can also be coordinated as part of a larger national strategy.

The emergence of these three policy instruments is due to two key reasons. First, WTO law contains only a limited set of legal disciplines to curtail each of their use. Thus, countries can seek to use these tools without fear of legal retribution. Second, each instrument offers a potential mechanism for states to expand domestic firms' share of the higher-value-added portion of technology GVCs and/or to protect that portion against challengers from overseas. In an age where competition between states is measured not by the absolute quantity of trade, but by its value addition, it is not altogether surprising that their use becomes more attractive.

---

[4] Ujal Singh Bhatia, *The Globalization of Supply Chains: Policy Challenges for Developing Countries*, *in* GLOBAL VALUE CHAINS IN A CHANGING WORLD 313–28 (Deborah K. Elms and Patrick Low eds., 2013); Gary Gereffi and Timothy Sturgeon, *Global Value Chains and Industrial Policy: The Role of Emerging Economies*, *in* GLOBAL VALUE CHAINS IN A CHANGING WORLD 329–60 (Deborah K. Elms and Patrick Low eds., 2013).

This chapter will discuss each of these three policy instruments in greater depth. It highlights how they are especially important when considering the competition in high-tech industries between the major trading powers: the United States, the European Union (EU), China, and Japan. After doing so, it will then explore potential ways in which the law might seek to further curtail their use for purely protectionist purposes. By no means is this development a certainty. But it is worth considering whether the trenches of competition over technology value chains requires further rules as the nature of such competition intensifies in the twenty-first century.

II. EXPORT POLICIES

When it comes to technology sectors, a persistent worry of developing countries is a fear that they will get locked into the lower-value-added portions of the value chain, without the ability to move up.[5] The fear is that global technology firms, based largely in advanced economies, will simply seek to exploit their cheaper labor costs and lax regulatory standards, without a desire to integrate these countries more deeply into the higher-value-added portions of their value chains.

To counter this concern, governments have employed different types of export policies designed to entice the higher value-added portions to their countries. One approach used is that of export restrictions. This can be enacted through an export tax, or less commonly, an export quota. Another strategy is to provide rebates of export value-added tax (VAT). Each is elaborated upon below.

1. Export Taxes

Export taxes impose a duty on the exportation of a particular good, to be imposed at the HS-6, HS-8, or HS-10 level. The net effect is to increase the cost of exportation, thereby causing more of the good to stay within a country's border than would otherwise be the case. Why might a government impose such a policy? One reason is simply to tap into a source of fiscal revenue. However, export taxes can also serve as a mechanism to attract foreign investment of downstream functions of a supply chain.

---

[5] This phenomenon is commonly referred to as the 'middle-income trap'. For further discussion, see Barry Eichengreen et al., *Growth Slowdowns Redux: New Evidence on the Middle-Income Trap*, 32 JAPAN & THE WORLD ECON. 65–84 (2014); Shekhar Aiyar et al., *Growth Slowdowns and the Middle-Income Trap* (IMF Working Paper No. WP/13/71, 2013).

This strategy is most effective when a country produces a significant quantity of a critical upstream input for that supply chain.

The export tax effectively drives up the cost of the input for foreign producers, providing domestic producers with a cost advantage. If the foreign producer has an alternative source for the input, it presumably will shift away to this other source, as the alternative upstream supplier now enjoys a relative cost advantage. In some instances, however, an alternative upstream supplier does not readily exist. A common reason is that it takes time for alternative sources to ramp up their production volume, due to the high fixed capital associated with the upstream production. Under this scenario, suppliers of downstream good will be tempted to shift more of their production to within the borders of the country imposing the export tax, so as to evade the higher cost of the export tax. By creating a cost wedge, the export tax can seek to advantage domestic producers of the downstream good.

Within technology sectors, China has become the most active and effective user of this policy instrument. Between 2013 and mid-2015, approximately 4.1 percent of all Chinese tariff lines at the HS-8 level were subject to export duties.[6] These are applied in accordance with the Regulation on Import and Export Tariffs. Among the products for which export taxes are imposed are minerals such as magnesia, antimony, and graphite. These minerals serve as critical inputs for the production of semiconductors that then serve as inputs into technology products. Hence, they are an important upstream component of technology GVCs, for which China seeks to capture a greater share of the downstream functions with higher-value addition.

At present, China controls a critical mass of the world's supply of several of these minerals. For example, China mined 76 percent of the world's antimony, 69 percent of magnesia, and 65 percent of graphite.[7] More often than not, China's control of the global supply of these upstream inputs is not due to any natural geological advantage, but rather its greater tolerance for the potential negative externalities associated with their production. The mining and processing of such minerals carry with it potentially harmful environmental and health risks for surrounding communities. With more countries choosing to disengage from mining and/or processing, on account of local political pressures or stronger regulations, China's share increases.

---

[6] Trade Policy Review Body, *Trade Policy Review, Report by the Secretariat–China*, WT/TPR/S/342, 73 (15 June 2016).

[7] Computations based on statistics provided by the US Geological Service, *Commodity Statistics and Information*, https://minerals.usgs.gov/minerals/pubs/commodity/ (last visited 10 September 2017).

The net effect of the export tax is to drive up the price for foreign semiconductors that rely upon these minerals for upstream inputs. Downstream consumers of the semiconductor will be tempted to buy greater quantities of Chinese-produced semiconductors, which are now effectively cheaper thanks to the export tax. Semiconductor companies that had produced overseas will now be tempted to shift more of their production to within China's borders, so as to not be placed at a cost disadvantage, or be forced to lose share to competitors that do. Overall, China achieves the desired result of capturing a greater share of a downstream slice of the GVC. This is particularly important in instances such as this where this downstream function (i.e., semiconductor production) constitutes a much greater proportion of the total value of the supply chain than the upstream function (i.e., mineral production).

In general, governments are not required under WTO rules to schedule their export taxes. Therefore, there are no inherent limits to the use of this strategy. However, certain countries may have chosen to undertake WTO-plus commitments as a result of their protocol of accession requiring them to do so. For example, China explicitly undertook a commitment not to impose any export taxes other than those listed in an Annex or in conformity with General Agreement on Tariffs and Trade (GATT), Article VIII.[8]

Because China's imposition of export taxes contravenes its WTO commitments, several governments have filed cases against it at the WTO. This includes *China—Raw Materials* and *China—Rare Earths*. In both instances, the WTO Appellate Body ruled against China, finding its policy to be a direct contravention of its Protocol of Accession commitments and disavowing China's argument that the taxes were motivated by environmental concerns.[9]

Nevertheless, these cases demonstrate the limits of WTO litigation. Because of the time-lag required to secure a positive ruling and lack of retrospective remedies, even if China loses the WTO case, it is still able to secure the desired outcome.[10] While the litigation was pending,

---

[8] Accession of the People's Republic of China, Decision of 10 November 2001 ('China Protocol of Accession'), WT/L/432, para. 11.3 (23 November 2001).

[9] Appellate Body Report, *China—Measures Related to the Exportation of Various Raw Materials*, WT/DS394/AB/R, WT/DS395/AB/R, WT/DS398/AB/R (adopted 22 February 2012) para. 362; Appellate Body Report, *China—Measures Related to the Exportation of Rare Earths, Tungsten, and Molybdenum*, WT/DS431/AB/R, WT/DS432/AB/R, WT/DS435/AB/R (adopted 29 August 2014), paras. 6.1–6.3.

[10] Mark Wu, *China's Export Restrictions and the Limits of WTO Law*, 16 World Trade Rev. 673 (2017).

downstream firms shifted their behavior so as to avoid any temporary cost disadvantage. Because these decisions may be 'sticky' in nature, even after the WTO rules against China, China continues to enjoy a portion of the positive impact of the firms' actions.[11]

More recently, two new additional cases have been filed, one by the United States and the other by the EU.[12] Both cases remain pending as of the time of writing.

2. Export VAT Rebates

While the section above discussed the use of policy instruments to constrain exports of certain essential inputs to technology supply chains, governments have also engaged in export-promoting policies. WTO law, however, does constrain the use of financial support instruments. Most notably, the Agreement on Subsidies and Countervailing Measures (SCM Agreement) prohibits the use of export subsidies.[13] In addition, the SCM Agreement allows for any subsidy which has an adverse effect on trade to be challenged through WTO dispute settlement.[14] Furthermore, governments possess the flexibility to impose countervailing measures against subsidized imports that cause harm or have the potential to cause harm to domestic competitors.[15]

Within the bounds of these legal constraints, governments have turned to export VAT rebates as an instrument to influence competition along technology GVCs. The export VAT rebates refers to the refund of tax paid by exporting firms to the tax authority for value-added components of the activity carried on by the firm within the authority's borders.

The goals of such a policy are often two-fold. First, a government may enact such a policy simply with the goal of enhancing the competitiveness of domestic firms seeking to export. The export VAT rebate lowers the firm's cost structure, thereby allowing it to charge lower prices overseas.

---

11 *Ibid.*; see also Mark Wu, *A Free Pass for China*, New York Times (2 April 2014), available at www.nytimes.com/2014/04/03/opinion/a-free-pass-for-china.html?mcubz =0 (last visited 10 September 2017).

12 Request for Consultations by the United States, *China—Export Duties on Certain Raw Materials*, WT/DS508/1 (14 July 2016); Request for Consultations by the European Union, *China—Duties and Other Measures Concerning the Exportation of Certain Raw Materials*, WT/DS509/1 (25 July 2016).

13 Agreement on Subsidies and Countervailing Measures, Art. 3.1, 15 April 1994, Marrakesh Agreement Establishing the World Trade Organization, Annex 1A, 1867 UNTS 14.

14 *Ibid.* Part III.

15 *Ibid.* Part V.

Second, the export VAT rebate can also serve to advance a government's industrial policy of attracting a greater share of the overall production related to the value chain. The goal is to ensure that the government's VAT policy does not serve as an impediment to attracting greater foreign investment for export processing activities. The export VAT rebate effectively neutralizes any tax impact that may dissuade a foreign investor, allowing the country to gain a toehold onto the GVC.

Again, China serves as an example of how this instrument can be used effectively to promote an industrial policy to attract a greater portion of a technology GVC. Unlike many other WTO members that enact a rather straightforward export VAT rebate policy, the Chinese scheme is fairly complicated. Instead of refunding the full value of the 17 percent VAT, the rate will vary across products and is subject to frequent change. These fluctuations allow the government to adjust the benefits enjoyed by producers over time in line with its trade and industrial policy goals.

Several recent economic studies have highlighted how this instrument has positively benefitted Chinese exporters. Using firm-level panel data for 2004–06, Chandra and Long find a positive correlation between a firm's export value and the average rebate rate.[16] Gourdon et al., using city-specific export-quantity data disaggregated at the HS-6 product level for 2003–12, find that export VAT rebate scheme is indeed an effective industrial policy and export competiveness strategy whose impact is magnified when applied to products with denser links to the local production structure.[17]

In the 2016 US Presidential debates, Donald Trump raised the issue of export VAT rebate as an unfair trade policy enacted by US trading partners to attract offshoring of US jobs.[18] Some have questioned President Trump's claims that the practice itself truly constitutes an unfair trade practice. But with the policy now rising to the fore of US monitoring of foreign trade, the export VAT rebates of governments pursuing technology-oriented industrial policies are certain to enjoy greater scrutiny in the years ahead.

---

[16] Piyush Chandra and Cheryl Long, *VAT Rebates and Export Performance in China: Firm-Level Evidence*, 102 J. PUB. ECON. 13 (2013).

[17] Julien Gourdon et al., *How Effective are VAT Export Taxes? Evidence from China* (Working Paper, February 2017), available at www.mwpweb.eu/1/58/resources/publication_2061_1.pdf (last visited 10 September 2017).

[18] For a transcript, see Aaron Blake, *The First Trump-Clinton Presidential Debate Transcript, Annotated*, WASHINGTON POST (26 September 2016), available at www.washingtonpost.com/news/the-fix/wp/2016/09/26/the-first-trump-clinton-presidential-debate-transcript-annotated/?utm_term=.0eaa1d43e28a (last visited 10 September 2017).

III. TECHNOLOGY TRANSFER POLICIES

Leadership in technology sectors today depends less on dominating the manufacturing and production of a given complex high-tech product and more on control over the intellectual property and know-how associated with the product, including its design. Countries increasingly utilize a range of policies to impact the flow of technology across borders. Those seeking to capture greater portions of the higher-value-added portions of GVCs may utilize a range of policies to induce firms to transfer technology to within its borders. Those with incumbent leaders, on the other hand, may enact policies to safeguard their technological leadership by restricting the outflow of such technologies. Each raises the ire of the other, generating increasing trade frictions associated with technology transfers.

1. Technology Transfer as a Condition for Investment Approval

While the WTO Agreement on Trade-Related Investment Measures (TRIMS) restricts the use of certain forms of performance requirements, such as local-content requirements, it does not bar a government from imposing, as a condition for granting regulatory approval for an investment concerning the production of a good, a requirement that the firm transfer certain technologies or base certain research and development activities within its borders.[19] The vast majority of WTO members are free to impose conditions of this sort, without violating their WTO treaty obligations. Unless a TRIMS-plus obligation has been adopted by a WTO member as part of its accession protocol, it is unlikely that a government is constrained by WTO law from adopting such conditionality as part of its inward investment policy.

One way to effectuate such a policy is to impose a cap on foreign ownership for a given sector. This will force any foreign investor interested in setting up operations in a given country to find a local partner, with whom it will inevitably have to share its technology and know-how. However, this is not the only method available. A government may also require that a firm obtain regulatory approval for an investment, which will be discussed in a subsequent section of this chapter. This again provides a government with the opportunity to impose conditionality requirements, should it so desire.

---

[19] See Agreement on Trade-Related Investment Measures, 15 April 1994, Marrakesh Agreement Establishing the World Trade Organization, Annex 1A, 1868 UNTS 186.

Simply because a government is free to impose a condition of technology transfer as a *quid pro quo* for investment approval, however, does not mean that it will readily do so. Some may lack bargaining power relative to the multinational corporations that possess the technology to make such a demand. Others may lack the absorptive capacity to make full use of the benefits of the technology. Furthermore, some may not wish to develop a reputation as being unfriendly or demanding of foreign investors.

However, countries with a large internal market and a strong human capital base may well be tempted to make such demands. While the track record of countries is mixed, several researchers have highlighted case studies of countries that have effectively utilized performance requirements, including technology transfer, to develop industries.[20] In addition, international agencies such as the United Nations Conference on Trade and Development (UNCTAD) and non-governmental organizations, such as the International Institute for Sustainable Development, have published reports touting the use and potential benefits associated with performance requirements.[21]

An example of how a large country can effectively leverage its size to demand technology transfer is India and the defense manufacturing industry. A McKinsey Global Institute report in 2014 highlighted the enormous potential of India's technology sector, but noted the need for India to attract greater foreign investment, particularly in private-sector research and development (R&D), and to strengthen cooperation between academic institutions and the private sector to encourage its technology transfer capacity.[22] In September 2014, India unveiled the 'Make in India' initiative, a comprehensive program to transform Indian manufacturing in priority sectors, one of which is defense manufacturing. Prime Minister Modi himself then emphasized the importance of re-orienting the criteria for evaluating foreign investments and contracts in the defense industry

---

[20] See e.g., GOEL COHEN, TECHNOLOGY TRANSFER (2004); Barry Bozeman, *Technology Transfer and Public Policy: A Review of Research and Theory*, 29 RES. POL'Y 627 (2000).

[21] See e.g., UNITED NATIONS CONFERENCE ON TRADE AND DEVELOPMENT (UNCTAD), FOREIGN DIRECT INVESTMENT AND PERFORMANCE REQUIREMENTS: NEW EVIDENCE FROM SELECTED COUNTRIES, UN Doc UNCTAD/ITE/IIA/2003/7 (2003); Aaron Cosbey, *Everyone's Doing It: The Acceptance, Effectiveness, and Legality of Performance Requirements*, INVESTMENT TREATY NEWS (19 February 2015), available at www.iisd.org/itn/2015/02/19/everyones-doing-it-the-acceptance-effectiveness-and-legality-of-performance-requirements/ (last visited 10 September 2017).

[22] NOSHIR KAKA ET AL., INDIA'S TECHNOLOGY OPPORTUNITY: TRANSFORMING WORK, EMPOWERING PEOPLE 1–42, 127 (2014).

to increase the emphasis on technology transfer.[23] In the intervening years since 2015, several leading manufacturers have announced plans to transfer technology for fighter planes, military platforms, and weapons systems to co-production facilities in India in a bid to gain advantage in the growing Indian market.[24]

To the extent that a government may be constrained in its ability to condition investment approval on technology transfer, it is likely a result of other treaties which the country has signed. As mentioned earlier, a government may have agreed to this additional obligation during the course of its WTO accession negotiations. China's Protocol of Accession, for example, includes a number of WTO-plus obligations.[25] This includes requirements tying the Chinese government's hand when it comes to requiring technology transfer. Paragraph 8.3 states that 'China shall ensure that the . . . right of importation or investment by national or sub-national authorities, is not conditioned on . . . performance requirements of any kind, such as the transfer of technology . . . or the conduct of research and development in China'.[26]

In addition, a government may have also agreed not to condition investment approval on technology transfer through a Bilateral Investment Treaty (BIT) or an investment chapter of a Free Trade Agreement (FTA). This is especially common in recent investment agreements between an advanced economy and a developing country. For example, the investment chapter of the EU-Vietnam FTA explicitly states that, for the sectors designated in the FTA's Annexes:

---

[23] Tommy Wilkes and Siva Govindasamy, *Modi Wants More Technology Transfer from Global Defence Firms*, Reuters (18 February 2015), available at http://uk.reuters.com/article/uk-airshow-india-modi/indias-modi-wants-more-technology-transfer-from-global-defence-firms-idUKKBN0LM0CY20150218 (last visited 10 September 2017).

[24] Manu Pubby, *For Make in India Fighter Plan, Will Create Factory Designed for Future Indian Combat Plane: Boeing*, Economic Times (17 November 2016), available at http://economictimes.indiatimes.com/news/defence/for-make-in-india-fighter-plan-will-create-factory-designed-for-future-indian-combat-plane-boeing/articleshow/55473572.cms (last visited 10 September 2017); Elizabeth Roche, *UK Offers Technology Transfer to India for Defence Manufacturing*, Live Mint (13 April 2017), available at www.livemint.com/Politics/VVxHieE3XVD8H2hmSdY1RN/UK-offers-technology-transfer-to-India-for-defence-manufactu.html (last visited 10 September 2017).

[25] For further analysis, see Julia Qin, *'WTO-Plus' Obligations and Their Implications for the WTO Legal System: An Appraisal of the China Accession Protocol*, 37 J. World Trade 483 (2003).

[26] China Protocol of Accession (n. 8 above) para. 7.3.

> neither party may impose, or enforce [a requirement] in connection with the establishment or operation of any investment of an investor of Party or of a non-Party in its territory . . . to transfer technology, a production process or other proprietary knowledge to a natural person or enterprises in its territory.[27]

Nevertheless, there is high variance in the substantive requirements of investment treaties. Some cover only post-establishment measures; others do not address performance requirements at all or may not include conditions for technology transfer on the list of prohibited performance requirements.

Even in instances where an explicit treaty obligation exists prohibiting the use of such conditionality, governments are often able to find a work-around to make its preferences for technology transfer known to the foreign investor. The next section details how this might take place.

2. Informal Linkages Between Technology Transfer and Government Action

A government need not go so far as to explicitly demand that a foreign firm transfer technology as a condition for certain government action. Instead, it can do so through much more informal, and more muted, mechanisms. It might choose to do so because, as noted earlier, it is prohibited through treaty obligations from imposing such conditions. However, even when its hands are not tied, a government nevertheless might prefer a more informal approach in order to create a semblance of being more 'investor-friendly' in its policy orientation. This is especially the case in instances where the desire for technology transfer is limited to only a small handful of sectors. Under these circumstances, the government might not wish to scare away foreign investors in other sectors.

This informal preference can be conveyed through both 'carrots' and 'sticks'. Which tool is employed will depend, in part, on the instrument that one thinks will be most effective in convincing a firm to undertake the desired technology transfer. Importantly, to avoid any risk of potential WTO litigation and/or an investor-state dispute settlement claim, the government may choose not to make the request directly or explicitly link the technology transfer as a *quid pro quo* bargain. Instead, the preference is made known informally, possibly through an intermediary without formal ties to the government or through vague statements. This avoids

---

[27] EU-Vietnam FTA, Chapter 8.2 Art. 6, agreed text as of January 2016, available at http://trade.ec.europa.eu/doclib/docs/2016/february/tradoc_154210.pdf (last visited 10 September 2017).

the formal appearance of a government measure and allows the government to maintain some degree of plausible deniability. It can simply claim that the firm misunderstood the business environment, possibly because of bad advice on the part of a business partner, lawyer, banker, or other intermediary. This makes it hard for counterparties (i.e., firms or other governments) to gather the evidence necessary to prove that there was any actual forced technology transfer.

An example of an informal 'carrot' that can be dangled before a firm is to link future government procurement with technology transfer. In evaluating bids between competing foreign firms, a government can make it known that it will give some positive weight to certain factors, such as the extent that a firm is willing to transfer technology. This may not be related to the quality of the good or service itself; however, the same would be true if a government were to consider factors such as whether a firm is minority-owned or the percentage of women on its board of directors. Nevertheless, the government can claim that consideration of such a factor reflects its broader public policy preference, just as would be the case for social factors such as gender, race, or redress for historical inequities. Furthermore, such a preference might not be stated explicitly, particularly if the government is a party to the WTO Government Procurement Agreement which imposes nondiscrimination requirements, but just understood informally.

Almost everywhere in the world, the government will be involved in decisions concerning purchases of software, electronic hardware, automobiles, aviation equipment, pharmaceuticals, to name but a few sectors where technology plays an important role. The government's influence can be even larger in economies with state-owned enterprises or tight linkages between the state and corporate conglomerates. This affords government the opportunity to dangle the prospect of greater near-term profits in a given market as a carrot in exchange for technology transfer. Again, technology transfer is not necessarily forced *per se*, but firms doing business understand the bargain necessary should it wish to secure a piece of the market.

On the flip-side, governments also retain a considerable amount of discretion over certain administrative actions, such as competition policy, national security review, and consumer protection. The possibility that a government might open an investigation for price-fixing, delay regulatory approval for a given product, or declare a given product to be unsafe can dampen a firm's profitability in that market. Again, a government can informally link its discretionary actions to the foreign firm's willingness to transfer technology. Here, instead of dangling the carrot of greater profits in a given market in exchange for technology transfer, the government carries a stick. Oftentimes, it will be the foreign firm that will proactively offer technology transfer as a means to stave off government action that will harm its profitability or as redress for past violations.

Several anecdotes of this sort flow from the Chinese market, but foreign firms are often hesitant to confirm any demands made of technology transfer informally by the Chinese government out of fear of retribution.[28] Qualcomm, a leading semiconductor manufacturer for mobile phones, was hit with a US$975 million fine by Chinese antitrust officials in 2015.[29] Qualcomm was also later fined in South Korea and has been under investigation in the United States, EU, and Taiwan.[30] To regain the good graces of the Chinese government, Qualcomm offered not only to lower its prices in China but also to shift more high-end manufacturing to Chinese partners and to upgrade China's technology capabilities by working with major Chinese firms such as Huawei, as well as start-ups such as Huaxintong Semiconductor.[31]

Another example is Apple, which has faced growing challenges from the Chinese government in recent years while its market share has stagnated. In the wake of the Snowden revelations, Chinese authorities began subjecting Apple and other US technology firms to security reviews to ensure that their products did not contain back-doors that could be used for monitoring purposes by foreign governments.[32] In 2017, Chinese government officials also challenged Apple over illegal content on its app stores

---

[28] Jack Corporal, *Fearing Chinese Reprisal, Companies Wary of Giving USTR Info in 301 Probe*, INSIDE U.S. TRADE (1 September 2017).

[29] Don Clark, *Qualcomm to Pay $975 Million Antitrust Fine to China*, WALL ST. JOURNAL (10 February 2015); Paul Mozur and Quentin Hardy, *China Hits Qualcomm with Fine*, NEW YORK TIMES (9 February 2015), available at www.nytimes.com/2015/02/10/business/international/qualcomm-fine-china-antitrust-investigation.html?mcubz=0 (last visited 10 September 2017).

[30] Tom Fairless and Don Clark, *EU Slaps Qualcomm with Antitrust Charges*, WALL ST. JOURNAL (8 December 2015); Eun-Young Jeong, *Qualcomm Faces $853 Million Fine from South Korea over Alleged Antitrust Violations*, WALL ST. JOURNAL (28 December 2016); Brett Kendall and Ted Greenwald, *Federal Trade Commission Files Antitrust Lawsuit against Qualcomm*, WALL ST. JOURNAL (17 January 2017).

[31] David Barboza, *How this U.S. Tech Giant is Backing China's Tech Ambitions*, NEW YORK TIMES (4 August 2017), available at www.nytimes.com/2017/08/04/technology/qualcomm-china-trump-tech-trade.html?mcubz=0 (last visited 10 September 2017).

[32] Paul Mozur and Jane Perlez, *China Quietly Targets U.S. Tech Companies in Security Reviews*, NEW YORK TIMES (16 May 2016), available at www.nytimes.com/2016/05/17/technology/china-quietly-targets-us-tech-companies-in-security-reviews.html?mcubz=0 (last visited 10 September 2017).

and for selling customer data illegally.[33] The same year, Apple announced plans to invest US$500 million and open four R&D centers in China.[34] It also agreed to open data centers in China to comply with the country's cybersecurity law.[35] While these may be a natural business moves for a leading technology company in the world's largest mobile phone market, it also raises concerns that Apple may be transferring technology to curry favor with the Chinese government in response to challenges by regulators.

Unlike the earlier instance where the demand for technology transfer is explicit, in these instances, it is difficult to prove that firms are not acting on their own accord out of their own business interests but in response to informal government pressure. Regardless of what is actually the case, the above examples highlight how certain governments with regulatory oversight over key markets do possess the ability to cajole foreign firms to transfer technology through informal channels and understood linkages between technology transfer and government actions.

Whether governments actually follow through with employing these informal carrots and sticks is up to each to decide. Depending on the country's size, market potential, factor endowments, industrial policy, and numerous factors, such informal policies may not necessarily be effective. Nevertheless, these informal mechanisms constitute yet another instrument in the arsenal of developing countries determined to capture a greater share of the value of global high-tech GVCs. As the Trump Administration's Section 301 investigation into China's 'forced' technology transfers highlights, they too will increasingly emerge as a tension point in trade relations in the coming era.[36]

---

33 Paul Mozur, *Apple Customer Data in China was Sold Illegally, Police Says*, New York Times (9 June 2017), available at www.nytimes.com/2017/06/09/business/china-apple-personal-data-sold.html?mcubz=0 (last visited 10 September 2017); Amy Qin, *China Casts a Wary Eye at an iPhone Cash Ccow, the App Store*, New York Times (10 August 2017), available at www.nytimes.com/2017/08/10/business/china-apple-app-store.html?mcubz=0 (last visited 10 September 2017).

34 Tripp Mickle, *Apple Pledges New Centers in China as Cook Set to Address Major Government Conference*, Wall St. Journal (17 March 2017).

35 Alyssa Abkowitz and Eva Dou, *Apple to Build China Data Center to Meet New Cybersecurity Law*, Wall St. Journal (12 July 2017).

36 Ana Swanson, *Trump Administration Goes after China over Intellectual Property, Advanced Technology*, Washington Post (14 August 2017), available at www.washingtonpost.com/news/wonk/wp/2017/08/14/trump-administration-goes-after-china-over-intellectual-property-advanced-technology/?utm_term=.93dd3a48efd3 (last visited 10 September 2017).

3. Technology Export Controls

While developing countries may employ policy instruments to spur the outflow of technology, governments in advanced economies also have tools at their disposal to stymie this flow. By far the most commonly employed instrument is that of technology export controls.

In the United States, three different government agencies have authority to issue export licenses: the Departments of State, Commerce, and Treasury. In addition to these three agencies, a number of others, including the Departments of Defense and Energy, are involved in maintaining the three major export control lists of items subject to regulatory oversight. These are the Department of Commerce's Export Administration Regulation, which includes the Commerce Control List concerning dual-use technologies; the US Munitions List, which includes those technologies that are developed or can be adopted/modified for military application; and the Nuclear Regulatory Commission Control, which includes technologies related to atomic energy activity. The stated goals of these export controls is to limit access to sensitive US technologies that impact national security, to comply with international commitments, and to prevent proliferation of such technologies to problematic parties.[37] However, the State Department also openly acknowledges that other goals include promoting regional stability and human rights considerations.[38]

These control lists and their review criteria allow the US government to limit the outflow of certain technologies by its firms to a number of countries; the specific countries to which export is banned will differ depending on the technology.[39] Because a number of dual-use technologies are subject to these controls, they can impact the range of choices available to a US technology firm when deciding where to establish overseas operations and/or joint ventures. Violation of the export control regulations is subject to civil and criminal enforcement, including fines and jail sentences. For example, in 2014, Wind River Systems, a wholly-owned subsidiary of Intel Corp., was fined US$750,000 for illegal sales of encryption software to

---

[37] See DEPARTMENT OF STATE, OVERVIEW OF U.S. EXPORT CONTROL SYSTEM, available at www.state.gov/strategictrade/overview/ (last visited 10 September 2017).

[38] *Ibid.*

[39] For an example of the complex administration of this program, see Department of Commerce, *Commerce Country Chart*, available at www.bis.doc.gov/index.php/documents/regulations-docs/federal-register-notices/federal-register-2014/1033-738-supp-1/file (last visited 10 September 2017).

governments and end-users in a wide range of countries, including China, Russia, Israel, South Africa, and South Korea.[40]

Not surprisingly, US export controls have been a persistent source of tension in US trade relations, including most notably with China. Chinese trade officials consistently attribute the bilateral trade imbalance to the fact that US export controls limit the export opportunities of American firms.[41] However, studies suggest that the policy is driven by foreign policy interests;[42] liberalizing the controls would have only a limited economic upside in the near-term while subjecting the United States to longer-term risks.[43]

Other major advanced economies also have developed export control regimes that regulate the outflow of dual-use technologies. In Japan, export controls are overseen by the Ministry of Economy, Trade, and Industry. The legal framework for the regime is extremely complicated as it is governed by a complex mix of laws, regulations, cabinet orders, ministerial ordinances, notifications, notices, and guidance, which may be intertwined with each other.[44] In the EU, the export control regime is governed by Council Regulation (EC) 428/2009: at the Community level, it provides for a common set of rules, a common list of technologies subject to export control, and harmonized implementation policies.[45]

---

[40] Bureau of Industry and Security, Department of Commerce, Press Release, *Intel Subsidiary Agrees to $750,000 Penalty for Unauthorized Encryption Exports* (8 October 2014), available at www.bis.doc.gov/index.php/about-bis/newsroom/press-releases/107-about-bis/newsroom/press-releases/press-release-2014/763-intel-subsidiary-agrees-to-750-000-penalty-for-unauthorized-encryption-exports (last visited 10 September 2017).

[41] Jesse Heatley, *After 100 Days and Much Hype, U.S.-China Talks Fall Flat*, FORBES (21 July 2017), available at www.forbes.com/sites/insideasia/2017/07/21/after-100-days-and-much-hype-u-s-china-talks-fall-flat/#1d92e5862010 (last visited 10 September 2017); Jessie Jang, *China and U.S. Diverge on High-Tech Trade in Economic Talks*, MORNING CONSULT (20 July 2017), available at https://morningconsult.com/2017/07/20/china-u-s-diverge-high-tech-trade-economic-talks/ (last visited 10 September 2017); Brian Spegele, *China Wants U.S. to Drop Tech Export Limits, or it Will Shop Elsewhere*, WALL ST. JOURNAL (14 April 2015).

[42] See HUGO MEIJER, TRADING WITH THE ENEMY: THE MAKING OF US EXPORT CONTROL POLICY TOWARD THE PEOPLE'S REPUBLIC OF CHINA (2016).

[43] Paul Eckert, *U.S. Export Controls have Small China Trade Impact*, REUTERS (22 May 2007), available at www.reuters.com/article/us-usa-china-technology/u-s-export-controls-have-small-china-trade-impact-idUSN1542500520070521 (last visited 10 September 2017). But see *contra* Bin Li and Xiao Yang, *Measuring Political Trade Barriers in US Exports to China*, 6 CHINESE J. INT'L POL. 133 (2013).

[44] For additional information, see CENTER FOR INFORMATION ON SECURITY TRADE CONTROL, OVERVIEW OF JAPAN'S EXPORT CONTROLS (4th ed., 2015).

[45] Council Regulation (EC) 428/2009 of 5 May 2009, [2009] OJ L134/1 (EU).

However, under certain circumstances each EU member is also free to subject additional technologies to control.

In each instance, countries implement export controls on dual-use technologies in order to comply with multilateral obligations, advance foreign policy goals, and protect national security interests. Because they restrict the transfer of technology abroad, they can also serve as a policy instrument for advanced economies to protect their dominance of high-value portions of technology value chains. They therefore can provide governments in advanced economies with a mechanism to enact industrial policy under the guise of national security.

IV. INVESTMENT REVIEWS

A third tool in the arsenal of governments in the quest for positioning along GVCs is the review of foreign investments. Governments are increasingly employing the regulatory power that they hold over acquisitions and greenfield investments to advance policy goals.

Fueling this trend is the rapid rise in outbound foreign investment from China. In a quest to gain access to leading-edge technologies, Chinese firms, oftentimes with indirect or informal links to the state, are actively buying up Western assets. In both Europe and the United States, Chinese investment hit record levels in 2016.[46] In Germany, during 2016, new acquisitions by Chinese firms are proceeding at a pace of one a week, with totals from the first half of 2016 hitting a record US$10 billion, more than the totals from all other years combined.[47]

Within advanced economies, there is rising concern that such acquisitions may lead to a gradual erosion of long-term competitiveness in advanced technology sectors.[48] Increasingly, individuals and trade unions are calling for stronger government scrutiny over such deals. There are rising concerns that corporate boards may be selling out the country's

---

For additional information, see European Parliament, Directorate-General for External Policies, Dual-Use Export Controls (2015).

46 Shawn Donnan, *Surge in Chinese Corporate Investment into the US*, Financial Times (2 January 2017); Tom Mitchell et al., *Chinese Investment in EU Dwarfs Flow the Other Way*, Financial Times (11 January 2017).

47 Guy Chazan, *German Angst over Chinese M&A*, Financial Times (9 August 2016).

48 Don Reisinger, *Here's the Latest on How Apple is Expanding in China*, Fortune (17 March 2016), available at http://fortune.com/2017/03/17/apple-rd-centers-china/ (last visited 10 September 2017); Abkowitz and Dou (n. 35 above).

long-term economic interests in exchange for short-term investment profits.

One of the highest-profile acquisitions in 2016 was the offer by the Chinese appliance maker, Midea, to purchase a controlling stake of the German robotics firm, Kuka. The deal valued Kuka at €4.6 billion, a 60 percent premium over its existing value. While some officials in Berlin and Brussels warned that the acquisition carried the risk of yielding an expanding high-tech sector to a Chinese firm, the German government nevertheless proceeded to approve the deal in August 2016.[49] The government noted that the law only allowed it to block an acquisition where it threatened core German interests concerning security and public order.

However, in the wake of this deal, European officials have sought to strengthen laws to increase regulatory oversight over deals involving promising technology industries. Previously, the rules allowed for a deal to be blocked only if it threatens energy security, defense, media concentration, or financial stability.[50] In July 2017, Germany adopted a new directive that expands the scope to include any attempt by a non-EU entity to acquire more than a 25 percent stake in critical infrastructure such as software for power plants, energy and water supply networks, electronic payments, hospitals, and transport systems, as well as for companies engaged in advanced defense technologies and surveillance equipment.[51]

In his State of the Union speech in September 2017, Jean-Claude Juncker, President of the European Commission, proposed a new EU-wide framework for investment screening.[52] The proposed draft framework would include an anti-circumvention clause to provide European governments with a basis to vet intra-EU takeovers in order to assess whether a non-EU investor is simply setting up a shell company to evade foreign

---

[49] Editorial, *Berlin approves Kuka sale to Midea*, DEUTSCHE WELLE (17 August 2016), available at http://dw.com/p/1JjVD (last visited 10 September 2017).

[50] Birgit Jennen et al., *German Push Grows for Chinese Investment Curbs as Aixtron Probed*, BLOOMBERG (23 October 2016), available at www.bloomberg.com/news/articles/2016-10-23/german-momentum-grows-for-curbs-on-chinese-overseas-investment (last visited 10 September 2017).

[51] Guy Chazan, *Germany Expands Powers to Block Takeovers*, FINANCIAL TIMES (12 July 2017).

[52] Jean-Claude Juncker, President of the European Commission, State of the Union Address 2017, 13 September 2017. For full details of the proposal, see Proposal for a Regulation of the European Parliament and of the Council Establishing a Framework for Screening of Foreign Direct Investments Into the European Union, COM(2017) 487 final (13 September 2017).

investment screening.[53] It would also require EU governments to share information on sensitive takeovers with each other and with Brussels, as well as also allow Brussels to weigh in with its own non-binding opinion for takeover deals likely to affect security or public order in one or more EU member states.[54] Whether the proposal will be adopted by the EU remains unclear as of this writing.

Foreign acquisitions of assets in the United States are subject to review by the Committee on Foreign Investment in the United States (CFIUS). The Committee consists of nine members[55] and two *ex officio* members,[56] along with five others whose role is to observe, and as appropriate, participate in and report to the President.[57] CFIUS is governed by the Foreign Investment and National Security Act of 2007. Its mandate allows it to review any transaction, merger, acquisition, or takeover that results in foreign control of any entity engaged in interstate commerce within the United States. CFIUS is tasked with analyzing whether the transaction implicates US national security, including but not limited to 'critical infrastructure' systems and assets. If so, CFIUS may requires steps be taken to mitigate the impact or bar the transaction outright. CFIUS operates through both a formal review process, as well as an informal process in which firms contemplating a transaction solicit input beforehand. The mere prospect of a CFIUS investigation can prove sufficient to derail the transaction.

Even prior to the recent wave of Chinese investment, CFIUS has not hesitated to step in to prevent US technology from being acquired by foreign entities. In 2006, for example, the Israeli firm, Check Point Software Technologies, abandoned its proposed US$225 million acquisition of Sourcefire, a US firm specializing in security appliances for protecting a firm's internal computer networks, due to the prospect of a CFIUS investigation.[58]

---

53 Jim Brunsden, *Brussels Prepares Powers to Block Foreign Takeovers*, Financial Times (12 September 2017).

54 *Ibid.*

55 These are the Secretaries of Commerce, Defense, Energy, Homeland Security, State, and Treasury, along with the Attorney General, the US Trade Representative, and the Director of the Office of Science and Technology Policy.

56 These are the Secretary of Labor and the Director of National Intelligence.

57 These are the Director of the Office of Management and Budget, the Chairman of the Council of Economic Advisors, the Assistant to the President for National Security Affairs, the Assistant to the President for Economic Policy, and the Assistant to the President for Homeland Security and Counterterrorism.

58 James Jackson, *The Committee on Foreign Investment in the U.S. (CFIUS)* 9 (Congressional Research Service Report, 12 August 2016).

In recent years, the prospect of a CFIUS review has served to hamper attempts by Chinese firms to acquire US technology. Several examples abound. In 2008, an attempt by Huawei to acquire 3Com was thwarted after the buyers failed to reach an agreement with CFIUS.[59] In 2010, Tangshan Caofedian Investment Corporation withdrew its bid to acquire Emcore, a US firm that makes components for fiber optics and solar panels, over CFIUS concerns.[60] More recently, in 2015, Tsinghua Unigroup Ltd. abandoned a proposed purchase of US semiconductor manufacturer, Micron Technologies, because of CFIUS concerns.[61] In 2016, Unisplendour, a division of Tsinghua Unigroup, also backed out of a proposed acquisition of Western Digital, a maker of hard drives, due to a pending CFIUS investigation.

Several of the deals above were thwarted prior to the actual commencement of a CFIUS investigation. However, not all deals for which an official investigation was conducted have resulted in a negative recommendation. For example, in January 2013, China's Wanxiang Group received approval to proceed with the acquisition of A123 Systems, an electric car battery maker, despite concerns raised that the deal might compromise US energy security. The deal also implicated competition in a potentially growing high-tech market, but CFIUS's current mandate only allows it to review a deal for national security reasons.

Just as is the case in Europe, some American officials have also proposed formally expanding CFIUS's mandate beyond national security. Academic work by Tingley et al. have highlighted how, in addition to national security concerns, economic distress and reciprocity are also key drivers to political opposition to proposed Chinese acquisitions of US firms.[62] In 2016, Congresswoman Rosa DeLauro (D-CT) introduced a Bill that would broaden CFIUS's power to review transactions not only for national security concerns but to more broadly 'determine whether

---

59 Steven Weisman, *Sale of 3Com to Huawei is Derailed by U.S. Security Concerns*, New York Times (21 February 2008), available at www.nytimes.com/2008/02/21/business/worldbusiness/21iht-3com.1.10258216.html?mcubz=0 (last visited 10 September 2017).

60 Stephanie Kirchgaessner, *U.S. Blocks China Fibre Optics Deal over Security*, Financial Times (30 June 2010).

61 Liana B. Baker and Greg Roumeliotis, *Exclusive: Micron does not Believe Deal with Tsinghua is Possible–Sources*, Reuters (20 July 2015), available at www.reuters.com/article/us-micron-m-a-tsinghua-exclusive/exclusive-micron-does-not-believe-deal-with-tsinghua-is-possible-sources-idUSKCN0PU1X120150720 (last visited 10 September 2017).

62 Dustin Tingley et al., *The Political Economy of Inward FDI: Opposition to Chinese Mergers and Acquisitions*, 8 Chinese J. Int'l Pol. 27 (2015).

such transaction is of net benefit to the U.S.'.[63] The draft Bill reportedly would expand CFIUS's mandate and require it to assess the impact of the proposed deal on factors such as employment and product innovation. Although the Bill did not gain traction in the Republican Congress, it highlighted the appetite of some in Washington to expand the powers of the government's investment review to prevent the aggressive moves by Chinese and other foreign firms to purchase key technologies and acquire a greater stake of the value chain.

Following President Trump's election in 2017, a bipartisan group of senators led by Senator John Cornyn (R-TX) introduced the Foreign Investment Risk Review Modernization Act to expand the scope of CFIUS review to include a broader range of deals, including joint ventures based outside of the United States and minority-stake investments which would give foreign investors access to sensitive information.[64] In addition, bipartisan legislation has been introduced by Senators Chuck Grassley (R-IA) and Debbie Stabenow (D-MI) to strengthen the focus on food security and expand the committee's membership.[65] As of this writing, neither piece of legislation has advanced through Congress yet. All of these legislative efforts, however, signal a desire to embark on some type of reforms to expand the reach of investment reviews.

In response, China has drafted its own national security law with the aim of equipping itself with a similar tool. In July 2015, the Standing Committee of the National People's Congress adopted a new National Security Law. Article 59 provides that the state shall engage in review of 'foreign investment that infringes upon, or may infringe upon, national security'.[66] Additional regulations serve to implement this directive;

---

[63] Diane Bartz, *U.S. Lawmaker to Introduce Bill to Broaden CFIUS Mandate beyond Security Concerns*, Reuters (25 February 2016), available www.reuters.com/article/us-usa-china-deals-congress/u-s-lawmaker-to-introduce-bill-to-broaden-cfius-mandate-beyond-security-concerns-idUSKCN0VY00U (last visited 10 September 2017).

[64] Diane Bartz, *Leading U.S. Senator Urges Changes in Foreign Investment Rules*, Reuters (26 June 2017), available at www.reuters.com/article/us-china-usa-investment-cornyn/leading-u-s-senator-urges-changes-in-foreign-investment-rules-idUSKBN19H2I5 (last visited 10 September 2017).

[65] Mercy Kuo, *CFIUS in US-China Relations*, The Diplomat (25 April 2017), available at http://thediplomat.com/2017/04/cfius-in-us-china-relations/ (last visited 10 September 2017).

[66] National Security Law of the People's Republic of China, art. 59 (promulgated by the Standing Committee, National People's Congress, 1 July 2015), art. 59, translated in China Law Translate, www.chinalawtranslate.com/2015nsl/?lang=en (last visited 11 September 2017).

these make clear that the government adopts a broad definition of national security. The 2011 Circular on the Establishment of a System for Security Review of Acquisition of Domestic Enterprises by Foreign Investors provided that mergers and acquisitions of firms engaged in key industries should be subject to national security review.[67] This was to be done through a joint agency process coordinated by the Ministry of Commerce and the National Development and Reform Commission. More recently, in May 2015, the State Council issued trial measures for the national security review of foreign investments in key industries located in the four coastal free trade zones. These trial measures explicitly identify 'IT products and services' as a sector where mergers and acquisitions of domestic enterprises will be subject to national security review.

V. PROSPECTS FOR FURTHER LEGAL DISCIPLINES

While the focus of this volume is on the so-called mega-regional trade agreements ('mega-RTAs'), these are but one mechanism that can be used to spur the creation of additional international economic law to govern the three categories of policy instruments discussed above that increasingly impact trade and investment in global high-tech goods and services. Other possibilities include traditional bilateral RTAs as well as BITs. Finally, governments may seek to shape policies not through treaty law, but rather the development of norms perpetuated through international forums. This final section examines the various ways in which each have been deployed to date.

The Comprehensive and Progressive Agreement for Trans-Pacific Partnership (CPTPP) serves as a quintessential example of how the range of issues discussed above can be tackled in a single mega-RTA. The CPTPP makes clear that, unless it has previously scheduled it in a designated Annex:

> no Party shall adopt or maintain any duty, tax or other charge on the export of any good to the territory of another Party, unless such duty, tax or other charge is adopted or maintained on that good when destined for domestic consumption.[68]

---

[67] For additional details, see WHITE & CASE, NATIONAL SECURITY REVIEWS: A GLOBAL PERSPECTIVE 5–6 (2016).

[68] CPTPP, to be signed 8 March 2018, art. 2.15.

Its Investment Chapter includes prohibition of a long list of performance requirements, including forced technology transfer.[69] In addition, its Electronic Commerce Chapter included a provision prohibiting a CPTPP Party from:

> requir[ing] the transfer of, or access to, source code of software as a condition for import, distribution, sale or use of such software, or of products containing such software, in its territory.[70]

The CPTPP also contains a number of other new innovations, such as a dedicated Chapter on state-owned enterprises and a more robust Competition Chapter.[71] All of these serve to limit the range of policy instruments discussed earlier that can be used to advantage domestic high-tech firms.

However, mega-RTAs are not the only possible means through which governments might seek to create new international economic law to curtail or discipline the growing use of the policy instruments described in this chapter. Trade negotiators also can resort to bilateral trade agreements to constrain the use of such policy instruments. Most US bilateral FTAs prohibit the use of export taxes between the parties to the agreement.[72] The same is true of several FTAs concluded by the EU and Japan.[73] In addition, they include robust Investment Chapters with limitations on performance requirements that cover technology transfer.[74]

Beyond trade agreements, countries can turn to other treaty instruments to constrain the practices of foreign governments. For example, BITs, as well as the Investment Chapters in FTAs, can include provisions prohibiting certain forms of performance requirements, including requiring technology transfer. To date, however, most BITs do not constrain investment reviews conducted on national security grounds. Most BITs by advanced economies include an exception for essential security interests, which, so far, has been deemed to be self-judging.[75] However, as outbound

---

[69] *Ibid.* art. 9.10.

[70] *Ibid.* art. 14.17.

[71] *Ibid.* chs. 16–17.

[72] See e.g., United States-Peru Trade Promotion Agreement, art. 2.11 (12 April 2006); United States-Korea Free Trade Agreement, art. 2.11 (30 June 2007).

[73] See e.g., Japan-Mexico Economic Partnership Agreement, art. 7 (17 September 2004); EC-Montenegro Stabilisation and Association Agreement, art. 22.1 (15 October 2007).

[74] See e.g., EU-Vietnam Free Trade Agreement, ch. 8.2, art. 6 (1 February 2016); Japan-Mongolia Economic Partnership Agreement, art. 10.7 (10 March 2015).

[75] Katia Yannaca-Small, *Essential Security Interests Under International Investment Law*, *in* International Investment Perspectives 2007 (OECD ed., 2007).

Chinese firms, including technology players, are negatively affected by national security reviews for foreign investment, China has sought to rethink the language of the national security exception of its BITs.[76] In the China-Japan-Korea Trilateral Investment Agreement, for example, it has injected additional language stating that the national security exception cannot be used 'as a means of avoiding its obligations' under the agreement.[77]

To summarize, as the dynamics of global high-tech production shift, so too will the policy instruments used by governments to ensure that they capture their share of the leading technology industries in the twenty-first century. This chapter has detailed several of the tools upon which governments increasingly rely as they seek to compete over the high-value portions of technology GVCs. As the contours and dynamics of competition shift, so too will the details of international economic law. While mega-RTAs are one possible outlet for the development of such a response, they are not the only possibility. Whether through treaties or unilateral actions, governments will increasingly find ways to address the growing use of strategic trade policies and industrial policies geared toward innovation and high-tech industries.

76 See generally Cai Congyan, *National Security Review in China-US Bilateral Investment Treaty* (draft manuscript, on file with the author).

77 China-Japan-Korea, Republic of, Trilateral Investment Agreement, art. 18.2 (13 May 2012).

6. China standard time: The boundary of techno-nationalism in megaregionals

Han-Wei Liu

I. INTRODUCTION

In the information and communication technology (ICT) industry, a typical market exhibits strong network externalities, and the rise and fall of an enterprise turns on the role of interoperability, enabling devices, services, and users to work together. One way to achieve interoperability is to develop standards to connect different systems.[1] In the past, most of these ICT standards were created by firms or government agencies from the West through formal standardization organizations or informal industry consortia.[2] In recent years, however, the paradigm has witnessed a sea-change, with emerging Asian economies seeking to shape the landscape with their Western counterparts. Besides Japan, an established player in the ICT standards world, other emerging Asian economies, notably, China, India, South Korea, and Taiwan, have stepped up their standards systems.[3] Of these new players, China's standards strategy has taken center stage since 2003, when it introduced the mandatory WLAN Authentication and Privacy Infrastructure

---

1 See John Palfrey and Usr Gasser, Interop: The Promise and Perils of Highly Interconnected Systems 137–8 (2012).

2 Han-Wei Liu, *International Standards in Flux: A Balkanized ICT Standard-Setting Paradigm and its Implications for the WTO*, 17 J. Int'l Econ. L. 551 (2014).

3 Heejin Lee et al., *The Rise of Asia in Global Standardization: A Threat, Opportunity or Something Else?*, 38 Telecom. Pol'y 851 (2014); Dieter Ernst et al., *Standards, Innovation, and Latecomer Economic Development: Conceptual Issues and Policy Challenges*, 38 Telecom. Pol'y 853 (2014); T. Ramakrishma et al., *Intellectual Property and ICT Standards in India*, available at http://sites.nationalacademies.org/cs/groups/pgasite/documents/webpage/pga_072484.pdf (last visited 23 August 2017).

(WAPI) standard, an incompatible alternative to the widely implemented Wi-Fi standard.[4]

China's interests in crafting a national standards strategy grew out of a complex, fluid environment. While China has successfully translated its abundance of cheap labor and natural resources into decades of double-digit economic growth, underneath this seemingly hegemonic dominance of the global manufacturing scene is a myriad of institutional challenges. China's aging population,[5] rising wages,[6] environmental crisis,[7] and many other socio-economic problems have eroded its comparative advantage vis-à-vis other emerging economies—primarily from Southeast Asia—in capturing a larger share of the manufacturing sector.[8] Despite China's decades-long economic growth, such a low valued-added model cannot sustain the nation in the long term. Reliance upon technologies created by its Western counterparts may place China in a subordinate role in both economic and geo-political terms.[9]

The confluence of these factors bred China's 'Indigenous Innovation Policies', a scheme that seeks to help the nation march towards the leading ranks of the most competitive economies. Government procurement, subsidies, and, more crucially for the present purpose, indigenous standards form the centerpiece of this scheme.[10] Often, these homegrown

---

4 See n. 5 below and accompanying text.

5 See e.g., Judith Banister et al., *Population Aging and Economic Growth in China*, *in* THE CHINESE ECONOMY: A NEW TRANSITION 114–49 (Masahiko Aoki and Jinglian Wu eds., 2012).

6 See generally Hongbin Li et al., *The End of Cheap Chinese Labor*, 26(4) J. ECON. PERSP. 57 (2012).

7 Elizabeth C. Economy, *The Great Leap Backward? The Costs of China's Environmental Crisis*, 86(5) FOREIGN AFF. 38 (2007).

8 See Robert D. O'Brien, *China's Indigenous Innovation: Origins, Components and Ramifications*, 6(3) CHINA SECURITY 51, 53 (2010).

9 See Greg Linden, *China Standard Time: A Study in Strategic Industrial Policy*, 6(3) BUS. & POLITICS 1, 3 (2004); Daniel C.K. Chow, *China's Indigenous Innovation Policies and the World Trade Organization*, 34 NW. J. INT'L L. & BUS. 81, 83 (2013) (noting that leading innovator countries like the United States are often reluctant to offer 'core' technologies to China in order to preserve competitive advantage); *ibid.* at 54 (arguing that indigenous innovation policy can 'ensure supply chain security and thereby increase their faith in the reliability of their utilities infrastructure, defense systems and information technology').

10 On China's government procurement, see e.g., S. James Boumil III, *China's Indigenous Innovation Policies Under the TRIPs and GPA Agreements and Alternatives for Promoting Economic Growth*, 12(2) CHI. J. INT'L L. 755 (2012); on the role of subsidies in China's indigenous innovation measures, see e.g., USHA C.V. HALEY AND GEORGE T. HALEY, SUBSIDIES TO CHINESE INDUSTRY: STATE CAPITALISM, BUSINESS STRATEGY, AND TRADE POLICY (2013).

standards are justified by the Chinese government in the name of public interest (e.g., privacy, cybersecurity, national security, etc.). Yet, the way in which standards are implemented has raised concerns about digital protectionism. The above-mentioned WAPI is an oft-criticized measure in point. While a series of Sino-United States political talks in 2004 paused the WAPI episode, similar measures persist. Today, China's indigenous standards policies have joined exchange rates and foreign direct investment as one of the hottest topics in United States-China economic relations, attracting attention from political scientists,[11] engineers,[12] and trade lawyers. Existing legal literature has addressed normative ramifications by considering the legality of the WAPI under the World Trade Organization (WTO regime).[13] While these scholars have aptly applied WTO laws and jurisprudence to China's indigenous standards, thus far none of these measures have been brought before WTO adjudicators. This may imply the practical limitations of using WTO dispute settlement in this context, given the rapidly evolving nature of the ICT sector and possible loopholes in current substantive WTO rules.[14] The same result may also suggest that

---

[11] See e.g., Scott Kennedy, *The Political Economy of Standards Coalitions: Explaining China's Involvement in High-Tech Standards Wars*, 2 ASIA POL'Y 41(2006); Richard P. Suttmeier et al., *Standards, Stakeholders and Innovation: China's Evolving Role in the Global Knowledge Economy* (Nat'l Bureau of Asian Res., NBR Special Report No. 15, September 2008); Richard P. Suttmeier et al., *Standards of Power? Technology, Institutions and Politics in the Development of China's National Standards Strategy* (Nat'l Bureau of Asian Res., NBR Report No. 10, June 2006); Dan Breznitz and Michael Murphree, *The Rise of China in Technology Standards: New Norms in Old Institutions* (US-China Econ. & Sec. Rev. Comm'n Research Report, 16 January 2013), available at www.uscc.gov/sites/default/files/Research/RiseofChinainTechnologyStandards.pdf (last visited 23 August 2017).

[12] See e.g., Robin Williams et al., *China and Global ICT Standardisation and Innovation*, 23(7) TECH. ANALYSIS & STRATEGIC MGNT. 715 (2011); Kai Jakobs, *The (Future) Role of China in ICT Standardisation: A European Perspective*, 38 TELECOM. POL'Y 863 (2014).

[13] See e.g., Zia K. Cromer, *China's WAPI Policy: Security Measure or Trade Protectionism?* 2005 DUKE L. & TECH. REV. 8 (2005); Christopher S. Gibson, *Globalization and the Technology Standards Game: Balancing Concerns of Protectionism and Intellectual Property*, 22 BERKELEY TECH. L.J. 1403 (2007); Shin-Yi Peng, *Standards as a Means to Technological Leadership? China's ICT Standards in the Context of the International Economic Order*, in CHINA IN THE INTERNATIONAL ECONOMIC ORDER: NEW DIRECTIONS AND CHANGING PARADIGMS 128 (Lisa Toohey et al. eds., 2015).

[14] Han-Wei Liu and Shin-Yi Peng, *Managing Trade Conflicts in the ICT Industry: A Case Study of EU–Greater China Area*, 19(3) J. INT'L ECON. L. 629 (2016) (identifying key variables that affect the EU's strategies to manage trade conflicts in the ICT industry).

China's indigenous standards are no longer perceived as a threat because of certain institutional changes.

These observations call for a reappraisal of the common perception that views the rise of China's indigenous standards as a critical threat to the international economic order. Presumably, because China has economically and legally been integrated into globalization, the reach of its standardization strategies hinges on complex internal and external forces. Internally, contrary to much of the legal literature that considers the Chinese standardization system as a unified whole with 'one voice', China's policy-makers face a rather complicated and sometimes confrontational setting that constrains the nation's capacity to leverage its standards policies as a trade protectionism tool. As the global value chain (GVC) has been fragmented, goods and services are no longer produced by vertically integrated, nationally oriented firms.[15] Such fragmentation implies that each firm's expertise is at different manufacturing stages, complicating ties with domestic and international counterparts and thwarting approaches to innovation and standardization. Diversified interests can also turn on power struggles between government agencies at various levels, affecting China's standards strategies.

External forces also play a role here. While the WTO is limited in addressing WAPI-type conflicts, efforts have been made in the context of preferential trade agreements (PTAs) and bilateral investment treaties (BITs) by adding new clauses to close loopholes. This is particularly so in PTAs/BITs led or signed by the United States—a nation with huge stakes in this high-tech sector. While China is not a party to many of these arrangements, certain new disciplines in the Trans-Pacific Partnership (TPP) Agreement and the US Model BIT, for example, may have some externalities that implicate China's indigenous standards policies.

At heart, the purpose of this chapter is to expand traditional discourse by unpacking internal and external factors that may constrain China's standards-based protectionism. While existing legal scholarship has aptly addressed the legality of WAPI-type measures through the lens of the WTO, these discussions appear to be based, at least in part, on flawed working assumptions by taking these standards initiatives as a given without examining the complexities of China's standardization system. None of the existing literature has addressed how major players, especially the

---

[15] See e.g., Timothy J. Sturgeon, *What Really Goes On in Silicon Valley? Spatial Clustering and Dispersal in Modular Production Networks*, 3 J. ECON. GEOGRAPHY 199 (2003); Michael Murphree and Dan Breznitz, *Innovation in China: Fragmentation, Structured Uncertainty, and Technology Standards*, 2013 CARDOZO L. REV. DE NOVO 196 205–8 (2013).

United States, respond to China's indigenous standards through the law-making process in the context of megaregionals. By exploring constraints that may reshape China's standardization strategies, this chapter seeks to identify new pathways to channel China's standards efforts away from 'techno-nationalism' and towards 'techno-globalism', reducing trade barrier concerns.[16] Against this backdrop, the rest of this chapter proceeds as follows. Section II sets the stage by outlining the evolution of China's standardization regime since 1949 and recapping the WAPI saga. Section III reassesses the prevailing perception that considers China's indigenous standards a threat to global trade by identifying internal and external forces that may well constrain such protectionism. We then highlight certain progress that seems to signal China's move towards 'techno-globalism', thereby reducing trade concerns. Section IV concludes.

II. CHINA, STANDARDS, AND DIGITAL WALL: CONTEXT AND PROBLEMS

1. A Snapshot of China's Evolving Standardization Regime

China's modern standardization system began in the 1930s, when the Republic of China (ROC) established the Committee of Industry Standards in 1931, which, together with the National Metrology Bureau, was consolidated as the 'Central Standard Bureau' in 1947 under the

---

[16] The terms 'techno-nationalism' and 'techno-globalism' were first coined by Robert Reich. Reich referred to the American approach to technologies by the mid-1980s as guided by techno-nationalism, an ideology that did not distinguish American technologies and those from others. As US hegemony declined, however, there was growing concern that national interests would be subordinated as a result of reliance on foreign, especially Japanese, technologies. According to this view, technologies were nationally-oriented. While such a distinction originally referred to Americans' shifted ideologies, techno-nationalism was later used to describe industrial policies adopted by East Asia economies, like China, Japan, Korea, and Taiwan. For the present purpose, we loosely understand the term of 'techno-nationalism' as government intervention that targets high-tech industries of strategic importance to secure national economic and security interests, while referring to 'techno-globalism' as those players who are more liberal and call for reductions in barriers to the transfer and diffusion of technology. In the former, governments often take the lead in innovation, while in the latter, global market forces play a central role. See Robert B. Reich, *The Rise of Techno-Nationalism*, 259 ATLANTIC MONTHLY 62–70 (1987); William W. Keller and Richard J. Samuels, *Innovation and the Asian Economies*, *in* CRISIS AND INNOVATION IN ASIAN TECHNOLOGY 1–22 (William W. Keller and Richard J. Samuels eds., 2003).

mandate of China's first Standards Act.[17] The establishment of the People's Republic of China (PRC) in 1949 marked a new chapter in the nation's standards system, which can be roughly divided into three major phases. In Phase I (1949–1960s), the Communist Party drew upon the experience of the former Soviet Union by formulating its standards regime to serve the planned economy.[18] The role of standards at this stage was, as China's standards experts describe, 'a measure for the government to organize large-scale production in a planned economy'; standards were therefore made 'mandatory'.[19]

Phase I came to an end when the devastating Cultural Revolution (1966–1976) largely destroyed the system.[20] It was not until Deng Xiaoping took over the administration in the 1970s that the nation began to resurrect science and technology policies. Several reforms marked a watershed for China's standards system.[21] In the late 1980s, China passed the Standardization Law,[22] and also the Regulation for Implementation of the Standardization Law as the new building block.[23] Hierarchically, the Standardization Law divides standards into four categories: 'national

---

[17] Biaozhun Fa [Standards Act] (promulgated by National Government of the Republic of China, 24 September 1946).

[18] In addition to the 'national standard', each of the industrial ministries issued compulsory 'ministry standards' governing the state-owned enterprises within the jurisdiction of each ministry. At the time, the aim of China's standards regime was to ensure product quality, make effective use of resources and enhance productivity. Wang Ping et al., *Standardization Strategy of China: Achievements and Challenges* (East-West Center Working Paper Econ. Series No. 107, 2010), available at www.eastwestcenter.org/publications/standardization-strategy-china-achievements-and-challenges (last visited 23 August 2017).

[19] Ping Wang and Zheng Laing, *Beyond Government Control of China's Standardization System: History, Current Status and Reform Suggestions* (Think Piece for EWC-NSF Workshop Mega-Regionalism, 20–21 January 2016), available at www.eastwestcenter.org/sites/default/files/filemanager/pubs/pdfs/6-3Wang.pdf (last visited 23 August 2017).

[20] For a recount, see e.g., Chun Tian Li, Biaozhunhua Gailun [Introduction to Standardization] (reporting that only around 400 standards were developed over this period).

[21] Chaoyi Zhao and John M. Graham, *The PRC's Evolving Standards System: Institutions and Strategy*, 2 Asia Pol'y 63, 65 (2006).

[22] Zhonghua Renmin Gongheguo Biaozhunhua Fa [Standardization Law of the People's Republic of China] ('Standardization Law') (promulgated by the Standing Comm. Nat'l People's Cong., 29 December 1988, effective 1 April 1989) 1988 Standing Comm. Nat'l People's Cong. Gaz. 8 (PRC).

[23] Zhonghua Renmin Gongheguo Biaozhunhua Fa Shishi Tiaoli [Regulation for Implementation of the Standardization Law] (promulgated by the St. Council, 6 April 1990) 1990(2) Zhonghua Renmin Gongheguo Fagui Huibian 63 (PRC).

standards', 'trade standards', 'local standards', and 'enterprise standards'.[24] National standards are at the top of the hierarchy; they are mandated for matters requiring consistency on a nationwide scale.[25] Trade standards are developed in areas where national standards do not exist, yet harmonization is required.[26] Absent these two standards, local standards kick in and are oftentimes formulated for safety and sanitation reasons.[27] At the bottom of the chain lie enterprise standards, set by individual companies to serve their specific needs.[28]

While the Chinese standardization regime in Phase II still carried the legacy of a planned economy,[29] there was progress signaling China's shift towards a Western model. First, the three types of government-issued standards have already been divided by the Standardization Law into 'compulsory' and 'voluntary': the former are issued to protect 'human health' and 'personal and property safety', while others were prescribed by laws and administrative rules.[30] Second, given the gap between China and its Western counterparts in technological capacities, the Standardization Law introduced the idea of a 'dual-track' strategy by extensively converting international standards and advanced standards set by the West into various Chinese standards.[31] Towards this end, China rejoined major international standardization bodies, including the International Organization for Standardization (ISO),[32] while following the Western practice by establishing technical committees (TCs) and subcommittees (SCs) that undertook technical works. It was reported that by the end of 1999, there were 243 TCs and 410 SCs.[33] In short, China's standards strategy at this stage was in line with its open-door policy; standards were considered a tool to transfer advanced Western technologies to relatively underdeveloped China.

Phase III began around the early 2000s, when China joined the WTO. Two developments are noteworthy and related to our discussion below. First, while the major instruments like the Standardization Law remain untouched, the Standardization Administration of China (SAC),

24 Standardization Law, art. 6.
25 Zhao and Graham (n. 21 above) 67.
26 Standardization Law, art. 6.
27 *Ibid.*
28 *Ibid.*
29 Wang et al. (n. 18 above) 4.
30 Standardization Law, art. 7.
31 *Ibid.*
32 Wang and Laing (n. 19 above) 3.
33 Wang et al. (n. 18 above) 2.

a new agency subordinated to the Administration for Quality Supervision Inspection and Quarantine (AQSIQ), has taken on the central role in developing the nation's standards agenda.[34] Second, and more crucially, the importance of the dual-track strategy has been gradually fading away.[35] In order to minimize the negative effects on its integration into the global economy, China's ruling elites explored alternatives to foreign technologies and standards. Its massive internal market, together with the decade-long accumulation of science, technology, and capital, boosted China's perception of its competence to establish homegrown standards. Several key policy documents reflect this perception.

The Tenth Five-Year Plan (2000–2005) underscored the strategic role of indigenous technologies and a national innovation system.[36] In 2006, a blueprint was introduced by the State Council called the National Mid-Term and Long-Term Science and Technology Development Plan (2006–2020), known as the MLP. The MLP's defining characteristic is its focus on the idea of '*zizhu chuangxin*', literally translated as 'indigenous innovation'.[37] China's expenditure in research and development (R&D) should, as envisaged by the MLP, account for at least 2.5 percent of the nation's gross domestic product (GDP) by 2020, while reducing its dependence on foreign technologies to less than 30 percent.[38] The MLP called for China not to rely on 'core technologies in key areas that affect the lifeblood of the national economy and national security', such as next-generation communication technologies, semiconductors, and high-end chipsets.[39] Other supporting documents, such as the Eleventh Five-Year

---

[34] China created the AQSIQ by consolidating the State Administration for Entry-Exit Inspection and Quarantine and the State Quality and Technical Supervision Bureau as a response to challenges in the post-WTO era.

[35] Wang and Laing (n. 19 above) 4. Legally speaking, however, the Dual-Adoption policy remains part of the Standardization Law, which has not been amended since 1989.

[36] Guomin Jingji he Shehui Fazhan Dishige Wunian Jihua Gangyao (2001–2005) [The Tenth Five-Year Plan for the Development of National Economy and Society (2001–2005)] (promulgated by the Ninth National People's Cong. Fourth Session, 15 March 2001), addressed www.people.com.cn/GB/shizheng/16/20010318/419582.html (last visited 23 August 2017). For an account of China's science and technology plan, see e.g., Sylvia Schwaag Serger and Magnus Breidne, *China's Fifteen-Year Plan for Science and Technology: An Assessment*, 4 Asia Pol'y 135 (2007).

[37] Guojia Zhongchangqu Keji Fazhan Guihua Gangyao (2006–2020) [The National Mid-Term and Long-Term Science and Technology Development Plan (2006-–2020)] (MLP) (promulgated by the St. Council, 9 February 2006), available at www.etiea.cn/data/attachment/123(7).pdf (last visited 23 August 2017) (PRC).

[38] *Ibid.*

[39] *Ibid.*

Plan (2006–2010) for Standardization Development, released by the SAC in the same year,[40] and the National Intellectual Property Strategy, issued by the State Council in 2008,[41] further confirmed this direction.

2. Logic of Indigenous Standards: WAPI and Beyond

China's evolving standards system features certain patterns. While the role of standards in Phase I was to serve the planned economy, standards in Phase II were considered tools to absorb foreign technologies to reverse the gap vis-à-vis China's Western counterparts. It was not until the post-WTO era that China began to leverage standards as an instrument to promote homegrown technologies and industries, competing with advanced economies in terms of productivity and wealth. Viewed in this light, it is often suggested that China has taken advantage of its top-down standardization system to protect the domestic ICT industry. Hence, many indigenous standards initiatives are depicted as techno-nationalism.[42] To see this perception and assess why and how China might have changed its approaches, as detailed in Section III below, let us recap the WAPI, an (in)famous initiative that has been a major target of criticism.

The earliest WAPI efforts can be traced to the late 1990s when a group of researchers at Xidian University (who in 2000 founded IWNCOMM, a private spin-off believed to have ties with military agencies) began work on the Chinese version of security protocol for wireless communication. The efforts gained momentum when the Ministry of Information Industry (MII), now renamed the Ministry of Industry and Information Technology (MIIT), in 2001 established the China Broadband Wireless Internet Protocol Standard Working Group (BWIPS) to draft an

---

[40] Guomin Jingji he Shehui Fazhan Di Shiyi Ge Wu Nian Guihua Gangyao (org.) [Outline of the Eleventh Five-Year Plan for National Economic and Social Development] (issued by Nat'l Dev. & Reform Comm'n of China [NDRC], 16 March 2006), available at www.gov.cn/ztzl/2006-03/16/content_228841.htm (last visited 23 August 2017) (PRC).

[41] Guowuyuan Guanyu Yinfa Guojia Zhishichanquan Zhanlue Gangyao De Tongzhi [Notice of the State Council on Issuing the Outline of the National Intellectual Property Strategy] (promulgated by the St. Council, 5 June 2008), available at www.gov.cn/zwgk/2008-06/10/content_1012269.htm (last visited 23 August 2017) (PRC).

[42] See Richard P. Suttmeier and Yao Xiangkui, *China's Post-WTO Technology Policy: Standards, Software, and the Changing Nature of Techno-Nationalism* 10–11 (Nat'l Bureau of Asian Res. NBR Special Report No. 7, May 2004), available at www.nbr.org/publications/specialreport/pdf/SR7.pdf (last visited 23 August 2017).

alternative to Wi-Fi.[43] The work of the BWIPS involved a narrow group of stakeholders. Besides government agencies, most notably the SAC and the MII, only a handful of Chinese firms and research institutes associated with the MII were invited to participate in the standard-setting process.[44]

In May 2003, citing cybersecurity concerns, AQSIQ approved the WAPI as a national standard and mandated all wireless devices placed in the Chinese market, domestically produced and imported, must incorporate the WAPI technology by the end of the same year, with the deadline later extended to mid-2004.[45] At the time, the 802.11 Wi-Fi standard, developed by the Institute of Electronical and Electronics Engineers (IEEE), was widely used in the global market. As the security technologies included in the WAPI were incompatible with the chips based on the Wi-Fi, mandatory implementation of the WAPI would effectively dissolve the global wireless market. Foreign firms that wished to maintain their businesses in China were left with a take-it-or-leave-it option: they could either redesign their (China-specific) products based on the WAPI or withdraw from this massive market altogether. To comply with the WAPI, foreign firms were required to obtain a license to use encryption technologies controlled by twenty-four Chinese companies by paying per-chip royalties for the WAPI and/or partnering with these local counterparts in development.[46] Cooperation involved the risk of disclosing technical specifications to their potential competitors.[47] Given that the algorithm used in the WAPI was controlled as a 'state secret' that could not leave the country, foreign companies produced relevant products in China,[48] facing an increase in

---

43 Brian DeLacey et al., *Government Intervention in Standardization: The Case of WAPI*, available at http://papers.ssrn.com/sol3/papers.cfm?abstract_id=930930 (last visited 23 August 2017).

44 *Ibid.* at 10.

45 Guojia Zhiliang Jiandu Jianyan Jianyi Zongju, Guojia Renzheng Renke Jiandu Guanli Weiyuanhui Gonggao 2003 Nian Di 113 Hao [No. 113 Announcement of 2003 of the General Administration of Quality Supervision, Inspection and Quarantine and Certification and Accreditation Administration], available at www.cnca.gov.cn/xxgk/ggxx/ggxx2004/201512/t20151230_44631.shtml (last visited 23 August 2017).

46 Michael Kanellos, *Divide between U.S. Tech Firms, China: A Great Wall?*, C/NET News (19 March 2004), available at www.cnet.com/news/divide-between-u-s-tech-firms-china-a-great-wall/ (last visited 23 August 2017).

47 Heejin Lee and Sangjo Oh, *The Political Economy of Standards Setting by Newcomers: China's WAPI and South Korea's WIPI*, 32 Telecom. Pol'y 662, 666 (2008).

48 Glen Fleishman, *Broadcom Threatens to Withhold Chips from China*, WNN Wi-Fi Net News (29 January 2004), available at http://wifinetnews.com/

manufacturing costs to maintain separate product lines. Additionally, adhering to the WAPI may arguably have undercut consumer welfare, as it was believed to be inferior to the Wi-Fi.[49] These concerns sparked resistance from Japan, Europe, and the United States.[50] High-tech firms from the United States were particularly frustrated with this initiative and called upon their government to take a hard stance against China. The collective outcry from the industry soon elevated this controversy to higher state-to-state level political discourse. Eventually, in April 2004, after a meeting of the United States-China Joint Commission on Commerce and Trade (JCCT), the Chinese government agreed to 'suspend indefinitely' the mandatory implementation of this WAPI policy.[51]

There are realties and puzzles behind the WAPI. What is evident from the above is the rationale behind this campaign: economic development and information security. Economically, when the WAPI was about to launch, while China lacked an extensive telephone landline infrastructure, it had one of the fastest-growing wireless markets in the world. It was thus argued that the WAPI would help China, on one hand, by reducing overall licensing costs while it expanded wireless telephony networks, and on the other, by removing the need to build redundant landline infrastructure.[52] A separate but related claim would be that the WAPI was used as a 'chip tax'. Yet, despite its remarkable growth in the ICT industry, China struggled with chip technology and remained a net importer of semiconductors for decades.[53] The WAPI would not only reduce the chip royalty payment, but also help local firms access foreign semiconductor technologies through forced partnerships.[54]

Cybersecurity is the other compelling reason underlying the WAPI

---

archives/2004/01/broadcom_threatens_to_withhold_chips_from_china.html (last visited 23 August 2017).

[49] Lee and Oh (n. 47 above) 666.

[50] For instance, the European Information and Communication Technology Association (EICTA) in February 2004 also requested the European Commission to take action against the WAPI. See Heejin Lee and Sangjo Oh, *A Standards War Waged by a Developing Country: Understanding International Standard Setting from the Actor-Network Perspective*, J. Strategic Info. Sys. 177, 181 (2006).

[51] DeLacey et al. (n. 43 above) 13; Kennedy (n. 11 above) 51.

[52] DeLacey et al. (n. 43 above) 11.

[53] At the time of the WAPI campaign, in fact, the United States in March 2004 filed a request for consultation relating to China's preferential value-added tax for domestically-produced integrated circuits. This dispute was later resolved by way of a mutually agreed-upon solution. See *China—Value-Added Tax on Integrated Circuits—Request for Consultations by the United States*, WTO Doc. WT/DS309/1, G/L/675, S/L/160 (23 March 2004).

[54] See Mike Clendenin and Patrick Mannion, *Wireless Security Tops U.S.-*

campaign. Security protocols used in the Wi-Fi (i.e., IEEE 802.11 series: a, b, and g) were the Wired Equivalent Privacy (WEP). The WEP helped encrypt data so as to protect wireless networks from intrusion as well as their wired counterparts. In 2001, however, the encryption key used by the WEP was weak and susceptible to interception.[55] In response, the IEEE and the Wi-Fi Alliance (a wireless industry consortium) launched a more robust encryption method, Wi-Fi Protected Access ('WPA'), which was approved and integrated into the 802.11 series as 802.11i in 2004.[56] While the IEEE was working on improvements, the security issue—a top concern of the Chinese government—offered a chance for intervention. For China, information security turned not merely on privacy protection, social order, or economic development, but was also, more critically, a national security concern. Concerns about security flaws or potential back-doors in the Wi-Fi elevated the WAPI beyond a purely commercial venture or an academic exercise.[57] Evidence shows that key actors behind the WAPI campaign included military and intelligence agencies.[58]

Beyond the WAPI, China has rolled out various initiatives over the past decade. Citing the need to protect social order, public interest, and national security, China in 2007 issued the Administrative Measures for the Graded Protection of Information Security, known to the West as the Multi-Level Protection Scheme (MLPS).[59] The MLPS divides the

---

China Trade Talks, EETimes (19 April 2004), available at www.eetimes.com/document.asp?doc_id=1192749 (last visited 23 August 2017).

[55] On the weakness of the WEP, see e.g., William A. Arbaugh et al., *Your 802.11 Wireless Network Has No Clothes*, 9(6) IEEE Wireless Comm. 44 (2002). The first versions of the WEP were particularly weak because, in large part, of the US restrictions on the export of advanced cryptographic technologies. See Jon Edney and William A. Arbaugh, Real 802.11 Security: Wi-Fi Protected Access and 802.11i 68–9 (2003).

[56] Eric Griffith, *802.11 Security Specification Finalized*, Wi-Fi Planet (25 June 2004), available at www.wi-fiplanet.com/news/article.php/3373441/80211i-Security-Specification-Finalized.htm.

[57] Kennedy (n. 11 above) 48.

[58] *Ibid.* at 48–9; DeLacey et al. (n. 43 above) 10.

[59] The MLPS was, in fact, issued based on the mandate of the Regulations of the People's Republic of China on Protecting the Safety of Computer Information Systems. See Zhonghua Renmin Gongheguo Xinxi Xitong Anquan Baohu Tiaoli [Regulation of the People's Republic of China on the Protecting the Safety of Computer Information Systems] (promulgated by St. Council, 18 February 1994), available at www.lawinfochina.com/Display.aspx?lib=law&Cgid=8918 (last visited 23 August 2017); Guanyu Yinfa 'Xinxi Anquan Dengji Baohu Guanli Banfa' De Tongzhi [Notice on Issuing the Administrative Measures for the Graded Protection of Information Security] (promulgated by the Ministry of Public Security, St. Secrecy Bureau, St. Cipher Code Admin. & Info. Office of the St. Council, 22 June

information systems into five levels, with each level assigned corresponding standards on cybersecurity. More specifically, those classified Grade III and above must meet certain mandatory technical requirements (e.g., the core technologies of the devices will have the Chinese indigenous intellectual property).[60] In other contexts, China promoted its indigenous standards in a softer manner. The Time Division-Synchronous Code Division Multiple Access (TD-SCDMA), the Chinese standard for 3G wireless communications, is a prime example. Despite the existence of two competing standards widely adopted in the global market—Europe's W-CDMA and America's CDMA-2000—the Chinese government launched its homegrown specification through Datang Corporation, a state-owned enterprise that held certain key patents of the TD-SCDMA.[61] While China did not mandate the TD-SCDMA as 'mandatory', the way it leveraged its wireless licensing process and public procurement raised trade barrier concerns.[62]

While these indigenous standards initiatives take different shapes, they nevertheless feature a common theme. Driven by concerns about economic development and information security, Chinese ICT standardization policies grew out of complex sentiments of national pride and distrust of foreign technologies. In no instance did the Chinese government take a hands-off approach to these ICT standards campaigns. Rather, standard-setting processes reveal the nation's preference for homegrown technologies. While China's standards strategies seem oriented to techno-nationalism, internal and external forces have led the nation towards techno-globalism.

III. NO MORE PROTECTIONISM? THE LIMITS OF CHINA'S TECHNO-NATIONALISM

The settlement of the WAPI controversy leaves more questions than it answers. As many trade lawyers have argued, Sino-US political dialogue thwarted this controversy. What remains puzzling is why China was

2007), available at www.lawinfochina.com/display.aspx?lib=law&id=6401&CGid= (last visited 23 August 2017).

[60] Notice on Issuing the Administrative Measures for the Graded Protection of Information Security, art. 21.

[61] See e.g., Xudong Gao and Jianxin Liu, *Catching up Through the Development of Technology Standard: The Case of TD-SCDMA*, 36 TELECOM. POL'Y 531, 534–7 (2012).

[62] See e.g., Shin-Yi Peng (n. 13 above) 134–6.

willing to settle this claim without a legal fight at all. While this may be the outcome of certain under-the-table deals between two major trading partners, China's retreat from the WAPI reflects the complex setting of the Chinese standardization regime. Moreover, while the United States has not initiated any WTO legal proceeding against China's indigenous standards, it has increased deterrence of the WAPI measures through PTAs/BITs. By revisiting the WAPI campaign, this section illustrates how these contextual constraints may help China transform its techno-nationalism-oriented standards policy in the megaregionals.

1. Market Mechanism and the Role of GVC

The WAPI grew out of the MII-funded BWIPS initiative. The BWIPS had only ten original members, including five public universities, four institutions controlled by the MII, and one research center affiliated with the SAC; shortly after the BWIPS was launched, other local firms, including three ICT giants, Founder, Lenovo, and Huawei, joined this initiative.[63] Despite the increase in number, there were only twenty-three participants, and no foreign stakeholders were invited to this standard-setting process.[64] The encryption algorithm used in the WAPI was considered a 'state secret' under the Regulation on the Administration of Commercial Cipher Codes;[65] thus, relevant technologies were authorized by the Chinese government only to eleven Chinese ICT firms, including Huawei and Lenovo.[66] Foreign firms were required to cooperate with these firms to comply with the WAPI.

Concerns about expensive royalties and the risk of disclosing proprietary technologies to Chinese competitors polarized industry stakeholders into three camps. Certain firms, including Hewlett-Packard (HP) and IBM, adopted a 'wait-and-see' strategy while the WAPI's future was in the dark.[67] By contrast, some Taiwanese manufacturers, including Acer, BenQ, Cybertan Technology, D-Link, Inprocomm (later acquired by MediaTek), and Silicon Integrated Systems, were prepared to implement

---

[63] Ping Gao, *Counter-Networks in Standardization: A Perspective of Developing Countries*, 17 Info. Sys. J. 391, 403 (2007).

[64] *Ibid.*

[65] Shangyong Mima Guanli Tiaoli [Regulation on the Administration of Commercial Cipher Codes] (promulgated by the St. Council, 7 October 1999), available at www.lawinfochina.com/display.aspx?lib=law&id=383&CGid= (last visited 23 August 2017).

[66] Gao (n. 63 above) 404.

[67] *Ibid.*

the WAPI.[68] A handful of American companies, including Linsys, Atheros, and Netgear, also expressed endorsement of this campaign.[69]

Still others stood as a large and unified group of multinational enterprises (MNEs) from Europe, Japan, and, in particular, the United States.[70] Several industry associations, including the Japanese Chamber of Industry and Commerce, the European Information and Communications Technology Industry Association, and the US Information Technology Office, began to lobby their respective governments to put pressure on China.[71] Another major blow came from certain key players in the field, including the IEEE, the Wi-Fi Alliance, and two US-based ICT giants, namely Intel and Broadcom. The IEEE, one of the largest not-for-profit international engineering institutions, created the Wi-Fi through the IEEE Standards Association (IEEE-SA).[72] In November 2003, Paul Nikolich, chairperson of the IEEE 802.11-series committee, wrote to the heads of China's SAC and MII, expressing his concerns about the fragmentation of the global wireless market:

> We are concerned regarding the requirement to support the new WAPI security protocol. We believe that globally-adopted standards provide great benefits both for manufacturers and users, and we have seen many examples of successes of our standards. Therefore, we are always concerned by activities that limit their global use. We believe that implementation of the WAPI protocols would unnecessarily fracture the world market for WLAN products. We are concerned that mandatory use of the standard would prohibit the use of 802.11 standard products and thereby limit choice and increase costs to users.[73]

The Wi-Fi Alliance took a similar stance. Founded in August 1999 as a joint effort among six companies (3Com, Aironet, Intersil, Lucent Technologies, Nokia and Symbol Technologies), the Wi-Fi Alliance was originally named the Wireless Ethernet Compatibility Alliance (WECA)

---

[68] See Mike Clendenin, *Beijing Backs off Proprietary Spec for Wireless LANs*, EETimes (26 April 2004), available at www.eetimes.com/document.asp?doc_id=1150032 (last visited 23 August 2017); DeLacey et al. (n. 43 above) 12.

[69] Gao (n. 63 above) 406.

[70] Kennedy (n. 11 above) 52.

[71] *Ibid.*

[72] For an overview of the IEEE, see Eliza Varney, *Institute of Electrical and Electronic Governance Regimes*, *in* Handbook of Transnational Economic Governance Regimes 561–72 (Christian Tietje and Alan Brouder eds., 2009).

[73] Letter from Paul Nikolich, Chairman, IEEE, 820 Local and Metropolitan Area Network Standards Committee, to Li Zhonghai, Chairman, Standardization Administration of China (SAC), and Wang Xudong, Minister of Ministry of Information Industry (MII) (23 November 2003), available at www.ieee802.org/16/liaison/docs/L80216-03_19.pdf (last visited 23 August 2017).

and was created to certify and support IEEE-802.11 compatible products.[74] Shortly after its establishment, the Wi-Fi Alliance expanded to include a group of industry leaders, including Alantro, Apple, Breezecom, Cabletron, Compaq, Dell, Intermec, No Wires Needed, Sharewave, Waypoint, and Zoom.[75] By 2002, when the Chinese government sponsored the establishment of the BWIPS, the Wi-Fi Alliance had grown to 200 firms from Asia, Europe, and North America, certifying over 500 Wi-Fi products.[76] The Wi-Fi Alliance mobilized key actors, including Broadcom and Intel, as noted below, who favored the Wi-Fi, convincing the industry that the WAPI was a threat, rather than a benefit, to their businesses.[77]

Additionally, a group of powerful market players teamed up to block the WAPI. Broadcom, the largest chipmaker in the world, was openly against the WAPI campaign. The CEO of Broadcom, Alan Ross, in early 2004 commented:

> We are not playing their game. We are not going to lose our technological edge through the risky disclosure of our intellectual property. To the extent that the only way to enter the Chinese market is using their encryption scheme, we are not committed to doing that today.[78]

His view was soon echoed by the Wi-Fi Alliance, the Information Technology Industry Council (ITI), the Semiconductor Industry Association (SIA), and the National Association of Manufacturers (NAM), among others.[79] Dennis Eaton, the chairperson of the Wi-Fi

---

[74] See generally, Wi-Fi Alliance, *Who We Are: History*, available at www.wi-fi.org/who-we-are/history (last visited 23 August 2017).

[75] See Wi-Fi Alliance, *Wireless Ethernet Compatibility Alliance (WECA) Announces Independent Test Lab and Wi-Fi Technology Brand* (15 September 1999), available at www.wi-fi.org/news-events/newsroom/wireless-ethernet-compatibility-alliance-weca-announces-independent-test-lab (last visited 23 August 2017).

[76] Wi-Fi Alliance, *Wi-Fi Certified Makes It Wi-Fi: An Overview of the Wi-Fi Alliance Approach to Certification* 5 (September 2006), available at www.senzafili consulting.com/downloads/Wi-Fi_Certified_Makes_it_Wi-Fi.pdf (last visited 23 August 2017).

[77] Shirley Chan et al., *An International Mobile Security Standard Dispute: From the Actor-Network Perspective*, *in* Designing Ubiquitous Information Environments: Social-Technical Issues and Challenges 301 (Carsten Sørensen et al. eds., 2005).

[78] Gao (n. 63 above) 405. Yet, some argued that Broadcom later took a softer stance on the WAPI. Peter White, *Broadcom and Washington Take Softer Stance on Chinese Wi-Fi*, Rethink (26 February 2004), available at http://rethinkresearch.biz/articles/broadcom-and-washington-take-softer-stance-on-chinese-wi-fi/ (last visited 23 August 2017).

[79] Gao (n. 63 above) 405.

Alliance, declared that if no compromise was reached, its members would stop selling WLAN equipment to China,[80] while the head of the ITI referred to the WAPI as unacceptable for requiring foreign firms to co-produce WAPI products with their local competitors to satisfy the Chinese regulation.[81]

The opposition of Intel, another industry giant, was the last straw for the WAPI campaign. By the time WAPI was in the making, Intel had invested massively in launching its Centrino processors based on the Wi-Fi standard. WAPI compliance would affect Centrino-enabled equipment, from which Intel's profits were primarily derived at that time.[82] Yet, given its interests in the Chinese market, Intel was cautious and did not rule out the WAPI at the outset. In March 2004, Intel joined the anti-WAPI coalition by announcing that 'it will not meet China's June 1 deadline to produce wireless chipsets that are compatible with China's security standards' allegedly because of the high royalty demanded by Chinese firms and unresolved technical issues.[83]

A crucial implication of this Wi-Fi/WAPI battle is the role of GVC in governing trade disputes in the globalized world. Indeed, market noises from these industry stakeholders led to the 2004 Sino-US political dialogue, thereby putting an end to this controversy, if only at face value. China's withdrawal from this campaign underscored the power of the expansive anti-WAPI network. Despite certain Taiwanese firms' endorsement, these supporters were relatively weak players in core technologies. Without the support of foreign ICT industry stakeholders, especially those controlling chip technologies, the WAPI was doomed to fail from the outset. In an interview conducted by a political scientist, an official from the MII lamented the failure of the WAPI:

> Chip technology is a bottleneck for the Chinese information industry. We have been unable to manufacture WLAN chips that are not only technologically advanced but also economically feasible. Some companies might have qualified WAPI products in their laboratories, but now they are definitely unable to start mass production of WAPI chips for commercial use.[84]

---

[80] *Ibid.*

[81] *Ibid.* Similar statements were made by the SIA and NAM; both criticized the WAPI as trade protectionism that violated the WTO rules.

[82] *Ibid.* at 406.

[83] See Laurie J. Flynn, *Intel Rejects China's Deadline on New Wireless Standard*, New York Times (10 March 2004), available at www.nytimes.com/2004/03/10/technology/intel-rejects-chinas-deadline-on-new-wireless-standard.html?_r=0 (last visited 23 August 2017).

[84] Gao (n. 63 above) 409.

Further complicating the matter is the diverging interests of Chinese ICT firms. While the WAPI may be welcome by domestic-oriented companies with limited export exposure, it can be rather problematic for China's MNEs.[85] For instance, although Lenovo joined the BWIPS, it was concerned about the costs of maintaining a China-specific product line given its greater interests in exportation.[86] Ironically, studies showed that Lenovo had been working closely with Intel for the next generation of the 802.11-based Centrino platform while the WAPI was about to be implemented.[87] Haiwei and ZTE, two powerhouses with significant stakes in overseas markets that joined the Wi-Fi network, faced a similar dilemma and were criticized by fellow participants for not taking this campaign seriously.[88] The views of China's MNEs were crucial, compelling the Chinese government to weigh in.[89] Thus, the suspension of the WAPI should not be considered a result of foreign pressure, but a response to the need of domestic industry stakeholders who have been integrated into the GVC. Figure 6.1 illustrates the relationship between the two camps and their respective supporters.

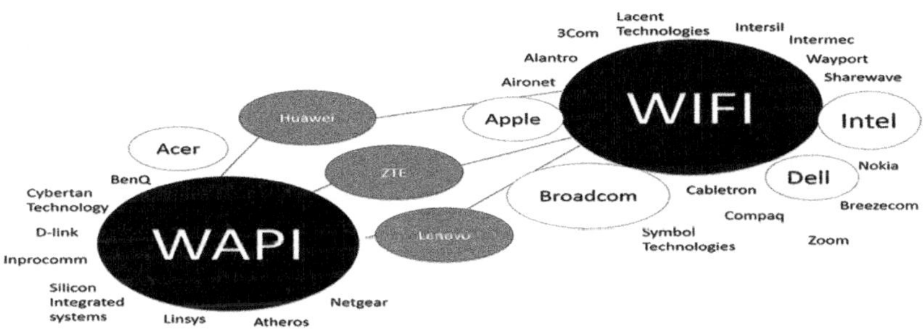

Figure 6.1 Two camps of the ICT industry in the Wi-Fi/WAPI battle

[85] See Dieter Ernst, Indigenous Innovation and Globalization: the Challenges for China's Standardization Strategy 31 (2011).

[86] Kennedy (n. 11 above) 53.

[87] Amy Bennett, *China's Lenovo Hedges Bets Against WAPI*, IT World (21 April 2004), available at www.itworld.com/article/2803325/mobile/china-s-lenovo-hedges-bets-against-wapi.html (last visited 23 August 2017).

[88] Stephen Bell and Hui Feng, *Made in China: IT Infrastructure Policy and the Politics of Trade Opening in Post-WTO China*, 14(1) Rev. Int'l Pol. Econ. 49, 64 (2007) (arguing that the WAPI put a group of Chinese companies in hot water, such as Huawei Technologies and ZTE Corporation who are also members of Wi-Fi).

[89] Kennedy (n. 11 above 53).

2. Bureaucratic Politics and Coordination Problems in China's Standardization Regime

On its face, China's top-down standardization system serves as a perfect tool for its government to pursue economic gains and defend national interests. As noted below, however, fragmented institutions and inter-agency politics render a single stance towards standardization in this globalized world problematic for China. This can in turn constrain the manner in which the Chinese government crafts its standards. To better understand, let's revisit the WAPI saga.

While the SAC approved the WAPI as a national standard, several key stakeholders stood behind the scenes, roughly falling into two camps. Led by the MII, the first camp was a group of supporters of the WAPI, including the Ministry of Science and Technology (MoST) and the State Encryption Management Commission (SEMC). The MII was the major sponsor, coordinating with other authorities responsible for national standardization, encryption control, quality management, and certification during the WAPI standard-setting process.[90] The MoST was in charge of the nation's R&D agenda and formed a coalition with the MII to promote indigenous standards, including the WAPI.[91] Another key agency was the SEMC, which acted under the mandate of the Regulation on the Administration of Commercial Cipher Codes.[92] While the intervention of these agencies was driven by different interests, all were strong advocates of the WAPI.[93] On the other end of the spectrum stood the Ministry of Commerce (MOFCOM) (formerly the Ministry of Foreign Trade and Economic Co-operation (MOFTEC)), which supervised China's trade policy. In contrast with the MII's traditional preference, promotion or sometimes protection of domestic industrial interests, the MOFCOM has been more cautious about international norms and foreign trade relations.[94] Given their different mandates, these two agencies have long been at odds with each other.[95] In the case of the WAPI, the MII took

---

[90] Bell and Feng (n. 88 above) 62.

[91] *Ibid.* at 61. *Cf.* Geerten van de Kaa et al., *Standards Battles in China: Opening Up the Black Box of the Chinese Government*, 25(5) TECH. ANALYSIS & STRATEGIC MGNT. 567 (2013) (arguing that the MOST was, in fact, with the MOFCOM).

[92] Regulation on the Administration of Commercial Cipher Codes (n. 65 above).

[93] Bell and Feng (n. 88 above) 61–2.

[94] See *ibid.*

[95] See generally Yuka Kobayashi, *The Impact of the World Trade Organization on China's Trade Policy: A Case Study of the Telecommunications Sector*, *in* CHINA'S FOREIGN TRADE POLICY: THE NEW CONSTITUENCIES 143–66 (Ka Zeng ed., 2008).

advantage of the MOFCOM's absence in pursuing industrial interests without taking into account implications for international trade.[96]

For certain Chinese experts, the flip side of the WAPI was that this campaign failed to gain full support from agencies with economic power. By contrasting the key event of the WAPI and the TD-SCDMA—no senior officials attended the meeting to announce the WAPI, while state leaders took part in the exhibitions of the homegrown 3G network—some scholars attributed the fate of the WAPI to 'strong disagreement and a lack of support within the Chinese government itself'.[97] While other political scientists perceive the nexus between Chinese corporate elites and foreign MNEs in the GVC as the major force underlying China's withdrawal from the WAPI initiative, they nevertheless pointed to the fact that no officials from the economic bureaucracy spoke on behalf of the WAPI.[98] Moreover, given the fact that Wu Yi had long served as the Minister of the MOFCOM, her appointment as the representative in the 2004 Sino-US meeting (though in her capacity of then Vice Premier) signaled top leadership's judgment call of how to resolve this high-profile trade conflict in China's early years following the WTO accession.[99]

While not conclusive, the above observations are consistent with the record that indicates turf battles often grip China's bureaucratic system. Unless Chinese leaders step in, coordination problems would become a major hurdle for any single agency to effectively leverage this top-down standardization regime in launching protectionist standards campaigns. As such, while trade lawyers applied the WTO rules to the WAPI-type initiatives, they seemed to take these episodes as a given without capturing the complete picture of China's inter-agency politics. Cross-sector bureaucratic cooperation, together with the dynamics in the private sector, would therefore constrain China's techno-nationalism.

3. US Pushback on Techno-nationalism in the Megaregionals

With significant national interests at stake in the ICT industry, the US government had pioneered among other trading partners in monitoring, and even combating, China's indigenous standards. Lobbyist efforts from the high-tech industry led the US embassy in Beijing and law-makers to

---

96 *Ibid.* at 62.

97 Gao (n. 63 above) 411. See also Van de Kaa et al. (n. 91 above) 576–7.

98 See Kennedy (n. 11 above) 53.

99 See Bell and Feng (n. 88 above) 67–8. *Cf.* Kennedy (n. 11 above) 53 (arguing instead that such an inter-agency politics explanation does not fully capture the complex context facing the Chinese government at the time).

express concern about the WAPI through various channels. This outcry eventually peaked with an unprecedented letter co-signed by three high-level officials (Colin Powell, Secretary of State, Robert Zoellick, United States Trade Representative, and Donald Evans, Secretary of Commerce) urged China to reconsider the WAPI's negative implications for global trade:

> If this [WAPI] policy goes into effect, China would be the only country in the world mandating a specific encryption standard for general consumer use. Since this standard is unique in China, implementation will impose a significant new burden on both foreign and Chinese domestic suppliers. Furthermore, implementation of this standard will make Chinese products incompatible with internationally-accepted standards, isolating China from the larger world market for these types of devices. We are particularly concerned that the new rules would require foreign suppliers to enter into joint ventures with Chinese companies and transfer technology to them. Such compelled investment and technology transfer would appear to be inconsistent with China's WTO commitments.[100]

As noted above, the letter led to high-level political talks. In April 2004, after a meeting of the United States-China Joint Commission on Commerce and Trade (JCCT), where Wu Yi, China's Vice Premier, and Robert Zoellick and Donald Evans chaired for each side. China agreed to 'suspended indefinitely' the mandatory implementation of this WAPI initiative.[101] Yet, while the WAPI conflict was successfully settled through diplomatic channels, the rise of China's indigenous innovation scheme underscored new challenges for trade negotiators. In this regard, what the United States has done relating to transparency and restrictions on the use of domestic technology through the 2012 US Model BIT and the TPP, for example, may implicate China's standards strategies. We discuss in turn.

(1) Enhanced transparency requirements and standardization clause

The BWIPS was founded 'silently' on the sponsorship of the MII. The BWIPS in turn created the WAPI silently, engaging a narrow group of government agencies and local companies. Throughout the standard-setting process, none of the foreign stakeholders in either private or public sectors were ever invited to contribute. Even at the stage where the SAC

---

[100] See Editorial, Online Extra, *Letter from Bush Administration Officials to Beijing Protesting Wi-Fi Encryption Standards*, Bloomberg Bus.Week Mag. (14 March 2004), available at www.bloomberg.com/news/articles/2004-03-14/online-extra-letter-from-bush-administration-officials-to-beijing-protesting-wi-fi-encryption-standards (last visited 23 August 2017).

[101] DeLacey et al. (n. 43 above) 13.

conducted administrative assessment and approval, the decision-making process remained closed.[102] For the United States, one way to manage protectionism arising from China's indigenous standards is to bring transparency and openness to the standardization process. Thus, while the United States and China were negotiating the text of the United States-China BIT, the 2012 US Model BIT was revised to include a novel clause, referred to hereinafter as the 'standardization clause'. Paragraph 8 of Article 11 (Transparency) of the 2012 US Model BIT reads in relevant part:

> Each Party shall allow persons of the other Party to participate in the development of standards and technical regulations by its central government bodies. Each Party shall allow persons of the other Party to participate in the development of these measures, and the development of conformity assessment procedures by its central government bodies, on terms no less favorable than those it accords to its own persons.[103]

This standardization clause expands transparency requirements under the Agreement on Technical Barriers to Trade (TBT Agreement) in several respects. For instance, TBT Agreement, Article 2.5 requires a WTO member to explain the justification while preparing, adopting, or applying a particular technical regulation only if such technical regulation 'may have a significant effect on trade of other Members' and 'upon the request of another Member'.[104] By contrast, Article 11.8 of the 2012 US Model BIT requires, without limitations as stipulated in TBT Agreement, Article 2.5, that the host state shall allow 'persons' from the other state party to participate in the standard-setting process conducted by central government bodies; the term 'persons' includes both natural persons and enterprises.[105] According to the footnote to Article 11.8, the host state may satisfy this requirement by, for example, 'providing interested persons a reasonable opportunity to provide comments on the measure it proposes to develop and taking those comments

---

[102] Gao (n. 63 above) 410.

[103] USTR, 2012 US Model Bilateral Investment Treaty, art. 11.8(a), available at www.state.gov/documents/organization/188371.pdf (last visited 23 August 2017).

[104] Agreement on Technical Barriers to Trade ('TBT Agreement'), 15 April 1994, Marrakesh Agreement Establishing the World Trade Organization, Annex 1A, 1868 UNTS 120.

[105] 2012 US Model BIT, art. 1. For an overview of this standardization clause, see e.g., Lise Johnson and Lisa Sachs, *International Investment Agreements, 2011–2012: A Review of Trends and New Approaches*, *in* Yearbook on International Investment Law and Policy 2012–2013, 257 (Andrea K. Bjorklund eds., 2014).

into account in the development of the measure'.[106] Moreover, if a technical regulation is issued in the form of 'laws, regulations, procedures and administrative ruling of general application', a set of notice and comments requirements under Article 11.3 of the 2012 US Model BIT (which are more stringent than those under the TBT Agreement) would come into play. Specifically, while TBT Agreement, Article 2.9 requires a WTO member to publish a notice about the proposed technical regulation 'at an early appropriate stage' so that interested parties in other WTO members can become acquainted with it, Article 11.3 provides that such publications shall be made 'in a single official journal of national circulation' and that host states 'should in most cases publish the proposed regulations not less than 60 days before the date public comments are due'.[107]

(2) Restrictions on domestic technologies

In addition to the standardization clause, provisions regarding the use of domestic technologies represent another new tool. Of particular relevance to our discussions is Article 8 of the 2012 US Model BIT and Annex 8 to the TPP Agreement. Article 8.1 of the 2012 US Model BIT on performance requirements imposes restrictions on the use of domestic technology, which provides in relevant part:

> 1. Neither Party may, in connection with the establishment, acquisition, expansion, management, conduct, operation, or sale or other disposition of an investment of an investor of a Party or of a non-Party in its territory, impose or enforce any requirement or enforce any commitment or undertaking. . .: (i) to purchase, use, or accord a preference to, in its territory, technology of the Party or of persons of the Party; or (ii) that prevents the purchase or use of, or the according of a preference to, in its territory, particular technology, so as to afford protection on the basis of nationality to its own investors or investments or to technology of the Party or of persons of the Party.[108]

Annex 8-B to the TPP Agreement goes further by including the 'Encryption Clause', representing certain new arrangements that touch upon the oft-cited justification of China's regulatory intervention, information security. Annex 8-B begins by clarifying its scope of application, extending to '[ICT] products that use cryptography' and defining certain technical terms including 'cryptography', 'encryption', 'cipher', and

---

106 2012 US Model BIT, note 14.
107 *Ibid.* art. 11.3(b).
108 *Ibid.* art. 8.1.

'key'.[109] Annex 8-B then establishes ground rules on how the TPP Parties govern encryption products:

> 3. With respect to a product that uses cryptography and is designed for commercial applications, no Party shall impose or maintain a technical regulation or conformity assessment procedure that requires a manufacturer or supplier of the product, as a condition of the manufacture, sale, distribution, import or use of the product, to: (a) transfer or provide access to a particular technology, production process or other information, for example, a private key or other secret parameter, algorithm specification or other design detail, that is proprietary to the manufacturer or supplier and relates to the cryptography in the product, to the Party or a person in the Party's territory; (b) partner with a person in its territory; or (c) use or integrate a particular cryptographic algorithm or cipher, other than where the manufacture, sale, distribution, import or use of the product is by or for the government of the Party.[110]

Indeed, the above-mentioned clauses are not without flaws. While the standardization clause can undercut the chance for China to adopt WAPI-type measures without engaging foreign stakeholders in advance, and it is not uncommon to discuss this provision against the backdrop of United States-China BIT negotiations,[111] it is not clear whether and how such mechanisms will be reflected in the text of the finalized BIT. Likely it may be equally or more problematic for the United States to invoke this provision to address China's standard-based protectionism under the name of cybersecurity. Although the encryption clause seeks to set a default rule by requiring the TPP parties not to interfere with the manner in which these ICT products incorporate encryption technologies, this clause applies to those products using 'cryptography and is designed for commercial applications'. However, the idea of 'commercial applications' is vague, and countries have been concerned with such technology given its 'dual-use' character. China is no exception and has at times designated a particular cryptography as a 'state secret' via the Regulation on the Administration of Commercial Cipher Codes, as noted above.[112] The

---

[109] See TPP, Annex 8-B, 4 February 2016, available at https://ustr.gov/sites/default/files/TPP-Final-Text-Technical-Barriers-to-Trade.pdf (last visited 1 November 2016).

[110] *Ibid.*

[111] See e.g., Sean Miner and Gary Clyde Hufbauer, *State-Owned Enterprises and Competition Policy: The U.S. Perspective*, *in* TOWARD A U.S.-CHINA INVESTMENT TREATY 16–18 (Peterson Institute for International Economics PIIE Briefing 15-1, February 2015).

[112] For a detailed account of the laws and politics of the TPP's encryption clause, see Han-Wei Liu, *Inside the Black Box: Political Economy of the TPP's Encryption Clause*, 51(2) J. WORLD TRADE 1117 (2017).

standardization clause, the encryption clause, and other supplemental rules that increase transparency and reduce regulatory intervention in selecting (local) technologies may serve as a solid starting point, pressing parties, including China, to adjust their approaches to standardization during integration into megaregionals.

IV. FINAL REMARKS

Having documented the main features and problems facing China's standardization regime, we may now conclude by demystifying some of the myths around the Chinese techno-nationalism-oriented indigenous standards policy. First, while it is true that China maintains a top-down, state-led standardization system, there is no guarantee that coordination problems do not exist. Contrary to much of the existing legal literature which takes China's standardization system as a given while criticizing Chinese standard-based protectionism, the SAC, China's standardization administrator, faces complicated contextual constraints. Such constraints come from both industry stakeholders and inter-agency politics. As shown in the WAPI saga, the lack of major suppliers of chipsets makes it economically and technically infeasible for China, a developing country without sufficient capacity to provide key components of wireless devices, to forge ahead with its homegrown standards. The fragmentation of GVC also highlights the diversified interests among industry stakeholders in China. While domestic-market-oriented companies may prefer the Chinese standards, MNEs with global reach are concerned about the costs of implementing different standards and have placed their bets on both sides. As shown in the WAPI campaign, Lenovo, Huawei, and ZTE, for instance, chose to work with foreign counterparts while at the same time taking part in this indigenous standards campaign. Support from industry at home and abroad, or the lack thereof, demonstrates the role of the GVC as an alternative to legal proceeding to manage trade disputes. Further complicating the matter are the differing preferences of key regulatory agencies towards the use of standards. While agencies such as the MII have historically pursued the national interest through various policy instruments, agencies with the mandate to oversee international economic relations are more concerned about the relevant implications for trade and investment. Inter-agency politics thus renders it problematic for the SAC to coordinate these regulators in the absence of aligned interests.

Second, while the coordination problem operates as an internal constraint that undercuts China's standard-based protectionism, the rise of the Chinese standards nevertheless prompted major trading powers, especially the United States, to fix possible loopholes through trade and investment arrangements. Among others, provisions on transparency requirements and restrictions on the use of domestic technologies in the 2012 Model BIT and the TPP, Annex 8-B are particularly relevant in addressing key issues of the WAPI-type standards: a closed standardization process and the preference for local technologies. Despite certain pitfalls, these arrangements represent a strong start in reducing trade concerns regarding China's homegrown standards initiatives. Although the question of whether and the extent to which China's standards strategies have moved towards techno-globalism is beyond the scope of this chapter, suffice it to say that the above-mentioned internal contextual constraints and new rules, when combined, form the boundary for a techno-nationalism-oriented standardization policy.

PART III

Environmental and energy policy

7. Trade and biological diversity governance in the age of megaregionalism

Won-Mog Choi

I. INTRODUCTION

Global trade and environmental regimes need to prevent clash between them. This possible clash goes back in the history to tensions between the Bretton Woods system and the New International Economic Order (NIEO).[1] The former system is based on the principles of nondiscrimination and market liberalization, whereas the principles of permanent sovereignty over natural resources and support for development define the latter. The Bretton Woods system and its principles have been successful in facilitating global trade and world economic betterment based on the economics of comparative advantage and the economics of competition.[2] On the other hand, while the NIEO initiative largely failed to achieve its professed goal of reforming the international economic system, it was successful in drawing third world countries politically together and forming a global environmental governance paradigm (in particular, a biological

[1] Declaration for the Establishment of a New International Economic Order ('NIEO Declaration'), adopted by the United Nations General Assembly in 1974, was a set of proposals put forward during the 1970s by some developing countries through the United Nations Conference on Trade and Development (UNCTAD) to promote their interests by improving their terms of trade, increasing development assistance, developed-country tariff reductions, and other means. It was meant to be a revision of the international economic system in favour of Third World countries, replacing the Bretton Woods system, which had benefited the leading states that had created it, especially the United States. See Declaration on the Establishment of a New International Economic Order, G.A Res. 3201(S-VI) (1 May 1974); also see WIKIPEDIA, NEW INTERNATIONAL ECONOMIC ORDER, available at https://en.wikipedia.org/wiki/New_International_Economic_Order (last visited 5 July 2017).

[2] John H. Jackson, *The WTO 'Constitution' and Proposed Reforms: Seven 'Mantras' Revisited*, 4(1) J. INT'L ECON. L. 67, 68 (2001).

diversity governance regime) by which future generations may counter the liberal economic paradigm under the Bretton Woods system.

As a successor agreement to an International Trade Organization (ITO) that failed to join the Bretton Woods system, the World Trade Organization (WTO)/General Agreement on Tariffs and Trade (GATT) Agreements made their own attempt to prevent this clash between trade and environmental governance. GATT, Article XX, in particular, had provisions for general exceptions to GATT obligations which applied to the entirety of the GATT provisions. According to this design, measures necessary to protect human, animal, or plant life or health and measures relating to the conservation of exhaustible natural resources, if such measures are made effective in conjunction with restrictions on domestic production or consumption, are exempted from disciplines under the trade governance. Another exception provision under the GATT regime, which relates to the NIEO, is Article XI:2(a). The provisions of paragraph 1 of this Article do not extend to the following: '(a) Export prohibitions or restrictions temporarily applied to prevent or relieve critical shortages of foodstuffs or other products essential to the exporting contracting party'.[3] This provision may well serve the purpose of protecting natural resources by many developing countries as a basis for prohibitions or restrictions of trade in natural resources that are currently in or may be in critical shortage.

Despite the utility of these provisions in multilateral trade agreements, developing countries might make attempts to use such countering mechanism built into the biological diversity regime in an aggressive manner. If this were to become a new prevalent trend, the NIEO idea would revive to engage in another round of clashes with the Bretton Woods paradigm. This time, the clash will be between the global trade system and the environmental governance regime.

II. THE NEW INTERNATIONAL ECONOMIC ORDER AND ITS IMPACT ON TRADE TREATIES

The post-World War II period generated new aspirations for developing countries including newly independent former colonies. Despite the prosperity and growth in overall economies of nations, a bloc of developing countries became vocal about the ways in which the Bretton Woods system failed to address existing inequalities in economic and political

[3] GATT, Art. XI:2(a).

power. Such developing countries perceived this failure as disadvantaging, with the lingering effects of colonialism and the international division of labor that relegated them to resource providers to the developed states (many of them former colonial powers) of raw materials at unfavorable and deteriorating terms of trade, which in turn rendered these developing countries unable to fulfill their development potential.[4]

These developing countries called for a more equitable international order that can reflect their political and economic interests. In the Asian-African Conference at Bandung, Indonesia in 1955, their goals were expressed in the form of a Final Communique, which was incorporated into the 1974 UN Declaration on the Establishment of a New International Economic Order ('NIEO Declaration').[5] The basic and ultimate goal of the NIEO was to improve developing countries' economic position in relation to developed countries, with the ultimate aim of gaining a parity of political power as well.[6] To achieve this, the main positions of the NIEO on international economic law can be summarized as follows.

1. Full Permanent Sovereignty over Natural Resources and Economic Activities

Developing countries considered that genuine self-determination is not achievable unless they can make demands for full sovereign control over their natural resources.[7] Resource-rich developing countries wished to exercise full control over the natural resources found on their territory,[8] including by means that were questionable under the classic principles

---

[4] Daniel J. Whelan, *'Under the Aegis of Man': The Right to Development and the Origins of the New International Economic Order*, 6(1) HUMANITY: INT'L J. HUM. RTS., HUMANITARIANISM, & DEV. 93 (2015).

[5] NIEO Declaration (n. 1 above).

[6] Jeehyung Lee, Trade and Environmental Governance Arising from the Convention on Biological Diversity and the Nagoya Protocol 29 (2016) (unpublished Ph.D Thesis, Ewha Womans University) (on file with the author).

[7] This view made its way into Art. 1(2) of both the Covenant on Civil and Political Rights and the Covenant on Economic, Social, and Economic Rights, which commonly reads: 'All peoples may, for their own ends, freely dispose of their natural wealth and resources without prejudice to any obligations arising out of international economic cooperation, based upon the principle of mutual benefit, and international law. In no case may a people be deprived of its own means of subsistence'. Also see Permanent Sovereignty over Natural Resources, GA Res. 1803 (XVII) (14 December 1962).

[8] NIEO Declaration (n. 1 above) para. 4(e).

of international law, such as nationalization without full or adequate compensation.[9] This was coming from a history of extractive policies on the part of developed countries, frequently executed through a conjunction of colonial rule and multinational corporations based in developed countries, and secured resource extraction deals with developing country governments.[10]

This principle of sovereignty over natural resources left its legacy in environmental treaties relating to cross-border resource extraction and use, including the UN Convention on the Law of the Sea[11] and Convention on Biological Diversity (CBD).[12] This was also echoed in the idea of historical responsibility in international environmental law, including the principle of common and differentiated responsibility in the climate change negotiations.[13] The Nagoya Protocol under the CBD system, dealing with the problem of developed and developing countries' comparative historical responsibility for the reduction in biological

---

9 Francisco V. Garcia-Amador, *The Proposed New International Economic Order: A New Approach to the Law Governing Nationalization and Compensation*, 12(1) Law. Am. 1, 29 (1980).

10 *Ibid.* at 27; Lee (n. 6 above) 21.

11 10 December 1982, 21 ILM 1261. The Declaration of Principles Governing the Sea-Bed and Ocean Floor, and the Subsoil Thereof, Beyond the Limits of National Jurisdiction, in the Twenty-fifth Session of the UN General Assembly, stated that 'The sea-bed and ocean floor, and the subsoil thereof (hereinafter referred to as the area), beyond the limits of national jurisdiction, as well as the resources of the area, are the common heritage of mankind' and that 'The area shall not be subject to appropriation by any means by States or persons, natural or juridical, and no State shall claim or exercise sovereignty or sovereign rights over any part thereof': GA Res. 2749 (XXV) (12 December 1970) paras. 1, 2. This would have the effect of stopping these resources from being effectively claimed by those entities and states, generally the developed states, that had the technology and capital to have first-mover advantage. See R.P. Anand, Studies in International Law and History: An Asian Perspective 186 (2013); Lee (n. 6 above) 21–2.

12 5 June 1992, 31 ILM 818. The CBD is an international agreement adopted at the Earth Summit, in Rio de Janeiro, in 1992. It has three main objectives: to conserve biological diversity, to use its components in a sustainable way, and to share fairly and equitably the benefits arising from the use of genetic resources. The CBD was negotiated under the guidance of the United Nations. It was signed by more than 150 government leaders at the Rio Earth Summit. The Convention is now one of the most widely ratified international treaties on environmental issues, with 194 member countries.

13 Center for International Sustainable Development Law, *The Principle of Common But Differentiated Responsibilities: Origins and Scope* (2002), available at http://cisdl.org/public/docs/news/brief_common.pdf (last visited 10 July 2017).

diversity[14] and elaborating on the access and benefit sharing mechanism to solve the problem, also traces its lineage to these principles and ideas.[15]

2. Regulation and Supervision of Transnational Economic Activities

In addition to proclaiming sovereignty over natural resources, regulating and supervising economic activities of transnational corporations was another major platform of the NIEO.[16] Multilateral control of selfish and predatory activities of transnational corporations that had been destructive to local economic sovereignty and markets was considered as a precondition to the principle of self-determination.

3. Just and Equitable Commodity Prices

Another principle of the NIEO Declaration was the:

> just and equitable relationship between the prices of raw materials, primary commodities, manufactured and semi-manufactured goods exported by developing countries and the prices of raw materials, primary commodities, manufactures, capital goods and equipment imported by them with the aim of bringing about sustained improvement in their unsatisfactory terms of trade and the expansion of the world economy.[17]

In the same spirit, the NIEO Declaration calls for improving the competitiveness of natural materials facing competition from synthetic substitutes.[18]

This principle is based on the experiences that colonial powers had historically imposed upon their colonies terms of trade in disfavor of raw materials and primary commodities. The colonial powers in the nineteenth century cultivated their colonies as both markets for expanding products and sources of raw materials, and the deluge of European manufactured goods into these colonies resulted in effective 'de-industrialization' of these colonies.[19] At the same time, most colonies in their role as the raw

---

[14] See e.g., SIMONE BILDERBEEK ET AL. (EDS.), BIODIVERSITY AND INTERNATIONAL LAW: THE EFFECTIVENESS OF INTERNATIONAL ENVIRONMENTAL LAW 18 (1992).

[15] Abdulqawi A. Yusuf, *International Law and Sustainable Development: The Convention on Biological Diversity*, 2 AFRICAN YEARBOOK OF INTERNATIONAL LAW 109, 124 (1994); Lee (n. 6 above) 21–2.

[16] NIEO Declaration (n. 1 above) para. 4(g); Lee (n. 6 above) 26–7.

[17] NIEO Declaration (n. 1 above) para. 4(j).

[18] *Ibid.* para. 4(m); Lee (n. 6 above) 27.

[19] WORLD TRADE ORGANIZATION, WORLD TRADE REPORT 2013: FACTORS SHAPING THE FUTURE OF WORLD TRADE 48 (2013).

material-supplying 'periphery' saw little to modest growth even into the twentieth century.[20]

Although this principle of the control of commodity prices was never fully materialized into the GATT and WTO trade regime, one of the general exceptions in Article XX of the GATT justifies any measure undertaken in pursuance of obligations under any intergovernmental commodity agreement on the condition that such agreement conforms to criteria approved by the GATT members.[21] In any case, this principle brings onto the agenda the issue of 'just and equitable relationship' between developed and developing countries engaging in trade of goods at different stages of processing or manufacturing.

4. International Cooperation and Aid for Development

Note that the NIEO was not against trade liberalization *per se*, and in fact advocated for the expansion and liberalization of trade.[22] The Charter of Economic Rights and Duties of States made it explicit that:

> Every State has the duty to cooperate in promoting a steady and increasing expansion and liberalization of world trade and an improvement in the welfare and living standards of all peoples, in particular those of developing countries.[23]

However, there was an emphasis on international cooperation, and preferential treatment and aid for development for developing countries.

The NIEO Declaration pronounces that: 'International co-operation for development is the shared goal and common duty of all countries'.[24] Accordingly, this duty can be fulfilled by:

> the broadest co-operation of all the States members of the international community, based on equity, whereby the prevailing disparities in the world may be banished and prosperity secured for all; strengthening, through individual and collective actions, of mutual economic, trade, financial and technical co-operation among the developing countries, mainly on a preferential basis; full and effective participation on the basis of equality of all countries in the solving of world economic problems in the common interest of all countries, bearing in mind the necessity to ensure the accelerated development of all the developing countries, and [e]xtension of active assistance to developing coun-

[20] *Ibid.* at 48–9.
[21] GATT, Art. XX(h).
[22] Lee (n. 6 above) 31.
[23] Charter of Economic Rights and Duties of States, GA Res. 3281 (XXIX), art. 14.
[24] NIEO Declaration (n. 1 above) para. 3.

tries by the whole international community, free of any political or military conditions.[25]

As a specific means to meet these duties, the NIEO Declaration indicates the reformation of the international monetary system, preferential and non-reciprocal treatment for developing countries in all fields of international economic cooperation, transfer of financial resources, and scientific and technological aid.[26]

III. EMERGING ISSUE OF TRADE AND BIOLOGICAL DIVERSITY GOVERNANCE

1. Convention on Biological Diversity and its Nagoya Protocol

The conclusion of the CBD in 1992 was a consequential response to the global decline of biological diversity. The threat to species and ecosystems had never been so great and species extinction caused by human activities continued at an alarming rate. As a result, there was a growing recognition that biological diversity is a global asset of tremendous value to present and future generations.[27] Even as biodiversity declined, however, the incentives for exploiting genetic resources increased with the development of modern biotechnology and the maturation of the pharmaceutical, agricultural, cosmetics and other industries that utilize the properties of genetic resources such as wild plants.[28]

Both issues, the loss of biodiversity and the potential gains to be made from genetic resources, affect different parts of the world in asymmetrical ways. Although the loss of biodiversity is a global phenomenon, the

---

[25] *Ibid.* para. 4(b)–(k). Lee (n. 6 above) 29–31.

[26] NIEO Declaration (n. 1 above) para. 4(l)–(p).

[27] CBD Secretariat, *History of the Convention: Introduction*, available at www.cbd.int/history/ (last visited 10 July 2017).

[28] The scale of industry utilizing biotechnology, or 'the application of science and technology to living organisms, as well as parts, products and models thereof, to alter living or non-living materials for the production of knowledge, goods and services', as defined by the OECD, grew by 7.7 percent in 2011 to reach a value of US$281.7 billion worldwide, and is forecast to have a value of US$453.3 billion, an increase of 60.9 percent since 2011, in 2016. OECD, *Statistical Definition of Biotechnology*, available at www.oecd.org/sti/biotech/statisticaldefinitionofbiotechnology.htm (last visited 10 July 2017); *Biotechnology: Global Industry Guide*, PR Newswire (8 January 2013), available at www.prnewswire.com/news-releases/biotechnology-global-industry-guide-186003832.html (last visited 10 July 2017); Lee (n. 6 above) 36–7.

gains from biotechnology are mainly concentrated in the developed and highly industrialized countries. Not only are their biotechnology sectors more developed, but their biotechnological inventions and discoveries are protected by strong regimes of protecting intellectual property rights. These regimes have been increasingly strengthened and harmonized in the multilateral conventions regarding intellectual property rights, including the WTO Agreement on Trade-Related Aspects of Intellectual Property Rights (TRIPS), that are also expanding their scope of application into the area of biotechnology.[29] This led to a deep contention and conflict of interests between developed and developing countries: developed countries reaped the major benefits from the use of genetic resources, due to their technological and economical capability to exploit genetic resources and a stronger intellectual property rights framework, while developing countries had the major burden of biodiversity conservation.[30]

Against this background of dwindling biological diversity and its increasing potential commercial value, developing countries demanded the recognition of sovereign rights to exploit and to control access to their own genetic resources and a fair sharing of the burdens and costs of biodiversity conservation, including the opportunity costs in developing countries' being obliged to forego rights to exploit their own biodiversity resources, as part of the CBD negotiations.[31] Also demanded were access to and transfer of biotechnology of developed countries, a funding mechanism including contribution by transnational companies, and fair and equitable sharing of benefits derived from utilization of genetic resources upon mutually agreed terms. These demands were by and large reflected in the CBD.[32]

After the CBD's entry into force in December 1993, discussions continued on making the access and benefit-sharing (ABS) provisions operational. A Working Group on Access and Benefit Sharing was established at the CBD's fifth Conference of the Parties with a mandate to develop 'guidelines, other approaches and their respective elements'

---

[29] Sebastian Oberthur and G. Kristin Rosendal, *Background and Analytical Framework*, *in* GLOBAL GOVERNANCE OF GENETIC RESOURCES: ACCESS AND BENEFIT SHARING AFTER THE NAGOYA PROTOCOL 4 (Sebastian Oberthur and G. Kristin Rosendal eds., 2014).

[30] *Ibid.* at 4–5; Lee (n. 6 above) 37–8.

[31] United Nations Environmental Programme, Ad Hoc Working Group of Experts on Biological Diversity Third Session, Geneva, 9–13 July 1990, UNEP/Bio-Div3/12, United Nations, 13 August 1990, para. 15.

[32] CBD, Arts. 15(1), (7), 16, 20.

on ABS, and the Bonn Guidelines were the result.[33] While industrialized countries mostly argued for voluntary provisions focusing on access, developing countries fought for a binding protocol obliging user countries to adopt domestic measures to support benefit sharing.[34] The negotiations on this new binding ABS Protocol began in 2004, and after six years of negotiations the resulting text was adopted by the tenth Conference of the Parties in 2010 at Nagoya, Japan.[35] The Nagoya Protocol on Access to Genetic Resources and the Fair and Equitable Sharing of Benefits Arising from their Utilization to the Convention on Biological Diversity ('Nagoya Protocol')[36] subsequently came into effect in October 2014 at the twelfth Conference of the Parties at Pyeongchang, Korea, ninety days after the fiftieth ratification.

The Protocol aims to provide a transparent legal framework for the effective implementation of one of the three objectives of the CBD: the fair and equitable sharing of benefits arising out of the utilization of genetic resources. To achieve this aim, the Nagoya Protocol sets out core obligations for its contracting parties to take measures in relation to access to genetic resources, benefit-sharing, and compliance as below:

- Access obligations: domestic-level access measures are to:
  - create legal certainty, clarity, and transparency;
  - provide fair and non-arbitrary rules and procedures;
  - establish clear rules and procedures for prior informed consent and mutually agreed terms;
  - provide for issuance of a permit or equivalent when access is granted;
  - create conditions to promote and encourage research contributing to biodiversity conservation and sustainable use;
  - pay due regard to cases of present or imminent emergencies that threaten human, animal, or plant health;

---

33 Stephen Tully, *The Bonn Guidelines on Access to Genetic Resources and Benefit Sharing*, 12(1) REV. EUR. COMMUNITY & INT'L EVNTL. L. 84, 85 (2003).

34 Linda Wallbott et al., *The Negotiations of the Nagoya Protocol: Issues, Coalitions and Process*, *in* GLOBAL GOVERNANCE OF GENETIC RESOURCES: ACCESS AND BENEFIT SHARING AFTER THE NAGOYA PROTOCOL 36 (Sebastian Oberthur and G. Kristin Rosendal eds., 2014).

35 Conference of the Parties to the Convention on Biological Diversity, Decision Adopted by the Conference of the Parties to the Convention on Biological Diversity at Its Tenth Meeting, 29 October 2010.

36 29 October 2010, available at www.cbd.int/abs/doc/protocol/nagoya-protocol-en.pdf.

  - consider the importance of genetic resources for food and agriculture for food security.
- Benefit-sharing obligations: domestic-level benefit-sharing measures are to provide for the fair and equitable sharing of benefits arising from the utilization of genetic resources with the contracting party providing genetic resources. Utilization includes research and development on the genetic or biochemical composition of genetic resources, as well as subsequent applications and commercialization. Sharing is subject to mutually agreed terms. Benefits may be monetary or non-monetary, such as royalties and the sharing of research results.
- Compliance obligations: specific obligations to support compliance with the domestic legislation or regulatory requirements of the contracting party providing genetic resources, and contractual obligations reflected in mutually agreed terms, are a significant innovation of the Nagoya Protocol. Contracting parties are to:
  - take measures providing that genetic resources utilized within their jurisdiction have been accessed in accordance with prior informed consent, and that mutually agreed terms have been established, as required by another contracting party;
  - cooperate in cases of alleged violation of another contracting party's requirements;
  - encourage contractual provisions on dispute resolution in mutually agreed terms;
  - ensure an opportunity is available to seek recourse under their legal systems when disputes arise from mutually agreed terms;
  - take measures regarding access to justice;
  - take measures to monitor the utilization of genetic resources after they leave a country, including by designating effective checkpoints at any stage of the value-chain: research, development, innovation, pre-commercialization or commercialization.[37]

2. Issue of Trade and Biological Diversity Governance

The successful conclusion of the Nagoya Protocol and its inclusion of binding obligations on access and benefit sharing means a global recognition of the interests of the developing countries in asserting their sovereignty over, and fair compensation for the use of, genetic resources.

---

[37] CBD Secretariat, *About the Nagoya Protocol*, available at www.cbd.int/abs/about/default.shtml/ (last visited 10 July 2017).

This echoes the demands of the non-aligned countries in the earlier discussion of the NIEO and its legacy, which include the assertion of permanent sovereignty over genetic resources, fair trade terms for commodity prices, and the overall programme of development emphasizing the transfer of technology that the NIEO strove for.[38]

In key aspects of the access and benefit-sharing rules, however, the industrialized countries' insistence on market mechanisms has shaped the final rules. The developing countries' call for a global biodiversity fund from the proceeds of genetic resource commercialization, for instance, gave way to private contracts (mutually agreed terms (MATs)) that would remunerate individual provider countries.[39] Despite the CBD and Nagoya Protocol obligating measures aiming at the fair and equitable sharing of benefits, the actual implementation of these obligations is done according to these private and commercial agreements, effectively leaving the determination of fairness and equity to individual provider and user negotiations.[40] The rules of access and benefit-sharing, therefore, are an amalgam of different demands for state sovereignty and control over genetic resources, on the one hand, especially on the access side of the rules, but also incorporating market principles in the benefit-sharing provisions.[41] This gives rise to at least two possible conflicts with the international governance of trade: on the one hand, the exercise of state sovereignty over access to genetic resources and the potential conflict with trade rules on quantitative restrictions; and on the other, state controls that may be placed on the mutually agreed terms of benefit-sharing with access restrictions as a leverage and the potential conflict with intellectual property and investment rules.[42]

Of course, it is common and widely accepted in modern societies for governments to intervene in markets in order to regulate them and to provide certain public goods.[43] Access measures and MATs are no different, considering that the provision of environmental goods, including biodiversity, is a prominent example of market failure and a valid area for government intervention.[44] The problem is that when these arrangements

---

[38] Lee (n. 6 above) 40.

[39] *Ibid.* 40–42.

[40] *Ibid.*

[41] *Ibid.*

[42] *Ibid.*

[43] See e.g., Kikolaos Karagiannis, *Key Economic and Politico-Institutional Elements of Modern Interventionism*, 50(3/4) Soc. & Econ. Stud. 17 (2001); Lee (n. 6 above) 40–42.

[44] See e.g., Alex Bowen et al., *Why Do Economics Describe Climate Change as*

take place across borders, they may come into conflict with the law of international trade. The interactions between international regimes are further complicated by the CBD's and Nagoya Protocol's own standards. On the access side, there is an obligation for CBD parties to create conditions to facilitate access to genetic resources for environmentally sound uses by other parties and not to impose restrictions that run counter to the objectives of the Convention,[45] and the Nagoya Protocol imposes obligations on provider states to provide for legal certainty, clarity, transparency, fair and non-arbitrary rules and procedures, information for applying for prior informed consent and other procedural guarantees.[46] Such facilitation and procedural guarantees are in general in keeping with the principles of the GATT and the WTO,[47] but warrant more scrutiny for compliance.[48]

Potential conflicts between the ABS regime and trade norms might arise in many ways. A user's access to biological resources for the purpose of obtaining genetic resources may be restricted by the provider country's access regulations in accordance with the CBD and Nagoya Protocol regimes. Also, without proper sharing of benefits arising from the utilization of genetic resources by a user, the provider country many deny any further access by such user to its own resources. If these restrictions and denials take the form of export prohibitions, the issue may well fall under the scrutiny of Article XI of the GATT. Because such export prohibitions are not justified as the exceptions under GATT, Article XI(2),[49] they seem to be inconsistent with the GATT principle of general elimination of quantitative restrictions.[50]

---

a 'Market Failure'?, THE GUARDIAN (4 May 2012), available at www.theguardian.com/environment/2012/may/21/economists-climate-change-market-failure; Lee (n. 6 above) 40–42.

[45] CBD, Art. 15(2); Lee (n. 6 above) 40–42.

[46] Nagoya Protocol, Art. 6(3); Lee (n. 6 above) 40–42.

[47] See e.g., GATT, Art. XIII:3.

[48] Lee (n. 6 above) 40–42.

[49] The exceptions include: (i) export prohibitions or restrictions temporarily applied to prevent or relieve critical shortages of essential products; (ii) import and export prohibitions or restrictions necessary to the application of standards or regulations for the classification, grading, or marketing of commodities in international trade; and (iii) import restrictions on any agricultural or fisheries product necessary to the enforcement of governmental measures which operate to restrict the quantities of the like domestic product, to remove a temporary surplus of the like domestic product, or to restrict the quantities permitted to be produced of any animal product.

[50] See Wonmog Choi, *Mutual Conflict and Harmony of the Nagoya Protocol of Access and Benefit Sharing of Genetic Resources and the International Trade Norms*, 19(2) EWHA L. J. 461 (2014).

Despite this inconsistency, the provider country implementing such export prohibitions might try to justify their measures by Article XX of the GATT. The general exception clause gives a general exemption from any obligations under the GATT to any measure that is 'necessary to protect human, animal or plant life or health' or 'relates to the conservation of exhaustible natural resources if such measures are made effective in conjunction with restrictions on domestic production or consumption'.[51] This exemption is conditioned upon the requirement that 'such measures are not applied in a manner which would constitute a means of arbitrary or unjustifiable discrimination between countries where the same conditions prevail, or a disguised restriction on international trade'.[52] Although export prohibitions to enforce the ABS mechanism might be able to be recognized as a trade measure 'necessary to protect animal or plant life or health' or 'relating to the conservation of exhaustible natural resources', it would be difficult for many of those measures to satisfy the requirement that:

> such measures are not applied in a manner which would constitute a means of arbitrary or unjustifiable discrimination between countries where the same conditions prevail, or a disguised restriction on international trade.[53]

Only some trade restriction measures that are carefully designed to be applied in a non-arbitrary and justifiable manner without creating disguised restriction in international trade might be able to pass the strict scrutiny.

ABS regime's conflict with the intellectual property provisions of TRIPS seem to be inevitable. Already, several developing countries have adopted domestic regulations requiring patent applicants to disclose the origin of genetic resources and/or biological resources that they have used to produce their inventions.[54] Moreover, any failure to obtain prior informed consents or to share benefits with the provider of genetic resources against domestic laws leads to the denial of patentability in some countries.[55] It is highly likely that this trend will spread into many developing countries.

---

[51] GATT, Art. XX(b), (g).

[52] The chapeau of GATT, Art. XX.

[53] GATT, Art. XX(b), (g).

[54] See Zhonghua Renmin Gongheguo Jhuanli Fa (2008 Sioujheng) [Patent Law of the People's Republic of China, 2008 Amendment] (promulgated by the Standing Comm. Nat'l People's Cong., 12 March 1984, effective 1 April 1985) (amended 2008), 2009 STANDING COMM. NAT'L PEOPLE'S CONG. GAZ. 27, art. 26(5) (China); Patent (Amendment) Act 2005, India Code (2005), art. 25 (India).

[55] Patent Law of the People's Republic of China, 2008 Amendment, art. 5.

This means that a general practice will be established, at least among developing countries, that patent rights are granted only for the applications that have satisfied ABS requirements.

According to Article 27.1 of TRIPS, 'patents shall be available for any inventions . . . that are new, involve an inventive step and are capable of industrial application', and patent rights shall be 'enjoyable without discrimination as to the place of invention, the field of technology and whether products are imported or locally produced'.[56] Any requirement of ABS as the precondition of patentability would be to establish an additional element that is not envisaged by Article 27.1, and if such a requirement is imposed only upon patent applicants whose invention is based on the use of foreign genetic resources, it would constitute a discrimination prohibited by Article 27.1.

It should be noted that TRIPS itself sets forth an exception from this general principle regarding patentability in Article 27.2. According to this, members may exclude from patentability:

> inventions, the prevention within their territory of the commercial exploitation of which is necessary to protect *ordre public* or morality, including to protect human, animal or plant life or health or to avoid serious prejudice to the environment.[57]

This interesting exception may play an important role in justifying the imposition of ABS requirements as a precondition of patentability. If the ABS regime could be widely recognized as a requirement to prevent the commercial exploitation of inventions that is 'necessary to protect animal or plant life or health or to avoid serious prejudice to the environment' within the meaning of Article 27.2, denials of patentability based on the failure of the disclosure or ABS obligations may be justified in their WTO consistency.

At any rate, all of these issues or points raise a pressing question of how to interpret these provisions under the GATT and TRIPS in relation to basic obligations in the Nagoya Protocol and CBD, and more broadly, how to establish trade and biodiversity governance in a mutually compatible way.

---

56 TRIPS Agreement, Art. 27.1.

57 *Ibid.* Art. 27.2.

IV. CONCLUSION: TRADE AND BIOLOGICAL DIVERSITY GOVERNANCE IN THE AGE OF MEGAREGIONALS

Given that the Trans-Pacific Partnership (TPP)[58] is the first mega-free trade agreement (FTA) among diverse economies, including developed and developing countries in the Asia-Pacific region, it is not surprising that the TPP has a provision entitled 'Trade and Biodiversity' in its Environmental Chapter. This provision begins with the recognition of 'the importance of conservation and sustainable use of biological diversity and their key role in achieving sustainable development'.[59] Accordingly, each party 'shall promote and encourage the conservation and sustainable use of biological diversity, in accordance with its law or policy'.[60] In doing so, the TPP parties recognize 'the importance of public participation and consultation, in accordance with their respective law or policy, in the development and implementation of measures concerning the conservation and sustainable use of biological diversity' and they must 'make publicly available information about its programmes and activities, including cooperative programmes, related to the conservation and sustainable use of biological diversity'.[61] The TPP also recognizes the importance of 'respecting, preserving and maintaining knowledge and practices of indigenous and local communities embodying traditional lifestyles that contribute to the conservation and sustainable use of biological diversity'.[62]

In order to realize these recognitions, the TPP acknowledges the importance of the new environmental governance system under the CBD and Nagoya Protocol. Accordingly, TPP parties must recognize 'the importance of facilitating access to genetic resources within their respective national jurisdictions, consistent with each Party's international obligations' and that:

---

[58] The Trans Pacific Partnership Agreement (TPP) is a trade agreement among twelve of the Pacific Rim countries (Brunei, Chile, New Zealand, Singapore, Australia, Canada, Japan, Malaysia, Mexico, Peru, United States, Vietnam — notably not including China and Korea). The finalized proposal was signed on 4 February 2016 in Auckland, New Zealand, concluding seven years of negotiations. It is currently awaiting ratification to enter into force.

[59] TPP, Art. 20.13, para. 1, available at https://ustr.gov/sites/default/files/TPP-Final-Text-Environment.pdf (last visited 10 July 2017).

[60] *Ibid.* Art. 20.13, para. 2.

[61] *Ibid.* Art. 20.13, para. 5.

[62] *Ibid.* Art. 20.13, para. 3.

> some Parties require, through national measures, prior informed consent to access such genetic resources in accordance with national measures and, where such access is granted, the establishment of mutually agreed terms, including with respect to sharing of benefits from the use of such genetic resources, between users and providers.[63]

For all of these activities, the parties should 'cooperate to address matters of mutual interest' and such cooperation may include:

> exchanging information and experiences in areas related to: the conservation and sustainable use of biological diversity; the protection and maintenance of ecosystems and ecosystem services; and access to genetic resources and the sharing of benefits arising from their utilization.[64]

Seemingly, these provisions appear largely hortatory in their binding effect, reflecting historical and fundamental philosophical tensions between the Bretton Woods trade liberalism and the New International Economic Order presenting a new paradigm of permanent sovereignty over natural resources. Nonetheless, the very existence of these provisions in the first mega-scale trade agreement is meaningful: it is an official acknowledgement that how to avoid clashes between trade and biodiversity paradigms and to achieve the goal of sustainable economic growth has become a primary issue in the era of mega-FTAs.

To avoid this possible clash, the TPP sets up multiple consultation mechanisms. It establishes the Environmental Committee and Contact Points in order to facilitate communication between the parties and to provide a forum to discuss, provide periodic reports, endeavor to resolve matters, and coordinate with other committees.[65] The environmental consultation mechanism is established to receive any requests from the parties regarding the operation of the Environmental Chapter, and to make every effort to arrive at a mutually satisfactory resolution.[66] If the consulting parties have failed to resolve the matter, the issue may be settled at the next level of senior representative consultations under which a consulting party may request that the Committee representatives from the consulting parties convene to consider the matter.[67] Even nongovernmental experts may be requested to provide relevant scientific and technical information and any Committee representatives from any other party may participate in the consultations to exert peer pressure.

---

63 *Ibid.* Art. 20.13, para. 4.
64 *Ibid.* Art. 20.13, para. 6.
65 *Ibid.* Art. 20.19.
66 *Ibid.* Art. 20.20.
67 *Ibid.* Art. 20.21.

If the consulting parties have failed to resolve the matter, a consulting party may refer the matter to the Ministerial Consultations hosted by the relevant Ministers of the consulting parties.[68] As a last resort, the TPP dispute settlement panel may handle the matter by issuing a binding decision.

By these series of multiple consultations and dispute settlement mechanisms, many clashes between trade and biodiversity regimes among TPP economies may be prevented or resolved, including disputes concerning export prohibition measures of biological resources on the ground of lack of prior informed consent (PIC) or MAT; the requirement of disclosure of origin of genetic resources and/or biological resources that a patent applicant has used to produce their inventions; and the denial of patentability against applicants who have not satisfied the MAT requirement.

Whether or not this soft approach through recognitions and consultations will work remains to be seen. Moreover, it is likely that the TPP might not be able to enter into force given the recent policy shift of Donald Trump's Administration in the United States.[69] Therefore, the trade and biodiversity provisions in the TPP are not likely to have the chance to be applied at all.

Nonetheless, an optimistic sign for the future is that the TPP has certainly taken a mega-step for the prevention of global clashes between trade and environment regimes toward the mutually non-exclusive trade and biodiversity governance in the twenty-first century. This step will certainly make an impact for future mega-FTAs because these provisions on trade and biodiversity are likely to be copied into other mega-FTAs. The global task to form a peaceful co-existence between the trade and environmental regimes is indeed a pressing need for all.

---

[68] *Ibid*. Art. 20.22.

[69] The new President of the United States signed executive orders to scrap the TPP on 23 January 2017. This means that the United States made a formal decision not to join the agreement. To take effect, the deal would have had to be ratified by February 2018 by at least six countries that account for 85 percent of the group's economic output. The United States would need to be on board to meet that last condition. Without some sort of alternative deal among the remaining countries, it is currently impossible to make the TPP enter into force.

8. Regulation of renewable energy trade in the megaregionals era: Current issues and prospects for rule-making reforms

Sherzod Shadikhodjaev*

I. INTRODUCTION

Energy is an indispensable prerequisite for any nation's socio-economic development. It can be derived from both fossil fuels and renewables. Many governments across the globe pursue renewable energy policies with mainly two purposes: to promote green growth and to ensure sustainable energy supplies from an increased utilization of virtually non-exhaustible renewable sources. Renewable energy typically includes solar energy, wind power, geothermal energy, hydropower, bioenergy, and ocean power, and finds its use in the electricity, heating, and cooling and transport sectors.[1]

Despite the utmost importance of renewable energy and the climate change agenda in today's international politics, the current World Trade Organization (WTO) rules do not address renewable energy *per se*. Even energy-related commitments of all acceded countries in the WTO have so far dealt with fossil fuels.[2] Nevertheless, a number of recent disputes and intensive forum discussions have raised the WTO's attention to renewable energy. In parallel, regional trade agreements (RTAs) these days tend to introduce renewables-specific rules, with some launching elaborate regulatory regimes and others encouraging intra-bloc cooperation in this sphere.

* This work was supported by the Ministry of Education of the Republic of Korea and the National Research Foundation of Korea (NRF–2016S1A3A2925230).

1 International Energy Agency, *Renewables*, available at www.iea.org/topics/renewables/ (last visited 15 July 2017).

2 Juneyoung Lee et al., *Energy-Related Rules in Accession Protocols: Where are They?*, *in* WTO ACCESSIONS AND TRADE MULTILATERALISM: CASE STUDIES AND LESSONS FROM THE WTO AT TWENTY 705 (Uri Dadush and Chiedu Osakwe eds., 2015).

Megaregionals, including, *inter alia*, the Trans-Pacific Partnership (TPP) and the Transatlantic Trade and Investment Partnership (TTIP), are not exceptions to this trend.

This chapter will examine multilateral and regional trade issues associated with renewables. It will show that, with respect to renewable energy, the movement towards regulatory convergence is detectable in some big economic blocs, while the legal regimes of the WTO and most of the RTAs remain largely divergent. After a brief introduction to the WTO and regional initiatives, this chapter will proceed with sector-specific topics discussing the status quo and areas for possible rule-making in the future. Due to space constraints, this analysis will address only localization measures, government support, infrastructural facilities, technical standards, and services.

II. RENEWABLE ENERGY INITIATIVES AT THE MULTILATERAL AND REGIONAL LEVELS

A trade-and-environment agenda of the Doha Ministerial Declaration (2001) envisages negotiations on 'the reduction or, as appropriate, elimination of tariff and non-tariff barriers to environmental goods and services'.[3] The Doha mandate anticipates achieving a 'win-win-win' outcome for (i) 'trade' through lowering the prices of green imports; (ii) 'environment' by improving access to eco-friendly technologies; and (iii) 'development' via assisting developing countries in obtaining tools for addressing their own environmental needs as part of their overall development policies. The World Bank predicts that the elimination of trade barriers could lead to a significant increase in the volume of clean energy technologies traded, from 7 percent in the case of tariff removal to 14 percent in the event of elimination of both tariffs and non-tariff restrictions.[4]

Since the negotiations in a multilateral framework have not progressed well, a group of WTO members launched a plurilateral Environmental Goods Agreement initiative in July 2014.[5] The talks, currently involving seventeen members, intend to remove tariff duties on green products on a

---

[3] WTO, Ministerial Declaration of 14 November 2001, WTO Doc. WT/MIN(01)/DEC/1, para. 31(iii).

[4] The World Bank, International Trade and Climate Change: Economic, Legal, and Institutional Perspectives 72 (2008).

[5] WTO, *Azevêdo Welcomes Launch of Plurilateral Environmental Goods Negotiations* (8 July 2014), available at www.wto.org/english/news_e/news14_e/envir_08jul14_e.htm (last visited 15 July 2017).

most-favored-nation (MFN) basis, provided that the critical mass of trade will be covered. About 340 tariff items are considered potential environmental goods placed under the categories of air pollution control, cleaner and renewable energy, energy efficiency, environmental monitoring and analysis, among other things. The negotiations mainly focus on the product scope and staging of tariff elimination. As for environmental and related services, they are covered by another ongoing plurilateral project on the Trade in Services Agreement, with twenty-three WTO members engaged.

Climate change and renewable energy has also been on the agenda of many regional fora. A very fresh example can be provided by the United States, Canada, and Mexico's joint commitment to deepen the North American alliance on the environmental front. In June 2016, they pledged to work closer on cutting greenhouse gas (GHG) emissions in the hydrocarbon industries, generating 50 percent of electricity in the region from clean sources by 2025 and building new cross-border transmission lines to boost capacity for green energy trading.[6]

Some international instruments like the North American Free Trade Agreement (NAFTA), the EU-Ukraine Associate Agreement, and the Japan-Australia Economic Partnership Agreement have energy-dedicated Chapters, but they do not specifically address renewables *per se*.[7] However, this is not the case for the trade arrangements falling within any of the following three groups which, with respect to renewable energy, either (i) pursue a common policy; or (ii) create specific trade and investment rules with no common policies; or (iii) simply support intra-governmental cooperation.

The European Union (EU) belongs to the first category above. The EU Renewable Energy Directive (2009/28/EC) establishes an EU-wide regime for the production and promotion of energy from renewable sources. In particular, it sets a regional target of fulfilling at least 20 percent of total energy needs with renewables by 2020 and specifies national targets ranging from a low of 10 percent in Malta to a high of 49 percent in Sweden. The

---

[6] Angela Greiling Keane and Josh Wingrove, *Three Amigos Unveil Climate and Energy Plan, NAFTA Changes*, Bloomberg (29 June 2016), available at www.bloomberg.com/politics/articles/2016-06-29/three-amigos-announce-new-north-american-climate-and-energy-plan (last visited 15 July 2017).

[7] See NAFTA, Chapter 6 (Energy and Basic Petrochemicals), 17 December 1992, 32 ILM 289; EU-Ukraine Association Agreement, Title I Chapter 11 (Trade-Related Energy), 21 March 2014, [2014] OJ L161/3); Japan-Australia Economic Partnership Agreement, Chapter 8 (Energy and Mineral Resources), 8 July 2014, available at http://dfat.gov.au/trade/agreements/jaepa/official-documents/Documents/jaepa-chapters-1-to-20.pdf (last visited 15 July 2017).

Member States must also ensure that by 2020 at least 10 percent of their transport fuels come from renewable sources. Implementation measures can be outlined in each Member State's renewable energy action plan.[8] The Association of Southeast Asian Nations (ASEAN) represents another example of a regional bloc pursuing a common policy. The ASEAN Plan of Action for Energy aims to integrate domestic energy markets and related policies over the 2016–2025 period, reduce energy intensity by 20 percent in 2020, and increase the share of renewable energy in the ASEAN energy mix to 23 percent by 2025. It focuses on seven program areas including, *inter alia*, ASEAN power grid, energy efficiency and conservation, and renewable energy.[9]

The second group includes the EU free trade agreements (FTAs) with Singapore and Vietnam that contain a special Chapter on 'Non-Tariff Barriers to Trade and Investment in Renewable Energy Generation' that hardly exists in other trade agreements. These FTAs are unique in combining trade and investment areas within the renewable energy context. The parties have committed themselves to cooperating towards removing or reducing related barriers and fostering regulatory harmonization, taking into account regional and international standards. The agreements in question specify the scope of application; principles of liberalizing the domestic regimes; provisions on standards, technical regulations and conformity assessment; exceptions; and areas of cooperation.[10]

The third group is wider, as many trade agreements tend to introduce more general—sometimes hortatory or 'best endeavor'—provisions on promotion of inter-state cooperation on renewable energy. For instance, the EU and Canada have pledged to 'pay special attention to facilitating the removal of obstacles to trade or investment in . . . renewable energy goods and related services' and cooperate on environmental matters, such

---

[8] See Directive 2009/28/EC of the European Parliament and of the Council of 23 April 2009 on the promotion of the use of energy from renewable sources and amending and subsequently repealing Directives 2001/77/EC and 2003/30/EC, [2009] OJ L140/16.

[9] See Christopher G. Zamora and ASEAN Member States (eds.), *ASEAN Plan of Action for Energy Cooperation (APAEC) 2016–2015, Phase 1: 2016–2020*, available at www.aseanenergy.org/wp-content/uploads/2015/12/HighRes-APAEC-online-version-final.pdf (last visited 15 July 2017).

[10] See EU-Singapore FTA, Chapter 7, authentic text as of May 2015, available at http://trade.ec.europa.eu/doclib/docs/2013/september/tradoc_151742.pdf (last visited 15 July 2017); EU-Vietnam FTA, Chapter 14, agreed text as of January 2016, available at http://trade.ec.europa.eu/doclib/docs/2016/february/tradoc_154228.pdf (last visited 15 July 2017).

as e.g. green technologies, renewables, and energy efficiency.[11] Energy cooperation between the EU and Chile aims to 'consolidate economic relations in key sectors such as hydroelectricity, oil and gas, renewable energy, energy-saving technology and rural electrification'.[12] Similar cooperation provisions can be found in other RTAs as well.[13]

The TPP also fits into the third category. Chapter 20 on Environment contains certain provisions concerning renewable energy. Acknowledging a need for collective action on transition to a 'low emissions economy', the parties agreed to cooperate over development of green technologies and 'clean and renewable energy sources', as well as other climate mitigation issues.[14] Cooperation must address 'matters of joint or common interest' and may proceed in a bilateral or plurilateral framework in the form of 'dialogues, workshops, seminars, conferences, collaborative programmes and projects; technical assistance to promote and facilitate cooperation and training; the sharing of best practices on policies and procedures; and the exchange of experts'.[15] As for 'environmental goods and services', the parties may engage in relevant cooperative projects, and the Committee on Environment is to address associated trade barriers and issues.[16]

In the TTIP negotiations, the EU insists on laying down specific rules

---

[11] EU-Canada Comprehensive Economic and Trade Agreement, Arts. 24.9, 24.12, 30 October 2016, available at http://ec.europa.eu/trade/policy/in-focus/ceta/ceta-chapter-by-chapter/ (last visited 15 July 2017).

[12] EU-Chile Association Agreement, Art. 22.1, 30 December 2002, [2002] OJ L352.

[13] See e.g., EU-Ukraine Association Agreement, Title IV, Art. 293; Framework Agreement Establishing a Free Trade Area between the Republic of Turkey and the Republic of Korea, Art. 5.6, 1 August 2002; Free Trade Agreement between the Republic of China (Taiwan) and the Republic of Guatemala, Art. 20.13, 22 September 2005, available at www.google.ch/url?sa=t&rct=j&q=&esrc=s&source=web&cd=3&ved=0ahUKEwit-tSN27DVAhXqCcAKHTblAVgQFgg2MAI&url=http%3A%2F%2Fwww.trade.gov.tw%2FApp_Ashx%2FFile.ashx%3FFilePath%3D..%2FFiles%2FTradeOldFile%2F17%2F30%2F88%2FFTA%2BBetween%2Bthe%2BROC%2Band%2Bthe%2BRepublic%2Bof%2BGuatemala.pdf&usg=AFQjCNFazX6E1dLJ17vAVeWxFXOY3beXKw (last visited 15 July 2017); Comprehensive Economic Partnership Agreement between Japan and the Republic of India, Art. 8, 16 February 2011, available at www.mofa.go.jp/region/asia-paci/india/epa201102/index.html (last visited 15 July 2017); Joint Statement on the Occasion of the Signing of the Agreement between Japan and Brunei Darussalam for an Economic Partnership, 18 June 2007, available at www.mofa.go.jp/region/asia-paci/brunei/epa0706/joint.html (last visited 15 July 2017).

[14] TPP, Art. 20.15, available at https://ustr.gov/sites/default/files/TPP-Final-Text-Environment.pdf (last visited 15 July 2017).

[15] *Ibid.* Art. 20.12.

[16] *Ibid.* Art. 20.18.

(possibly a discrete Chapter) on energy and raw materials, as it believes that the current WTO rules are not adequate enough to handle trade and investment issues in this field.[17] The newly-introduced disciplines would ensure free access to energy and raw materials, eliminate existing restrictions, and promote the development of green energy. With respect to renewable energy and energy efficiency, the TTIP text will likely foresee bans on localization measures and forced transfer of technology, and obligate the parties to work towards making domestic green standards converge.[18] A Chapter on Trade and Sustainable Development could stress the shared objective to promote trade and investment in environmental (renewable energy) goods and services, including through addressing non-tariff barriers.[19]

III. LOCAL CONTENT REQUIREMENTS

Stone et al. (2015) identified 146 localization measures implemented by about forty economies between 2008 and 1 April 2014 as a response to the 2007–2008 global financial crisis.[20] Localization policies have restrictive impacts on international trade. According to Hufbauer et al. (2013), local content requirements (LCRs) affected nearly 5 percent of the US$18.5 trillion of total global trade and would reduce world trade by as much as US$93 billion annually.[21]

Kuntze and Moerenhout (2013) found LCRs on renewables in more than ten economies, including Canada, some EU Member States, the United States, China, Turkey, Brazil, India, South Africa, and so on.[22]

---

[17] European Commission, *EU-U.S. Transatlantic Trade and Investment Partnership: Raw Materials and Energy*, Initial EU Position Paper, 1–2, available at http://trade.ec.europa.eu/doclib/docs/2013/july/tradoc_151624.pdf (last visited 15 July 2017).

[18] *Ibid.* at 3.

[19] European Commission, *Trade and Sustainable Development Chapter/Labour and Environment: EU Paper Outlining Key Issues and Elements for Provisions in the TTIP*, available at http://trade.ec.europa.eu/doclib/docs/2015/january/tradoc_153024.pdf (last visited 15 July 2017).

[20] Susan Stone et al., *Emerging Policy Issues: Localisation Barriers to Trade* (OECD Trade Pol'y Papers, No. 180, 2015).

[21] Gary Clyde Hufbauer et al., Local Content Requirements: A Global Problem 37–8 (2013).

[22] Jan-Christoph Kuntze and Tom Moerenhout, *Local Content Requirements and the Renewable Energy Industry: A Good Match?* 21–31 (International Centre for Trade and Sustainable Development Working Paper, 2013).

As of 1 January 2016, the WTO Committee on Trade-Related Investment Measures (TRIMS) addressed LCRs under six national schemes affecting the renewable energy sector, notably: Clean Development Mechanism projects on renewable energy (China);[23] solar power generation projects (India);[24] the Jawaharlal Nehru National Solar Mission (India);[25] renewable electricity generation (Turkey);[26] wind power equipment (Uruguay);[27] and regional renewable energy programs (the United States).[28] Among them, the Jawaharlal Nehru National Solar Mission was examined in panel and appellate decisions.[29]

Six subsidy-related disputes—all initiated from 2010 onwards—targeted public support for renewable energy contingent upon the use of local content.[30] At issue were government incentives granted in relation to

---

[23] Committee on Trade-Related Investment Measures, Minutes of the Meeting Held on 1 November 2007, Note by the Secretariat, WTO Doc. G/TRIMS/M/26 (9 November 2007); Committee on Trade-Related Investment Measures, Minutes of the Meeting Held on 25 October 2006, Note by the Secretariat, WTO Doc. G/TRIMS/M/25 (27 October 2006).

[24] Committee on Trade-Related Investment Measures, Minutes of the Meeting Held on 5 October 2015, WTO Doc. G/TRIMS/M/39 (2 February 2016); Committee on Trade-Related Investment Measures, Minutes of the Meeting Held on 16 April 2015, WTO Doc. G/TRIMS/M/38 (27 July 2015).

[25] Committee on Trade-Related Investment Measures, Minutes of the Special Meeting Held on 1 October 2012, Note by the Secretariat, WTO Doc. G/TRIMS/M/33 (22 November 2012); Committee on Trade-Related Investment Measures, Minutes of the Special Meeting Held on 4 May 2012, Note by the Secretariat, WTO Doc. G/TRIMS/M/32 (14 June 2012); Committee on Trade-Related Investment Measures, Minutes of the Meeting Held on 3 October 2011, Note by the Secretariat, WTO Doc. G/TRIMS/M/31 (10 November 2011).

[26] WTO Doc. G/TRIMS/M/38.

[27] Committee on Trade-Related Investment Measures, Minutes of the Meeting Held on 20 June 2014, WTO Doc. G/TRIMS/M/36 (5 September 2014); Committee on Trade-Related Investment Measures, Minutes of the Meeting Held on 4 October 2013, WTO Doc. G/TRIMS/M/35 (20 December 2013).

[28] WTO Doc. G/TRIMS/M/35; WTO Doc. G/TRIMS/M/39; WTO Doc. G/TRIMS/M/38; Committee on Trade-Related Investment Measures, Minutes of the Meeting Held on 8 October 2014, WTO Doc. G/TRIMS/M/37 (21 November 2014); WTO Doc. G/TRIMS/M/36; Committee on Trade-Related Investment Measures, Minutes of the Meeting Held on 30 April 2013, Note by the Secretariat, WTO Doc. G/TRIMS/M/34 (19 June 2013).

[29] See Sherzod Shadikhodjaev, *India—Certain Measures Relating to Solar Cells and Solar Modules*, 111 Am. J. Int'l L. 139 (2017).

[30] These disputes dealt with subsidy issues as reflected in consultation requests (and panel/appellate decisions for some of them). These are: *European Union and Certain Member States—Certain Measures on the Importation and Marketing of Biodiesel and Measures Supporting the Biodiesel Industry*, WTO Doc. WT/DS459/

renewable energy (e.g. biodiesel) and/or power generating inputs and equipment (e.g. solar cells). The *Canada—Renewable Energy* / *Canada—Feed-In Tariff Program* case dealt with Ontario's Feed-in Tariff (FIT) program under which the government paid, on a long-term basis, guaranteed prices to eligible generators of solar- or wind-power-based electricity if they met the 'minimum required domestic content level' for installation of related equipment.[31] Similarly, the Indian authorities in *India—Solar Cells* entered into long-term purchase agreements with solar power developers subject to the mandatory 'domestic content requirement' for using solar cells and modules.[32] In both cases, the complainants stressed that they were not questioning the legitimacy of environmental and renewable energy policies as such, but rather trade-restrictive LCRs imposed thereby.[33] The Canadian and Indian localization measures were eventually found to be in violation of the national treatment provisions of the General Agreement on Tariffs and Trade (GATT) and the TRIMS Agreement. The public procurement derogation under Article III:8(a) of the GATT was found to be inapplicable to the measures at issue, because the government was actually purchasing electricity while discriminating against another product, namely, power-generating equipment.[34]

Since LCRs are generally considered as a bad industrial policy contrary to the national treatment principle, there is some room for elaborating on such anti-LCR stance for renewables in more detail. In this regard, some lessons can be drawn from the EU FTAs with Singapore and Vietnam.

(request for consultation received 15 May 2013); *India—Certain Measures Relating to Solar Cells and Solar Modules* ('*India–Solar Cells*'), WTO Doc. WT/DS456 (adopted 14 October 2016); *European Union and Certain Member States—Certain Measures Affecting the Renewable Energy Generation Sector*, WTO Doc. WT/DS452 (request for consultation received 5 November 2012); *Canada—Measures Relating to the Feed-in Tariff Program*, WTO Doc. WT/DS426 (adopted 24 May 2013); *China—Measures Concerning Wind Power Equipment*, WTO Doc. WT/DS419 (request for consultation received 22 December 2010); *Canada—Certain Measures Affecting the Renewable Energy Generation Sector* ('*Canada—Renewable Energy*'), WTO Doc. WT/DS412 (adopted 24 May 2013).

[31] Panel Reports, *Canada—Renewable Energy* (n. 30 above); *Canada—Measures Relating to the Feed-in Tariff Program* ('*Canada—Feed-In Tariff Program*'), WTO Docs. WT/DS412/R, WT/DS426/R (adopted 24 May 2013), paras. 7.64–7.68.

[32] *India—Solar Cells* (n. 30 above) paras. 7.1–7.14.

[33] *Canada—Renewable Energy* (n. 30 above) para. 7.7; *India—Solar Cells* (n. 30 above) para. 7.18.

[34] Appellate Body Reports, *Canada—Renewable Energy*; *Canada—Feed-In Tariff Program*, WTO Docs. WT/DS412/AB/R, WT/DS426/AB/R (adopted 24 May 2013), paras. 5.79, 5.84; Appellate Body Report, *India—Solar Cells*, WT/DS456/AB/R (adopted 14 October 2016), para. 5.40.

With respect to renewable energy generation, these agreements urge the parties to 'refrain from adopting measures providing for local content requirements or any other offset affecting the other Party's products, service suppliers, investors or investments'.[35] An LCR in this context means:[36]

(i) with respect to goods, a requirement for an enterprise to purchase or use goods of domestic origin or from a domestic source, whether specified in terms of particular products, in terms of volume or value of products, or in terms of a proportion of volume or value of its local production;
(ii) with respect to services, a requirement which restricts the choice of the service supplier or the service supplied to the detriment of services or service suppliers from the other party.

For goods, the definition largely resembles that in the Annex to the TRIMS Agreement. While the LCR definition for services cannot be found in the General Agreement on Trade in Services (GATS), it appears to be formulated quite broadly going beyond the actual 'anti-localization' purpose, as a requirement to use services from a particular foreign country (as a trade preference) other than the party to the FTA(s) in question can also be captured by this definition. The EU Agreements with Singapore and Vietnam also disallow requirements to establish 'partnerships' (joint legal entities) with local companies unless they are otherwise necessary for 'technical reasons' to be demonstrated by the imposing party upon request.[37] In a sense, these definitional elements for renewables-related LCRs are 'WTO-plus' descriptions. One of the merits of such RTA-inserted LCR bans for renewable energy 'investment' projects is the possibility for the investor's government (if foreseen by the text) to rely on RTA's dispute settlement remedies, including trade sanctions if applicable, against a wrongdoing host party, something which is typically not available under bilateral investment treaties.

35 EU-Singapore FTA, Art. 7.4(a); EU-Vietnam FTA, Ch. 14, Art. 4(1)(a).
36 EU-Singapore FTA, Art. 7.2(a); EU-Vietnam FTA, Ch. 14, Art. 2(a).
37 EU-Singapore FTA, Art. 7.4(b); EU-Vietnam FTA, Ch. 14, Art. 4(1)(b).

IV. PUBLIC SUPPORT

According to REN21 (2016), in 2015, 146 countries had renewable energy support policies at the national or state/provincial level. Feed-in policies or quota schemes for utilization of green electricity were implemented in over 100 jurisdictions, followed by sixty-six countries with biofuel mandates and sixty-four countries with the public competitive bidding system in place. Governments have also resorted to various fiscal incentives for the production and deployment of related equipment.[38]

Since companies do not consider societal benefits of renewables, they will not normally engage in renewable energy projects on their own, as production costs there tend to exceed private benefits. Therefore, economic theory justifies subsidies in this sector for their ability to correct such a market failure. While the WTO Subsidies and Countervailing Measures (SCM) Agreement does not provide explicit flexibilities for promotion of renewable energy, the Appellate Body in *Canada—Renewable Energy / Canada—Feed-In Tariff Program* took bold efforts to interpret the existing disciplines in a way that offers some policy space.[39] There, the Appellate Body concluded that the wind power and solar energy segments of the entire blended electricity market were themselves separate markets for the sake of comparing the government-supported prices at issue with other relevant prices in the same markets. Although consumers do not distinguish electricity by its source of generation (be it renewable or conventional energy), the Appellate Body emphasized the supply-side factors—'important differences in cost structures and operating costs and characteristics among generating technologies'—that actually enable suppliers to differentiate between conventional and renewable electricity so as to consider the latter to be in a distinct market.[40] Moreover, the Appellate Body observed that the role of the government in *creating* a renewable electricity market would not automatically amount to a subsidy disciplined in the WTO.[41]

With these Appellate Body findings, it is arguably more difficult to successfully challenge a foreign FIT or other public support schemes in

---

[38] REN21, RENEWABLES 2016: GLOBAL STATUS REPORT 19–20 (2016), available at www.ren21.net/wp-content/uploads/2016/06/GSR_2016_Full_Report.pdf (last visited 15 July 2017).

[39] See Sherzod Shadikhodjaev, *First WTO Judicial Review of Climate Change Subsidy Issues*, 107 AM. J. INT'L L. 864 (2013).

[40] *Canada—Renewable Energy*; *Canada—Feed-In Tariff Program* (n. 30 above) paras. 5.170–5.178.

[41] *Ibid*. para. 5.188 (emphasis original).

the renewable energy sector. Perhaps for this reason, the United States did not invoke the SCM Agreement in the panel proceedings on the Jawaharlal Nehru National Solar Mission in *India—Solar Cells*, although it did so in its first consultation request when the Appellate Body ruling in *Canada—Renewable Energy / Canada—Feed-In Tariff Program* had not yet been issued.[42]

Absent any export promotion or localization elements, renewable energy programs can, in principle, avoid many WTO challenges. Trade frictions can also be avoided if such schemes are open to all eligible operators inside and outside of the 'subsidizing' country, as one may infer from the EU case law.[43] In *PreussenElectra*, the German scheme that required regional electricity distributors to purchase renewable electricity at fixed above-market prices was not applicable to imports of renewable electricity. In the *Ålands* case, Swedish green certificates, which could be sold to local suppliers and users who had a quota obligation for the purchase of renewable electricity, were not available to renewable electricity generators operating outside Sweden. The *Essent* case dealt with a similar scheme in Belgium. The Court of Justice of the European Union (CJEU) eventually rejected the claim that such territorial restrictions in question violated the EU's principle of free movement of goods, partially on the grounds that the electricity markets in the region had not yet fully merged.[44] But the Advocate General took the opposite view, saying that the limited access to national support schemes would contradict a key goal of the EU renewable energy policy to 'promote cross-border exchanges of green electricity'.[45] He also argued that trade in green electricity resulting from opening national support schemes to foreign electricity producers could contribute to the 'prudent and *rational* utilisation of natural resources' in line with the EU environmental policy, as it could facilitate the optimal distribution of production across the region.[46]

---

[42] The United States made its first and second consultation requests on 6 February 2013 and 10 February 2014, respectively, and a panel request on 14 April 2014. The Appellate Body issued its reports in *Canada—Renewable Energy*; *Canada—Feed-In Tariff Program* on 6 May 2013.

[43] This part on EU case law is drawn from Sherzod Shadikhodjaev, *Promotion of 'Green' Electricity and International Dispute Settlement: Trade and Investment Issues*, 49 INT'L L. 343, 352–6 (2016).

[44] C-573/12 *Ålands vindkraft AB* v. *Energimyndigheten* [2014] ECR I-000 (nyr), paras. 49–54, 94.

[45] C-573/12 *Ålands vindkraft AB* v. *Energimyndigheten*, Opinion of Advocate General Bot (2014), para. 87.

[46] *Ibid.* para. 109 (emphasis original).

The text of the SCM Agreement, on its face, fails to accommodate many climate change mitigation actions, including renewable energy subsidies. Thus, many commentators suggest that the subsidy rule book should be amended accordingly.[47] One possible approach here could be creation of a legislative temporary carve-out for green energy subsidies to the extent of each member's real needs. In other words, product-specific green subsidies would be permitted up to the scheduled caps, to be phased out over time as the subsidized product becomes competitive in the marketplace.[48] Otherwise, the Appellate Body's attempt in *Canada—Renewable Energy / Canada—Feed-In Tariff Program* to make the current rules more responsive to the current environmental challenges should arguably act as an encouraging signal to many national authorities in pursuing their climate policies.

Interested countries can agree to create a common renewable energy market with joint public stimulus programs. In this regard, a useful reference point could be the EU Renewable Energy Directive that foresees three mechanisms of cooperation among EU Member States (and with non-EU countries) to help them meet their renewable energy targets. Under 'statistical transfers', one member can purchase the statistical value of renewable energy produced in another member to reach its target, with no physical imports involved.[49] The cooperating members can also launch 'joint projects' to share renewable energy, notably green electricity, heating, or cooling. In the case of joint projects with third countries, renewable electricity produced there must be consumed inside the EU.[50] Finally, under 'joint support schemes' (common FIT programs, quota or certificate trading schemes, etc.) governments co-finance renewable energy production within their territories and the renewable energy generated in one participating member may count towards another participating member's national target via statistical transfers or pursuant to a predetermined distribution rule for the allocation of renewable energy amounts.[51] Since 2012, Sweden and Norway have had a common green certificate

---

[47] See e.g., Sherzod Shadikhodjaev, *Renewable Energy and Government Support: Time to 'Green' the SCM Agreement?*, 14 WORLD TRADE REV. 479 (2015); Aaron Cosbey and Petros C. Mavroidis, *A Turquoise Mess: Green Subsidies, Blue Industrial Policy and Renewable Energy: The Case for Redrafting the Subsidies Agreement of the WTO*, 17 J. INT'L ECON. L. 11 (2014); Luca Rubini, *Ain't Wastin' Time No More: Subsidies for Renewable Energy, the SCM Agreement, Policy Space, and Law Reform*, 15 J. INT'L ECON. L. 525 (2012).

[48] Shadikhodjaev (n. 47 above) 495–6.

[49] Directive 2009/28/EC, art. 6.

[50] *Ibid.* arts. 7–10.

[51] *Ibid.* art. 11.

support scheme in place, under which certificates for renewable electricity can be obtained and traded across the bilateral common market.[52]

International rules facilitating cross-border trade in renewable energy through, *inter alia*, harmonization of related support measures would maximize the benefits from clean energy in a more cost-efficient way.[53] Indeed, since production of solar energy in one country can be more expensive than in another country, while this can be vice versa in the case of wind power, bilateral trade could be a solution for both countries in nurturing their own comparative advantages in renewables while meeting their national greening targets. Moreover, cross-border exchanges of electricity may stimulate greater penetration of intermittent renewables to the energy-supply mix, as the cooperating countries will have more diversified access to electricity.[54]

Besides integrating renewables markets and related support programs, trade agreements including megaregionals can provide a platform for restricting fossil fuel subsidies. This issue failed to gain momentum at the WTO level in the past despite earlier calls from the G-20 and Asia-Pacific Economic Cooperation leaders.[55] Fossil fuel subsidies boost the production of 'dirty' energy, but their global amount exceeds that of renewable energy subsidies by several times.[56] The TPP provisions calling for elimination of agricultural export subsidies and prohibiting certain fisheries subsidies[57] should inspire governments to take similar actions against harmful fossil fuel subsidies. Intensive public support for renewables, on the one hand, and restriction of fossil fuel promotion, on the other, would increase the competitiveness of renewable energy in the world marketplace and make climate mitigation actions more efficient.

---

[52] International Energy Agency, Norway-Sweden Green Certificate Scheme for Electricity Production, available at www.iea.org/policiesandmeasures/pams/norway/name-21865-en.php (last visited 15 July 2017).

[53] For instance, an increased cooperation on renewable energy within the EU can lead to up to 6 percent lower support cost, 5 percent lower generation cost, and 3 percent less capital expenditure. See European Commission Staff Working Document, *Guidance on the Use of Renewable Energy Cooperation Mechanism*, SWD(2013)440 final, 3.

[54] See Heymi Bashar and Jehan Sauvage, *Cross-Border Trade in Electricity and the Development of Renewables-based Electric Power: Lessons from Europe* 7 (OECD Trade and Environment Working Papers, 2013/02, 2013).

[55] Shadikhodjaev (n. 47 above) 483.

[56] *Ibid.*

[57] See TPP, Arts. 2.21, 20.16(5).

V. GREEN POWER INFRASTRUCTURE

The internationalization of domestic electricity transmission lines enables cross-border movement of green electricity that, in the long run, may possibly occur via an inter-continental (or 'global') grid.[58] Electricity can be distributed only through fixed infrastructure (electrical grid) that has a more limited transportation capacity than vessels, airplanes, ships, or trains carrying other 'conventional' goods.

Trade in electricity necessitates the installation of interconnectors between national grids. For instance, the construction of the ASEAN regional power grid started with the implementation of bilateral interconnection projects to be followed by building of multilateral interconnections across the bloc in order to facilitate cross-border flows on a bilateral, sub-regional, and eventually a fully-integrated regional basis.[59] If one country supplies energy to another via the territory of a third country, two former countries will rely on the transit capacity of the latter. Therefore, it is suggested that trade agreements provide for (i) free access to in-country electricity-related infrastructure, and (ii) free transit where a transit country is a party to the same agreement.

With respect to the first issue above, the EU Renewable Energy Directive obliges Member States to provide priority or guaranteed access to the grid of electricity produced from renewable energy sources.[60] The EU FTAs with Singapore and Vietnam require that authorization, certification, and licensing procedures applicable to renewable energy-generating 'equipment, plants and associated transmission network infrastructures' should be objective, transparent, non-arbitrary, and non-discriminatory against the counterpart's applicants. In the same vein, electric grids must be accessible to the counterpart's suppliers on transparent and nondiscriminatory terms.[61]

As for the second issue, Article V of the GATT recognizes freedom of transit via 'most convenient' routes for 'goods (including baggage), and also vessels and other means of transport' involved in 'traffic in transit', subject to reasonable and non-discriminatory charges and regulations (if any). As interpreted by the panel in *Colombia—Ports of Entry*, freedom of transit implies 'unrestricted access via the most convenient routes for the passage of goods in international transit whether or not the goods have

---

[58] See Thomas Cottier, *Renewable Energy and WTO Law: More Policy Space or Enhanced Disciplines?*, 5 Renewable Energy L. & Pol'y Rev. 40, 48–9 (2014).

[59] See Zamora and ASEAN Member States (n. 9 above) 15–19.

[60] See Directive 2009/28/EC, art. 16.2.

[61] EU-Singapore FTA, Art. 7.4; EU-Vietnam FTA, Ch. 14, Art. 4.

been trans-shipped, warehoused, break-bulked, or have changed modes of transport'.[62] Article 11 of the Agreement on Trade Facilitation goes one step further in minimizing the use of restrictions (fiscal charges, formalities, etc.) on traffic in transit and detailing some applicable customs procedures. Neither of these WTO provisions on international transit makes reference to energy products and related transportation infrastructure as such, although some members put forward relevant proposals in the course of drafting of the trade facilitation rules.[63] Ukraine was the first country in the WTO—followed by Montenegro, Russia and Tajikistan—which made an explicit accession commitment to abide by Article V of the GATT and other relevant multilateral trade disciplines in application of an internal regime for transit of goods 'including energy'.[64]

Whereas the WTO provisions above are worded in a quite neutral way to accommodate energy transit in principle, some aspects of the current regulation are not clear enough. For example, it is questionable whether freedom of transit includes the right of the exporting country to build transit infrastructures for electricity (transmission lines or interconnections) in the territory of the transit country which itself does not possess transmitting capacity.[65] Given the uniqueness of energy transit through the fixed infrastructure, it would make sense to introduce tailor-made provisions in trade agreements. Perhaps a most relevant model for rule-making in this sphere would be the Energy Charter Treaty (1994), an international agreement among fifty-plus governments on trade and investment issues in the energy sector.[66] One of the most salient features of the energy transit regime there is that it addresses not only the existing transport infrastructure but also the possibility of expanding the transit capacity. According to Article 7(10) of the Energy Charter Treaty, 'energy transport facilities' necessary for energy transit refer to pipelines, 'high-voltage electricity transmission grids and lines', and 'other fixed facilities' for handling energy materials and products (i.e., nuclear energy, oil, gas, coal, and electrical energy). Article 7(2) states that the parties 'shall encourage

---

[62] Panel Report, *Colombia—Indicative Prices and Restrictions on Ports of Entry*, WTO Doc. WT/DS366/R (adopted 20 May 2009), para. 7.401.

[63] See e.g., Negotiating Group on Trade Facilitation, Communication from the Former Yugoslav Republic of Macedonia, Mongolia, Switzerland, and Swaziland–Revision, WTO Doc. TN/TF/W/133/Rev.3 (26 June 2009).

[64] Lee et al. (n. 2 above) 711.

[65] *Ibid.* at 709.

[66] For a detailed analysis of the Energy Charter Treaty provisions on energy transit and comparison with the GATT regime, see e.g., Lothar Ehring and Yulia Selivanova, *Energy Transit*, *in* REGULATION OF ENERGY IN INTERNATIONAL TRADE LAW: WTO, NAFTA AND ENERGY CHARTER 81–102 (Yulia Selivanova ed., 2011).

relevant entities' to cooperate in modernizing and developing the energy transport facilities, facilitating the interconnection of these facilities and mitigating the effects of interruptions in energy supply. Pursuant to Article 7(4)–(5) and the related understanding, a party cannot, in principle, object to the construction of new infrastructure for transit if its existing facilities are not sufficient, unless the valid legislation on environmental protection, land use, safety or technical standards would provide otherwise, or the construction would 'endanger the security or efficiency of its energy systems'. Article 7(7) establishes conciliation procedures for resolving disputes between the contracting parties over energy transit matters. Article 7(6) provides that, prior to the conclusion of such a dispute, a transit party cannot, as a rule, interrupt or reduce the existing transit flows.

Finally, since green electricity fed into the grid is blended with conventional electricity, there is a need for a mechanism that would verify the existence, type, and amount of the green power in the grid to check whether and to what extent national renewable energy targets are met. The European Commission in *PreussenElectra* stated that a system of certifying the green nature of electricity was essential in order to make trade in renewable electricity both reliable and possible in practice.[67] As a first step in this regard, trading countries can set up the EU-like regime for so-called 'guarantees of origin', an electronic document that proves to a final consumer that a given quantity of the purchased electricity (or heating/cooling) was produced from renewable sources. In *Essent*, the CJEU observed that guarantees of origin serve to prove the renewable sources of electricity, to facilitate trade in green electricity, and to increase transparency for the consumer's choice between green and conventional electricity.[68]

VI. TECHNICAL STANDARDS

According to the International Renewable Energy Agency's database (2013), there are at least 573 technical standards in the field of renewable energy, mostly developed by regional or global standard-making agencies, dealing with the product characteristics, performance, manufacturing, (pre)installation, testing, sustainability, and other aspects.[69] For instance,

---

[67] C-379/98 *PreussenElektra AG* v. *Schhleswag AG* [2001] ECR I-2099, para. 80.

[68] C-204/12 and C-208/12 *Essent Belgium NV* v. *Vlaamse Reguleringsinstantie voor de Elektriciteits-en Gasmarkt* [2014] ECR I-2192, para. 79.

[69] INTERNATIONAL RENEWABLE ENERGY AGENCY, INTERNATIONAL STANDARDISATION IN THE FIELD OF RENEWABLE ENERGY 36–9 (2013), available at

in order to receive government favors or count towards national renewable energy targets at the EU level, bioenergy (biofuels (used in transport) and bioliquids (used for electricity and heating or cooling)) must comply with the Renewable Energy Directive's 'sustainability criteria' of having GHG emission savings of at least 35 percent (or 60 percent from 2018 onwards) in comparison to fossil fuels and being made from raw materials obtained from sustainably managed lands. Companies can prove compliance with the sustainability criteria through national systems or voluntary schemes recognized by the European Commission.[70]

The Technical Barriers to Trade (TBT) Agreement allows mandatory 'technical regulations' or voluntary 'standards' to pursue certain legitimate policy objectives, such as e.g. protection of the environment through energy-efficiency labelling requirements or technical specifications for renewables. But overly burdensome or discriminatory TBT measures restrict international trade and may cause inter-state frictions. In 2012 and 2013, Argentina requested consultations with the EU with respect to its regulatory policy and some Member States' measures on biodiesels, alleging violations of nondiscrimination and TBT-related provisions, among other things.[71] Moreover, WTO members have frequently used the TBT Committee as a discussion forum for specific trade concerns in this field. In particular, Argentina, Indonesia, Malaysia, and the United States took issue with the EU over the above-mentioned regime for sustainable bioenergy, pointing to discrimination, lack of transparency or unnecessary barriers to trade and asking for more clarity on conformity assessment procedures and other aspects.[72] Allegations of trade-restrictiveness were also raised in relation to the US renewable fuel standards that affected palm-oil-derived biofuels from Indonesia and Malaysia.[73] Argentina, Mexico, and the EU questioned the validity of Colombia's regulation under which all gasoline-engine motor vehicles in the future must be flexible-fuel vehicles, with their engines being capable of using bioethanol.[74]

---

www.irena.org/DocumentDownloads/Publications/International_Standardisation_%20in_the_Field_of_Renewable_Energy.pdf. (last visited 15 July 2017).

[70] Directive 2009/28/EC, arts. 17–19.

[71] *European Union and a Member State—Certain Measures Concerning the Importation of Biodiesels*, WTO Doc. WT/DS443 (request for consultation received 17 August 2012); WTO Doc. WT/DS459/ (n. 30 above).

[72] See e.g., WTO Doc. G/TBT/M/54 (20 September 2011), paras. 67–73; WTO Doc. G/TBT/M/57 (18 September 2012), paras. 253–6.

[73] See e.g., Committee on Technical Barriers to Trade, Minutes of the Meeting of 30–31 October 2013, Chairperson: Mr. Jingo Kikukawa, Note by the Secretariat, WTO Doc. G/TBT/M/61 (5 February 2014), paras. 2.41–2.43.

[74] See e.g., Committee on Technical Barriers to Trade, Minutes of the Meeting

As for renewable energy-generating equipment, the United States raised its concern over Korea's standard for thin-film solar panels (KS 61646). The US representative argued that the Korean standard based on the international standard IEC 61646 accepted only one type of solar panels (amorphous silicon type thin-film solar panels) produced by local companies, while excluding other types of thin-film solar panels of foreign origin and thereby restricting market access, as the latter types could not be certified appropriately in Korea. But Korea responded that this was a voluntary standard with no market-closing effect and that it excluded other types of thin-film panels because they used some environment-threatening toxic substances. This issue has remained on the agenda for five years.[75]

With the increasing number of renewable energy standards, there is huge potential for regulatory misalignment across the globe. For example, the aforementioned EU minimum threshold for sustainable bioenergy GHG emission savings (35 percent) does not coincide with the respective level (20 percent) under the US Environmental Protection Agency's renewable fuel standard for biofuels.[76] The International Organization for Standardization (ISO) issued 'Sustainability Criteria for Bioenergy' (ISO 13065:2015) on 15 September 2015 which applies to all forms of bioenergy, irrespective of raw material, geographical location, technology or end use. But it does not establish any thresholds, nor does it describe specific bioenergy processes and production methods. The ISO states that compliance with ISO 13065:2015 does not determine the sustainability of processes or products.[77] Since this international standard was published very recently, it will take some time for national standards to adapt thereto accordingly.

---

of 18–19 March 2009, Note by the Secretariat, WTO Doc. G/TBT/M/47 (5 June 2009), paras. 79–80; Committee on Technical Barriers to Trade, Minutes of the Meeting of 15–16 June 2011, Note by the Secretariat, WTO Doc. G/TBT/M/54 (20 September 2011), paras. 187–90; Committee on Technical Barriers to Trade, Minutes of the Meeting of 20–21 March 2012, Note by the Secretariat, WTO Doc. G/TBT/M/56 (16 May 2012), paras. 72–3.

[75] See Committee on Technical Barriers to Trade, Minutes of the Meeting of 23–24 June 2010, Note by the Secretariat, WTO Doc. G/TBT/M/51 (1 October 2010), paras. 33–5; Committee on Technical Barriers to Trade, Minutes of the Meeting of 19–20 March 2014, Note by the Secretariat, WTO Doc. G/TBT/M/62 (20 May 2014), paras. 2.89–2.90.

[76] For the US standard in question, see e.g., WTO Doc. G/TBT/M/61, para. 2.41.

[77] See ISO, ISO 13065:2015, Sustainability Criteria for Bioenergy, available at www.iso.org/iso/home/store/catalogue_tc/catalogue_detail.htm?csnumber=52528 (last visited 15 July 2017).

Chapter 8 of the TPP contains horizontal provisions on TBT measures as well as specific provisions tailored to particular products, such as wine, pharmaceuticals, medical devices, prepackaged foods, organic products, and others. The same approach can be followed for renewable energy products to address at least four issues below.

First, many voluntary standards may act as *de facto* market restrictions, but the TBT Agreement has certain constraints in capturing all standards. In particular, compared to local governments and non-governmental bodies' standards, the TBT Agreement imposes a stronger obligation on WTO members to ensure the acceptance of the Code of Good Practice for voluntary standards developed by 'central government' standardizing bodies. But this obligation should arguably be extended to local governments with respect to all or at least renewable energy standards. In the RTA context, the parties may identify some regulatory non-mandatory schemes on renewable energy that they commit to bringing into compliance with the Code of Good Practice.

Second, the WTO principles of harmonization, equivalence, and (mutual) recognition of conformity assessment results can be strengthened at a regional level. The EU FTAs with Singapore and Vietnam require that the parties base their technical measures in the field of renewable energy generation on related international standards, notably those set by the ISO and the International Electrotechnical Commission.[78] In addition, the EU and Singapore agreed to mutually recognize compliance testing results for virtually all goods in HS Chapter 84 (boilers, steam turbines and other machinery and mechanical appliances, electrical equipment, etc.), solar panels and wind-powered generators.[79]

Third, since renewable energy used in the manufacturing is not detectable in a final product, it constitutes non-product-related process and production method which some consider as being outside of the TBT Agreement disciplines.[80] But the number of environmentally conscious consumers is steadily increasing. As 2010 and 2011 surveys reveal, 80 percent of consumers view renewable energy favorably and 65 percent of consumers worldwide prefer products made with wind power.[81] This suggests that

---

[78] EU-Singapore FTA, Art. 7.5.1; EU-Vietnam FTA, Ch. 14, Art. 5.2.

[79] EU-Singapore FTA, Art. 7.5.3.

[80] For a review of this issue, see e.g., Christiane R. Conrad, Processes and Production Methods (PPMs) in WTO Law: Interfacing Trade and Social Goals 376–81 (2011).

[81] Deborah Baker Brannan et al., *Made with Renewable Energy: How and Why Companies are Labelling Consumer Products* 1 (National Renewable Energy Laboratory Technical Report, NREL/TP-6A20-53764, 2012).

green energy labeling programmes (e.g. Green-e Marketplace, Windmade, RenewablePLUS, etc.) that affect marketability of related products need to be addressed more properly. Therefore, the time is ripe for legislative reforms in the TBT area to accommodate such programs as well.

Fourth, discrepancies in the standard-setting on renewable energy can be reconciled through enhanced cooperation between national regulators. The TTIP negotiations intend to insert a discrete Chapter on regulatory cooperation with a view to making EU and US standards more compatible with each other. The anticipated Chapter will address both horizontal and sectoral cooperation to identify shared principles and best practices, reduce unnecessary duplication of regulatory requirements in particular sectors, and set an agenda for future work.[82] Alternatively, a higher-level regulatory cooperation can follow Australia and New Zealand's approach in relation to food stuff. As the parties to the Closer Economic Relations Trade Agreement, they operate a bi-national government agency to develop and administer unified food standards.[83] Common standards created at a regional level could eventually be 'multilateralized', i.e., spread across the web of RTAs and/or inserted into the international standardization process at the global level.

VII. RENEWABLE ENERGY SERVICES

Neither the WTO's services classification system W/120 nor the related CPC provisional system makes an explicit reference to renewable energy services as such.[84] Energy services identifiable in W/120—services incidental to mining (CPC 883+5115), services incidental to energy distribution (CPC 887), and transportation of fuels (CPC 7131)—fall short of mentioning renewables. Environmental services (CPC 9401-9403 including sewage services, refuse disposal services, sanitation services and 'other') do not appear to accommodate renewable energy either.

Apart from the absence of a recognized classification for renewable energy

---

82 See European Commission, TTIP and Regulation: An Overview (2015), available at http://trade.ec.europa.eu/doclib/docs/2015/february/tradoc_153121.pdf (last visited 15 July 2017).

83 See Food Standards Australia and New Zealand, available at www.foodstandards.gov.au/Pages/default.aspx (last visited 15 July 2017).

84 See Services Sectoral Classification List, WTO Doc. MTN.GNS/W/120 (10 July 1991); United Nations Statistics Division, *Provisional Central Product Classification*, available at http://unstats.un.org/unsd/CR/Registry/regcst.asp?Cl=9&Lg=1 (last visited 15 July 2017).

services, there are two more scoping problems. First, some renewables- or climate-related services cut across several W/120 sectors. For instance, smart grid services comprise some elements of telecommunication services, computer services, and services incidental to energy distribution.[85] A smart grid is 'an electricity network that uses digital and other advanced technologies to monitor and manage the transport of electricity from all generation sources to meet the varying electricity demands of end-users'. It enables integration of variable renewable energy resources into the electricity system.[86] Another example is carbon capture and storage (capturing CO_2 before it is emitted and storing it in geological sinks on a long-term basis) which also involves business, transport, and other services. Some argue that it constitutes a new service not covered by the W/120 regime.[87] But the development of novel technologies diversifying or updating the ways of supply of already existing services will not automatically imply the emergence of a new type of service. Indeed, the panel in *US—Gambling* held that mode 1 under the GATS encompasses 'all possible means of supplying services' in line with the principle of 'technological neutrality' that 'seems to be largely shared among WTO Members'.[88]

Second, many existing services involved in generation of clean energy can be extended to other sectors as well, raising a so-called 'dual use' problem. Pursuant to the US International Trade Commission, renewable energy services embrace services related to generation, transmission, distribution, and sale of green electricity and/or heat.[89] These also cover some services not confined to renewables, such as planning, design, and

---

[85] UN Department of Economic and Social Affairs, *New Issues Requiring Guidance in the Central Product Classification (CPC)*, UN Doc. ESA/STAT/AC.289/20 (Meeting of the Expert Group on International Statistical Classifications, 2015), para. 1.21, citing WTO, Committee on Specific Commitments, Energy Services, Overview of Classification Issues, Informal Note by the Secretariat, WTO Doc. JOB/SERV/94 (5 March 2012), para. 22.

[86] International Energy Agency, Technology Roadmap: Smart Grids 5–6 (2011), available at www.iea.org/publications/freepublications/publication/smartgrids_roadmap.pdf (last visited 15 July 2017).

[87] UN Department of Economic and Social Affairs (n. 85 above) para. 1.17, citing WTO, Committee on Specific Commitments, Environmental Services Overview of Classification Issues, Informal Note by the Secretariat, WTO Doc. JOB/SERV/84 (31 August 2011), paras. 27–8 and WTO Doc. JOB/SERV/94, para. 21.

[88] Panel Report, *United States—Measures Affecting the Cross-Border Supply of Gambling and Betting Services* ('*US–Gambling*'), WTO Doc. WT/DS285/R (adopted 20 April 2005), para. 6.285.

[89] USITC, *Renewable Energy and Related Services: Recent Developments*, USITC Pub. 4421, Inv. No. 332-534, para. 2-12 (August 2013).

engineering, construction, maintenance, and financial services that may be provided throughout the entire lifecycle of a renewable energy project.[90] Consultancy, research and development, legal services related to green energy can also be added to such dual-use services.

It follows that market openings for renewable energy services would affect many sectors, which may discourage countries from assuming specific commitments. Where trade liberalization is not possible for all activities in such services (banking, construction, etc.), negotiating parties could limit their commitments to activities associated with renewables only. This is quite possible as some GATS schedules occasionally contain sectoral headnotes or footnotes that limit the scope of services under committed sub-sectors.[91]

Typical examples of trade barriers to renewable energy services and suppliers include LCRs (e.g. use of local labour); investment restrictions (prescribed forms of legal entities, ownership restrictions, foreign equity limits or economic needs tests); technology transfer obligations; limitations on temporary movement of foreign workers-suppliers; cumbersome and non-transparent project approval or licensing procedures.[92] Some restrictions in the goods sector affect services as well. For instance, an LCR on equipment may act as a market barrier to foreign services, as many wind or solar power equipment producers supply services together with their technologies. Similarly, TBT measures on green equipment can restrict market access of associated foreign services.[93] Therefore, for the sake of effective trade liberalization in the renewable energy sector, negotiations on improving market access should cover both goods and services, and address tariff issues as well as regulatory restrictions.[94]

VIII. CONCLUDING REMARKS

While big economic blocs such as the EU and ASEAN pursue a common renewable energy policy, neither WTO law nor the majority of RTAs

---

90 See also Joachim Monkelbaan, *Trade in Sustainable Energy Services* 10–28 (International Centre for Trade and Sustainable Development Working Paper, 2013).

91 For the case of environmental services, see Council for Trade in Services, Background Note on Environmental Services, Note by the Secretariat, WTO Doc. S/C/W/320 (20 August 2010), paras. 90–91.

92 See USITC (n. 89 above) paras. 2-21–2-22, 4-26.

93 *Ibid.* paras. 2-22, 3-25–3-26, 4-25.

94 See also Monkelbaan (n. 90 above) 4.

contain renewables-specific provisions. This represents regulatory convergence and divergence as regards the subject matter of this chapter. Since renewable energy will only grow in importance in the future, the time is ripe for meaningful legislative reforms at both multilateral and regional levels to make the international trading system more responsive to the needs and challenges arising throughout the entire chain of greening activities. In particular, the WTO should work towards adopting a separate renewable energy agreement or otherwise renewables-dedicated provisions under existing agreements. By the same token, RTAs should include a relevant discrete Chapter (section) or provisions across existing Chapters. A sector-based regulatory approach is not new to the multilateral and regional trade practice,[95] so the establishment of a tailor-made regime will help handle generation, distribution, consumption, and cross-border supply of renewable energy more appropriately. It is hoped that the issues reviewed in this chapter will become potential areas for consideration in designing such rules in the future.

---

[95] In the WTO system, such sectoral agreements have dealt with agriculture, textiles and clothing, information technology, civil aircraft, among other things.

9. The promotion of renewable electricity technology in the mega-RTA era: A preliminary evaluation of the potential effects on regulatory convergence or divergence

Anton Ming-Zhi Gao

I. INTRODUCTION

Recent extreme weather and disasters have raised awareness regarding the serious issue of climate change.[1] As a response to these challenges, the international legal regime of the United Nations Framework Convention on Climate Change (UNFCCC) was initiated and put into force on 21 March 1994.[2] The famous Kyoto Protocol of 1997[3] and the recent Paris Agreement of 2015[4] can be viewed as continuing and enduring support from the international community on this important issue. The attainment of low-carbon energy, especially in renewable electricity (RE), is a key mitigation and adaptation goal under the UNFCCC and is therefore

[1] See, e.g., SCIENTIFIC AMERICAN EDITORS, STORM WARNINGS: CLIMATE CHANGE AND EXTREME WEATHER (2012); DAVID A. RELMAN ET AL., GLOBAL CLIMATE CHANGE AND EXTREME WEATHER EVENTS: UNDERSTANDING THE CONTRIBUTIONS TO INFECTIOUS DISEASE EMERGENCE: WORKSHOP SUMMARY (2008).

[2] United Nations Framework Convention on Climate Change (UNFCCC), *Paris Agreement, Status of Ratification*, available at http://unfccc.int/2860.php (last visited 18 August 2017); UNFCCC, *First Steps to a Safer Future: Introducing the United Nations Framework Convention on Climate Change*, available at http://unfccc.int/essential_background/convention/items/6036.php (last visited 18 August 2017).

[3] UNFCCC, Kyoto Protocol, available at http://unfccc.int/kyoto_protocol/items/2830.php (last visited 18 August 2017).

[4] UNFCCC, The Paris Agreement, available at http://unfccc.int/paris_agreement/items/9485.php (last visited 18 August 2017).

central to the implementation of the Paris Agreement.[5] Following recent developments in Germany and France, an energy transition from traditional electricity to an RE-based supply system has become the central theme of climate change and energy policy.[6]

In general, policies to promote RE have produced uncoordinated and frequently high-cost measures. Large subsidies are usually necessary to give impetus to RE development[7] and are considered valuable and necessary instruments to facilitate the climate change mitigation work of the UNFCCC. However, such a subsidy-thirsty regime may threaten the important world order of international economic law (IEL) and trade law. Recent cases brought before the World Trade Organization (WTO) concerning green-power industrial policies have signaled a paradigm shift in the conflict between trade and the environment.[8] How to strike a balance between the international climate law regime and IEL will become more and more important in the future. The current IEL approach to RE subsidy, including the relevant provisions of the General Agreement on Tariffs and Trade (GATT), the Agreement on Subsidies and Countervailing Measures (SCM) and the General Agreement on Trade in Services (GATS), cannot effectively address issues regarding trade in energy or renewable energy. Thus, an alternative approach to facilitating the integration of RE in the broader context of IEL has been heavily discussed recently. Countries are increasingly making use of regional trade agreements (RTAs) to advance environmental and climate objectives.[9]

---

5 ORGANISATION FOR ECONOMIC CO-OPERATION AND DEVELOPMENT (OECD), OECD BUSINESS AND FINANCE OUTLOOK 2016 143 (2016).

6 Miranda A. Schreurs, *The German Energiewende in a European Context*, *in* GERMANY'S ENERGY TRANSITION: A COMPARATIVE PERSPECTIVE 102 (Carol Hager and Christoph H. Stefes eds., 2016); Hans Günter Brauch and Ursula Oswald Spring, *Sustainability Transition and Sustainable Peace: Scientific and Policy Context, Scientific Concepts and Dimensions*, *in* HANDBOOK ON SUSTAINABILITY TRANSITION AND SUSTAINABLE PEACE 41 (Hans Günter Brauch et al. eds., 2016).

7 OECD, SUSTAINABLE DEVELOPMENT: CRITICAL ISSUES 197 (2001).

8 See Yifan Zhou, *The WTO Appellate Body's Subsidy Analysis in Canada-Renewable Energy / FIT*, U. PA. J. INT'L L. (August 2016), available at http://pennjil.com/the-wto-appellate-bodys-subsidy-analysis-in-canada-renewable-energy-fit/ (last visited 18 August 2017). See also Mark Wu and James Salzman, *The Next Generation of Trade and Environment Disputes: The Rise of Green Industrial Policy*, 108 NW. U. L. REV. 401 (2014).

9 Markus W. Gehring et al., *Climate Change and Sustainable Energy Measures in Regional Trade Agreements (RTAs): An Overview* 6 (ICTSD Programme on Global Economic Policy and Institutions Issue Paper No. 3, August 2013), available at www.ictsd.org/downloads/2013/08/climate-change-and-sustainable-energy-measures-in-regional-trade-agreements-rtas.pdf (last visited 18 August 2017).

One way in which an RTA can be better than a multilateral IEL is that countries striving to include sustainable development in all of their policies will find greater success pursuing it through RTAs rather than multilaterally.[10] The wind is also blowing in favor of the recent mega-RTAs, such as the Transatlantic Trade and Investment Partnership (TTIP)[11] and the Trans-Pacific Partnership (TPP).[12] The inclusion of an Environmental Chapter in the TPP and the emphasis on 'sustainable development' and 'energy and raw materials' in the TTIP can be regarded as a sign to consider and advance the role of renewable energy.

The primary purpose of this chapter is to answer the core question: Can an RTA, particularly a mega-RTA, contribute to RE development? If the answer is 'yes', the question then becomes, in what manner? Can it reduce tariffs or non-tariff barriers? This chapter also analyzes the dynamic interaction between the IEL/RTA system and the regulatory regime of RE, where the regulatory regime involves incentives for and the regulation of RE development. The second research question is: How are regulatory divergence and convergence affected by the IEL/RTA system?

II. PROMOTION OF RENEWABLE ELECTRICITY TECHNOLOGY UNDER THE IEL REGIME: TRADE REMEDIES

1. Anti-subsidy and Local Content Requirement

Generally, the primary purpose of IEL is to facilitate the development of trade.[13] The promotion of RE is not necessary to its agenda. On the issue of the relationship between IEL versus environmental protection/ sustainable energy/climate change, the exception clauses of Article XX(b)

---

[10] Ministry for the Environment, *Free Trade and Environmental Cooperation Agreements*, available at www.mfe.govt.nz/more/international-environmental-agreements/free-trade-and-environmental-cooperation-agreements (last visited 18 August 2017); Rafael Leal-Arcas, *Mega-regionals and Sustainable Development: The Transatlantic Trade and Investment Partnership and the Trans-Pacific Partnership*, 4 Renewable Energy L. & Pol'y Rev. 248, 254 (2015).

[11] European Commission, *In Focus: The Transatlantic Trade Investment Partnership*, available at http://ec.europa.eu/trade/policy/in-focus/ttip/.

[12] US Trade Representative (USTR), The Trans-Pacific Partnership, available at https://ustr.gov/tpp/ (last visited 18 August 2017).

[13] Teresa Gramm, *The Development of Trade Institutions and the Advent of Globalization, in* Routledge Handbook of Major Events in Economic History 354 (Randall E. Parker and Robert M. Whaples eds., 2013).

and (g) of the GATT are the provisions most often cited.[14] For a trade-related environmental measure to be eligible for an exception under Article XX(b) or (g), a member must establish a connection between its stated environmental policy goal and the measure at issue. The measure must be either:[15]

- necessary for the protection of human, animal or plant life or health (paragraph (b)); or
- related to the conservation of exhaustible natural resources (paragraph (g)).

Regarding RE, the main justifying reasons concern 'the conservation of exhaustible natural resources'.[16] In addition, a time-limited environmental exception clause was provided in the SCM Agreement. Environmental subsidies that met the requirements in the SCM were non-actionable.[17] However, as of 1 January 2000, the provision on such non-actionable subsidies and the exemption expired because WTO members decided not to extend it. Finally, the Agreement on Trade-Related Investment Measures ('TRIMS Agreement') is also relevant to subsidies for RE.[18]

2. Anti-dumping

Apart from such an anti-subsidy (AS) regime and its exceptions, local content requirement (LCR), anti-dumping (AD) usually coincides with the AS regime. AD measures are covered by Article VI of the GATT and the Agreement on the Implementation of Article VI of the GATT ('AD Agreement'). These agreements permit a WTO member to implement AD measures if imported products have been 'dumped' onto its market,

---

[14] See, e.g., BRADLY J. CONDON AND TAPEN SINHA, THE ROLE OF CLIMATE CHANGE IN GLOBAL ECONOMIC GOVERNANCE 61 (2013); Martijn Wilder Am and Lauren Drake, *International Law and the Renewable Energy Sector*, *in* THE OXFORD HANDBOOK OF INTERNATIONAL CLIMATE CHANGE LAW 372 (Kevin R. Gray et al. eds., 2016).

[15] WTO, *WTO Rules and Environmental Policies: GATT Exceptions*, available at www.wto.org/english/tratop_e/envir_e/envt_rules_exceptions_e.htm.

[16] Rolf H. Weber, *Renewable Energy: Subsidies and Taxes as Competition Distortion*, *in* ENVIRONMENTAL PRICING: STUDIES IN POLICY CHOICES AND INTERACTIONS 170 (Larry Kreiser et al. eds., 2015).

[17] CONDON AND SINHA (n. 14 above) 63.

[18] Debra P. Steger, *International Trade and Investment: Towards a Common Regime?*, *in* PROSPECTS IN INTERNATIONAL INVESTMENT LAW AND POLICY: WORLD TRADE FORUM 160 (Roberto Echandi and Pierre Sauvé eds., 2013).

causing material injury, or the threat thereof, to the domestic industry that produces like products.[19]

3. Practice

What does the implementation of these regimes look like in reality? Table 9.1[20] shows related AD and AS cases in recent years, up to July 2015.

III. RTAS AND RE: RTAS AS A WAY OUT?

While the mandate has clear implications for climate change, progress in negotiations to date has been limited, even in the liberalization of environmental goods and services (EG&S).[21] The WTO Doha Round mandate includes negotiations on EG&S liberalization, calling in paragraph 31(iii) for the 'reduction or, as appropriate, elimination of tariff and non-tariff barriers to environmental goods and services'.[22]

Despite this directive, the negotiations appear to be stalled precisely over the method of classification of EG&S for the purpose of liberalization. A great deal has been written about how to classify environmental goods and services. The fact that the negotiations are stalled on this matter is unfortunate.[23]

Nonetheless, the further development of RTAs and free trade agreements (FTAs) seems to be shedding some light on the development of EG&S provisions, climate change measures, sustainable development, and RE.

---

19 Am and Drake (n. 14 above) 371.

20 Among all twenty-five cases in this table, eighteen relate to photovoltaic (PV) systems, while sixteen and seven cases are relevant to biofuel and wind power, respectively. Interestingly, these cases have been brought within the previous ten years. If focusing on RE, then most of the cases occurred within the past five years. Perhaps these trends are relevant to the intensive measures to promote RE after the effective date of the Kyoto Protocol in 2005 and the 2010/2020 RE or emission reduction policy targets in many countries.

21 ICTSD, *Capping Unusually High Tariffs: The WTO Doha Round and 'Tariff Peaks'* (Information Note No. 9, November 2009), available at www.ictsd.org/downloads/2011/12/capping-unusually-high-tariffs-the-wto-doha-round-and-tariff-peaks.pdf (last visited 18 August 2017); David Laborde, *Looking for a Meaningful Duty Free Quota Free Market Access Initiative in the Doha Development Agenda* (ICTSD Programme on Global Economic Policy and Institutions Issue Paper No. 4, December 2008), available at www.ictsd.org/downloads/2009/01/labrodeweb.pdf (last visited 18 August 2017).

22 WTO, Ministerial Declaration Adopted on 14 November 2001, WTO Doc. WT/MIN(01)/DEC/1, 41 ILM 746 (2002).

23 Gary P. Sampson, The WTO and Sustainable Development 64 (2005).

Table 9.1 Trade remedies on clean energy

Product	Country	Trade remedy	Initiation of investigation	Year since trade remedy measures
EU				
Biodiesel	United States	AD+AS	2008	2009
	Canada	AD+AS	2010	2011
	Singapore	~~AD+AS~~	2010	–
	Argentina	AD+~~AS~~	2012	2013
	Indonesia	AD+AS	2012	2013
Bioethanol	United States	AD+~~AS~~	2011	2013
Glass fibres	China	AD	2009	2010
Solar panels	China	~~AD+AS~~	2012	Resolved through price undertaking agreement in 2013. Non-participating producers/exporters in agreement still facing duties.
Solar glass		AD+AS	2013	2013
Peru				
Biodiesel	United States	AD	2013	
Australia				
Biodiesel	United States	AD+AS	2009	2010
Wind towers	China and Korea	AD	2010	2014
Solar modules/ panels	China	AD	2013	
United States (2014)				
Wind towers	China	AD+AS	2011	2012
Wind towers	Vietnam	AD+AS	2011	2012
Solar panels	China	AD+–AS	2011	2012
Solar panels	China and Chinese Taipei	AD	2014	2014
Solar panels	China	AS	2014	2014
Canada				
Solar photovoltaic (PV) modules and laminates	China	AD+AS	2014	[2015]
China				
Polysilicon	United States	AD+AS	2012	2013
	EU	AD+AS	2012	2014
	South Korea	AD+AS	2012	2013

Table 9.1 (continued)

Product	Country	Trade remedy	Initiation of investigation	Year since trade remedy measures
India				
Solar cells/ modules	China	AD	2012	–
	United States	AD	2012	–
	Malaysia	AD	2012	–
	Taiwan	AD	2012	–

Sources: JONAS KASTENG AND CAMILLA PRAWITZ, ELIMINATING ANTI-DUMPING MEASURES IN REGIONAL TRADE AGREEMENTS: THE EUROPEAN UNION EXAMPLE (2013); Ricardo Meléndez-Ortiz, *Enabling the Energy Transition and Scale-up of Clean Energy Technologies: Options for the Global Trade System* 13 (E15 Expert Group on Clean Energy Technologies and the Trade System Policy Option Paper, January 2016).

1. Asia-Pacific Economic Cooperation (APEC) List of Environmental Goods

As a result of such deadlocks, there is a trend toward a regional approach. The APEC Environmental Goods Agreement and the APEC List of Environmental Goods ('APEC List') are considered to represent vital regional initiatives. At the APEC Summit in Vladivostok in 2012, the APEC economies agreed on a list of fifty-four environmental goods on which they would cut tariffs to 5 percent or less by the end of 2015.[24] Of all fifty-four environmental goods, the renewable energy category has the greatest number (seventeen) on the list.[25]

2. Environmental Goods Agreement

Since July 2014, the EU and other members of the WTO (named below) have been negotiating the Environmental Goods Agreement (EGA) to remove barriers to trade in environmental or 'green' goods that are crucial for environmental protection and climate change mitigation.[26] So far,

24 Joshua P. Meltzer, *The Trans-Pacific Partnership Agreement, the Environment and Climate Change*, *in* TRADE LIBERALISATION AND INTERNATIONAL CO-OPERATION: A LEGAL ANALYSIS OF THE TRANS-PACIFIC PARTNERSHIP AGREEMENT 221 (Tania Voon ed., 2013).

25 See www.ictsd.org/sites/default/files/news/2012/11/apec-figure01.jpg (last visited 18 August 2017).

26 European Commission, *The Environmental Goods Agreement (EGA):*

seventeen WTO members are involved.[27] The purpose of the EGA is to enhance trade in environmental goods and technologies contributing to environmental protection, and in particular to combat climate change and to accelerate the uptake of environmental technologies.[28] This would include RE technologies. There have been sixteen rounds of negotiations since July 2014, with the latest round taking place in October 2016.[29] This agreement builds on APEC's Early Voluntary Sectoral Liberalization initiative and, specifically, APEC's 2012 agreement to reduce applied tariffs on fifty-four environmental goods to a maximum of 5 percent by the end of 2015. In terms of RE, the EU actively supports the reduction and/or elimination of barriers to RE-related goods, services, and technologies, both in its RTAs and in the context of multilateral and plurilateral trade negotiations.[30]

3. A Wide Range of other RTAs and FTAs

(1) Renewable energy RTAs and FTAs concluded by the EU

One study also investigated the role of renewable energy in the EU's thirty-seven signed FTAs and twelve planned FTAs.[31] Regarding the relationships of these RTAs/FTAs to renewable energy, the results are not very promising:[32]

Liberalising Trade in Environmental Goods and Services, available at http://trade.ec.europa.eu/doclib/press/index.cfm?id=1116 (last visited 18 August 2017).

[27] Claudia Weiss, Environmental Goods Agreement (EGA), the Technology-Trade Nexus: A Key Enabling Force for Achieving the SDGs (2016), available at http://staging.unep.org/energy/Portals/50177/documents/Session%203%20-%20Claudia%20Weiss.pdf (last visited 18 August 2017).

[28] *Ibid.*

[29] European Commission, Environmental Goods Agreement: Report from the 16th Round of Negotiations, available at http://trade.ec.europa.eu/doclib/docs/2016/october/tradoc_154996.pdf (last visited 18 August 2017).

[30] Rafael Leal-Arcas et al., *Renewables, Preferential Trade Agreements and EU Energy Security*, *in* Energy Security, Trade and the EU: Regional and International Perspectives 321 (Rafael Leal-Arcas et al. eds., 2016).

[31] The twelve that are planned are: (1) Comprehensive Economic and Trade Agreement (CETA); (2) EU-East African Community (EAC) Economic Partnership Agreement (EPA); (3) EU-India Preferential Trade Agreement (PTA); (4) EU-Japan PTA; (5) EU-Malaysia PTA; (6) EU-Morocco PTA; (7) EU-Southern African Development Community (SADC) EPA; (8) EU-Singapore PTA; (9) EU-Thailand PTA; (10) TTIP; (11) EU-Vietnam PTA; and (12) EU-West Africa EPA. See Rafael Leal-Arcas et al., *Renewables, Preferential Trade Agreements and EU Energy Security*, 4(3) Laws 472, 482 (2015).

[32] *Ibid.* at 505.

- fifteen of the RTAs do not provide for any renewable energy-related provisions;
- twenty-two of the RTAs include renewable energy-related provisions, even though only three of them contain legally enforceable obligations, whereas the remaining nineteen EU RTAs provide for general and unenforceable commitments; and
- the only legally enforceable renewable energy-related provisions found in EU RTAs are those of the EU's Renewable Energy Directive (2009/28/EC) (RED), as three of the RTAs expressly require parties to implement the RED (namely, the Agreement on the European Economic Area ('EEA Agreement'),[33] the EU-Moldova RTA,[34] and the EU-Georgia RTA).[35]

To summarize, despite the EU's active role in trying to push forward the renewable energy agenda in these RTAs/FTAs, these agreements seem to be primarily soft law in a sense that the relevant commitments are general and unenforceable. The only legally binding instrument, the RED, seems to be associated with access to the EU market from non-EU countries. Thus, this special EU situation is not applicable to the rest of the world. This means that the role of renewable electricity in the EU, a much narrower version of renewable energy, is inapplicable as well.

(2) RTAs and FTAs on environment, climate change, and sustainable development around the world

Apart from the lessons of the EU, the ICTSD Report of August 2013[36] examined RTAs and FTAs around the world to extract their ideas on the related subjects of environment, climate change, and sustainable development.

To summarize the findings from this report, there are three main points, including:

---

[33] *Ibid.*

[34] *Ibid.*

[35] *Ibid.*

[36] Markus W. Gehring et al., *Climate Change and Sustainable Energy Measures in Regional Trade Agreements (RTAs): An Overview*, International Centre for Trade and Sustainable Development (ICTSD), ICTSD Programme on Global Economic Policy and Institutions, Issue Paper No. 3 (August 2013) at 6, available at www.ictsd.org/downloads/2013/08/climate-change-and-sustainable-energy-measures-in-regional-trade-agreements-rtas.pdf.

- Not an explicit concept: the promotion of RE is usually subject to the broader concept of environment, sustainable development, or low carbon/climate change. There is usually no independent role of RE in these RTAs. Only on rare occasions do the RTAs even mention the term 'renewable energy'.[37]
- Not specific: the articles relating to renewable energy are usually not very specific in nature. Usually they refer to abstract principles (investment, trade, environment) or measures (law, finance). This also indicates that the actions in the EGA and the APEC List could be more specific.[38]
- Soft measures: the measures to implement renewable energy are primarily soft measures, such as technology promotion in the Guatemala-Taiwan FTA,[39] or cooperation.[40]

4. Would Mega-RTAs Do Better?

As noted in section I, countries are increasingly making use of RTAs to advance environmental and climate objectives.[41] But does this really provide a specific role for RE? From the findings noted, it seems that the role of RE is relatively clearer in 'tariff-based' RTAs, including the EGA and the APEC List, than in other RTAs. We now move on to analyze the role of RE in the recently created mega-RTAs.

(1) Trans-Pacific Partnership

The TPP is a free trade agreement concluded amongst twelve Asia-Pacific nations.[42] The negotiation was concluded on 5 October 2015, after several years of secretive negotiations.[43]

The goal of the TPP is to create a platform for economic integration across the Asia-Pacific region. The aim is to establish a foundation for economic growth for the development and creation of employment in the member countries.[44] The TPP includes an Environmental Chapter that

---

37 *Ibid.*

38 *Ibid.*

39 *Ibid.*

40 *Ibid.*

41 Gehring et al. (n. 9 above) 6.

42 Note that the United States has withdrawn from the TPP.

43 USTR, *Summary of the Trans-Pacific Partnership Agreement*, available at https://ustr.gov/about-us/policy-offices/press-office/press-releases/2015/october/summary-trans-pacific-partnership (last visited 18 August 2017).

44 Organization of American States (OAS), Trans Pacific Partnership Agreement (TPP): Australia, Brunei Darussalam, Canada, Chile, Japan, Malaysia, Mexico,

requires the commitment by all parties to be involved in the trades of environmental goods or services.

The Environmental Chapter of the TPP consists of twenty-three articles that address different environmental issues. Various articles deal with environment, trade, and sustainable development.[45] Yet the TPP's Environmental Chapter demonstrates a lack of clarity about the environment and sustainability. While the Chapter touches upon crucial areas of environmental protection that may pave the way for future talks, it does not inspire.[46]

There is only one Article explicitly mentioning 'renewable energy' in Article 20.15, which provides as follows:

> Transition to a Low Emissions and Resilient Economy
> 1. The Parties acknowledge that transition to a low emissions economy requires collective action.
> 2. . . . Areas of cooperation may include, but are not limited to: . . . clean and renewable energy sources; . . . Further, the Parties shall, as appropriate, engage in cooperative and capacity-building activities related to transitioning to a low emissions economy.

From this Article, we can see the supplementary nature of renewable energy in climate change/sustainable development. Also, there is no further specific role for RE. Finally, the nature of the provision is rather soft, even though the TPP does include a section on 'Transition to a Low Emissions and Resilient Economy'.[47]

(2) Transatlantic Trade and Investment Partnership

The TTIP aims to further economic growth, investment, and trade between the EU and the United States by reducing or eliminating tariffs and by removing 'behind the border' technical barriers to export.[48] The EU has released initial position papers on several topical areas of the TTIP. Among such papers, the most relevant for the purposes of this

---

New Zealand, Peru, Singapore, the United States, and Vietnam, available at www.sice.oas.org/TPD/TPP/TPP_e.ASP (last visited 18 August 2017).

[45] Leal-Arcas (n. 10 above) 257.

[46] *Ibid.* at 263.

[47] Ricardo Meléndez-Ortiz, *Enabling the Energy Transition and Scale-up of Clean Energy Technologies: Options for the Global Trade System* 20 (E15 Expert Group on Clean Energy Technologies and the Trade System Policy Option Paper, January 2016).

[48] Leal-Arcas (n. 10 above) 250; European Commission, *About TTIP*, available at http://trade.ec.europa.eu/trade/policy/in-focus/ttip/about-ttip/.

chapter are those relating trade to 'sustainable development' and to 'raw materials and energy'.[49]

Even if the TTIP could represent a new paradigm for the energy issue as a whole, it is relatively uncertain with regard to the disputed role of renewable energy.[50] According to the literature, this is a very important negotiation issue on the EU side.[51] The most likely Chapter to mention the role of renewable energy would be a Chapter on sustainable development or 'energy and raw materials'. To date, however, the role of renewable energy is only mentioned briefly in the position paper on sustainable development, and it is missing from the documents on the latter topic.[52]

It is unclear what will be the final form of the provision in the TTIP. One way in which the TTIP could support these goals would be to build upon the work of the APEC List.[53] In this respect, the role of RE in the TTIP could be more advanced than what is provided by the EGA and APEC List, in terms of 'tariff liberalization'.

(3) Regional Comprehensive Economic Partnership (RCEP)

The RCEP is a proposed FTA between the ten member states of the Association of Southeast Asian Nations (ASEAN) and the six states with which ASEAN has existing FTAs. Negotiations were formally launched in

---

[49] European Commission, *Trade and Sustainable Development Chapter/Labour and Environment: EU Paper Outlining Key Issues and Elements for Provisions in the TTIP* (EU Position Paper, 2015), available at http://trade.ec.europa.eu/doclib/docs/2015/january/tradoc_153024.pdf (last visited 18 August 2017); European Commission, *EU-U.S. TTIP—Trade and Sustainable Development* (Initial EU Position Paper, 2013), available at http://trade.ec.europa.eu/doclib/docs/2013/july/tradoc_151626.pdf (last visited 18 August 2017); European Commission, *EU-U.S. TTIP—Raw Materials and Energy* (Initial EU Position Paper, 2013), available at http://trade.ec.europa.eu/doclib/docs/2013/july/tradoc_151624.pdf (last visited 18 August 2017); European Commission, *TTIP—EU Textual Proposal: Energy and Raw Materials* (EU Position Paper, 2016), available at http://trade.ec.europa.eu/doclib/docs/2016/july/tradoc_154801.pdf (last visited 18 August 2017).

[50] European Commission, *Energy and Raw Materials in TTIP* (2015), available at http://trade.ec.europa.eu/doclib/docs/2015/january/tradoc_153015.2%20Energy%20and%20raw%20materials.pdf (last visited 18 August 2017); European Commission, *Trade and Sustainable Development Chapter/Labour and Environment* (n. 49 above) (EU paper outlining key issues and elements for provisions of the TTIP).

[51] *Ibid.* See also Tim Smedley, *TTIP: What Does the Transatlantic Trade Deal Mean for Renewable Energy?*, The Guardian (5 August 2015), available at www.theguardian.com/public-leaders-network/2015/aug/05/ttip-free-trade-deal-renewable-energy-transatlantic-partnership-eu-us (last visited 18 August 2017).

[52] European Commission, *Raw Materials and Energy* (n. 49 above) ('There is nothing in TTIP on renewable energy').

[53] Leal-Arcas (n. 10 above) 255.

November 2012 at the ASEAN Summit in Cambodia.[54] The RCEP strives to progressively eliminate tariff and non-tariff barriers on substantially all trade in goods to establish a free trade area among the parties.[55]

Compared with the comprehensive nature of the TPP and TTIP noted above, the scope of the RCEP is much narrower and more focused on the 'economic integration' aspect. Additionally, although recent RTAs tend to at least refer to 'environment', 'climate change', or 'sustainable development', the RCEP refers primarily to the 'investment environment'.[56] Thus, the role of renewable energy is only implicitly integrated into the related talks on goods trade, service trade, and investment issues. For instance, New Zealand wishes to use the RCEP to export related 'renewable energy services'.[57]

IV. REGULATORY RESPONSE: DIVERGENCE OR CONVERGENCE

1. Subsidy and Incentive Scheme

(1) Choices among the primary subsidy tools

Over the past few decades, we have witnessed a change in the subsidy paradigm for RE. In the 1980s and 1990s, the primary subsidy tool continued to be the investment grant/demonstration subsidy. What implications does the rise and fall of RE incentive schemes have for IEL? Because the technology is expensive, it usually requires a heavy subsidy to make it happen. Yet the use of large amounts of government money to subsidize the development would definitely lead to IEL issues. Before January 2000, however, large early subsidies, particularly investment grants, were

---

[54] Rahul Mishra, *RCEP: Challenges and Opportunities for India*, in RSIS COMMENTARIES, available at www.files.ethz.ch/isn/172081/RSIS1402013.pdf.

[55] Japan Ministry of Economy, Trade and Industry (METI), Guiding Principles and Objectives for Negotiating the Regional Comprehensive Economic Partnership, Final 1 (30 August 2012), available at www.meti.go.jp/policy/trade_policy/east_asia/dl/RCEP_GP_EN.pdf.

[56] Kristy Hsu, *ASEAN Centrality: A Quest for Leadership Role in East Asian Economic Integration*, *in* ASIAN LEADERSHIP IN POLICY AND GOVERNANCE 84 (Evan Berman and M. Shamsul Haque eds., 2015); DAVID A. GANTZ, LIBERALIZING INTERNATIONAL TRADE AFTER DOHA: MULTILATERAL, PLURILATERAL, REGIONAL, AND UNILATERAL INITIATIVES 261 (2013).

[57] New Zealand Foreign Affairs and Trade, Regional Comprehensive Economic Partnership (RCEP), available at www.mfat.govt.nz/en/trade/free-trade-agreements/agreements-under-negotiation/rcep/.

shielded by the exemption in the SCM Agreement.[58] Thus, it seems that the SCM Agreement exemption led to the regulatory convergence on investment grants in the 1990s.

A feed-in tariff (FIT) is an energy supply policy that promotes the rapid deployment of renewable energy resources. A FIT offers a guarantee of payments to renewable energy developers for the electricity they produce. These payments are generally awarded as long-term contracts set over a period of fifteen to twenty years.[59] Germany's Renewable Energy Act (EEG) of 2000[60] launched the era of a new RE promotion scheme: feed-in tariffs.[61] Germany began implementing FITs in its 1991 Feed-in Act.[62] Unlike the investment subsidy provided by government money, the FIT scheme passed the cost to final customers via a system surcharge.[63] In this way, a FIT leads not only to sustainable financial sources for RE development, but also to fewer conflicts with IEL over government subsidy concerns.

A typical FIT scheme has been tested against IEL in the European court system, in the *PreussenElektra* case of 2001.[64] The Court of Justice of the European Union (CJEU) rejected the claim that a state subsidy existed as defined in Article 887 ff. of the Treaty Establishing the European Economic Community ('EC Treaty'). The Court reasoned that this was not state aid because it did not lead to a direct or indirect transfer of state funds to the corporation producing this electricity.[65] It is unclear whether this CJEU decision gives impetus to the further

---

[58] SCM Agreement, Art. 27.3.

[59] A feed-in tariff (FIT) is an energy supply policy that promotes the rapid deployment of renewable energy resources. A FIT offers a guarantee of payments to renewable energy developers for the electricity they produce. Payments can be composed of electricity alone or of electricity bundled with renewable energy certificates. These payments are generally awarded as long-term contracts set over a period of fifteen to twenty years.

[60] Renewable Energy Sources Act 2000 (EEG 2000), available at www.erneuerbare-energien.de/EE/Redaktion/DE/Dossier/eeg.html?cms_docId=71110.

[61] Hannes Weigt and Florian Leuthold, *Experience with Renewable Energy Policy in Germany*, *in* Harnessing Renewable Energy in Electric Power Systems: Theory, Practice, Policy 286 (Boaz Moselle et al. eds., 2010).

[62] Craig Morris and Arne Jungjohann, Energy Democracy: Germany's Energiewende to Renewables 169 (2016).

[63] OECD, *Germany: Keeping the Edge Competitiveness for Inclusive Growth* 24 (Better Policies Series, February 2104).

[64] ECJ NVwZ 2001, 665/666, PreussenElektra AG/Schleswag AG. See Ulrich Steger et al., Sustainable Development and Innovation in the Energy Sector 147 (2005).

[65] *Ibid.*

adoption and development of the FIT scheme after the regulatory convergence of 2005.

Since 2010, because the 'standard FIT' passed all of the high RE costs to the final customer and led to the Solar PV boom, there was an outcry from the public, followed by an effort to reform the FIT scheme. Subsequently, the quantity control approach of tendering schemes came to be favored. For instance, Taiwan and France established a combination scheme of FIT and tendering for PV in March 2011.[66] The tendering mechanism even affected the FIT founding country, Germany, in which its EEG 2014 changed from the central administration of tariff rates to a tendering scheme.[67] The move to a combined scheme of FIT and tendering could also be seen as 'regulatory divergence'. As such, it may be affected by the recent WTO rulings against Canada[68] and India.[69] The IEL provisions involved in those cases are the national treatment clauses of Article 3.4 of the GATT and Article 2.1 of the TRIMS Agreement. Thus, it is uncertain whether there is a 'safe harbor' for LCR. But does the tendering scheme totally shield RE from the IEL concerns?

---

[66] See Anton Ming-Zhi Gao, Assistant Professor, Ching-Hua University, *Feed-in Tariff Reform in PV Sector: What's the Next Step?*, presentation at the 7th International Scientific Conference on Energy and Climate Change (8–10 October 2014), available at www.promitheasnet.kepa.uoa.gr/images/files/3_20141009%20KEPA%20conference%20Anton%20GAO.ppt (last visited 18 August 2017). See also Anton Ming-Zhi Gao, *A More Sustainable Way to Promote PV: Transformations from FIT to FIT/FIT Tendering Schemes in Taiwan and France*, *in* Legal Issues of Renewable Electricity in Asia Region: Recent Development at a Post-Fukushima and Post-Kyoto Protocol Era 47–84 (Anton Ming-Zhi Gao and Chien Te Fan eds., 2014); Anton Ming-Zhi Gao et al., *Sustainable Photovoltaic Technology Development: Step-by-Step Guidance for Countries Facing PV Proliferation Turmoil under the Feed-in Tariff Scheme*, 43 Renewable & Sustainable Energy Rev. 156 (2015).

[67] Alexandra Purkus, Concepts and Instruments for a Rational Bioenergy Policy A New Institutional Economics Approach 227 (2016).

[68] Panel Report, Canada—Certain Measures Affecting the Renewable Energy Generation Sector ('Canada–Renewable Energy'); Canada—Measures Relating to the Feed-in Tariff Program ('Canada–Feed-In Tariff Program'), WTO Doc. WT/DS412/R, WT/DS426/R (adopted 24 May 2013); Appellate Body Report, Canada—Renewable Energy, Canada—Feed-In Tariff Program, WTO Doc. WT/DS412/AB/R, WT/DS426/AB/R (adopted 24 May 2013).

[69] Panel Report, India—Certain Measures Relating to Solar Cells and Solar Modules ('India–Solar Cells'), WTO Doc. WT/DS456/R (adopted 14 October 2016); Appellate Body Report, India—Solar Cells, WTO Doc. WT/DS456/AB/R (adopted 14 October 2016).

(2) FIT

The original design of FIT does not discriminate as to whether the product is imported or locally manufactured. As long as RE installations meet basic environmental, health, and safety (EHS) technical standards, they can qualify for long-term contracts and FIT rate subsidies. Examples of this style of FIT are Germany's EEG, Taiwan's Renewable Energy Act of 2009, Japan's FIT law, and a number of FIT laws in Europe.[70] This could be regarded as the regulatory convergence of IEL-compatible FITs.

However, FITs of this style do not provide special protection to local industries. Many countries began to integrate LCR into the FIT design. This also led to the aforementioned cases in Canada and India. Apart from LCR, there is also a very interesting 'regional' content requirement in Italy based on guidelines established by the Italian government as part of its Conto Energia 4 ('CE4') FIT program.[71]

Regarding onshore wind power, Turkey's government has sought to encourage this by offering a higher FIT of up to US$0.11 per kW-hour for five years if the entire turbine is manufactured in Turkey.[72] From these examples, we can see a trend of regulatory divergence from the standard FIT design by incorporating LCR.

Does this divergence really lead to extra protection for local industry? From Canada's experience, it seems the primary beneficiary of the policy is not local Canadian industry but, rather, Korean industry: Samsung has agreed to build plants to manufacture components for wind and solar projects in Ontario.[73] Also, in Turkey, US-based General Electric and Portugal-based Tegopi are benefiting from that country's LCR FIT.[74] It

---

[70] For further information on the FIT in Europe, see Europe's database on RE promotion measures, RES legal, www.res-legal.eu/.

[71] The CE4 program intends to encourage the use of components 'made in Europe', rewarding projects that contain at least 60 percent local content with a 10 percent premium over normal feed-in tariff rates.

[72] Turkey already has a thriving tower production business, and blades can also be sourced locally. The highest FIT theoretically now available using these components is US$0.087/kWh. Heather O'Brian, *Turkish Minister Praises Local Content*, WIND POWER MONTHLY (25 February 2013), available at www.windpowermonthly.com/article/1171995/turkish-minister-praises-local-content (last visited 18 August 2017).

[73] Huaxia Lai, *The Climate-Trade Conundrum: A Critical Analysis of the WTO's Jurisprudence on Subsidies to Renewable Energy*, *in* EMERGING ISSUES IN SUSTAINABLE DEVELOPMENT 305 (Mitsuo Matsushita and Thomas J. Schoenbaum eds., 2016). See also Matthew Paterson, *Automobility: Culture, (Re-)production, and Sustainability*, *in* HANDBOOK OF THE INTERNATIONAL POLITICAL ECONOMY OF PRODUCTION 44 (Kees van der Pijl ed., 2015).

[74] Ayla Jean Yackley, *GE invests $515 Million in Turkish Energy and Other*

seems that governments have risked violations of IEL not for the benefit of local industry, but instead for local job opportunities.

(3) Tendering

The original design of a tendering scheme is supposed to facilitate trade and competition among all RE products around the world. The most transparent form of a tendering scheme is 'price-based' tendering. Under such a tendering scheme, the purchase price of RE is primarily determined by the tendering price. Normally, the lowest price is awarded the bid.[75] An example can be seen in Taiwan's tendering scheme for ground-type and rooftop (30kW) PV products since 2011.[76] Countries including the United Kingdom, Ireland, France, the United States, and China have used tendering schemes for the supply of RE.[77] Thus, there has been regulatory convergence of price-based tendering over the past few decades.

However, such an open and transparent scheme once again is flawed by its inability to promote national industry. Thus, a recent development is the 'open' or 'secret' integration of a non-price component into the design of tendering schemes. This can also be viewed as regulatory divergence from the original price-based tendering scheme.

(a) 'Open' integration of LCR in tendering In 2003, China launched the first concession tendering scheme, mandating local content in turbines to promote the country's wind-power industry. From 2003 to 2008, five concession tendering schemes were organized, first mandating 50 percent local content, then 70 percent. However, this requirement was later removed because it was construed as a breach of WTO rules.[78]

Projects, REUTERS (26 September 2013), available at www.reuters.com/article/us-ge-turkey-idUSBRE98P12S20130926 (last visited 18 August 2017).

75 See, e.g., DONALD N. ZILLMAN ET AL. (EDS.), BEYOND THE CARBON ECONOMY: ENERGY LAW IN TRANSITION 199 (2008).

76 See also Anton Ming-Zhi Gao, *A More Sustainable Way to Promote PV: Transformations from FIT to FIT/FIT Tendering Schemes in Taiwan and France, in* LEGAL ISSUES OF RENEWABLE ELECTRICITY IN ASIA REGION: RECENT DEVELOPMENT AT A POST-FUKUSHIMA AND POST-KYOTO PROTOCOL ERA 47–84 (Anton Ming-Zhi Gao and Chien Te Fan eds., 2014). Related Ordinances in Taiwan include PV Tendering Ordinance of Phase I of 2011, PV Tendering Ordinance of Phase II of 2011, PV Tendering Ordinance of Phase III of 2011, PV Tendering Ordinance of 2012, PV Tendering Ordinance of 2013, etc.

77 Zillman et al. (n. 75 above) 199.

78 MARIA VAGLIASINDI, REVISITING PUBLIC-PRIVATE PARTNERSHIPS IN THE POWER SECTOR 65 (2013).

In 2010, the South Korean government set a target for offshore wind power of 2.5 gigawatts by 2030. The plan was modified in April 2015 to include a new timeline for 80 megawatts to be operational by 2018. Most of the projects under the 2.5-GW plan will follow the private-public partnership model, in which the Korea Electric Power Corporation will be a leading developer, together with Doosan Heavy Industries and Construction.[79]

(b) 'Secret' integration of non-price LCRs in tendering South Africa has a very comprehensive selection scoreboard composed of multiple elements for that country's Renewable Energy IPP Procurement Program. The LCR is listed as 25 percent of the value of local content expenditure (LCE) divided by the total project value (TPV), (LCE/TPV)*0.25. The aim is to promote the local onshore wind industry.[80]

Such a scoreboard approach to hide the LCR is also very often found in France's PV and offshore wind projects. For instance, there is a complex scoreboard, including price, environmental impact, industrial risk, carbon emission evaluation, project feasibility and completion times, and contributions to research and development ('R&D'), under the 2011 and 2013 Complex Tendering Schemes.[81] In France, such a protectionist tendering scheme is also applicable to offshore wind development. Again, under the scoreboard of the first phase of offshore wind power tendering specifications,[82] the tender price accounts for only 40 percent, while the remainder represents 40 percent for effects on industry and 20 percent for existing activities and environmental impact.[83] The emergence of

---

79 David Foxwell, Offshore Wind Boosted by Significant Investment in Renewables, Asia/Middle East Maritime Focus (25 July 2016), available at http://www.amemaritime.com/news/view,offshore-wind-boosted-by-significant-investment-in-renewables_43910.htm.

80 Anton Eberhard et al., South Africa's Renewable Energy IPP Procurement Program: Success Factors and Lessons 45 (2014), available at www.gsb.uct.ac.za/files/ppiafreport.pdf (last visited 18 August 2017).

81 Gao (n. 76 above).

82 Ministère de l'Écologie, du Développement durable et de l' Énergie, *Cahier des charges de l'appel d'offres portant sur des installations éoliennes de production d'électricité en mer en France métropolitaine*, available at www.cre.fr/documents/appels-d-offres/appel-d-offres-portant-sur-des-installations-eoliennes-de-production-d-electricite-en-mer-en-france-metropolitaine2/cahier-des-charges (last visited 18 August 2017) (Fr.).

83 Editorial, *EDF and Alstom Big Winners in French Offshore Wind Farm Tender*, BusinessGreen (10 April 2012), available at www.businessgreen.com/bg/news/2166602/edf-alstom-winners-french-offshore-wind-farm-tender (last visited 18 August 2017).

non-price elements in tendering could very well be related to substantial litigation against LCR FIT schemes in PV and wind power. Thus, in search of a new safe harbor, countries use this more implicit approach of LCR and national protectionism. It appears that such an approach works very well.

France's offshore wind power experience provides protection not only to local industry, but also to local jobs. The same is true for the onshore wind industries of South Africa (I-WEC), China (Goldwind, Sinovel), and South Korea (Hyundai, etc.). It seems that national protectionism works much better in a tendering scheme than in a FIT subsidy scheme, as it actually creates both local jobs and local industries. However, over-protective LCR-based tendering in China for offshore wind power appears to be in violation of the GATT, TRIMS, and SCM Agreement. Does the excuse those countries give—that their use of such tendering constitutes 'pilot and test demonstrations'—shield their regime from violations of IEL? This remains to be seen.

(4) Renewable electricity portfolio standards (RPS)

The various RPS schemes oblige electricity retailers[84] or generators[85] to buy a certain percentage of renewable electricity. Such schemes are widely used in the United States.[86] The purest form of an RPS scheme is merely to set the percentage target without any further details. For instance, Hawaii has set RPS targets of 30 percent by 2020, 40 percent by 2030, 70 percent by 2040, and 100 percent by 2045.[87] Thus, under this regime, as long as there is no further LCR requirement, it seems that all RE is treated equally. Such an approach is non-discriminatory in nature and thus is largely compatible with IEL. It seems to be the norm, and there is regulatory convergence of such technology-neutral RPS schemes.

However, such a technology-neutral approach is not very helpful in promoting specific types of RE. Therefore, some governments have adopted a set-aside[88] mechanism. For instance, in Maryland, the RPS goal is set at 20

---

[84] The most often-used model around the world, e.g., in the United States, United Kingdom, etc.

[85] E.g., in South Korea.

[86] See NC Clean Energy Technology Center, Database of State Incentives for Renewables and Efficiency, available at www.dsireusa.org/ (last visited 18 August 2017).

[87] HAW. REV. STAT. § 269-91 *et seq.*; HAW. H.B. NO. 623 (2015) (U.S.).

[88] The introduction of set-asides in the United States: 'Many state programs promote particular technology types by establishing sub-targets known as carve outs or set-asides. In addition to meeting the overall RPS targets, energy supply companies need to show that they have acquired a particular percentage of their power sales from the designated technology type. In some instances, multiple

percent by 2022. Yet among that 20 percent, special protection is given to solar PV (2 percent by 2020) and offshore wind (2.5 percent maximum by 2017).[89] Of course, as long as there is no LCR for PV and offshore wind, such strategic industry promotion appears to remain compatible with IEL. Nevertheless, we can detect implicit local protectionism behind the establishment of these set-asides.

The multipliers[90] under an RPS scheme may also be used to promote relatively stronger local RE industries. For instance, Nevada's Energy Portfolio Standard has a credit multiplier for PVs and on-peak energy savings, along with a set-aside for solar (5 percent of the annual requirement through 2015, 6 percent for 2016–2025).[91] Such provisions may be relevant to the industrial policy of the local PV industry.

In the latest survey of state RPS programs in June 2016, we find that regulatory convergence of RPS accompanies either multipliers or set-asides.[92] The RPS schemes may be used to promote relatively stronger local RE industries, such as in the US practice of protecting 'the state's own interest' in RE.[93]

---

technology types are bundled together in 'tiers' or 'classes' with similar effect. Not all states have set-asides or tiers (some preferring to promote particular technologies through credit multipliers) and each state that groups technologies together in a tier does so differently'. See SourceWatch, *Renewable Portfolio Standards*, available at www.sourcewatch.org/index.php/Renewable_portfolio_standard (last visited 18 August 2017).

89 Md. Code Ann., Pub. Util. Cos. § 7-701 ff. (US).

90 The introduction of the multiplier in the United States is as follows: 'For states with REC trading programs, a Renewable Energy Certificate is issued to eligible producers for each MWh of renewable energy production. Some state programs, in order to promote specific renewable technology types, apply a credit multiplier by which a MWh of electricity produced by a particular technology receives more than one REC. For example, a wind multiplier of three means that one MWh of electricity produced with wind technology provides the producer of that electricity with three certificates'. See SourceWatch (n. 88 above).

91 Nev. Rev. Stat. § 704.7801 *et seq.* (US).

92 Jocelyn Durkay, *State Renewable Portfolio Standards and Goals*, Nat'l Conf. St. Legis. (27 July 2016), available at www.ncsl.org/research/energy/renewable-portfolio-standards.aspx (last visited 18 August 2017).

93 MJ Beck Consulting, *Renewable Portfolio Standards (RPS)*, available at http://mjbeck.emtoolbox.com/?page=Renewable_Portfolio_Standards. See also, Anton Ming-Zhi Gao, *Promotion of Renewable Electricity: Free Trade and Domestic Industrial Development*, *in* Research Handbook on International Energy Law 424 (Kim Talus ed., 2014).

(5) Supplementary scheme

(a) Loan scheme In terms of loan flow, there are primarily two types of loans or loan guarantee schemes. The first type is the loan for local installations. For a technologically advanced RE country such as Germany, loans are usually provided under the banking and loan scheme of domestic policy. For instance, KfW Bank financed the first offshore wind farm in the North Sea in Germany.[94] In the United Kingdom, the Green Investment Bank provided a loan scheme to facilitate the adoption and kick-off of Siemens' offshore wind installations.[95] Such an approach could be seen as IEL-compatible development.[96] This relatively softer trade distortion scheme (a loan) instead of direct investment in a non-payback grant, coupled with non-discrimination toward foreign investors, could be a win-win solution for both IEL and the local prosperity of RE. In most of the RE-promoting countries, it seems that this reciprocal approach is prevailing, and such regulatory convergence represents a phenomenon of 'You do good for my industry, and I return a benefit to you in my home country'.

Yet a loan scheme could also represent an element of trade distortion. The most famous example is China's over-generous loan scheme extended to its local industry. China's policies to promote renewable energy have long included mandates and incentives to support the development of domestic technologies and industries.[97] Taiwan has also begun to consider including LCR elements on a very small scale in loan requirements: a zero-interest loan could be provided for two LCR offshore wind turbines.[98]

---

[94] KfW, Press Release, *Impetus for Energy Turnaround: KfW Finances First Offshore Wind Farm in the North Sea* (5 August 2011), available at www.kfw.de/s/enkE1Tj.Cfz (last visited 18 August 2017) ('Today KfW has signed the financing agreement for the two offshore wind farms Meerwind Ost and Meerwind Süd (288 MW). The project is one of the most demanding German projects and, given the investment volume of almost EUR 1.3 billion, it is one of Germany's largest offshore project financing transactions.').

[95] Green Investment Bank, Press Release, *PGGM & Ampere Equity Fund GBP 224M Refinancing of their 24.8% Stake in the 367 MW Walney Offshore Wind Farm in the Irish Sea* (20 December 2012), available at www.greeninvestmentbank.com/media/5267/walney_opw_refinancing_press_release1.pdf (last visited 18 August 2017).

[96] International Energy Authority Renewable Energy Technology Deployment (IEA-RETD), Offshore Renewable Energy: Accelerating the Deployment of Offshore Wind, Tidal, and Wave Technologies 178 (2012).

[97] Joanna I. Lewis, *The Rise of Renewable Energy Protectionism: Emerging Trade Conflicts and Implications for Low Carbon Development*, 14(4) Global Environmental Politics 10, 15 (2014).

[98] Fengli Fadian Lian Xitong Shifan Jiangli Banfa [Offshore Wind Power

The integration of LCR into the primary promotion scheme (FIT, RPS, tendering, etc.) can raise serious conflicts with IEL. Thus, it seems that countries increasingly use the softer loan scheme to launch LCR or protectionism. Such regulatory divergence from the original IEL-compatible practice seems to be very popular.

Apart from the local trend, the use of export loans to support the deployment of local industry appears to be a widespread phenomenon. Large offshore and onshore wind export countries, such as Denmark and Germany, all provide export loans to assist in the export of their industries. For instance, KfW Bank provided an export loan to assist Taiwan's development of onshore wind power.[99] So did Denmark's Export Credit Agency (EKF) in assisting the Danish wind industry in exporting.[100] In recent years, there appears to be regulatory convergence to establish export loans to support RE exports around the world.

(b) Investment grants As noted above, the 1980s–1990s was an era with a large number of LCR-based investment subsidies or demonstration grants, either before or in the early stages of IEL development. For instance, the government of Denmark put into place a system of fixed incentives in 1985 to favor the early development of wind power for local communities.[101] There is regulatory convergence in the use of such schemes to promote local industry.

Demonstration Subsidy Ordinance] art. 18(2), available at https://web3.moeaboe.gov.tw/ECW/populace/Law/Content.aspx?menu_id=1850 (last visited 18 August 2017) (Taiwan).

[99] *KfW IPEX-Bank, Press Release, KfW IPEX-Bank Finances Tongyuan Wind Farm in Taiwan* (24 September 2012), available at www.kfw-ipex-bank.de/International-financing/KfW-IPEX-Bank/Presse/News/Newsdetails_6689.html (last visited 18 August 2017).

[100] E.g., the EKB and EIB of Denmark provide loans for Belgian offshore wind projects: Belwind (2009, Belgium, 165 MW, Vestas V90, EUR 544 M financing): first deal post-financial crisis allowed to confirm that the early structures were sound (construction risk, some merchant risk) while increasing the size thanks to heavy multilateral involvement; three MLAs, EIB and EKF, no syndication. See Jérôme Guillet, Managing Director of Green Giraffe, pre-seminar presentation at EWEA Offshore 2011, available at www.ewea.org/offshore2011/fileadmin/eow2011_documents/WETF/EWEA%20OFFSHORE%202011%20pre-event%20semainar%20-%203.3%20Jerome%20Guillet%20-%20Finance.pdf (last visited 18 August 2017).

[101] M. Mustafa Erdoğdu and Coşkun Karaca, *A Road Map for a Domestic Wind Turbine Manufacturing Industry in Turkey*, *in* ECONOMIC BEHAVIOR, GAME THEORY, AND TECHNOLOGY IN EMERGING MARKETS 70 (Bryan Christiansen and Muslum Basilgan eds., 2014).

With the emergence of other generation-based strategies, the investment subsidy is only applied to RE in very exceptional cases. However, it is still very often applied in R&D and demonstration projects. For instance, Japan's demonstration offshore wind power project is funded by the Ministry of Economy, Trade and Industry and the Ministry of the Environment. Japan-based Mitsubishi and Hitachi are funded to set up 7-MW[102] and 5-MW[103] floating offshore wind turbines, respectively.

Usually such projects are small in scale, making them relatively IEL-compatible; however, IEL concerns increase with these commercialized projects. In some regimes, domestic-made RE installations can receive higher electricity-production-based investment subsidies[104] or capital grants[105] than non-local installations. This could be regarded as regulatory divergence to an IEL-concerned investment subsidy.

2. Regulatory Scheme

(1) Tax and tariff barriers

Among all of the regulatory schemes, the most relevant may be the RE tariff and the tax barrier. These two barriers create disadvantages for foreign-imported RE and create advantages for local industry.

Tax credit regimes are usually IEL compatible, but there are still a few exceptions. For instance, Washington State in the United States uses a tax credit scheme that allows a higher tax credit for PV products made in that state.[106] These issues could be the toughest issues for IEL and

---

102 *MHI floating 7MW ready for deployment* (22 June 2015), available at www.windpoweroffshore.com/article/1352499/mhi-floating-7mw-ready-deployment; *Latest Japan Offshore Wind Power Articles*, Windpower Offshore, available at www.windpoweroffshore.com/japan (last visited 18 August 2017).

103 Ines Heger, *Japan Industry and Policy News: Offshore Wind Technology*, EU-Japan Centre for Industrial Cooperation News, available at www.eu-japan.eu/news/japan-industry-and-policy-news-offshore-wind-technology (last visited 18 August 2017).

104 Under the ODOD, Wind Production and Manufacturing Incentive Program (Ohio)+, for generators in Ohio, installers will receive a production incentive of US$0.01 per kWh for up to five years, or until the entire amount of the grant approved has been earned by the wind-energy project, whichever occurs first. A higher incentive rate of US$0.012 is available for projects that use 'Ohio-manufactured' wind 'turbines', see http://en.openei.org/w/index.php?title=Property:Incentive/Summary&until=Ohio+Biomass+Energy+Program+(Ohio).

105 USTR, *China Ends Wind Power Equipment Subsidies Challenged by the United States in WTO Dispute*, available at www.ustr.gov/about-us/press-office/press-releases/2011/june/china-ends-wind-power-equipment-subsidies-challenged.

106 Washington State Department of Revenue, *Renewable Energy Cost Recovery*

RTAs.[107] On the other hand, tariffs or excise duties significantly affect the free movement of RE goods. Thus, as noted above for most RTAs and FTAs, particularly for the EGA and the APEC List, the focus is always on the RE tariff as a first priority. Thus, there is regulatory convergence to reduce tariffs for the key RE, such as PV and wind-powered goods.[108]

With regard to solar cells (APEC List HS 854140), according to the latest survey,[109] the most-favored nation (MFN) duty is generally reduced to 0 percent. Only a few countries impose rates of 1, 3, 2.5, 5, or 6 percent, while only one country imposes 22 percent, and three countries impose 10 percent. However, the picture is different for wind power:[110] even though about sixty countries have a 0 percent MFN duty for wind turbine generators, there are seventy countries for which the MFN tariff is between 1 percent and 10 percent, and five countries with tariffs ranging from 12 to 20 percent. From this, we can find regulatory divergence between wind power and PV in the reform of MFN duties.

(2) Other general and non-tariff barriers

Other non-tariff barriers may also be relevant to the development of RE, although usually there is much regulatory divergence in this area, particularly in terms of EHS regulations. For instance, regarding the environmental impact assessment threshold for wind power, the following divergent regulations are in place:[111]

- height (>15 m in the United Kingdom; >80 m in Denmark; 35 m in Germany);

Incentive Program, available at http://apps.leg.wa.gov/documents/WSLdocs/2009-10/Pdf/Bills/Session%20Law%202010/6658-S.SL.pDf. https://energy.gov/savings/renewable-energy-cost-recovery-incentive-payment

107 See Gehring et al. (n. 9 above) 13.

108 Wind Energy table in ICTSD, *Renewable Energy Technologies: Tariffs and Trade Flows* 7, available at http://citeseerx.ist.psu.edu/viewdoc/download?doi=10.1.1.614.7116&rep=rep1&type=pdf.

109 *HS Tariff Codes, Import Duty and Taxes and Restrictions for Solar Panels*, available at www.dutycalculator.com/hs-code-duty-rate-import-restrictions/854140/solar-panels/8541.40.6020/8541.40.9029/1018/.

110 *HS Tariff Codes, Import Duty and Taxes and Restrictions for Wind Turbine Generator*, available at www.dutycalculator.com/hs-code-duty-rate-import-restrictions/850231/wind-turbine-generator/8502.31.0000/8502.31.0090/2723/.

111 Anne-Charlotte Vaissière et al., *Biodiversity Offsets for Offshore Wind Farm Projects: The Current Situation in Europe*, 48 Marine Pol'y 172, 175 (2014).

- number of plants (five in the United Kingdom; three in Denmark; twenty in Germany; three in Sweden; ten in the Netherlands; five in Ireland);
- installation capacity (>5 MW in the United Kingdom and Ireland; 10 MW in Germany; >10 MW in Sweden and the Netherlands).

In short, as stressed by Gehring:

> states have further adopted specific exceptions in RTAs regarding areas where it is possible that trade rules on inter alia *sanitary and phytosanitary standards, TBT, intellectual property rights, public procurement, services or investment*, might constrain the use of climate-change measures, including those related to promotion of sustainable energy, and climate change induced environmental emergencies. (emphasis added)

These issues could be the toughest issues for IEL and RTAs.[112]

V. CONCLUSION

With a view toward harmonizing the international law order of UNFCCC and IEL, RTAs seek to integrate additional elements through the concepts of environment, climate change, and sustainable development. Yet when it comes to the role of RE in these RTAs, it remains obscure even in the face of the flood of cases on PV and wind power in recent years. It seems that techniques to raise the role of RE in these RTAs could be very important in the post-Paris Agreement era.

Nevertheless, the role of RTAs in certain areas cannot be underestimated. In particular, the reform of tariffs under the EGA and the APEC List appears to lead to further advances of global trade and development in PV and wind power.

Despite progress, given the increasing trade in PV and wind power, disputes are also increasing. From the cases, it seems that in the PV area, lower tariffs lead to a greater need to use subsidy schemes to protect local industry. Thus, there are relatively more cases on AD and AS for PV than for wind power. On the other hand, higher tariffs for wind power seem to be sufficient in providing protections to local industry and blocking the invasion of foreign products. Additionally, the relatively higher 'other general and non-tariff barriers' in wind power as opposed to PV may lead to fewer AD and AS cases. However, as noted in this chapter, more

---

112 See Gehring et al. (n. 9 above) 13.

and more AS and LCR concerns are being raised in attempts to protect local offshore wind industries. A forthcoming high volume of cases over offshore wind power is very much expected by this author.

Are mega-RTAs helpful in resolving the impasse over RE? The author remains quite negative. In recent mega-RTAs, the role of RE remains unclear. Most of the provisions relevant to RE are 'soft' in nature. The only hope is the TTIP, which has the potential to become a highly successful and influential RTA, with its terms possibly becoming a model structure for future trade negotiations.

The regulatory trend sends a rather worrisome signal that more and more countries are adopting explicit or implicit incentive regimes and diverging from more IEL-concerned incentives. In other words, the non-tariff barrier and protectionism are back. However, the LCR experience with RE seems to send a mixed message regarding the effectiveness of these LCR measures in achieving local protection goals. Without LCR, of course, local industry and jobs would be highly likely to suffer from global competition—for example, cheap solar cells from China and advanced wind power technology from Germany and Denmark. Even with LCR in place, however, this is not necessarily a guarantee of the success of local protection. For instance, Canada's government seems to violate IEL to protect Samsung, and the LCRs of Turkey and Brazil seem to benefit foreign wind power companies such as GE, Enercon, etc. Thus, it seems that the application of LCR in the RE sector shows the double-edged sword effect. From this chapter, it appears that only the LCR tendering scheme could really be protective of local industry and jobs at the same time. It remains unclear, however, whether the widespread deployment of such a scheme could be helpful in achieving the goals of the UNFCCC.

At this post-Paris Agreement moment, the Agreement suggests a new business future for RE development. It is unclear whether most countries will take this opportunity to implement more LCR, dumping, or subsidies to circumvent IEL. The international legal order may lose its balance and incline toward the UNFCCC instead of the IEL. On the one hand, the rise of national protectionism in RE may make it appear that IEL is the loser. On the other hand, because RE is a very technology-driven and capital-intensive industry, foreign RE companies may also benefit from LCRs and national protectionism. From this perspective, IEL may not be the total loser.

PART IV

Food safety and public health

10. Food and product safety issues in the TPP*

Yoshiko Naiki

I. INTRODUCTION

Japan is the first and only country so far which has completed a ratification of the Trans-Pacific Partnership (TPP) Agreement out of the twelve parties which signed the TPP Agreement. In October 2016, when Japan's Lower House was discussing the Bill for TPP ratification, one of the issues was whether the TPP Agreement would affect Japan's food safety. It was discussed whether imported foods from the TPP parties, such as hormone-treated beef or genetically modified salmon, could put food safety at risk.[1] Among the twelve parties which signed the TPP Agreement, Japan was the only country in which food and product safety issues were debated so extensively in the context of the TPP's impacts. Such consumers' concerns regarding sanitary and phytosanitary (SPS) measures and technical barriers to trade (TBT) measures have been a sensitive issue for the government of Japan during the TPP negotiations and after their conclusion. However, a few weeks after such debates in Japan's Lower House, Donald Trump won the presidential election in the United States. If the TPP Agreement were to enter into force, for Japan, it would be its sixteenth regional trade agreement (RTA).

Existing studies have examined provisions and practices in the Chapters on SPS measures ('SPS Chapter') and TBT measures ('TBT Chapter') under current RTAs.[2] Variations among these regional experiences

* Section II of this chapter draws on the author's earlier article, written in Japanese: *TPP to Shoku no Anzen* [*The TPP and Food Safety*], 44(12) KOKUSAI SHOJI HOMU [Journal of the Japanese Institute of International Business Law], 1820–27 (2016).

[1] The House of Representatives, Japan, Special Committee on the TPP (31 October 2016), available at www.shugiin.go.jp/internet/itdb_kaigiroku.nsf/html/kaigiroku/030519220161031010.htm (last visited 6 August 2017) (Japan).

[2] Gonzalo Villalta Puig and Eric D. Dalke, *Nature and Enforceability of*

make a comparison with such existing practices and the TPP Agreement a challenging task, even just in terms of their SPS and TBT Chapters. The analytical view of this chapter builds mainly on Japan's existing regional experiences and the World Trade Organization (WTO)'s Agreement on the Application of Sanitary and Phytosanitary Measures ('SPS Agreement') and Agreement on Technical Barriers to Trade ('TBT Agreement'): it considers whether and in what way the TPP's SPS and TBT Chapters are different from and go beyond the WTO Agreements and Japan's regional experiences.

Generally, Japan's economic partnership agreements (EPAs) contain both an SPS Chapter and a TBT Chapter, but there are some exceptions.[3] Moreover, the SPS and TBT Chapters in Japan's EPAs are structured in a simple manner and not subject to a built-in dispute settlement procedure. Neither the SPS nor the TBT Chapters in Japan's EPAs have significant WTO-plus provisions. Normally, the SPS Chapters are simpler than the TBT Chapters, which reaffirm the rights and obligations in the WTO TBT Agreement but also contain several WTO-plus provisions[4] (such as mutual recognition of the results of conformity assessment procedures).

Overall, the TPP's SPS and TBT Chapters appear more comprehensive and innovative for Japan vis-à-vis Japan's previous EPAs. When Japan joined the TPP negotiations in 2013, concerns about food and product safety were already raised by the public (especially consumers). For example, whether Japan's food additive regulations or genetically modified organisms (GMOs) labeling requirements might be changed in response to the US demands during the TPP negotiations was deliberated. In addition to the SPS and TBT Chapters, there are other parts of the TPP Agreement—the market access Chapter, Chapter annexes, or bilateral side-letters—addressing food safety and product standards. These specific

---

WTO-plus SPS and TBT Provisions in Canada's PTAs: From NAFTA to CETA, 15 WORLD TRADE REV. 51 (2016); Andrew L. Stoler, *TBT and SPS in Practice*, *in* PREFERENTIAL TRADE AGREEMENT POLICIES FOR DEVELOPMENT: A HANDBOOK 217 (Jean-Pierre Chauffour and Jean-Christophe Maur eds., 2011).

[3] The Japan-Singapore EPA, the Japan-Philippines EPA, and the Japan-Thailand EPA have Chapters on mutual recognition, instead of TBT Chapters. The Japan-Singapore EPA, the Japan-Philippines EPA, and the Japan-Thailand EPA do not have SPS Chapters. The Japan-Indonesia EPA and the Japan-Brunei EPA have neither SPS nor TBT Chapters.

[4] In particular, the TBT Chapter of the Japan-Peru EPA contains provisions going beyond the WTO's TBT Agreement. See JAPAN MINISTRY OF TRADE, ECONOMY, AND INDUSTRY, 2015 REPORT ON COMPLIANCE BY MAJOR TRADING PARTNERS WITH TRADE AGREEMENTS-WTO, FTA, AND IIA 903 (2016), available at www.meti.go.jp/english/report/data/2015WTO/03_01.pdf (last visited 20 July 2017).

provisions relate to products such as GMOs, used and remanufactured goods, motor vehicles, cosmetics, organic products, and food additives. These various product-specific provisions are a unique characteristic of the TPP Agreement, reflecting trade interests and concerns of exporting parties.

This chapter will address these specific provisions, as well as the SPS/TBT Chapters under the TPP Agreement, and analyze how such provisions will affect food and product safety of the TPP parties, in particular, that of Japan. Thus, this chapter does not intend to examine and explain the TPP's SPS and TBT Chapters in a general and comprehensive manner. Rather, the focus is on the provisions concerning food safety and product standards.

II. SPS CHAPTER AND OTHER FOOD SAFETY-RELATED PROVISIONS

1. SPS Chapter

As noted, under Japan's EPAs, an SPS Chapter is normally not subject to a dispute settlement procedure. In contrast, TPP Article 7.18.1 provides that the SPS Chapter is subject to the Dispute Settlement Chapter, with timelines and several exceptions. Furthermore, before having recourse to the Dispute Settlement Chapter, a TPP party is required to seek to resolve a matter through 'cooperative technical consultations' (CTC) as per Article 7.17.8. This CTC system can be used to discuss any matter arising from the SPS Chapter. The CTC system appears to be a similar mechanism to that of 'specific trade concerns' (STC) developed under the WTO SPS Committee. However, one notable feature of the CTC system is that it provides steps and timelines for the consultation process, which do not exist for the STC system under the WTO's SPS Committee.

A major feature of the TPP's SPS Chapter is the extensive provisions on procedures, such as transparency, audits, and import checks. This point will be addressed in Chapter 11 of this volume, so instead, this chapter focuses on substantive provisions related to food safety. In terms of substantive provisions, the TPP's SPS Chapter builds on and reaffirms the rights and obligations of the WTO SPS Agreement (Article 7.4); however, there are some differences and also provisions going beyond the text of the WTO's SPS Agreement.

One notable provision is Article 7.9, titled 'Science and Risk Analysis'. The concept of 'risk analysis' is defined in Article 7.1, meaning 'the process that consists of three components: risk assessment; risk management;

and risk communication'.[5] There are also definitions of these three components. In this regard, the WTO SPS Agreement only uses the wording 'risk assessment'. It can be recalled that, in the *EC—Hormones* case, while the Panel employed the two concepts of 'risk assessment' and 'risk management', the Appellate Body refused to use the concept of 'risk management', stating 'the Panel's distinction . . . has no textual basis'.[6] The WTO SPS Committee has not adopted any decision and recommendation but has organized a workshop on risk analysis twice, in 2000 and 2014.[7]

Article 7.9 addresses similar issues to those under Article 3 (Harmonization) and Article 5 (Assessment of Risk) in the WTO SPS Agreement. According to a document published by the government of Japan,[8] the government paid attention especially to the current Article 7.9.2 before entering into the negotiations, as regards whether the terms of this Article might cause difficulties to the country. Article 7.9.2 is a similar provision to Article 3 of the WTO SPS Agreement, addressing the use of international standards and deviation from international standards. Initially, Japan was concerned whether this provision might involve a strong preference for harmonization of international standards and would not allow deviation from international standards, contrary to Article 3.3 of the WTO SPS Agreement.

However, Article 7.9.2 in fact requires parties to ensure that their measures conform to international standards, but if the measures do not conform to international standards, it requires parties to ensure that the measures 'are based on documented and objective scientific evidence that is rationally related to the measures'.[9] Thus, the provision allows deviation from international standards under certain conditions. However, the wording of the conditions under Article 7.9.2—that measures are based on documented and objective scientific evidence that is rationally related to the measures—is different from Article 3.3 of the WTO SPS Agreement,

---

5 TPP, Art. 7.1, available at https://ustr.gov/sites/default/files/TPP-Final-Text-Sanitary-and-Phytosanitary-Measures.pdf (last visited 20 July 2017).

6 *European Communities—Measures Concerning Meat and Meat Products (Hormones)* ('*EC—Hormones*'), Appellate Body Report, WTO Doc. WT/DS26/AB/R, WT/DS48/AB/R (adopted 13 February 1998), para. 181.

7 The second workshop was proposed by the US Committee on Sanitary and Phytosanitary Measures, Review of the Operation and Implementation of the SPS Agreement, Draft Report of the Committee, Revision, WTO Doc. G/SPS/W/280/Rev.2 (6 November 2014), at 26.

8 Naikaku Kanbo [Cabinet Secretariat], TPP Kyotei Kosho no Bunya Betsu Jokyo [Current Sectoral Situation of the TPP Negotiations] 17 (2011), available at www.cas.go.jp/jp/tpp/pdf/2012/1/20111021_1.pdf (last visited 20 July 2017) (Japan).

9 TPP, Art. 7.9.2.

which provides that the deviation must be based on a scientific justification or Article 5 of the SPS Agreement.

There are some views that this wording goes further than Article 3.3 of the WTO SPS Agreement.[10] However, it is doubtful how far Article 7.9.2 goes beyond the WTO SPS Agreement. For example, in terms of 'rationally related', the WTO's Appellate Body in the *EC—Hormones* case stated, in the context of Article 5.1 of the SPS Agreement, that being based on risk assessment requires 'a rational relationship between the measure and risk assessment'.[11] Therefore, 'rationally related' is not a new concept, and the Appellate Body also stated that 'determination of the presence or absence of that relationship can be done on a case-to-case basis'.[12] With regard to 'documented and objective scientific evidence', there have been some occasions for the Appellate Body to qualify the notion of scientific evidence. For example, in the *EC—Hormones* case, the Appellate Body stated that if a scientific opinion comes from 'qualified and respected sources', that opinion, either being the mainstream or the divergent view, could form a risk assessment.[13] Also, the Appellate Body noted that a risk assessment should be 'sufficiently specific' but 'general studies' do not suffice.[14] Similarly, in the *Australia—Salmon* case, it suggested that 'some evaluation' is not sufficient, either.[15] Thus, in the light of the Appellate Body's observation, the conditions under Article 7.9.2—that measures are based on documented and objective scientific evidence that is rationally related to the measures—do not necessarily sound new. Lastly, Article 7.9.2 is exempted from the Dispute Settlement Chapter.[16] This implies difficulties in and disagreements over this provision, and probably, exempting this provision from the dispute settlement procedure was a political compromise by negotiators.

Furthermore, while the WTO SPS Agreement contains a provision on

---

[10] Trans-Pacific Partnership Agreement: Likely Impact on the U.S. Economy and on Specific Industry Sectors, USITC Pub. No. 4607, Inv. No. TPA-105-001, 419 (May 2016), available at www.usitc.gov/publications/332/pub4607.pdf (last visited 20 July 2017); Hogan Lovells, *TPP: New Markets Opening Up for U.S. Food Products* (22 January 2016), available at http://ehoganlovells.com/rv/ff0024f902e6f-61f12e9131e2f479605707e6985 (last visited 20 July 2017).

[11] *EC—Hormones* (n. 6 above) para. 193.

[12] *Ibid.* para. 194.

[13] *Ibid.*

[14] *Ibid.* para. 200.

[15] *Australia—Measures Affecting Importation of Salmon*, Appellate Body Report, WTO Doc. WT/DS18/AB/R (adopted 6 November 1998), para. 124.

[16] TPP SPS, footnote 3.

equivalence (Article 4 of the SPS Agreement),[17] the TPP's SPS Chapter contains a more extensive provision on equivalence. Article 7.8 of the SPS Chapter, addressing equivalence, mostly covers the procedures for requesting an equivalence assessment and making the determination between an exporting member (a requesting member) and importing member (a member receiving the request). Such procedural issues are partly based on the SPS Committee's decision on equivalence[18] as well as the Codex guidelines on equivalence.[19]

With regard to the substantive condition of determining equivalence, Article 4 of the WTO SPS Agreement provides that 'if the exporting Member objectively demonstrates to the importing Member that its measures achieve the importing Member's appropriate level of sanitary or phytosanitary protection', a determination of equivalence should be made by the importing member. Achieving the appropriate level of sanitary or phytosanitary protection (ALOP) of the importing member is a common requirement and understanding for making such a determination; however, the TPP's SPS Chapter added another option. Article 7.8.6 addresses this issue, and its paragraph (a) is the same as Article 4 of the WTO SPS Agreement concerning the ALOP. Then, its paragraph (b) states another condition for the determination of equivalence, namely, if the exporting party's measure 'has the same effect in achieving the objective as the importing Party's measure'.

But again, this 'same effect' condition is not entirely new, because it is already referred to in the SPS Committee's decision[20] and the Codex guidelines.[21] The underlying thought seems to be that achieving the ALOP is possible by demonstrating that the measure has the same effect. Further,

---

[17] WTO SPS Agreement, Art. 4.

[18] Committee on Sanitary and Phytosanitary Measures, Decision on the Implementation of Article 4 of the Agreement on the Application of Sanitary and Phytosanitary Measures, Revision, WTO Doc. G/SPS/19/Rev.2 (23 July 2004).

[19] Codex Alimentarius Commission, Guidelines on the Judgement of Equivalence of Sanitary Measures Associated with Food Inspection and Certification Systems, FAO Doc. CAC/GL 53-2003 (2003).

[20] SPS Committee Decision (n. 18 above) para. 7 ('If the exporting Member demonstrates by way of an objective basis of comparison or similar approach established by a relevant international organization that its measure has the same effect in achieving the objective as the importing Member's measure, the importing Member should recognize both measures as equivalent.').

[21] Codex Guidelines (n. 19 above) section 6(15) ('an exporting country may demonstrate achievement of the importing country's ALOP by demonstrating that the measures it proposes as equivalent have the same effect, relative to the achievement of the importing country by using an objective basis of comparison').

both the SPS Committee's decision and the Codex guidelines stipulate that the measure's same effect should be demonstrated by using 'an objective basis of comparison', and the Codex guidelines provide the details on such a comparison.[22] On the other hand, Article 7.8.6 simply mentions the 'same effect' condition and does not elaborate further. On this point, it should be noted that the provision of the 'same effect' is exempted from the TPP Dispute Settlement Chapter.[23] It seems that negotiators could not agree upon the details of this provision, and, therefore, gave up attempts to make this provision enforceable by backing it up with the use of dispute settlement procedures.

2. Trade in GM Products in the Market Access Chapter

In Japan, there have been concerns that provisions concerning GM products in the Market Access Chapter may increase the import of GM plants and products.[24] To begin with, a question would be raised as to why provisions regarding GM products are contained in the Market Access Chapter, instead of the SPS Chapter addressed above. The TPP provisions on GM products are not addressing the quality or safety of GMOs. Rather, they are about 'transparency, cooperation and exchanging information'[25] related to trade in GMOs, which is the reason why the provisions are located in Section C: Agriculture, Chapter 2 on Market Access.

To be precise, Article 2.27 is titled 'Trade of Products of Modern Biotechnology'. 'Modern Biotechnology' sounds new. Article 2.19 defines it as 'agricultural goods, as well as fish and fish products, developed using modern biotechnology', but does not include medicines and medical products.[26] Similar wording can be found on activities in the Asia-Pacific Economic Cooperation (APEC).[27] In the APEC, there has been a meeting

---

22 *Ibid.* section 6(16).

23 TPP SPS, note 2.

24 Naikaku Kanbo [Cabinet Secretariat], TPP ni Kansuru Q&A: Zentai-ban [Q & A regarding the TPP: Full Version] 14 (October 2016), available at www.cas.go.jp/jp/tpp/qanda/pdf/161007_tpp_qanda_zentai.pdf (last visited 20 July 2017) (Japan).

25 TPP, Art. 2.27.1.

26 *Ibid.* Art. 2.19, available at https://ustr.gov/sites/default/files/TPP-Final-Text-National-Treatment-and-Market-Access.pdf (last visited 20 July 2017). It also defines 'modern biotechnology' as 'the application of . . . techniques . . . that overcome natural physiological reproductive or recombinant barriers and that are not techniques used in traditional breeding and selection'.

27 Other than the work of the APEC, the Canada-EU Comprehensive Economic and Trade Agreement (CETA) also contains provisions on cooperation

known as the 'High Level Policy Dialogue on Agricultural Biotechnology' (HLPDAB) since 2002, with the aim to 'develop regulatory frameworks, facilitate technology transfers, encourage investment and strengthen public confidence in biotechnology'.[28] Also, the APEC Ministerial Meeting held in 2015 had an agenda on 'Food Security, Agricultural Technical Cooperation, and Agricultural Biotechnology', stating that 'we encourage APEC member economies to enhance cooperation in maximizing the benefits of biotechnology for improved resiliency, inclusive growth, sustainable agriculture development, and food security'.[29]

How much then is the APEC work reflected in Article 2.27 of the TPP? Article 2.27 paragraphs 2 and 3 are confirmations of the rights of parties: 'Nothing in this Article shall prevent a Party from adopting measures in accordance with its rights and obligations under the WTO Agreement or other provisions of this Agreement',[30] and '[n]othing in this Article shall require a Party to adopt or modify its laws, regulations and policies for the control of products of modern biotechnology within its territory'.[31]

Furthermore, the Article is concerned with 'low level presence' (LLP) occurrences. 'LLP occurrence' is explained in a footnote as an 'inadvertent low level presence in a shipment of plants or plant products . . . of rDNA plant material that is authorized for use in at least one country, but not in the importing country'.[32] In short, usually, when GM products are exported, this product must be authorized in an importing country. However, LLP occurs when GM products are exported without the authorization of the importing country.

One effective way to prevent trade disruption from LLP occurrences is to increase the chances for authorization of GM products in importing parties. On this point, the key provision for the authorization is Article 2.27 paragraph 8. It states that on the exporting side, 'each exporting Party shall . . . endeavour to encourage technology developers to submit applications to Parties for authorization', and on the importing side, 'a Party . . . shall endeavour to . . . allow year-round submission and

and information exchange concerning biotechnology products in the Chapter on bilateral dialogues and cooperation. See CETA, Ch. 25, available at http://ec.europa.eu/trade/policy/in-focus/ceta/ceta-chapter-by-chapter/ (last visited 20 July 2017).

[28] APEC, *Agricultural Biotechnology*, available at www.apec.org/Groups/Other-Groups/Agricultural-Biotechnology (last visited 4 August 2017).

[29] APEC, *2015 APEC Ministerial Meeting* (November 2015), para. 128, available at https://www.apec.org/Meeting-Papers/Annual-Ministerial-Meetings/2015/2015_amm (last visited 13 February 2018).

[30] TPP, Art. 2.27.2.

[31] *Ibid.* Art. 2.27.3.

[32] *Ibid.* Art. 2.27.5 note 14.

review of applications for authorization'.[33] Note that the wording of 'shall endeavor to' is used; thus, this is not something legally required, but merely best-efforts. It appears that the provision for authorization is carefully crafted, considering interests and concerns of both exporting and importing parties: on the one hand, interests of exporting parties which want to increase the chances of authorization in importing parties, and on the other hand, concerns of importing parties which want to be cautious in issuing the authorization.

3. A Side-letter Between the United States and Japan

TPP parties agreed on a number of side-letters on food safety, and one example is the agreement made by the United States with other parties.[34] With Japan, the United States made three agreements, concerning post-harvest fungicides, food additives, and gelatin/collagen. These agreements are contained in the United States-Japan Letter Exchange on Non-Tariff Measures,[35] following agreement between the two governments at the time of Japan's joining the TPP negotiations in 2013 that the SPS issues would be included as one of the non-tariff barriers measures.[36]

Before concluding the negotiations, in Japan, there were a number of concerns reported by newspapers and magazines regarding the possibility that Japan's food safety regulation might be made weaker in response to the US demands.[37] In fact, the three issues—post-harvest fungicides, food additives, and gelatin/collagen—had already been mentioned in the US Trade Representative (USTR)'s *2015 National Trade Estimate Report on Foreign Trade Barriers* as SPS barriers that the US government was concerned about.[38]

---

[33] *Ibid.* Art. 2.27.8.

[34] See USITC (n. 10 above) 422–3 (see Table 6.3: Selected bilateral SPS outcomes addressed in TPP side-letters).

[35] Letter from Kenichiro Sasae, Ambassador of Japan, to Michael B.G. Froman, US Trade Representative (4 February 2016), available at www.cas.go.jp/jp/tpp/naiyou/pdf/side_letter_en/side_letter_en21.pdf (last visited 20 July 2017) (regarding US-Japanese parallel negotiations on non-tariff measures).

[36] See letter from Kenichiro Sasae, Ambassador of Japan, to Demetrios Marantis, acting US Trade Representative (12 April 2013), available at www.cas.go.jp/jp/tpp/pdf/2013/4/130412_syokan(e).pdf (last visited 20 July 2017).

[37] See, e.g., *Shoku No Anzen Wa Mamorareruno? [Will Food Safety be Protected?]*, Asahi Shimbun (Morning ed., 15 October 2015) at 7 (Japan).

[38] Michael B.G. Froman, *2015 National Trade Estimate Report on Foreign Trade Barriers*, 211–12, available at https://ustr.gov/sites/default/files/2015%20NTE%20Combined.pdf (last visited 20 July 2017).

However, when we look at the outcomes of the bilateral negotiations, it does not seem that Japan faced hard bargaining negotiations. With regard to post-harvest fungicides, the United States was complaining that 'Japan classifies fungicides that are applied pre-harvest as pesticides, and fungicides that are applied post-harvest as food additives', and therefore 'each designation requires a separate review' which causes 'the lengthy review process' for 'fungicides that may be used both pre- and post-harvest'.[39] On this issue, the side-letter simply states that Japan's relevant Ministry 'will implement a streamlined approval process for fungicides that may be applied both pre-harvest and post-harvest by utilizing a unified application and deliberation process for approval of pesticides and food additives'.[40]

In terms of food additives, the United States was complaining that a number of food additives that 'are widely-used in the [United States] and other markets are not permitted in Japan' thereby restricting the US imports to Japan.[41] On this point, according to the side-letter, the government of Japan 'will faithfully implement the Cabinet Decision' (of 10 July 2012) 'which determined that the Government of Japan would, within approximately one year . . . complete approval of all four not-yet-designated food additives'.[42]

Finally, in terms of gelatin/collagen, the United States was concerned about Japan's ban on gelatin/collagen for human consumption since 2003 due to the rise of BSE in the United States.[43] However, in March 2015, just before the TPP's conclusion, Japan lifted the import restriction following the risk assessment done by Japan's food safety committee. Thus, the side-letter only states the following outcome: the relevant Ministry 'has eased restrictions on imports of gelatin and collagen'.[44]

Overall, it can be said that the terms of the side-letter between the United States and Japan were quite different from the concerns expressed in newspapers and magazines in Japan, and there was no risk of Japan's food safety regulations being changed and made weaker in response to US demands.

---

39 *Ibid.* at 212.
40 Letter from Kenichiro Sasae (n. 35 above) 17.
41 Froman (n. 38 above) 212.
42 Letter from Kenichiro Sasae (n. 35 above) 17.
43 Froman (n. 38 above) 212.
44 Letter from Kenichiro Sasae (n. 35 above) 17.

III. TBT CHAPTER AND OTHER PRODUCT SAFETY-RELATED PROVISIONS

1. TBT Chapter

As noted, the TBT Chapters in Japan's EPAs are normally not subject to a dispute settlement procedure. In contrast, the TPP's TBT Chapter is subject to the TPP Dispute Settlement Chapter, with one exception.[45] The TBT Chapter contains a provision on 'technical discussions', aiming to resolve any matters arising from this Chapter.[46] Different from the CTC in the TPP's SPS Chapter, these 'technical discussions' in the TBT Chapter are not a precondition to recourse to the Dispute Settlement Chapter.

In comparison with the TPP's SPS Chapter, the TBT Chapter has a similar feature whereby the provision on transparency procedures is enhanced, while substantive provisions are less ambitious. In fact, issues covered in the transparency provisions of the TBT Chapter are similar to those in the SPS Chapter[47]: both cover notification, notice and comment, and compliance period, which were already addressed in the WTO TBT Committee's decisions and recommendations.[48]

One remarkable difference between the TBT and SPS Chapters regarding the procedures is a provision on the involvement and participation of interested parties. In the TBT Chapter, Article 8.7.1—the first paragraph of the transparency provision—states:

> Each Party shall allow persons of another Party to participate in the development of technical regulations, standards . . . on terms no less favourable than those that it accords to its own persons.[49]

A similar participation provision exists in the first paragraph of the transparency provision in the SPS Chapter; however, the wording is less exact:

---

[45] TPP, Art. 8.4.2 ('No Party shall have recourse to dispute settlement under Chapter 28 (Dispute Settlement) for a dispute that exclusively alleges a violation of the provisions of the TBT Agreement incorporated under paragraph 1.'), available at https://ustr.gov/sites/default/files/TPP-Final-Text-Technical-Barriers-to-Trade.pdf (last visited 20 July 2017).

[46] TPP, Art. 8.10.

[47] *Ibid.* Art. 8.7.

[48] Committee on Technical Barriers to Trade, Decisions and recommendations adopted by the WTO Committee on Technical Barriers to Trade since 1 January 1995, Note by the Secretariat, Revision, WTO Doc. G/TBT/1/Rev.12 (21 January 2015).

[49] TPP, TBT Art. 8.7.1.

> The Parties recognise the value of . . . providing interested persons and other Parties with the opportunity to comment on their proposed sanitary and phytosanitary measures.[50]

In this regard, the participation requirement in Article 8.7.1 of the TBT Chapter has raised a concern in Japan that this provision may make it difficult for the government to introduce more stringent labeling requirements.[51] Before joining the negotiations, the government of Japan also seemed to be concerned about the inclusion of this provision, considering how to ensure foreign participation in the development processes of regulations and standards.[52]

However, the final text of Article 8.7.1 added a footnote, stating that a party can satisfy this participation requirement by providing interested persons a reasonable opportunity to provide comments on measures and taking those comments into account in the development of the measures.[53] The government of Japan explains that this opportunity for interested persons to provide comments is a regular procedure already in use in Japan.[54] Again, adding this footnote seems to be a political compromise among negotiators, not to require too many changes in the procedures of developing regulations and standards.

On product safety, the TPP's TBT Chapter builds on the definitions in the WTO TBT Agreement's Annex 1[55] and reaffirms the rights and obligations of the WTO TBT Agreement.[56] The government of Japan was initially concerned whether a specific annex on the labeling of GMOs might be attached to the TBT Chapter in response to US demands in the negotiations.[57] In Japan, food labeling is required if foods contain GMOs; however, the United States complained that its imports are treated less favorably under such a GM labeling requirement. As the purpose of GM labeling is to provide information to consumers, the labeling requirement is normally subject to the WTO TBT Agreement.[58] In the event, the

---

50 TPP, SPS Art. 7.13.1.

51 Naikaku Kanbo (n. 24 above) 17.

52 Naikaku Kanbo (n. 8 above) 20.

53 TPP, TBT note 3. Note that TPP, TBT Art. 8.7.1 is similar to Art. 11.8 (a) of the 2012 US Model Bilateral Investment Treaty, available at https://ustr.gov/sites/default/files/BIT%20text%20for%20ACIEP%20Meeting.pdf (last visited 20 July 2017).

54 Naikaku Kanbo (n. 24 above) 17.

55 TPP, TBT Art. 8.1.

56 TPP, TBT Art. 8.4.

57 Naikaku Kanbo (n. 8 above) 20.

58 David Morgan and Gavin Goh, *Genetically Modified Food Labelling and the WTO Agreements*, 13(3) Rev. Eur. Community & Int'l Envtl. L. 306, 312 (2004).

TPP's TBT Chapter did not add anything on this labeling issue; thus, if the issue of GM labeling is raised, it falls under the scope of Article 2.1 of the WTO's TBT obligation, being subject to requirements of 'like products' and 'no less favourable treatment'.

With regard to harmonization and mutual recognition, the TPP's TBT Chapter does not seem to go beyond the WTO. Article 8.5 of the TPP's TBT Chapter addresses international standards, but the wording is weaker than the language in the SPS Chapter (TPP SPS Article 7.9.2): the provision only asks the parties to recognize the important role of international standards in reducing unnecessary technical barriers to trade. Thus, the provision does not require the parties to use international standards, while it is important to note that Article 2.4 of the WTO TBT Agreement is incorporated through Article 8.4.1 of the TPP's TBT Chapter. One notable point is that Article 8.5.2 refers to the WTO TBT Committee's decision in determining the existence of international standards and recommendations. That TBT Committee's decision provides six principles—transparency, openness, consensus, effectiveness, coherence, and development dimension—that should be observed in the development processes of international standards. This decision was also referred to in *United States—Tuna II (Mexico)* as a 'subsequent agreement between the parties regarding the interpretation of [the TBT Agreement]' in Article 31(3)(a) of the Vienna Convention on the Law of Treaties.[59]

In terms of mutual recognition, it is addressed in the provision on cooperation and trade facilitation;[60] however, it remains simple commitments. The provision simply points out that mutual recognition arrangements between accreditation bodies/conformity assessment bodies are an important mechanism to facilitate the acceptance of conformity assessment results.[61] Also, the provision states that accepting technical regulations as equivalent is one important mechanism to eliminate unnecessary technical barriers to trade.[62] Notably, another provision requires a party to explain the reasons why it has not accepted a technical regulation of equivalence,[63] which is a WTO-plus obligation. The obligation to provide reasons is also set out where a party declines to enter into negotiations to conclude a

---

59 *United States—Measures Concerning the Importation, Marketing and Sale of Tuna and Tuna Products* ('*United States–Tuna II (Mexico)*'), Appellate Body Report, WTO Doc. WT/DS381/AB/R (adopted 13 June 2012), para. 372.
60 TPP, Art. 8.9.
61 *Ibid.* Art. 8.9.1(a).
62 *Ibid.* Art. 8.9.2(d).
63 *Ibid.* Art. 8.9.6.

mutual recognition agreement or to use mutual recognition arrangements in the context of conformity assessment.[64]

2. Annexes to the TBT Chapter

The TBT Chapter contains seven sector-specific Annexes: wine and distilled spirits; information and communications technology products; pharmaceuticals; cosmetics; medical devices; proprietary formulas for prepackaged foods and food additives; and organic products. Article 8.12.3(b) indicates that annexes covering other sectors may be developed in the future.

Overall, it seems that these seven sectors were chosen because there have been concerns with removing barriers and reducing costs in these sectors. Thus, it does not seem to raise product safety concerns as regards these sectors. However, consumers may be interested in and concerned about, for example, what is agreed upon in the Annexes concerning organic products, proprietary formulas for prepackaged foods and food additives, pharmaceuticals, cosmetics, and medical devices. This chapter will take a quick look at these consumer concerns.

With regard to organic products, there have been concerns over trade barriers concerning organic products because each country has its own organic standards and exporting products need to be certified under different standards. On this point, the importance of promoting mutual recognition or equivalence has been argued. The Annex contains a provision to encourage parties to 'consider, as expeditiously as possible, a request for recognition or equivalence' and 'accept as equivalent or recognise' the standards of organic products of other parties.[65] Also it includes an obligation to explain reasons when a party refuses equivalence or recognition of the other party's standards, on request.

Turning to proprietary formulas for prepackaged foods and food additives, this Annex concerns information gathering relating to proprietary formulas. There have been concerns that confidentiality of the information relating to proprietary formulas is not maintained in applying regulations and standards of foods and food additives. The United States has raised its concerns in the USTR's *2015 National Trade Estimate Report* against Japan's disclosure requirements that new food products entering

---

[64] *Ibid.* Arts. 8.6.14 and 8.6.12. The obligation to provide reasons is also established where a party refuses to accept the results of a conformity assessment procedure. See TPP, Art. 8.6.13.

[65] TPP, TBT Annex 8-G, para. 4.

the market provide a list of all ingredients and food additives. The United States claimed that 'this process risks the release of proprietary information to competitors'.[66] The Annex contains a provision to require each party to ensure that 'its information requirements are limited to what is necessary to achieve its legitimate objective'.[67] Another provision in the Annex requires that 'the confidentiality of information about products originating in the territory of another Party . . . is respected in the same way as for domestic products and in such manner that legitimate commercial interests are protected'.[68]

Finally, in terms of pharmaceuticals, cosmetics, and medical devices, these three-sector Annexes have a similar structure. One feature of the Annexes is that the Annex applies to regulations, standards, and 'marketing authorization'. The definition of marketing authorization is given at the beginning of the TBT Chapter: 'the process or processes by which a Party approves or registers a product in order to authorize its marketing, distribution or sale'.[69] There are concerns about marketing authorization functioning as trade barriers in these three sectors. Thus, the three Annexes contain several provisions relating to marketing authorization that have been creating trade barriers for exporters. In addition, the three Annexes contain the same provision on the preparation of marketing authorization (which also applies to a technical regulation and standard). It provides the factors that should be considered in the preparation and development of marketing authorization in view of reducing trade barriers, namely:

> the evaluation of the risks involved, the need to adopt a measure to address those risks, the review of relevant scientific or technical information, and the consideration of the characteristics or design of alternative approaches.[70]

3. Product Standard Topics in the Market Access Chapter

In addition to the TBT Chapter, the TPP Agreement addresses product standard issues in another part—in the Market Access Chapter. It contains two topics which are worth noting: one is concerning remanufactured goods and the other is regarding motor vehicles. The US government had strong export interests in both topics in respect of Asian countries and Japan.

---

66 Froman (n. 38 above) 226.
67 TPP, TBT Annex 8-F, para. 3(a).
68 TPP, TBT Annex 8-F, para. 3(b).
69 TPP, Art. 8.1.
70 TPP, TBT Annexes 8-C, 8-D, and 8-E, para. 2.

(1) Prohibition on the import restrictions of remanufactured goods

A provision on remanufactured goods,[71] contained in the Market Access Chapter, raises an interesting topic in view of product safety. Article 2.11.1 prohibits import and export restrictions on remanufactured goods. Furthermore, even in a case where a party applies import restrictions on used goods, Article 2.11.2 emphasizes the prohibition of import restrictions on remanufactured goods. Thus, the Article distinguishes between two concepts: 'used goods' and 'remanufactured goods'.

Some countries apply import bans against used goods because of product safety concerns. Used goods are sometimes unsafe and not sanitarily cleaned compared with new ones. Another reason for applying import bans is that used goods have a shorter useful life and easily lead to waste—for developing countries, without capacities of recycling such waste disposal, the importation of used goods may put their human health and their environment at risk.

'Remanufactured goods' are different products from such used goods. Generally, the remanufacturing process is described as 'a manufacturing process that restores used or end-of-life products to original working condition or better ("like new")'.[72] The market in remanufactured goods has been growing and the United States is a major country producing and exporting such goods. While there seems to be various existing definitions of 'remanufactured goods' among sectors and countries, the USTR defined the concept as follows:

> non-agricultural goods that are entirely or partially comprised of parts that (i) have been obtained from the disassembly of used goods; and (ii) have been processed, cleaned, inspected, and tested to the extent necessary to ensure they have been restored to original working condition or better; and for which the remanufacturer has issued a warranty.[73]

---

[71] I am grateful to Prof. Tsuyoshi Kawase for bringing this issue to my attention. See, Tsuyoshi Kawase and Fujio Kawashima, *Web Kaisetsu TPP Kyotei–2.1 Nai Kokumintaigu Oyobi Buppin no Shijyo Akusesu (honsoku)* [*TPP Agreement Web Commentary–Chapter 2.1: National Treatment and Market Access for Goods*] 11 (2016), available at www.rieti.go.jp/jp/projects/tpp/pdf/2.1_ma_and_nt_v2.pdf (last visited 20 July 2017) (Japan). See also, Michikazu Kojima, *Kokusai Reuse wo Meguru Ronten [Issues Concerning International Reuse]* (Institute of Developing Economies, 2013), available at http://www.ide.go.jp/library/Japanese/Publish/Download/Report/2012/pdf/C35_ch1.pdf (last visited 20 July 2017) (Japan).

[72] *Remanufactured Goods: An Overview of the U.S. and Global Industries, Market, and Trade*, USITC Pub. No. 4356, Inv. No. 332-525, 1–6 (October 2012), available at www.usitc.gov/publications/332/pub4356.pdf (last visited 20 July 2017).

[73] *Ibid.* at 1-1–2.

There are a number of industry sectors engaging in remanufactured goods, such as electronics, computers, medical devices, motor vehicle parts, which raise product safety concerns. The United States has been concerned that foreign custom authorities treat remanufactured goods as used goods, and that therefore US remanufactured goods oftentimes face import bans.[74]

The United States has expressed its interests on this topic since 2005 at the WTO Doha negotiations[75] and has already included a provision on remanufactured goods in its free trade agreements (FTAs).[76] Furthermore, at the APEC Ministerial Meeting held in 2011 in Honolulu, Hawaii, the 'Pathfinder on Facilitating Trade in Remanufactured Goods'[77] was agreed: it prohibits import prohibitions on remanufactured goods and promotes treating such goods as new goods.

Thus, the United States was very keen to include a provision in the TPP on the prohibition on import restrictions concerning remanufactured goods and to raise awareness that remanufactured goods are not used goods, but more like new ones. In TPP Chapter 1, a definition of remanufactured goods is included,[78] thus, the scope of goods is now

---

74 *Ibid.* at xx.

75 Negotiating Group on Market Access, Market Access for Non-Agricultural Products, Negotiating NTBs Related to Remanufacturing and Refurbishing, Communication from the United States, Addendum, WTO Doc. TN/MA/W/18/Add.11 (5 December 2005).

76 See, e.g., United States–Colombia Trade Promotion Agreement, Art. 2.8 note 1 (22 November 2006), available at https://ustr.gov/sites/default/files/uploads/agreements/fta/colombia/asset_upload_file145_10148.pdf (last visited 20 July 2017); United States-Korea Free Trade Agreement, Art. 2.8 note 1 (30 June 2007), available at https://ustr.gov/sites/default/files/uploads/agreements/fta/korus/asset_upload_file904_12701.pdf (last visited 20 July 2017); United States-Singapore Free Trade Agreement, Annex 3C (6 May 2003), available at https://ustr.gov/sites/default/files/uploads/agreements/fta/singapore/asset_upload_file965_4043.pdf (last visited 20 July 2017).

77 APEC, *2011 Ministerial Meeting, Annex D-Pathfinder on Facilitating Trade in Remanufactured Goods*, available at https://www.apec.org/Meeting-Papers/Annual-Ministerial-Meetings/2011/2011_amm/annex-d (last visited 13 February 2018).

78 According to TPP, Art. 1.3, remanufactured goods means 'a good classified in HS Chapters 84 through 90 or under heading 94.02 except goods classified under HS headings 84.18, 85.09, 85.10, and 85.16, 87.03 or subheadings 8414.51, 8450.11, 8450.12, 8508.11, and 8517.11, that is entirely or partially composed of recovered materials and: (a) has a similar life expectancy and performs the same as or similar to such a good when new; and (b) has a factory warranty similar to that applicable to such a good when new', see https://ustr.gov/sites/default/files/TPP-Final-Text-Initial-Provisions-and-General-Definitions.pdf (last visited 20 July 2017).

clarified.[79] If goods have a similar life expectancy and perform the same as new ones, coming with a factory warranty, such goods are treated as remanufactured goods. At the same time, note that the right of importing countries is also ensured: a footnote to Article 2.11 of the TPP indicates that importing countries can demand remanufactured goods to be identified, for example by labeling, in order to distinguish them from used goods and to meet all technical requirements that apply to new goods.

(2) Motor vehicle trade (United States-Japan)

When Japan joined the TPP negotiations, the United States and Japan agreed to 'conduct negotiations on motor vehicle trade in parallel to the TPP negotiations', including the issue on safety standards.[80] Since then, in Japan, there have been concerns about safety standards of motor vehicles—the United States may demand the lowering of Japan's safety standards in order to promote US exports.

As an outcome, the TPP's Market Access Chapter contains the agreement between the United States and Japan on motor vehicles ('Appendix D-1'), which is attached to a party-specific Annex to that Chapter.[81] With regard to this Appendix, the United States and Japan concluded several side-letters on motor vehicles for the purpose of elaborating and qualifying the agreement.

During the negotiations with the United States, Japan's concern was to avoid accepting demands from the United States that were similar to those agreed upon by Korea in the United States-Korea Free Trade Agreement. Still, we can see some influences from the United States-Korea FTA on TPP Appendix D-1. For instance, in Appendix D-1, there is a provision on an interval between the date of the publication and the date of compliance with technical regulation and conformity assessment procedures that would require a substantial change in motor vehicle design or technology—it sets such a period as 'usually not less than 12 months' (Article 2.1). This is longer than the interval specified in Article 8.8.2 of the TPP's TBT Chapter, which provides a period of 'more than 6

[79] However, see a lengthy list of exemptions for Vietnam in TPP, Annex 2-B.

[80] This bilateral agreement was made during the US-Japanese bilateral consultations on Japan's interests in joining the TPP negotiations. See *Motor Vehicle Trade, Terms of Reference* (12 April 2013), available at www.cas.go.jp/jp/tpp/pdf/2013/4/130412_tor(e).pdf (last visited 20 July 2017).

[81] TPP, Annex 2-D, Appendix D-1, available at https://ustr.gov/sites/default/files/TPP-Final-Text-Japan-Appendix-D-1-Appendix-between-Japan-and-the-United-States-on-Motor-Vehicle-Trade.pdf (last visited 20 July 2017).

months'. It is apparent that the interval of twelve months was taken from the provision in the United States-Korea FTA.[82]

In terms of safety requirements on motor vehicles, under the United States-Korea FTA, the United States and Korea reached an agreement that motor vehicles from the United States:

> sold no more than 25,000 . . . in the territory of Korea during the previous calendar year shall be deemed to comply with Korean Motor Vehicle Safety Standards (KMVSS) if the manufacturer certifies that the motor vehicle complies with U.S. Federal Motor Vehicle Safety Standards (FMVSS).[83]

This provision was understood to have resulted in laxer Korean safety standards, because importation of a certain volume of US motor vehicles to Korea was automatically treated as the United States being in compliance with Korean safety standards—in other words, the US safety requirements were regarded as sufficiently stringent as Korean requirements without examining the differences between each requirement. Japan was concerned about such an outcome and was determined not to accept a similar provision in the negotiations with the United States.[84]

Appendix D-1 addresses various kinds of trade barriers on motor vehicles, and in particular, Article 3 is concerned with technical regulations. Notably, Article 3.6(a) of Appendix D-1 addresses how Japan treats the differences in safety standards between the two countries. It states that if the competent authority of Japan finds that:

> a requirement of the U.S. FMVSS is no less stringent than the requirement under [Japan's] Road Vehicle Law to which it corresponds, originating motor vehicles from the U.S. . . . that comply with such a requirement of the U.S.

---

[82] Exchange of Letters between US Trade Representative Ron Kirk and Korean Trade Minister Kim Jong-Hoon (includes English translation) on 10 February 2011, Section C: Transparency, 1 ('each Party shall provide an interval between the date of publication of the technical regulation or conformity assessment procedure and the date on which compliance with the measure becomes mandatory that is usually not less than 12 months'), available at https://ustr.gov/sites/default/files/uploads/Countries%20Regions/africa/agreements/korus/2011_02_10_Kim-Kirk%20Response.pdf (last visited 7 August 2017).

[83] *Ibid.* Section B: Safety Standards, 1.

[84] *TPP: Beikokusha no Anzenkijyun Shouten* [*TPP: The Issue is Safety Standards of US Autos*], MAINICHI (Morning ed., 10 June 2014) at 7 (Japan). See also, Hisashi Shibata, *TPP niokeru Jidoushagoui to Kongo no Tenbou* [*Motor Vehicle Agreements under the TPP and Future Prospects*], 45(3) KOKUSAI SHOJI HOMU [Journal of the Japanese Institute of International Business Law], 393, 396 (2017) (Japan).

> FMVSS shall be deemed to comply with that requirement under the Road Vehicle Law.[85]

Thus, unlike the United States-Korea FTA, Japan's competent authority will decide on a case-by-case basis whether a requirement of the US FMVSS is as stringent as one of Japan's safety requirements. To elaborate on Article 3.6(a), there exists a side-letter that identified seven US FMVSS requirements that were found to be as stringent as Japan's safety requirements.[86] Related to Article 3 of the Appendix D-1, another side-letter addresses technical regulations concerning motor vehicles that will ensure or have ensured conformity with international standards (such as a UN Regulation or Global Technical Regulation), and which were already or will be revised.[87] This is to show that the government of Japan is making efforts to avoid creating unnecessary obstacles to trade by its motor vehicle technical regulations.

IV. CONCLUSION

In view of regulatory divergence and convergence, it can be said that the TPP's provisions on food and product safety are attempting regulatory convergence to some extent in that these provisions rely on past experiences at other forums or bilateral negotiations—incorporating obligations under those WTO Agreements, adopting the WTO Committees' decisions and recommendations, following discussions in the APEC, and also bringing in own trade concerns and interests expressed in past bilateral interactions. Thus, the TPP's outcome concerning food and product safety is a mixture and combination of past experiences and issues, and in that sense, the TPP's provisions on food and product safety contribute to regulatory convergence.

Looking at the TPP's SPS and TBT Chapters, a number of WTO-plus provisions are found in procedural provisions (in particular, the transparency provision) rather than in substantive provisions concerning food and

---

[85] TPP, Annex 2-1, Appendix D-1, Art. 3.6(a).

[86] Letter from Kenichiro Sasae, Ambassador of Japan, to Michael B.G. Froman, US Trade Representative (4 February 2016), available at www.cas.go.jp/jp/tpp/naiyou/pdf/side_letter_en/side_letter_en18.pdf (last visited 20 July 2017).

[87] Letter from Kenichiro Sasae, Ambassador of Japan, to Michael B.G. Froman, US Trade Representative (4 February 2016): Motor Vehicle Technical Regulations, Standards and Conformity Assessment Procedures, available at https://www.cas.go.jp/jp/tpp/naiyou/pdf/side_letter_en/side_letter_en17.pdf (last visited 20 July 2017).

product safety. It seems that the existence of extensive provisions in transparency is a trend in negotiating FTAs.[88] While agreeing on procedural issues is easier than agreeing on substantive ones, procedural obligations can also generate convergence. It has been pointed out that 'provisions that promote information exchange and introduce notification and comment periods can provide an opportunity for convergence' because such provisions can increase the chances for cooperation to reduce barriers to trade.[89]

While it has become extremely uncertain whether the TPP Agreement will enter into force after the withdrawal of the United States, the TPP's outcomes will not just go away. Food and product safety issues addressed in this chapter will be raised again in future trade negotiations, and legal provisions (or even political compromises) under the TPP Agreement can emerge as a focal point in bargaining. On that point, experiences and knowledge gained from the TPP negotiations would remain.

---

[88] Stoler (n. 2 above) 219 (see Table 11.1 Comparison of main features relating to TBT and SPS measures).

[89] Puig and Dalke (n. 2 above) 83.

11. Megaregional transformation of global food safety governance: Normative roots and ramifications

Ching-Fu Lin

I. INTRODUCTION

The conclusion of the Trans-Pacific Partnership (TPP) negotiations in October 2015 represents a defining moment in international trade and regulatory governance. Historically, the TPP has its root in the Trans-Pacific Strategic Economic Partnership Agreement concluded by Brunei, Chile, New Zealand, and Singapore in 2006. The United States' participation in 2008 served as a major catalyst, leading to further expansion of membership[1]—with Australia, Peru, Malaysia, Vietnam, Peru, Mexico, Canada, and Japan successively joining in the negotiations. Although the TPP has yet to enter into force and the United States has formally withdrawn,[2] its signatories represent a considerable share of global gross domestic product (GDP) and world trade,[3] and the 'gold standards' enshrined in the TPP may likely find their way through other channels and continue to exert significant normative influence in current and future negotiations.

The depth and breadth of this megaregional agreement, as well as the diversity of its parties, pose a challenge not only to trade policies

[1] Ian F. Fergusson et al., *The Trans-Pacific Partnership (TPP) Negotiations and Issues for Congress* (Congressional Research Service Report, 20 March 2015).

[2] Singapore Ministry of Trade and Industry, Press Release, Joint Statement by TPP Partners (21 May 2017), available at www.mti.gov.sg/MTIInsights/SiteAssets/Pages/TPP/Statement%20on%20the%20Trans-Pacific%20Partnership%20(21%20May%202017).pdf (last visited 26 August 2017); Tomohiro Ebuchi and Ryohei Yasoshima, *The TPP 11 Agree to Move Forward with Minimal Tweaks*, Nikkei Asian Review (20 July 2017).

[3] Press Release, Trans-Pacific Partnership Ministers' Statement (4 February 2016), available at www.mti.gov.sg/MTIInsights/SiteAssets/Pages/TPP/Joint%20Statement%20by%20Ministers%20on%20TPP%20Signing_FINAL.pdf (last visited 26 August 2017).

in the conventional sense, but also to many other cross-cutting issues. Envisioned by its parties as 'a comprehensive, next-generation regional agreement that liberalizes trade and investment',[4] the TPP includes thirty Chapters that address both traditional trade issues and new challenges. On the one hand, the TPP covers the full spectrum of regional trade agreement (RTA) matters, including *inter alia* trade in goods and services,[5] technical barriers to trade (TBT) and sanitary and phytosanitary (SPS) measures,[6] and intellectual property.[7] On the other hand, the TPP takes a step forward by adopting horizontal rules to address cross-cutting issues such as regulatory coherence,[8] labor and environment,[9] state-owned enterprises (SOEs) and designated monopolies,[10] and small and medium-sized enterprises (SMEs).[11]

Remarkably, it is expected that there will be an increase of overlaps and normative interactions between the traditional and sectoral as well as the novel and horizontal rules, which will likely generate complex impacts—mutually reinforcing or conflicting—on the dynamic balance between regulatory autonomy and cooperation. Given the institutional design of the TPP, food safety governance is destined to be configured and reconfigured not only by the SPS Chapter alone, but also by other horizontal rules. For example, while harmonization with international standards, scientific principle, risk analysis, and transparency still serves as the fundamental rubric of SPS (and SPS-plus),[12] cooperation among

---

4 Press Release, Trans-Pacific Partnership Leaders Statement (12 November 2011), available at www.whitehouse.gov/the-press-office/2011/11/12/trans-pacific-partnership-leaders-statement (last visited 26 August 2017).

5 Trans-Pacific Partnership (signed on 4 February 2016, yet to be ratified), full text available at https://ustr.gov/trade-agreements/free-trade-agreements/trans-pacific-partnership/tpp-full-text (last visited 26 August 2017) (TPP), Chs. 2–6, 10–13.

6 *Ibid.* Chs. 7 and 8.

7 *Ibid.* Ch. 18.

8 *Ibid.* Ch. 25.

9 *Ibid.* Chs. 19 and 20.

10 *Ibid.* Ch. 17.

11 *Ibid.* Ch. 24.

12 SPS issues are addressed in TPP, Ch. 7 (SPS Chapter), see https://ustr.gov/sites/default/files/TPP-Final-Text-Sanitary-and-Phytosanitary-Measures.pdf (last visited 26 August 2017). Positioning the TPP as a high standard FTA for full market liberalization during the SPS Chapter negotiations, the parties have struggled to find a proper balance between the promotion of trade and the protection of public health. As a result, there are a number of SPS-plus provisions in the final text of the SPS Chapter, ranging from 'pro-trade' to 'pro-health', that go beyond the scope and depth of the World Trade Organization (WTO) Agreement on the

TPP members and cross-cutting of regulatory coherence rules, such as the notice-and-comment requirement, cost-benefit analysis, and regulatory impact assessment, will come into play with significant relevance and importance. What are the SPS-plus rights and obligations of the TPP? Will such SPS-plus provisions pose pro-trade or pro-health ramifications for countries within and beyond the scope of the TPP? How will the rules under the SPS Chapter and the Regulatory Coherence Chapter interact and work together to create an optimal institutional design that can simultaneously strengthen trade liberalization and ensure adequate food safety protection? How will the diversity of the TPP parties in terms of legal systems and stages of development affect the implementation of relevant rules? Last but not least, will the TPP platform for SPS cooperation produce constructive or destructive effects on the World Trade Organization (WTO) multilateral trading system?

To explore the theoretical and practical importance of such questions, this chapter endeavors to explore these issues by closely examining the TPP Chapters on SPS Measures (and Regulatory Coherence). Section II briefly reviews the negotiation history of the SPS Chapter, sorting out the development of some contentious issues, which then serves as a vantage point to analyze the main provisions of the final text. Section III identifies the SPS-plus provisions incorporated in the TPP by referencing the WTO SPS Agreement, characterizing the provisions along a pro-trade versus pro-health continuum. The study then examines the implications of the TPP for global food safety governance, offering some preliminary observations for future discussions in comparable settings. Section IV concludes.

II. AN OVERVIEW OF MEGAREGIONAL SPS PROVISIONS

The TPP negotiations on the SPS Chapter involved a number of SPS-plus issues, covering various proposals that extended beyond the rights and obligations under the WTO Agreement on the Application of Sanitary and Phytosanitary Measures (SPS Agreement).[13] Similar to most of the RTAs currently in force, the TPP SPS Chapter mirrors the WTO SPS

Application of Sanitary and Phytosanitary Measures ('SPS Agreement'). See the discussion in Section III below.

[13] For a comprehensive analysis of the SPS Agreement, see JOANNE SCOTT, THE WTO AGREEMENT ON SANITARY AND PHYTOSANITARY MEASURES: A COMMENTARY (2007); LUKASZ GRUSZCZYNSKI, REGULATING HEALTH AND ENVIRONMENTAL RISKS UNDER WTO LAW: A CRITICAL ANALYSIS OF THE SPS AGREEMENT (2010).

Agreement in terms of its fundamental objectives, which seek to protect human, animal, or plant life or health in the territories of the parties, while facilitating and expanding trade.[14] The advent of the multilateral trading system—in conjunction with the globalization of economic activities, advancements in food science, development of transportation technology, and integration and consolidation of agri-food industries—has significantly transformed the production, distribution, and consumption of food worldwide.[15] Such transformed patterns have posed new challenges to food safety governance, evidenced in the intensified scale, severity, frequency, and impact of food-borne illness outbreaks, especially in the cross-border context.[16] Risks posed by unsafe food products can originate from a producer in one country and quickly spill over to many others, evolving from a local problem to a global concern through international trade channels within a short period of time.[17] In light of the globalized food-borne risk landscape, as well as heightened public criticism,[18] there has been considerable demand for more stringent regulation (i.e., SPS

---

14 TPP, Art. 7.2(a). Jackson and Vitikala have reviewed 256 RTAs currently in force and found that most of them mirror the objectives to protect human, animal, or plant life or health stipulated in the SPS Agreement. For their comprehensive survey, see Lee Ann Jackson and Hanna Vitikala, *Cross-Cutting Issues in Regional Trade Agreements: Sanitary and Phytosanitary Measures*, *in* REGIONAL TRADE AGREEMENTS AND THE MULTILATERAL TRADING SYSTEM 230–315 (Rohini Acharya ed., 2016).

15 See World Economic Forum, *Global Risk 2008: A Global Risk Network Report*, available at www.weforum.org/pdf/globalrisk/report2008.pdf (last visited 26 August 2017); Yasmine Motarjemi et al., *Future Challenges in Global Harmonization of Food Safety Legislation*, 12(6) FOOD CONTROL 339, 340–41 (2001); Fritz K. Käferstein et al., *Foodborne Disease Control: A Transnational Challenge*, 3(4) EMERGING INFECTIOUS DISEASES 503, 503–10 (1997); Fritz K. Käferstein and Mohammed Abdussalam, *Food Safety in the 21st Century*, 77(4) BULLETIN OF WORLD HEALTH ORG. 347, 347–51 (1999).

16 See generally Ching-Fu Lin, *Global Food Safety: Exploring Key Elements for an International Regulatory Strategy*, 51(3) VA. J. INT'L L. 637 (2011).

17 *Ibid*. See also Kenneth A. Bamberger and Andrew T. Guzman, *Importers as Regulators: Product Safety in a Globalized World*, *in* IMPORT SAFETY: REGULATORY GOVERNANCE IN THE GLOBAL ECONOMY 193–214 (Cary Coglianese et al. eds., 2009); Praveen Gangahar, *Food Safety and Management System*, *in* FOOD SAFETY, QUALITY ASSURANCE AND GLOBAL TRADE: CONCERNS AND STRATEGIES 25 (S.P. Singh et al. eds., 2009); Derek Yach and Douglas Bettcher, *The Globalization of Public Health I: Threats and Opportunities*, 88 AM. J. PUB. HEALTH 735 (1998) (discussing the effects of globalization on public health issues).

18 See e.g., ED RANDALL, FOOD, RISK AND POLITICS: SCARE, SCANDAL AND CRISIS—INSIGHTS INTO THE RISK POLITICS OF FOOD SAFETY (2009); MARION NESTLE, SAFE FOOD: THE POLITICS OF FOOD SAFETY (2010).

measures)[19]—posing grand challenges for governments as well as the WTO in distinguishing between genuine public health protection and disguised trade protectionism.[20]

On the one hand, the SPS Chapter of the TPP recognizes the need and the right of the parties to formulate SPS measures in order to protect the health and lives of their citizens from risks posed by imported food and agricultural products. On the other hand, considering the potentially restrictive effect that SPS measures may have on international trade, the Chapter builds on the SPS Agreement and devises more specific or additional rules to impose discipline on such measures. The next section provides an overview of such rules under the SPS Chapter in its final text, which may serve as a premise for discussion below.

1. Scientific Justification and Risk Analysis

To strike a proper balance between the liberalization of trade in food and parties' right to regulate for the purpose of public health protection,[21] science continues to serve as the benchmark to distinguish between legitimate protection and disguised protectionist measures.[22] Article 7.9 of the TPP, which is the central provision of the SPS Chapter, requires SPS measures to be based on scientific principles.[23] Parties must either 'conform to the relevant international standards, guidelines or recommendations' or base their measures on 'documented and objective scientific evidence' in light of the risk assessment obligations under the SPS Agreement.[24]

When conducting a risk assessment, the parties shall 'take into account reasonably available and relevant scientific data', which may be in the form

---

[19] See e.g., Alberto Alemanno, *The European Food Import Safety Regime under a 'Stress Test': The Melamine Contamination of the Global Food Supply Chain*, 3(4) Erasmus L. Rev. 203, 213–15 (2010).

[20] See generally Scott (n. 13 above); Gruszczynski (n. 13 above).

[21] See generally Denise Prévost, Balancing Trade and Health in the SPS Agreement: The Development Dimension (2009).

[22] In the area of food safety, an unchallenged premise is that a state has the right to take into account its special concerns and to establish legitimate but differentiated rules and standards in order to protect the health of its citizens. See Paul Martin, *Sovereignty and Food Safety in a NAFTA Context*, 24 Can.-U.S. L.J. 369 (1998). See also generally Gabrielle Marceau and Joel P. Trachtman, *The Technical Barriers to Trade Agreement, the Sanitary and Phytosanitary Measures Agreement, and the General Agreement on Tariffs and Trade*, 36(5) J. World Trade 811 (2002).

[23] TPP, Art. 7.9.1.

[24] *Ibid.* Art. 7.9.2.

of qualitative or quantitative information.[25] In terms of risk management, the parties are to consider options for SPS measures, which can achieve the appropriate level of protection while being 'not more trade restrictive than required', and especially the option of taking no measures.[26] All in all, throughout the process of risk analysis,[27] the parties must document the entire course,[28] offer other parties and interested persons 'an opportunity to comment',[29] and 'take into account relevant guidance of the WTO SPS Committee and international standards, guidelines and recommendations'.[30] Apart from the rules set forth in Article 7.9, when a party adopts an emergency measure to protect human, animal, or plant life or health, it is also required to review the scientific basis of the measure within six months.[31]

2. Harmonization

Many RTAs contain SPS provisions that make reference to harmonization in a manner mirroring Article 3 of the SPS Agreement,[32] and the TPP is no exception. To facilitate a greater level of harmonization among the parties, the TPP goes beyond the harmonization requirement established in the SPS Agreement,[33] asking the parties to 'conform

---

25 *Ibid.* Art. 7.9.5.

26 *Ibid.* Art. 7.9.6 and note 5.

27 The concept of 'risk analysis' contains three basic components: risk assessment, risk management, and risk communication. The TPP's SPS Chapter specifically addresses risk assessment and risk management, but leaves the component of risk communication intact. For relevant discussions, see Lukasz Gruszczynski, *Science in the Process of Risk Regulation under the WTO Agreement on Sanitary and Phytosanitary Measures*, 7 GERMAN L.J. 371, 371–98 (2006).

28 TPP, Art. 7.9.4(b).

29 *Ibid.*

30 *Ibid.* Arts. 7.9.6(a), 7.9.7, and 7.9.8.

31 *Ibid.* Art. 7.14.2.

32 See Jackson and Vitikala (n. 14 above) 324–7. Among those RTAs containing harmonization provisions, most do not go beyond the requirement stipulated in Article 3 of the SPS Agreement. See also John G. Surak, *Harmonization of International Standards*, *in* ENSURING GLOBAL FOOD SAFETY: EXPLORING GLOBAL HARMONIZATION 340–41, 349–50 (Christine E. Boisrobert et al. eds., 2010).

33 The SPS Agreement requires WTO members to 'harmonize [SPS] measures on as wide a basis as possible, [and] base their [SPS] measures on international standards, guidelines or recommendations, where they exist'. SPS Agreement, Arts. 3.1 and 3.2 (15 April 1994), Marrakesh Agreement Establishing the World Trade Organization, Annex 1A, 1867 UNTS 493. Such international standards, guidelines, or recommendations refer to those adopted by the 'three sister' organizations, i.e., the Codex Alimentarius Commission ('Codex') relating to food safety, the International Office of Epizootics (OIE) relating to animal health, and

to'[34] (see the discussion below in Section III) relevant international standards, recommendations, or guidelines adopted by the Codex Alimentarius Commission ('Codex'), the International Office of Epizootics ('OIE'), and the International Plant Protection Convention ('IPPC').[35] Note that, however, the SPS Chapter does not strive for complete harmonization. Rather, it allows for SPS measures that deviate from international standards, guidelines, or recommendations if there is scientific justification, as required under Article 7.9.[36] The right of the parties to establish their own appropriate level of protection, which may differ from protection at the international level, is also recognized.[37]

It should be noted that on many other occasions, the Chapter explicitly requires the parties to 'take into account the relevant guidance of the WTO SPS Committee', as well as that of 'international standards, guidelines and recommendations'.[38] In areas including equivalence determination,[39] risk analysis procedures,[40] audit and certification,[41] and transparency,[42] the parties bear a legal obligation to consider the guidance of not only the 'three sisters', but also the SPS Committee of the multilateral trading system.

3. Equivalence and Mutual Recognition

The TPP SPS Chapter provides the parties with different channels to determine equivalence while achieving one another's chosen levels of protection and urges them to 'apply equivalence to a group of measures or on a systems-wide basis, to the extent feasible and appropriate'.[43] More specifically, when an exporting party objectively demonstrates that its SPS

---

the International Plant Protection Convention (IPPC) relating to plant health: SPS Agreement, Annex A.

[34] For a discussion on the difference between 'based on' and 'conform to', see e.g., Scott (n. 13 above) 199–200; Dale E. McNeil, *The First Case Under the WTO's Sanitary and Phytosanitary Agreement: The European Union's Hormone Ban*, 39 Va. J. Int'l L. 89, 123 (1998); Ryan David Thomas, *Where's the Beef: Mad Cows and the Blight of the SPS Agreement*, 32 Vand. J. Transnat'l L. 487, 509 (1999).

[35] TPP, Art. 7.9.2.

[36] See above for the discussion on scientific principle and risk assessment.

[37] TPP, Arts. 7.9.2 and 7.9.3(a).

[38] See the examples and footnotes referred to below.

[39] TPP, Art. 7.8.1.

[40] *Ibid.* Art. 7.9.6(a).

[41] *Ibid.* Arts. 7.10.3 and 7.12.6.

[42] *Ibid.* Art. 7.13.

[43] *Ibid.* Art. 7.8.1.

measure 'achieves the same level of protection' or 'has the same effect in achieving the objective' set by the importing party's measure, the importing party shall recognize the equivalence of such measures.[44]

To facilitate the process of equivalence assessment, Article 7.8 imposes specific obligations on the importing party. For example, an importing party is required, upon the request of an exporting party, to provide an explanation of 'the objective and rationale of its SPS measure and clearly identify the risk the SPS measure is intended to address'[45] and its 'process and plan for making the equivalence determination'.[46] In addition, an exporting party has the right to request an equivalence assessment by an importing party, and the importing party 'shall initiate the assessment within a reasonable period of time' when sufficient information is provided.[47] If an importing party reaches a conclusion of equivalence determination, it must provide the requesting party a written communication about the measure and implement it in a reasonable time span.[48]

4. Import Check, Audit, and Certification

Considering the regulatory challenges confronted by importing parties in the face of the complex global food supply chain, the SPS Chapter specifies three types of SPS measures parties can adopt in order to ensure food safety: import check, audit, and certification. Nonetheless, as these systems may in some cases unjustifiably impede international trade, parties are required to administer their control and approval procedures in a manner that is not more burdensome than reasonable and necessary.

First, to determine an exporting party's capacity to meet the SPS measures of the importing party, each importing party has the right to conduct system-based audits to evaluate the effectiveness of the regulatory system of the exporting party.[49] The audit may cover an assessment of an exporting party's control programs, including reviews of the inspection and audit programs, as well as on-site inspections of facilities.[50] Again, the importing party shall explain to and discuss with its counterpart 'the objectives and scope of the audit; the criteria or requirements against which the exporting Party will be assessed; and the itinerary and procedures for conducting the

44 *Ibid.* Art. 7.8.6.
45 *Ibid.* Art. 7.8.2.
46 *Ibid.* Art. 7.8.4.
47 *Ibid.* Art. 7.8.3.
48 *Ibid.* Art. 7.8.7.
49 *Ibid.* Art. 7.10.1.
50 *Ibid.*

audit'.[51] The auditing party is further obliged to provide the audited party the opportunity to comment on the findings of the audit and to take any such comments into account before the former renders its conclusions.[52]

With regard to import checks, the parties must base their measures on the risks associated with the imported products, carry out import checks 'without undue delay', and make available relevant information such as sampling procedures, rationale for determining the frequency of checks, analytical methods, and even the facilities that they use to test.[53] Importing parties shall also ensure that final decisions with regard to a finding of nonconformity are reasonable and necessary, and are 'rationally related to the available science'.[54] When a party decides to prohibit or restrict the importation of a product of another party, the importing party bears an obligation to notify the importer or its agent, the exporter, the manufacturer, or the exporting party within seven days, and to provide an opportunity for review.[55]

Finally, assurance with respect to SPS requirements may be provided through certificates. The importing party shall ensure that 'the certificate requirement is applied . . . only to the extent necessary to protect human, animal or plant life or health'.[56] Furthermore, the attestations and information required on the certificates should be limited to essential information related to the SPS objectives of the importing party.[57] Similarly, an importing party is obliged to provide to another party, upon request, the rationale for relevant requirements.[58] In addition to the harmonization requirements mentioned above, parties may work cooperatively to develop model certificates and promote electronic certification or other technologies to facilitate trade.[59]

---

51 *Ibid.* Art. 7.10.4.

52 More specifically, the auditing party's 'decision or action taken . . . as a result of the audit shall be supported by objective evidence and data that can be verified, taking into account the auditing Party's knowledge of, relevant experience with, and confidence in, the audited Party'. The auditing party also has to 'provide a report setting out its conclusions in writing to the audited Party within a reasonable period of time'. TPP Arts. 7.10.5 and 7.10.6.

53 *Ibid.* Arts. 7.10.1, 7.10.2, and 7.10.4.

54 *Ibid.* Art. 7.11.5.

55 The notification should include: (a) the reason for the prohibition or restriction; (b) the legal basis or authorization for the action; and (c) information on the status of the affected goods and their disposition. TPP, Arts. 7.11.6–7.11.8.

56 *Ibid.* Art. 7.12.2.

57 *Ibid.* Art. 7.12.4.

58 *Ibid.* Art. 7.12.5.

59 *Ibid.* Arts. 7.12.6 and 7.12.7.

5. Institutionalized Cooperation and Technical Assistance

Without an effective platform to serve as the normative infrastructure for SPS cooperation, the objectives of this Chapter could not be adequately fulfilled.[60] Therefore, the TPP devised a series of mechanisms to 'strengthen communication, consultation and cooperation between the Parties'.[61] First, similar to the SPS Agreement, the parties must provide a written description of their contact points, as well as competent authorities with regard to relevant SPS responsibilities.[62] Moreover, Article 7.5 establishes a Committee on Sanitary and Phytosanitary Measures ('TPP SPS Committee')—comprised of government representatives of each party—as a forum to exchange information, establish working groups and projects, and enhance understanding on issues related to the implementation of the SPS Agreement and this Chapter, as well as SPS measures and regulatory processes of the parties.[63] The TPP SPS Committee may also 'identify and develop technical assistance and cooperation projects' to facilitate SPS cooperation among parties.[64]

Remarkably, with respect to international cooperation, this Committee 'may consult on matters and positions' for relevant meetings of the WTO SPS Committee, and those held under the auspices of the Codex, OIE, and IPPC.[65] Additionally, the Committee is expected to meet regularly (at least once a year) so as to serve as a channel for quick handling of SPS issues.[66] Finally, the parties shall explore opportunities for further cooperation, collaboration and information exchange, including trade facilitation initiatives and technical assistance.[67]

---

[60] With regard to the benefits of having an institutional mechanism to discuss special trade concerns, apply peer pressure, and facilitate cooperation, see e.g., Yoshiko Naiki, *Accountability and Legitimacy in Global Health and Safety Governance: The World Trade Organization, the SPS Committee, and International Standard-Setting Organizations*, 43(6) J. World Trade 1255 (2009); Andrew Lang and Joanne Scott, *The Hidden World of WTO Governance*, 20(3) Eur. J. Int'l L. 575 (2009).

[61] TPP, Art. 7.2(c).

[62] *Ibid.* Art. 7.6.

[63] *Ibid.* Art. 7.5.3(a)–(f).

[64] *Ibid.* Art. 7.5.3(e).

[65] *Ibid.* Art. 7.5.3(g).

[66] *Ibid.* Art. 7.5.5.

[67] *Ibid.* Art. 7.15.

6. Transparency

To enhance mutual understanding of each party's SPS measures, and to strengthen the role interested persons can play in the policy-making process, the SPS Chapter requires parties to provide information related to proposed and final SPS measures for interested parties to comment. More specifically, unless there are urgent SPS problems or the measure is trade-facilitating, a party shall notify the other parties of a proposed SPS measure that may have an effect on trade by way of the existing WTO SPS notification system and allow at least sixty days for written comments.[68] The party shall also make available to the public the proposed SPS measure, the legal basis for the measure, and the written comments (or a summary) received.[69] When proposing to adopt an SPS measure, a party shall also discuss with another party, upon request or under appropriate circumstances, scientific or trade concerns that may emerge, as well as available, less trade-restrictive alternatives.[70] Finally, if the final form of an SPS measure is 'substantively altered' vis-à-vis the proposal, the party must offer an explanation in conjunction with the publication of the final measure.[71]

7. Dispute Resolution

According to Articles 7.17 and 7.18, the SPS Chapter covers three arrangements for the resolution of disputes: the prioritized use of domestic and bilateral remedies, the cooperative technical consultations (CTC), and the dispute settlement mechanism as provided under Chapter 28. Although this structural design resembles that of the WTO SPS Agreement, the emphasis on domestic and bilateral remedies, as well as the significantly elaborate CTC, may serve as a more proactive and progressive channel to address potential disputes.

When any matter arises under the auspice of the SPS Chapter, a concerned party shall endeavor to address the issue via available administrative procedures of the other party, as well as existing bilateral or other mechanisms, as the first venue.[72] Yet, the concerned party may resort to the CTC as long as it considers that the above approaches would not resolve the issue.[73] In that case, the parties shall meet within thirty days of the

---

68 *Ibid.* Arts. 7.13.3–7.13.5.

69 *Ibid.*

70 *Ibid.* Arts. 7.13.6 and 7.13.7.

71 *Ibid.* Art. 7.13.10.

72 *Ibid.* Art. 7.17.1.

73 *Ibid.* More specifically, parties may initiate CTC with another party 'to

responding party's acknowledgement of the consultation request to discuss the issue, endeavor to reach a mutually agreed resolution within 180 days if possible, and 'ensure the appropriate involvement of relevant trade and regulatory agencies in meetings'.[74] As a general principle, all communications relevant to the process of the CTC and documents produced therein shall be made confidential.[75] Because the CTC serves as a compulsory precondition for resources to dispute settlement, it is only when the CTC meetings are finished or such meetings do not take place within a specified period of time that the requesting party can resort to Chapter 28.[76]

III. SPS-PLUS INSTITUTIONAL DESIGNS AND NORMATIVE IMPLICATIONS FOR GLOBAL FOOD SAFETY GOVERNANCE

'WTO-Plus' generally refers to rights or obligations in an RTA that go beyond the baseline set in the WTO multilateral trading system, namely, when RTA parties assume greater obligations or enjoy extra rights vis-à-vis those under the relevant WTO agreements.[77] Hence, 'SPS-plus' denotes:

> legal instruments that are signed by countries and that include *more detailed or demanding provisions* than the multilateral rules under the SPS Agreement, or that contain other regulatory or cooperative elements *beyond the scope* of the SPS Agreement. (emphasis added)[78]

---

discuss any matter arising under this Chapter that the requesting Party considers may adversely affect its trade by delivering a written request to the responding Party, and the responding Party shall acknowledge the request in writing within seven days of the date of its receipt'. TPP, Arts. 7.17.2 and 7.17.3.

[74] *Ibid.* Arts. 7.17.4 and 7.17.5.

[75] *Ibid.* Art. 7.17.6.

[76] *Ibid.* Arts. 7.17.7 and 7.17.8. According to Art. 7.18, the provisions of dispute settlement under Ch. 28 apply to the SPS Chapter. However, the rights and obligations under two specific provisions of the SPS Chapter are exempted from such application. One is Art. 7.6(b): whether the exporting party's SPS measure has the same effect as the importing party's, any disputes deriving from the assessment are not subject to dispute settlement. The other is Art. 7.9.2: each party shall ensure that its SPS measures either conform to the relevant international standards, guidelines, or recommendations or, if they don't, that the measures are based on documented and objective scientific evidence that is rationally related to the measures, while recognizing the parties' obligations regarding risk assessment: TPP, Art. 7.18.

[77] See CHANG-FA LO, WTO-PLUS IN FREE TRADE AGREEMENTS 1 (2010).

[78] Ching-Fu Lin, *SPS-Plus and Bilateral Treaty Network: A 'Global' Solution to the Global Food Safety Problem?*, 29(4) WIS. INT'L L.J. 694, 714 (2012).

The former may be regarded as a 'vertical' and the latter a 'horizontal' SPS-plus institutional design, each of which deepens or widens contracting parties' rights and obligations, respectively. More specifically, vertical SPS-plus provisions tend to elaborate on the SPS Agreement, limit room for discretion enjoyed by parties, and extend the scope of application, while horizontal provisions usually establish innovative mechanisms that are not covered by the SPS Agreement, incorporating additional rights, obligations, norms, or guidance.[79]

In addition, as the SPS Agreement aims to strike a balance between trade liberalization and WTO members' right to regulate for public health objectives,[80] SPS-plus provisions can also be categorized depending on their 'pro-trade' or 'pro-health' nature (in a relative sense) in weighing and balancing the interests of international trade and public health.[81] Pro-

---

[79] Instead of viewing different SPS-plus institutional designs as 'vertical v. horizontal', some may prefer regarding them as 'SPS-plus v. SPS-extra'. Both uses of terms basically indicate the same approach to analyzing different natures of SPS provisions in RTAs. See e.g., Chad P. Bown, *Mega-Regional Trade Agreements and the Future of the WTO* 2–3 (Part of Discussion Paper Series on Global and Regional Governance, Council on Foreign Relations, September 2016), available at http://i.cfr.org/content/publications/attachments/Discussion_Paper_Bown_Mega-Regionals_OR.pdf (last visited 26 August 2017); Joost Pauwelyn and Wolfgang Alschner, *Forget About the WTO: The Network of Relations Between PTAs and Double PTAs*, *in* TRADE COOPERATION: THE PURPOSE, DESIGN AND EFFECTS OF PREFERENTIAL TRADE AGREEMENTS 500–501 (Andreas Dür and Manfred Elsig eds., 2015).

[80] See e.g., TRACEY EPPS, INTERNATIONAL TRADE AND HEALTH PROTECTION: A CRITICAL ASSESSMENT OF THE WTO'S SPS AGREEMENT (2008). *Cf.* Bruce A. Silverglade, *The WTO Agreement on Sanitary and Phytosanitary Measures: Weakening Food Safety Regulations to Facilitate Trade?*, 55 FOOD & DRUG L.J. 517, 518–24 (2000); Alan O. Sykes, *Exploring the Need for International Harmonization: Domestic Regulation, Sovereignty, and Scientific Evidence Requirements—A Pessimistic View*, 3 CHI. J. INT'L L. 353, 354 (2002).

[81] The SPS Agreement, through harmonization, scientific justification, and transparency etc., seeks to prevent countries from taking a protectionist approach to SPS measures to unjustifiably restrict trade so as to minimize the market-access impacts when exercising regulatory autonomy. In this sense, the term 'SPS-plus' might appear to some trade lawyers as an expansion of rules in favor of trade liberalization (as the case 'TRIPS-plus' illustrates) and any pro-health provisions that may loosen trade-centered obligations are better framed as 'SPS-minus'. However, this chapter is of the view that the SPS Agreement, though a trade agreement under the WTO regime, aims at striking a balance between trade and health (leave aside the issue whether the balance is properly established or maintained), as set out in its Preamble. Therefore, SPS-plus can refer to pro-trade rules that require the consideration of published and compelling scientific evidence prior to the implementation of any measures; SPS-plus

trade SPS-plus measures, despite their vertical or horizontal nature, seek to lower or eliminate non-tariff barriers to trade, avoid protectionism, and pursue a more liberalized trade environment. Pro-health SPS measures, despite their vertical or horizontal nature, aim to better protect human, animal, or plant life or health in the territories of the parties in response to prevalent global food safety crises. It should be noted that in practice, the four dimensions (vertical, horizontal, pro-trade, and pro-health) are not necessarily mutually exclusive and may overlap. For the purpose of this chapter, the discussion will focus on the SPS-plus elements along the continuum from pro-trade to pro-health (see also the discussion above and Figure 11.1) to assess the normative implications of the SPS Chapter for global food safety governance.

1. SPS-plus Institutional Designs in the TPP

First, while many RTAs have the same risk assessment provisions as those of the SPS Agreement, approximately a few dozen include temporal limits and additional procedures.[82] The TPP SPS Chapter raises the threshold for considering scientific evidence and lays out more specific components of risk analysis when compared to the baseline of the SPS Agreement. Under the SPS Agreement, when conducting risk assessments, members are to consider 'available scientific evidence',[83] while in the SPS Chapter, parties are required to take into account 'documented and objective scientific evidence that is rationally related to the measures'.[84] This elaboration of the rule substantially raises the standard for scientific evidence and potentially reduces the latitude enjoyed by parties in adopting SPS measures that do not conform to international standards. The SPS Chapter also includes additional obligations of importing parties in the course of risk assessment, such as scheduling work in accordance with procedures and laws, as well as informing exporting parties of progress and any delays that may occur.[85] Additionally, the SPS Agreement requires members to ensure that their measures are not more trade restrictive than required to achieve the appropriate level of protection and to take into account technical and

can also refer to pro-health cooperative mechanisms such as a certification program, Hazard Analysis Critical Control Point (HACCP) preventive requirements, or a rapid alert system of information exchange. See Lin (n. 78 above) 714–18.

[82] Jackson and Vitikala (n. 14 above) 334.

[83] SPS Agreement, Art. 5.2.

[84] TPP, Art. 7.9.2.

[85] *Ibid.* Arts. 7.9.7–7.9.8.

economic feasibility,[86] whereas the SPS Chapter further points out that risk management options may include the facilitation of trade by not taking any measure.[87]

Second, because the existence or spread of pests and diseases respects no national borders, WTO members are required to take into account geographic and ecological conditions, as well as pest- and disease-free areas, so as to adapt their measures according to the regionalization approach.[88] More than fifty RTAs appear to go beyond Article 6 of the SPS Agreement by including more specific and systematic requirements that facilitate the implementation of regionalization.[89] With regard to the determination of regional conditions, the SPS Chapter stipulates several new requirements on importing parties that are not covered by the SPS Agreement. For example, when an exporting party requests a determination of regional conditions, an importing party 'shall initiate an assessment within a reasonable period of time' if it determines that information submitted is sufficient.[90] In the process of assessment, both parties may agree in advance on 'the risk management measures that will apply . . . in the event of a change in the status'.[91] Similar to the practices of a number of RTAs, such as Nicaragua-Taiwan and Peru-Korea,[92] the TPP includes an obligation of the importing party to explain when a regionalization request is denied. Finally, if there is a serious food safety incident or change of pest/disease conditions and the importing party must modify or revoke the regionalization determination, both sides 'shall cooperate to assess whether the determination can be reinstated'.[93]

Third, as previously discussed, many RTAs contain harmonization provisions that simply mirror Article 3 of the SPS Agreement.[94] However, very few actually go beyond the WTO's harmonization requirements.[95] The TPP SPS Chapter imposes detailed harmonization obligations on parties in various provisions for the purpose of trade liberalization and facilitation. For example, the SPS Chapter not only reaffirms the

---

86 SPS Agreement, Art. 5.6.

87 TPP, Art. 7.9.6.

88 SPS Agreement, Art. 6. See also GRUSZCZYNSKI (n. 13 above) 251.

89 Jackson and Vitikala (n. 14 above) 338.

90 TPP, Art. 7.7.4. Note that some RTAs further include a specific timeframe for determination, such as EU-Georgia Agreement, Arts. 58, 59, and 62; Jackson and Vitikala (n. 14 above) 340.

91 TPP, Arts. 7.7.6 and 7.7.8.

92 Jackson and Vitikala (n. 14 above) 339.

93 TPP, Arts. 7.7.10 and 7.7.11.

94 See Jackson and Vitikala (n. 14 above) 324–7.

95 *Ibid.*

importance of international standards, guidelines, and recommendations, but also on many occasions asks the parties to consider the relevant guidance of the WTO SPS Committee, seeking to increase the referral power and harmonization impact of non-binding instruments such as decisions and guidelines adopted by the Committee. Notably, the SPS Chapter requires parties to 'conform to' international standards, guidelines, or recommendations or otherwise undergo the avenue of risk assessment and 'documented and objective scientific evidence'.[96] This SPS-plus institutional design arguably limits the range of choice and discretion enjoyed by parties vis-à-vis that under Article 3 of the SPS Agreement, where WTO members' measures need only be 'based on' international standards, guidelines, or recommendations.

Fourth, the existing RTAs include significantly different approaches to equivalence, and only nineteen go beyond Article 4 of the SPS Agreement.[97] According to Article 4 of the SPS Agreement, when an exporting WTO member 'objectively demonstrates . . . that its measures achieve the importing Member's appropriate level of [SPS] protection, the importing Member is obliged to accept such measures as equivalent'.[98] To facilitate the process, Article 4 also requires the requesting member to provide the importing member with 'reasonable access . . . for inspection, testing and other relevant procedures',[99] while at the same time imposing the 'duty of negotiation' on the importing member.[100] The TPP SPS Chapter embraces the 'duty of negotiation' and goes further to require that equivalence assessments shall be undertaken in a fair and timely manner and that importing parties shall explain their SPS measures and applicable procedures for equivalence determination. It should be noted that the Chapter incorporates almost the exact language specified in Decision G/SPS/19 of the WTO SPS Committee as a binding obligation, which asks parties to accept equivalence if the exporting party can objectively demonstrate that its measure 'has the same effect in achieving the objective as the importing party's measure'.[101] Finally, the SPS Chapter explicitly expands the scope

---

96 TPP, Art. 7.9.2.
97 See Jackson and Vitikala (n. 14 above) 327–8.
98 SPS Agreement, Art. 4.1.
99 *Ibid.*
100 *Ibid.* Art. 4.2.
101 TPP, Art. 7.8.6(b); Committee on SPS Measures, *Decision on the Implementation of Article 4 of the SPS Agreement*, WTO Doc. G/SPS/19/Rev.2, para. 7 (23 July 2004) (stating that if the exporting WTO member can objectively demonstrate that 'its measure has the same effect in achieving the objective as the importing Member's measure, the importing Member should recognize both measures as equivalent').

of application of the equivalence provision to include not only a specific measure as stipulated in the SPS Agreement, but also 'groups of measures' and 'on a system-wide basis'.[102]

Fifth, from a pro-health perspective, the SPS Chapter details three types of regulatory measures that importing parties can adopt to ensure the importation meets their appropriate levels of SPS protection, i.e., import checks, auditing, and certification.[103] As such, parties have access to a more elaborate and strengthened toolkit to ensure food safety and achieve other SPS objectives. At the same time, from a pro-trade perspective, the SPS Chapter imposes more obligations on the importing parties than those under Annex C to the SPS Agreement,[104] such as the importing party's duty to explain the rationale for certificate information requirements and to provide the exporting party with opportunities to comment in the decision-making process and seek review afterwards.[105]

Sixth, like many other RTAs,[106] the SPS Chapter introduces a range of new transparency obligations that exceed the existing requirements in the SPS Agreement.[107] To begin, concerning the duty of notification, the SPS Agreement only requires members to notify their proposed measures when there exists no international standard, guideline, or recommendation or the SPS measures are 'not substantially the same' as such instruments.[108] In contrast, according to the SPS Chapter, even when the proposed measure conforms to relevant international instruments, parties are obliged to notify.[109] Moreover, where the SPS measures do not conform to relevant international instruments, parties must provide relevant documentation

---

[102] TPP, Art. 7.8.1.

[103] See relevant discussions above in Section II; TPP, Arts. 7.10–7.12.

[104] SPS Agreement, Annex C, governs members' control, inspection, and approval procedures.

[105] TPP, Arts. 7.10.5, 7.11.2, 7.11.8, and 7.12.5.

[106] Some RTAs have a general and separate chapter on transparency (e.g. United States-Australia, United States-Bahrain, and United States-Chile; note that TPP, Ch. 25 on regulatory coherence also touches upon transparency issues in a more general sense), and over seventy RTAs include SPS-specific transparency provisions, many of which exceed WTO commitments; see Jackson and Vitikala (n. 14 above) 341.

[107] For relevant discussions, see Terry Collins-Williams and Robert Wolfe, *Transparency as a Trade Policy Tool: The WTO's Cloudy Windows*, 9(4) World Trade Rev. 551 (2010).

[108] SPS Agreement, Annex B, para. 5. See also Committee on Sanitary and Phytosanitary Measures (SPS Committee), *Recommended Procedures for Implementing the Transparency Obligations of the SPS Agreement*, WTO Doc. G/SPS/7/Rev.3 (20 June 2008).

[109] TPP, Art. 7.13.3.

(such as objective scientific evidence) they have considered in the decision-making process.[110] In addition to the notification obligation, the SPS Agreement merely asks WTO members to provide comment opportunities to other members,[111] while the SPS Chapter extends such procedural access to all interested persons.[112] Upon request, a party shall also make available to another party significant written comments and relevant documentation considered to support the final measure.

Another noteworthy aspect of the SPS-plus institutional design is the pro-health transparency requirement, which imposes notification responsibilities on exporting parties with an aim toward preventing the entry, establishment, and spread of food-borne and other SPS hazards. More specifically, an exporting party shall notify relevant contact points when any of the following five situations emerges: a significant SPS risk related to its exportation of goods; urgent situations of change in animal or plant health status within an exporting party's territory; a major change in regionalization; new and important scientific findings related to food safety, pests, or diseases regulation; and substantial changes in food safety or other SPS risk management policies or practices.[113] This appears to be an uncommon practice in RTA design,[114] but essentially allows the importing party to take preventive measures to ensure more effective and efficient food safety governance.

Last but not least, the SPS Chapter includes other important SPS-plus institutional designs, such as those related to emergency measures and a dispute settlement timeline.[115] The SPS Chapter not only reaffirms parties' rights under the SPS Agreement to adopt a provisional SPS measure,[116] but also allows parties to take an emergency measure that is necessary for the protection of human, animal, or plant life or health.[117] The Chapter,

---

110 *Ibid.* Art. 7.13.6.

111 SPS Agreement, Annex B, para. 5(d).

112 TPP, Art. 7.13.4.

113 *Ibid.* Art. 7.13.11.

114 Very few RTAs include such a notification obligation on exporting parties, yet a few similar practices exist, as the Chile-Mexico and Hong Kong-Chile RTAs include provisions on notification of disease breakout; see Jackson and Vitikala (n. 14 above) 344.

115 To be sure, there exist other SPS-plus institutional designs at different levels in the TPP, yet this chapter cannot examine each and every one of them here due to their varied relevance, as well as space limits.

116 TPP, Art. 7.9.3(c).

117 *Ibid.* Arts. 7.14.1 and 7.14.2. When taking an emergency measure, nonetheless, the party shall promptly notify the other parties and take into consideration any information provided by other parties in response to the notification. Additionally,

however, provides no further guidance on the relationship between provisional and emergency measures. As for dispute settlement, as noted, parties must first endeavor to address any SPS issue via available administrative procedures and bilateral mechanisms, and must then exhaust the possibilities of resolutions with the framework of CTC under a certain timeframe (if possible, within 180 days) before being allowed recourse to formal dispute settlement. While the majority of RTAs feature certain forms of consultation mechanisms to resolve SPS issues, only some exceptions include specific timeframes.[118] This institutional design under the SPS Chapter urges parties to prevent and mitigate potential trade disputes as early as possible.

2. Normative Implications for Global Food Safety Governance

Premised on the above analysis of SPS-plus rights and obligations under the TPP, this chapter moves on to examine the implications of the TPP for global food safety governance and to offer some preliminary observations. In particular, this section focuses on the TPP SPS Chapter's theoretical and practical implications in the following respects. How will these SPS-plus provisions—pro-trade or pro-health—impact the regulatory approaches adopted by governments within and beyond the TPP? Do the SPS-plus elements introduce regulatory uncertainty in the course of implementation due to the diverse legal systems and developmental states of parties? Furthermore, how will the Chapters on SPS and regulatory coherence interact to prevent potential disputes? Finally, what is the future relationship between the TPP and the WTO with regard to SPS cooperation in the age of megaregionals?

(1) Is SPS-plus good for food safety governance?

If the TPP enters into force, the SPS-plus institutional designs analyzed above will certainly result in significant impacts on parties' food safety regulations, risk analysis systems, and even rule-making procedures. How parties will implement such provisions on the ground remains to be seen, taking into account their diverse legal and developmental backgrounds. Nevertheless, this chapter endeavors to provide a preliminary assessment of the SPS Chapter's public health and international trade ramifications (see Figure 11.1).

---

the party 'shall review the scientific basis of that measure within six months and make available the results of the review to any Party on request'. If the measure is maintained after the review, the party should review the measure periodically; *ibid.*

118 Jackson and Vitikala (n. 14 above) 349–53.

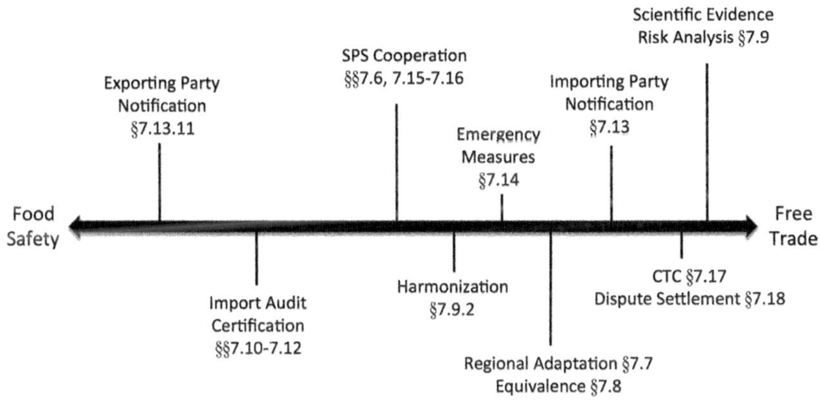

Figure 11.1 *TPP SPS-plus provisions along the food safety-free trade spectrum*

First, from the right end of the spectrum, there are the provisions tilting in favor of trade liberalization, such as those pertaining to scientific justification and risk analysis, regional adaptation and equivalence, and strengthened transparency and dispute settlement. With SPS-plus elements such as the heightened threshold of scientific evidence, duty of negotiation and explanation, explicit timelines, and heavy procedural requirements, the parties will arguably be discouraged from proactively adopting food safety or other SPS measures. Second, in the central area of the spectrum are the provisions on emergency measures, harmonization, and cooperation. While the Chapter confirms the parties' right to adopt emergency measures to ensure food safety, it also stipulates safeguards to avoid abuse of that right. The provisions on harmonization and cooperation are rather general, with a certain level of flexibility, and this chapter therefore assigns them to the center of the spectrum. Third, there are two other provisions placed to the left of the spectrum, tilting towards public health protection. The notification obligation imposed on the exporting parties is supposed to be the most pro-health SPS-plus provision. The rules under the SPS Agreement imply that 'importing' countries typically bear the cost of ensuring import safety, since the customary practice of discovering unsafe products has traditionally rested on border inspections.[119] Remarkably, however, the SPS Chapter obliges the 'exporting' parties to notify regarding significant cases of SPS risks in a timely manner, so as to shift from a response-oriented to a more preventive approach to food

[119] See Lin (n. 78 above) 716.

safety. The SPS Chapter further specifies (if not encourages) three import control approaches—audit, import check, and certificate—available for adoption by importing parties to strengthen their ability in the areas of food safety surveillance and response, provided that they act in line with necessity, proportionality, and reason.

To be sure, the TPP is a trade agreement that is ambitious enough to address other cross-cutting and even non-trade (subject to debate) issues.[120] It would therefore not be surprising to find out that pro-trade SPS provisions outnumber pro-health provisions in the TPP context. Nevertheless, as the SPS Chapter incorporates substantial rules to ease barriers to trade, it adds to the plate various practical tools to safeguard food safety. All in all, the SPS Chapter seems to have reconfigured the balance (again, subject to debate) struck by the SPS Agreement—not in a manner that favors either trade liberalization or health protection, but in a manner that broadens the room for maneuver enjoyed by parties to achieve both objectives.

(2) Dispute resolution, transformed

Traditional barriers to trade, such as tariffs and quotas, have been significantly reduced after decades of trade liberalization at the multilateral level, but non-tariff barriers (NTBs) to trade, usually in the form of domestic standards, regulations, and even red tape, have stepped in to replace and have also become prominently important as the major hurdle to market access.[121] The conventional dispute settlement mechanism may work well for issues of traditional and relatively 'static' barriers to trade, but it fall shorts as an effective forum to address the issues of the more 'dynamic' NTBs, due to factors such as technical and scientific complexity, political and social uncertainties, and usually opaque policy-making processes. Against such a backdrop, the TPP (through the Chapters on SPS Measures and Regulatory Coherence) arguably transforms the

---

[120] Indeed, as can be seen in the multilateral context, food safety and public health issues have not been the core considerations of the covered agreements throughout the WTO's history. See Huei-chih Niu, *A Comparative Perspective on the International Health Regulations and the World Trade Organization's Agreement on the Application of Sanitary and Phytosanitary Measures*, 1 ASIAN J. WTO & INT'L HEALTH L. & POL'Y 513, 515 (2006).

[121] For instance, unclear requirements, regulatory changes adopted without prior notice, and redundant conformity procedures all disadvantage foreign suppliers due to the lack of inside knowledge and increased compliance costs. See e.g., Thomas J. Bollyky, *Regulatory Coherence in the Trans-Pacific Partnership Talks*, *in* THE TRANS-PACIFIC PARTNERSHIP: A QUEST FOR A 21ST CENTURY TRADE AGREEMENT 172–3 (Chin Leng Lim et al. eds., 2012).

'behind the border' struggle over issues regarding domestic standards and regulations by moving the lens of scrutiny upstream to cover 'behind the order' phases of policy-making.

The TPP Chapter on Regulatory Coherence requires parties to implement good regulatory practices in their rule-making processes for more effective and efficient achievement of parties' policy objectives, as well as facilitation of international trade, investment, economic growth, and employment.[122] While the Chapter leaves the scope of application for the parties to determine, they are expected to achieve 'significant coverage' of their regulatory measures.[123] Given the crucial importance of SPS issues in the region and the *softer* nature of the Regulatory Coherence Chapter,[124] SPS measures, and many other issues, are likely to be covered.

Although much of the Regulatory Coherence Chapter must be further clarified,[125] it refers to 'good regulatory practices' that aim to discipline

---

[122] TPP, Art. 25.2. For an earlier discussion on the Regulatory Coherence Chapter of the TPP, see e.g., Elizabeth Sheargold and Andrew D. Mitchell, *The TPP and Good Regulatory Practices: An Opportunity for Regulatory Coherence to Promote Regulatory Autonomy?*, 15(4) World Trade Rev. 587 (2016). For more comprehensive analyses, see e.g., Petros C. Mavroidis, *Regulatory Cooperation: Lessons from the WTO and the World Trade Regime* (E15 Task Force on Regulatory Systems Coherence Policy Options Paper, January 2016).

[123] TPP, Art. 25.3.

[124] According to TPP, Art. 25.11, for any issue arising under the Regulatory Coherence Chapter, parties are not entitled to have recourse to the dispute settlement mechanism established in Ch. 28. Many legal scholars use a binary lens to distinguish 'binding' hard law from 'non-binding' soft law. However, when designing a global institution or an international legal instrument, an exclusive focus on the binding/non-binding dichotomy would not be practically helpful for states to further their goals. This chapter adopts a softer-to-harder-law spectrum approach, taking into account the dimensions proposed by Abbott and Snidal—that 'obligation' (legally binding force), 'precision' (specificity of treaty language), and 'delegation' (such as third-party review or adjudication) define the level of 'legalization' of a legal instrument. As the dispute settlement provisions do not apply to issues regarding regulatory coherence under Ch. 25 and the language used therein tends to be general, the Chapter seems to fall on the softer side of the spectrum. See Kenneth W. Abbott et al., *The Concept of Legalization*, 54(3) Int'l Org. 401, 401 (2000); Kenneth W. Abbott and Duncan Snidal, *Hard and Soft Law in International Governance*, 54(3) Int'l Org. 421, 424 (2000). *Cf.* Jan Klabbers, *The Redundancy of Soft Law*, 65(2) Nordic J. Int'l L. 167, 168 (1996); Wolfgang Reinicke and Jan Martin Witte, *Interdependence, Globalization, and Sovereignty: The Role of Non-binding International Legal Accords*, *in* Commitment and Compliance: The Role of Non-binding Norms in the International Legal System 76 (Dinah Shelton ed., 2000).

[125] See e.g., Shin-yi Peng, *Regulatory Coherence in the TPP: The Laws Governing Unsolicited Commercial Electronic Messages as a Case Study* (draft

government actions in the entire rule-making process. Good regulatory practices apply to the planning, design, issuance, implementation, and review of covered regulatory measures, where parties must enhance stakeholder engagement, respond to comments and explain regulatory rationale, and review and revise regulatory measures.[126] The regulatory coherence rules, together with the transparency requirements of the SPS Chapter, will embed good regulatory practices—such as notice and comment procedures, stakeholder participation, duty to explain, access to information, and mutual consultation—into parties' SPS rule-making processes. With enhanced stakeholder involvement (comment, respond, and consultation) and parties' commitment to conduct *ex-post* assessments, potential causes of disputes could be identified and addressed in earlier phases, which in turn reduces the likelihood of unpleasant surprises and trade conflicts after a measure is adopted and implemented.[127] The increased transparency and predictability in the rule-making process, together with the CTC discussed above, may help parties to prevent unnecessary disputes, resolve frictions within a definite timeframe, and move away from lengthy and costly dispute settlement.

(3) Exporting US regulatory models

As we can see from the negotiation history, the United States played the lead in setting the agenda and crafting the texts, and there are fingerprints of the United States throughout the TPP, including the SPS Chapter. Taking a closer look at the SPS Chapter, it seems clear that the United States has pushed to incorporate some key elements of its newest food safety law, the Food Safety Modernization Act (FSMA),[128] into this twenty-first century agreement (note that the Administrative Procedure Act[129] and certain executive orders have also found their way into the TPP

---

presented at the Workshop, 'Governing Science and Technology in the Mega-RTA Era: Regulatory Divergence and Convergence', 17–18 November 2017, National Tsing Hua University, Taiwan).

[126] TPP, Arts. 25.5.6, 25.5.7, and 25.8.

[127] See Andrew T. Guzman, *Food Fears: Health and Safety at the WTO*, 45 VA. J. INT'L L. 1, 34–5 (2004); Robert Howse, *Democracy, Science, and Free Trade: Risk Regulation on Trial at the World Trade Organization*, 98(7) MICH. L. REV. 2329, 2330 (2000).

[128] Food Safety Modernization Act (FSMA), Pub. L. No. 111-353, 124 Stat. 3885 (2011). For an introduction, see e.g., Debra M. Strauss, *An Analysis of the FDA Food Safety Modernization Act: Protection for Consumers and Boon for Business*, 66 FOOD & DRUG L.J. 353 (2011).

[129] Administrative Procedure Act (APA), Pub. L. No. 79-404, 60 Stat. 237 (1946).

Chapter on Regulatory Coherence, although this chapter does not discuss another example here due to space limitations).

The FSMA was signed into law by President Obama in January 2011, striving to revamp the outdated set of provisions in the Federal Food, Drug, and Cosmetics Act (FFDCA) promulgated in 1938[130] and the Pure Food and Drug Act in 1906.[131] The FSMA is expected to bring major reforms to the FFDCA and to expand the Food and Drug Administration (FDA)'s authority,[132] including preventive control and industry responsibility, *ex-post* enforcement tools, import safety and international cooperation, and enhanced partnership. The FSMA's institutional design on import safety, especially its third-party certification requirements for certain imported food products, is of significant relevance here.

Recognizing the FDA's administrative inability to rely almost solely on border inspection for a sufficient portion of food imports, the FSMA significantly strengthens the FDA's power over food imports in Title III, 'Improving the Safety of Imported Food'.[133] Under its Foreign Supplier Verification Program, the FSMA requires food importers to assess and verify that their partner suppliers in other countries have designed and implemented risk-based preventive control plans to maintain a level of safety equivalent to that found in the United States.[134] The FDA is also allowed to require certifications from importers as a condition for entry, and such certifications may be issued by accredited third-party auditors.[135] It should be noted that the scope of accredited third-party auditors includes foreign governments, foreign cooperatives, or other third parties.[136] In addition, the FSMA authorizes the FDA to establish a Voluntary Qualified Importer Program, under which some importers may be rewarded for taking more stringent food safety measures by accepting expedited review and entry of their shipments.[137]

While the FSMA may encounter legal challenges in the WTO dispute

---

130 Federal Food, Drug, and Cosmetics Act, Pub. L. No. 75-717, 52 Stat. 1040 (1938).

131 Pure Food and Drug Act, Pub. L. No. 59-384, 34 Stat. 768 (1906).

132 Margaret A. Hamburg, *Food Safety Modernization Act: Putting the Focus on Prevention*, WHITE HOUSE BLOG (3 January 2011, 4:53 p.m.), www.whitehouse.gov/blog/2011/01/03/food-safety-modernization-act-putting-focus-prevention (last visited 26 August 2017).

133 FSMA, Title III.

134 *Ibid.* §301.

135 *Ibid.* §303.

136 *Ibid.* §307.

137 *Ibid.* §302.

settlement system,[138] all such regulatory tools have found their way—as explicitly recognized and (implicitly) encouraged approaches to food safety regulation—into the TPP. The United States may have exported its regulatory models to other TPP parties out of rational self-interest considerations, but encouraging trading partners to adopt the FSMA approach will likely have positive impacts on food safety governance in the region. One caveat is that given the massive diversity of the TPP parties in terms of legal systems, administrative capacity, market structure, technical capacity, and stages of development, the real impacts remain to be seen.

(4) A multilateral anchor

Last but not least, the TPP platform for SPS cooperation appears to be able to produce constructive effects on the WTO multilateral trading system. The work of the SPS Committee serves as a normative benchmark of the SPS Chapter, as the Chapter incorporates in its formal texts the same or similar language from a number of decisions, guidelines, and recommendations adopted by the Committee. Examples can be found in *inter alia* the Decision on the Implementation of Article 4 of the SPS Agreement (TPP, Articles 7.8.1, 7.8.2, and 7.8.6(b)),[139] Guidelines to Further the Practical Implementation of Article 6 of the SPS Agreement (TPP, Article 7.7.5–7.7.7),[140] and Recommended Procedures for Implementing the Transparency Obligations of the SPS Agreement (TPP, Articles 7.8.2 and 7.13.4).[141] The SPS Chapter utilizes such instruments to expand, elaborate on, supplement, or clarify the baseline rules established in the SPS Agreement. While the decisions and recommendations adopted by the SPS Committee do not have legally binding force on WTO members,[142]

---

138 At least China, Brazil, Belize, and Korea have raised specific trade concerns over FSMA—in particular its outsourced audits and certification—consistent with the obligations under the SPS Agreement. See WTO, *Record Number of Concerns Raised on Food Safety, Animal-Plant Health Measures*, WTO News (16–17 October 2013). See also Ching-Fu Lin, *FDA Food Safety Modernization Act Might Raise Trade Concerns?*, Bill of Health Blog (6 November 2013), http://blogs.harvard.edu/billofhealth/2013/11/06/fda-food-safety-modernization-act-might-raise-trade-concerns/ (last visited 26 August 2017).

139 See Committee on SPS Measures (n. 101 above).

140 Committee on SPS Measures, *Guidelines to Further the Practical Implementation of Article 6 of the SPS Agreement*, WTO Doc. G/SPS/W/218 (25 February 2008).

141 Committee on SPS Measures, *Recommended Procedures for Implementing the Transparency Obligations of the SPS Agreement (Article 7)*, WTO Doc. G/SPS/7/Rev.3 (20 June 2008).

142 For a discussion of the legal status of the SPS Committee's decisions, recommendations, and guidelines, see generally Chris Downes, The Impact of

the TPP's direct incorporation of texts effectively transforms these softer multilateral rules into harder, binding obligations in the megaregional setting.

Furthermore, as noted previously, the SPS Chapter makes explicit reference to the WTO SPS Committee on a number of occasions and requires parties to actively take into account the Committee's 'relevant guidance'. This can also be regarded as a built-in multilateral anchor in a megaregional RTA, which links and updates parties' rights and obligations with the present and future developments of the WTO SPS Committee. The TPP SPS Chapter is therefore an evolving, organic body of rules. Most importantly, given the massive coverage and instrumental position of the TPP, the relevance and the importance of the multilateral norm-setting activities of the WTO SPS Committee are expected to grow over time.

IV. CONCLUSION

The TPP indeed represents a defining moment in international trade and regulatory governance. The depth and breadth of this megaregional agreement, as well as the diversity of its parties, pose a challenge not only to trade policies in the conventional sense, but also to many other cross-cutting issues. As noted above, normative interactions between traditional and sectoral, as well as novel and horizontal, rules will likely generate complex impacts on the dynamic balance between regulatory autonomy and cooperation. Accordingly, food safety governance will be configured and reconfigured not only by the SPS Chapter alone, but also by the Regulatory Coherence Chapter.

WTO SPS Law on EU Food Regulations 35 (2014); Gruszczynski (n. 13 above) 45–7; Patrick F. J. Macrory et al., The World Trade Organization: Legal, Economic and Political Analysis 332, note 497 (2005); George A. Bermann and Petros C. Mavroidis, Trade and Human Health and Safety 41, note 139 (2006).

12. How are package-related food safety issues addressed in the TPP?

Chang-Fa Lo

I. INTRODUCTION

Different views exist as to whether the Trans-Pacific Partnership (TPP) Agreement helps or undermines food safety control in its participating countries (especially in the United States, which was the original participating country but has been subsequently withdrawn from the TPP by President Trump). The positive view concerning the usefulness of the TPP in food safety control has been that the TPP not only allows the United States to continue enforcing its strict food safety laws and regulations, but also helps other TPP parties improve their food safety systems, the enhancement of which in turn will help improve food safety control in the United States.[1] An opposing argument that the TPP is unfriendly to food safety control contends that the TPP 'only permits food safety standards that facilitate and expand trade', and additionally, 'rules that interfere with the speedy shipment of suspicious or unsafe food could be called illegal trade barriers'.[2] Examining discussions regarding the relationship between the TPP and food safety issues, it is apparent that people have very diverse views about the TPP's impact on food safety issues.

But if we turn to the real text of the TPP, it is apparent that foods and food safety issues were not the main focus of the negotiators' concerns. The TPP's text does not identify food safety issues as its core element. The food safety concerns are not reflected in the TPP text.

Having said this, it must be noted that the TPP still has close ties to food safety problems. Food safety issues are genuinely important from all

---

[1] See United States Trade Representative (USTR), *The TPP: Ensuring Food Safety*, available at https://ustr.gov/sites/default/files/TPP-Ensuring-Food-Safety-Fact-Sheet.pdf (last visited 29 August 2017) (US).

[2] Food and Water Watch, *The TPP Assault on Food Safety* 1 (Factsheet, April 2016), available at www.foodandwaterwatch.org/sites/default/files/fs_1604_tpp-food-safety-web_0.pdf (last visited 29 August 2017).

perspectives in and for TPP countries, including the perspective of their potential effects on every person in the jurisdictions of all of the TPP countries, as well as the close connection between food safety issues and the trade rules provided in the TPP. Hence, examining the TPP's provisions, which have implications for food safety controls, is of high importance.

Additionally, food safety issues are not limited to the safety of foods themselves, but are also related to the packaging of foods. This is primarily because foods and food products are quite different from other products in that the former almost invariably require packages and these packages may have an effect on the safety of the products, whereas the latter might also need packages (depending on the type of product), but these packages generally do not have such a direct impact on the safety of the products.

In this chapter, discussions will focus on food packages and their relationship to food safety in the context of the TPP. Section II of the chapter discusses the importance of packaging in food safety issues, including food safety issues arising from food packages (as opposed to food safety issues arising from the foods themselves) and various food hazards caused by packages. Since food packages are closely related to the safety of foods, countries adopt various package-related measures (PRMs) to address package-related food safety issues. Hence, section III will explain those PRMs that serve as overall regulatory measures and, more specifically, PRMs adopted to address various food hazards. The text of the TPP is said to be of high quality in the liberalization of regional trade and in the protection of intellectual property rights and foreign investment. However, whether or not the TPP has properly addressed food safety issues is another problem. Section IV will examine relevant TPP rules concerning package-related food safety issues to determine whether the TPP has properly addressed or can be properly applied to cope with food safety problems, and especially food package problems. For food safety issues, the most relevant chapters in the TPP are Chapter 7 on Sanitary and Phytosanitary Measures ('SPS Chapter'), and Chapter 8 on Technical Barriers to Trade ('TBT Chapter'). As a result, in this part, the discussion of the TPP's provisions will focus on the TBT and SPS Chapters in the TPP.[3] The author will explain that the application of the TBT Chapter should be preferred and is interpretatively possible. Section V concludes by reiterating that package-related food safety issues are not properly

[3] It must be noted that for PRMs designed for the purpose of tobacco control, there could also be involvement of TPP's Intellectual Property Chapter (because a PRM for tobacco control could include limiting the use of trademarks of a tobacco company) and its Investment Chapter.

addressed by the TPP because it does not make any significant distinctions from the Agreement on the Application of Sanitary and Phytosanitary Measures ('SPS Agreement')[4] and the Agreement on Technical Barriers to Trade ('TBT Agreement')[5] under the WTO, and by explaining a manner of interpreting the relevant text of the TPP to make it easier for parties to the Agreement to implement effective food safety control measures (especially the PRMs).

II. IMPORTANCE OF PACKAGES IN FOOD SAFETY ISSUES

1. Food Safety Concerns Arising from Foods and Food Packages

Food safety issues involve many different issues. Most often when food safety issues are discussed, the focus is on safety concerns arising from the foods themselves. For instance, a wide range of discussions about food safety issues focus on food contamination and proper measures to prevent contamination and control the spread of contaminated foods; on food additives and whether and to what extent certain kinds of additives added by the producers or processers in foods are safe for human consumption; on genetically modified foods (GMFs)[6] and whether GMFs are safe for human consumption from a long-term perspective; and on adulteration and whether and to what extent the adulteration of certain materials in foods is safe/unsafe for human consumption and should/should not be permitted.

Another very important aspect of food safety issues (which is not so commonly discussed) is the 'packages' that hold foods or food products. Food packages serve various functions. One very important function of food packages is to preserve the soundness of foods so as to prevent physical hazards to consumers and to prevent contamination or the introduction of other hazards from external sources.

Food packaging issues are not limited to the materials (which have potential impacts on human health) used in the packages, however. They also include information or images included on the packages. The design

---

[4] Marrakesh Agreement Establishing the World Trade Organization, Annex 1A, 15 April 1994, 1867 UNTS 493.

[5] *Ibid.* at 120.

[6] WHO, *Food Safety: Frequently Asked Questions on Genetically Modified Foods* (May 2014), available at www.who.int/foodsafety/areas_work/food-technology/faq-genetically-modified-food/en/ (last visited 29 August 2017).

of food packages and information placed on them can be used to attract consumers or to better preserve foods. In other words, there is a consumer-attracting function and a food preserving function in the design of food packages. Information on food packages can also include the origin or source of the products and information about materials and ingredients in food products, as well as uses, functions, and nutritional values of foods. Hence, there is the transparency function of food packaging. It is also very important to ensure that such information on food packages is correct and is not false or misleading indications. These are all related to the safe preservation and consumption of foods.

2. Importance of Packages in Food Safety and Categories of Food Hazards

The importance of food packages concerning food safety issues can also be explained by the categorization of food hazards.

One categorization of food hazards is the nature of food hazards. This includes physical hazard (such as foreign objects in the food item that can cause injuries to consumers); biological hazard (such as bacteria, viruses, yeasts, molds and parasites); and chemical hazard (such as pesticides, antimicrobial residues and chemicals used on processing equipment).[7] Although such hazards are not necessarily caused by food packages, food packages can contribute and very often can lead to such hazards. For instance, packages that have direct contact with foods can emit chemicals or spread biologicals if the packages are produced with chemically unsafe materials or with biologically contaminated materials. Additionally, for instance, if food packages are not strong enough to support the food, it is likely that it could become physically or biologically unsafe for consumers.

Another categorization of food hazards is intentional and unintentional hazards caused by producers, suppliers, transporting parties, and others. Most of the time, intentional hazards are the result of the adulteration of certain undesirable substances (for economic or other purposes), while unintentional hazards are caused by contamination.[8] From a regulatory

---

[7] Jeannine Schweihofer and Sarah Wells, *Biological, Chemical and Physical Hazards Assessed with HACCP*, Mich. St. U. Extension (18 July 2013), available at http://msue.anr.msu.edu/news/biological_chemical_and_physical_hazards_assessed_with_haccp (last visited 29 August 2017).

[8] Markus Lipp, *A Closer Look at Chemical Contamination*, Food Safety Mag. (August/September 2011), available at www.foodsafetymagazine.com/magazine-archive1/augustseptember-2011/a-closer-look-at-chemical-contamination/ (last visited 29 August 2017).

standpoint, both intentional and unintentional hazards are of the same critical importance for the purpose of ensuring public health and consumer health and life. These categories of food hazards also have a close connection to food packages. For instance, if the producers intentionally or unintentionally use unsafe chemical materials for food packages, food safety concerns could arise from chemical emissions caused by the packaging.

Yet another category of food hazards is food hazards caused by or arising from different stages of the food supply chain (including harvesting, manufacturing, processing, transporting, importing, preparing, storing, and serving). Food packages are constantly used in the stages that follow harvesting. In the course of manufacturing and processing, food packages are normally used to preserve the freshness, flavor, and even physical soundness of foods. Even in the downstream stages of the food supply chain (including the stages of transporting, importing, preparing, storing, and serving), both original packages (used by the manufacturers or processers) and new packages (used by the parties who engage in transporting, importing, storing, and serving) may be sources for contamination or hazardous emissions.

III. PACKAGE-RELATED MEASURES TO ADDRESS FOOD SAFETY IN GENERAL

1. Package-related Measures are Part of Food Safety Control Measures and are Trade-related

A wide variety of food safety control measures exist. For foods themselves, such measures can be designed to control the contents, processes, and production methods, contamination and additives related to foods or food products, and GMFs. For food packages, package-related control measures can be designed to address intentional and unintentional physical, biological, and chemical hazards caused in different stages of the food supply chain. Food package requirements are a very important component of food safety control.

It must be noted that not all food safety control measures are trade-related. However, many are directly or indirectly related to trade. In particular, measures specifically addressing packages (i.e., package-related measures, or PRMs) can be very closely related to trade rules. As a result, these measures are regulated under trade agreements, especially the TBT or SPS portions of trade rules.

2. Package-related Measures to Address Various Food Hazards

Increasing numbers of PRMs are being developed and adopted for various regulatory purposes. Some PRMs are developed to address the correctness and sufficiency of the message reflected on the packages and to prevent false or misleading indications. For instance, in most jurisdictions, consumer products (including food products) are commonly required to have labels indicating the contents of the products and to place these labels on the packages. PRMs can also be used to require disclosure of nutritional information (such as calories and nutrients), safety information (such as food safety inspection information), and other necessary information (such as whether the product is GMF) concerning the food products. It is a common requirement in most jurisdictions that food packages must include information about the producer and the supplier of the product. A PRM can also be designed to help consumers identify the products and their sources and ensure the correctness of the source of a product.[9]

Some others PRMs are imposed to prevent physical hazards to consumers. For example, there could be the hazard of glass fragments (which can cause injury to consumers) resulting from the use of glass containers. Such glass fragments can be incorporated in the stages of manufacturing and processing. Regulatory measures to address such a hazard include regulation against products with glass in certain specifications and the

---

[9] Concerning the identifying function of food packages, food package requirements are primarily designed to enhance the identification of the sources and producers. For tobacco products, however, the identifying function is 'de-emphasized' by the producers. A PRM can also be used to dilute the identifying function by restricting the use of trademarks or designs. This will reduce the appeal of such products and the distinctiveness and identities of specific products. Such measures have an apparent impact on the protection of trademarks, as it can reduce a trademark's functions of indicating the origin of products and of conveying the messages of brand image. For instance, the plain package requirement is to restrict the use of trademarks and other designs on the package so that the producers and their attractive designs will not be used to attract smokers or potential smokers. A PRM can be used to reduce the attractiveness of packaging designs. This is particularly relevant to the interests of tobacco and alcohol companies, which intensively use packaging designs to attract existing and potential consumers. A PRM can also be used to govern the marketing function of packaging by restricting the use of trademarks or requiring a warning function to dissuade or discourage existing and potential consumers from consuming certain products. In most jurisdictions, there are requirements including pictorial warnings on the surface of cigarette packets to intensify the adverse image of tobacco products. The excessive requirement of warning signs on packaging can certainly affect the design and the use of trademarks.

application of food adulteration regulations to foods containing potential foreign objects (including glass fragments).[10]

Many PRMs are developed to prevent contaminants from packages and from food contact materials. This is because hazardous chemicals are present in many kinds of food contact materials (which are made of plastics and other substances). The hazardous chemicals in these materials can migrate from the containers and other packages into food and then into human bodies.[11] For instance, in the United States, food contact substances which are intended for 'use as a component of materials used in manufacturing, packing, packaging, transporting, or holding food if such use of the substance is not intended to have any technical effect in such food' are regulated by the Federal Food, Drug, and Cosmetic Act.[12] Also, for instance, a Canadian law prohibits anyone from selling 'any food in a packaging that may yield to its contents any substance that may be injurious to the health of a consumer of the food'.[13]

IV. TPP RULES PERTAINING TO PACKAGE-RELATED FOOD SAFETY AND THEIR RESPECTIVE ISSUES

1. Overall Perspectives of TPP and 'Product Packages'

If we examine 'product packages' from a broader perspective and do not limit our examination to 'food packages', it is apparently that additional trade rules could possibly be involved. For instance, the Australian plain packaging requirement imposed on tobacco products 'prohibits the use of logos, brand imagery, and promotional text on tobacco products and packaging, and includes restrictions on colour, size, format and materials

---

[10] Food and Drug Administration (FDA), *Chapter 21, Glass Inclusion*, available at www.fda.gov/downloads/Food/GuidanceRegulation/UCM252441.pdf (last visited 29 August 2017) (US).

[11] Health and Environment Alliance (HEAL), *Food Contact Materials and Chemical Contamination* (Briefing February 2016), available at www.env-health.org/IMG/pdf/15022016_-_heal_briefing_fcm_final.pdf (last visited 29 August 2017).

[12] FDA, *Food Ingredients and Packaging Terms*, available at www.fda.gov/Food/IngredientsPackagingLabeling/Definitions/default.htm (last visited 29 August 2017) (US).

[13] George G. Misko, *Regulation of Food Packaging in Canada*, Food Safety Mag. (October/November 2014), available at www.foodsafetymagazine.com/magazine-archive1/octobernovember-2014/regulation-of-food-packaging-in-canada/ (last visited 29 August 2017).

of packaging, as well as the appearance of brand and variant names'.[14] Such packaging requirements could involve intellectual property rights rules (because the regulations can be argued to restrict the use of trademark rights) and investment provisions (because the regulations can be argued to have an equivalent effect of expropriation of foreign investment) provided in trade agreements. Also, for instance, many countries require pharmaceutical products to be placed in medicine bottles which have childproof packaging designs. Such designs could involve patent rights.[15]

However, for package requirements imposed on food packages, the involvement of intellectual property rights (either trademark or patent rights) or investment issues is not obvious.

2. TPP's SPS Chapter

There are two related chapters in the TPP, i.e., Chapter 7 ('SPS Chapter') and Chapter 8 ('TBT Chapter'). They are mutually exclusive in their respective applications.

Article 8.3.5 provides '[The TBT Chapter] shall not apply to sanitary and phytosanitary measures. These are covered by Chapter 7 (Sanitary and Phytosanitary Measures)'. Article 7.3 provides '[The SPS Chapter] shall apply to all sanitary and phytosanitary measures of a Party that may, directly or indirectly, affect trade between the Parties'.[16] Hence, if a measure falls within the scope of the SPS Chapter, the TBT Chapter will not apply, even though it is possible that the same measure could fall within the scope of the definitions of the technical regulations provided in the TBT Chapter. This represents a means of prioritizing the application of the SPS Chapter provisions. Hence, it is important to decide the scope of regulation of the SPS Chapter to in turn determine whether the PRMs for food safety purposes are regulated under this Chapter.

In this regard, Article 7.1 provides that the definitions in Annex A to

---

14 See Tobacco Plain Packaging Act 2011, No. 148, www.legislation.gov.au/Details/C2013C00190 (last visited 29 August 2017) (Austl.).

15 See e.g., the patent for childproof cap for medicine bottles, US Patent No. 3679085 A (filed 16 April 1971), www.google.com/patents/US3679085 (last visited 29 August 2017) (US).

16 These provisions are similar to the relationship provisions between the TBT Agreement (Art. 1.5, which provides that 'The provisions of this Agreement do not apply to sanitary and phytosanitary measures as defined in Annex A of the Agreement on the Application of Sanitary and Phytosanitary Measures') and the SPS Agreement (which provides, in part, in Art. 1.1, that 'This Agreement applies to all sanitary and phytosanitary measures which may, directly or indirectly, affect international trade').

the SPS Agreement are incorporated into the SPS Chapter. Annex A to the SPS Agreement provides in paragraph 1, in part, that SPS measures include any measure applied 'to protect human . . . life or health within the territory of the Member from risks arising from additives, contaminants, toxins or disease-causing organisms in foods, beverages' and 'include all relevant laws, decrees, regulations, requirements and procedures including, *inter alia*, end product criteria; processes and production methods; testing, inspection, certification and approval procedures; . . . and packaging and labelling requirements directly related to food safety'. Apparently, food safety issues are regulated by the SPS Chapter in the TPP, notwithstanding that there are only two other provisions in Article 7.13 which specifically mention 'food safety' a few times.[17]

Under the SPS Chapter, the general principles required for a party to adopt an SPS measure are that 'sanitary or phytosanitary measures implemented by a Party do not create unjustified obstacles to trade',[18] 'that their respective sanitary and phytosanitary measures are based on scientific principles',[19] that their 'sanitary and phytosanitary measures either conform to the relevant international standards, guidelines or recommendations or, if its sanitary and phytosanitary measures do not conform to international standards, guidelines or recommendations, that they are based on documented and objective scientific evidence that is rationally related to the measures',[20] and that when a party adopts an SPS measure, it shall 'ensure that its sanitary and phytosanitary measures do not arbitrarily or unjustifiably discriminate between Parties where identical or similar conditions prevail' and 'conduct its risk analysis in a manner that is documented and that provides interested persons and other Parties an opportunity to comment'.[21]

3. TPP's TBT Chapter

As indicated above, the international trade rules that are among the most relevant to PRMs are the provisions on TBT. The TBT Chapter

---

[17] TPP, Art. 7.13, available at https://ustr.gov/sites/default/files/TPP-Final-Text-Sanitary-and-Phytosanitary-Measures.pdf (last visited 28 August 2017) (which requires an exporting TPP party to notify the importing party in a timely and appropriate manner 'of new scientific findings of importance which affect the regulatory response with respect to food safety, pests or diseases' and 'of significant changes in food safety, pest or disease management, control or eradication policies or practices that may affect current trade').

[18] TPP, Art. 7.2(d).

[19] *Ibid.* Art. 7.9.1.

[20] *Ibid.* Art. 7.9.2.

[21] *Ibid.* Art. 7.9.4.

addressed the TBT issues. The only provision in the TBT Chapter that mentions the issue of 'food' is Annex 8-F (titled 'Proprietary Formulas for Prepackaged Foods and Food Additives'). This Annex addresses the preparation, adoption, and application of technical regulations and standards related to packaged foods and food additives. Although the Annex is about packaged foods and food additives, the main issue here is only about the requirement that TPP parties respect the confidentiality of information about such products. It does not directly address food packages. As a result, we must turn to examine the general provisions in the TBT Chapter to determine how the PRMs can be brought under the TPP's TBT Chapter.

The TPP adopts the definition of the TBT Agreement.[22] Under Annex 1 to the TBT Agreement, 'technical regulation' is defined as a:

> [d]ocument which lays down product characteristics or their related processes and production methods, including the applicable administrative provisions, with which compliance is mandatory. It may also include or deal exclusively with terminology, symbols, packaging, marking or labelling requirements as they apply to a product, process or production method.

Under this definition, most package requirements would fall within the scope of technical regulation (unless such requirements fall within the scope of Article 8.3.5 as mentioned above), because they are primarily mandatory packaging, marking, or labeling requirements that apply to a product, process, or production method.

The objective of the TBT Chapter 'is to facilitate trade, including by eliminating unnecessary technical barriers to trade, enhancing transparency, and promoting greater regulatory cooperation and good regulatory practice'.[23] The following Articles concerning the preparation, adoption, and application of technical regulations by central government bodies in the TBT Agreement are incorporated into the TBT Chapter: Articles 2.1, 2.2, 2.4, 2.5, 2.9, 2.10, 2.11, 2.12.[24]

The TPP also requires its parties to recognize the important role that international standards, guides, and recommendations can play in supporting greater regulatory alignment, good regulatory practice, and reducing unnecessary barriers to trade.[25] However, it also stipulates that '[n]o Party shall have recourse to dispute settlement under Chapter 28

22 See *ibid.* Art. 8.1.
23 *Ibid.* Art. 8.2.
24 *Ibid.* Art. 8.4.1(a).
25 *Ibid.* Art. 8.5(1).

(Dispute Settlement) for a dispute that exclusively alleges a violation of the provisions of the TBT Agreement incorporated under paragraph 1'.[26] Article 8.3.6 provides:

> For greater certainty, nothing in this Chapter shall prevent a Party from adopting or maintaining technical regulations, standards or conformity assessment procedures in accordance with its rights and obligations under this Agreement, the TBT Agreement and any other relevant international agreement.

4. Distinctions Between the SPS and TBT Chapters Concerning their Application

From the above provisions in the respective Chapters on the SPS and TBT measures, it can be further elaborated as follows: first, concerning the basic requirements related to international trade, both the SPS and TBT Chapters similarly require that the adoption and implementation of the measures do not create unjustifiable or unnecessary obstacles to international trade.[27]

Second, concerning the role of 'international standards', the TPP's SPS rules require the parties to conform to relevant international standards (as provided in Article 7.9.2). This is similar to the TPP's TBT rules, which require its parties to recognize the important role of international standards, guides, and recommendations (as provided in Article 8.5(1)) and to employ international standards (as provided in Article 2.4 of the TBT Agreement, which is incorporated in TPP, Article 8.4.1(a)).

Third, as to whether a PRM may become either an unjustified or unnecessary obstacle to international trade or a necessary measure to fulfill the legitimate objective of the 'protection of human health or safety', both the SPS Chapter and the TBT Chapter strive to balance the need to eliminate trade barriers against the need to protect human health. The balance struck by the TPP is similar to that found in the TBT and SPS Agreements. On the one hand, the TPP requires its parties not to adopt an SPS or TBT regulation to create unjustified or unnecessary obstacles to international trade, as provided in TPP, Articles 7.2(d) and 8.2, as well as Article 2.2 of the TBT Agreement (which is incorporated in TPP, Article 8.4.1(a)). On the other hand, the TPP allows its parties to adopt a measure which serves the legitimate objective of protecting human health, as provided in TPP, Article 7.2(a) and Article 2.2 of the TBT Agreement

---

26 *Ibid.* Art. 8.4.1(b).

27 *Ibid.* Art. 7.2(d); *ibid.* Art. 8.2.

(which is incorporated in TPP, Article 8.4.1(a)). The TBT Chapter further establishes a 'rebuttable presumption' that measures adopted in accordance with relevant international standards, as provided in Article 2.5 of the TBT Agreement (which is also incorporated in TPP, Article 8.4.1(a)), do not create an unnecessary obstacle to international trade. Although there is no specific wording in the SPS Chapter granting the 'rebuttable presumption' of not creating an unjustified barrier to international trade, the effect of presumption in the SPS Chapter should either be similar or even stronger because of the provision in Article 7.9.2, which requires that:

> sanitary and phytosanitary measures either conform to the relevant international standards, guidelines or recommendations or, if its sanitary and phytosanitary measures do not conform to international standards, guidelines or recommendations, that they are based on documented and objective scientific evidence that is rationally related to the measures.

In other words, for those areas where international standards have been adopted, it should be very safe for a country to adopt such standards as its mandatory requirements, based on either the SPS provisions or the TBT provisions. If there is not an international standard to be followed, then the country adopting a PRM will not enjoy such presumption and hence will be required to justify the use of certain PRMs. For those areas of PRMs that already have international standards, it does not matter whether such standards are considered as the standards being governed by the SPS rules or as standards being governed by the TBT rules.

For instance, some package-related guidelines have been developed by the Codex Alimentarius, such as the Code of Practice for Packaging and Transport of Fresh Fruit and Vegetables[28] to address the packaging issues of fresh fruits and vegetables, and the Code of Hygienic Practice for Bottled/Packed Drinking Water (Other Than Natural Mineral Waters)[29] to address the hygiene issues of water supply. There is also the General Standard for the Labelling of Prepackaged Foods[30] to require

---

[28] CAC/RCP 44-1995, available at www.fao.org/fao-who-codexalimentarius/sh-proxy/en/?lnk=1&url=https%253A%252F%252Fworkspace.fao.org%252Fsites%252Fcodex%252FStandards%252FCAC%2BRCP%2B44-1995%252FCXP_044e.pdf (last visited 29 August 2017).

[29] CAC/RCP 48-2001, available at www.fao.org/fao-who-codexalimentarius/sh-proxy/en/?lnk=1&url=https%253A%252F%252Fworkspace.fao.org%252Fsites%252Fcodex%252FStandards%252FCAC%2BRCP%2B48-2001%252FCXP_048e.pdf (last visited 29 August 2017).

[30] Codex Stan 1-1985, available at www.fao.org/fao-who-codexalimentarius/sh-proxy/en/?lnk=1&url=https%253A%252F%252Fworkspace.fao.org%252Fsites%25

that prepackaged foods 'shall not be described or presented on any label or in any labelling in a manner that is false, misleading or deceptive or is likely to create an erroneous impression regarding its character in any respect' and 'shall not be described or presented on any label or in any labelling by words, pictorial or other devices which refer to or are suggestive either directly or indirectly, of any other product with which such food might be confused, or in such a manner as to lead the purchaser or consumer to suppose that the food is connected with such other product'. These standards serve as a strong basis for countries to adopt related measures.

Nonetheless, international standards that specifically address the wider scope of food safety issues arising from packages have yet to be comprehensively developed.[31] Hence, the current TPP provisions concerning the recognition of the important role of international standards might not be very helpful in addressing many aspects of the PRMs for food safety purposes. In those areas where international standards have already been provided, there is not much difference in the application of TPP SPS and TBT provisions. However, for those areas where international standards are still lacking, often there is a significant difference in the application of SPS and TBT provisions.

Fourth, concerning the scientific principles or scientific evidence and the risk analysis, the TPP parties must base their SPS measures on scientific principles or evidence and must also conduct risk analysis, whereas they are not required to meet such requirements when adopting TBT measures. Apparently, the requirements for a TPP country to adopt an SPS measure are stricter than the requirements for the adoption of a TBT measure.

5. Should Package-related Food Safety Measures be Subject to the SPS or the TBT Chapter?

As indicated above, the SPS and TBT Chapters in the TPP have some critical differences in their requirements for the adoption of package-related food safety measures. Also, the definitions of SPS measures and TBT measures (i.e., technical regulations) in the respective SPS and TBT Chapters can literally include PRM. An issue arises as to whether there is room to interpret whether certain PRMs for food safety purposes should

2Fcodex%252FStandards%252FCODEX%2BSTAN%2B1-1985%252FCXS_001e.pdf (last visited 29 August 2017).

[31] For current international food standards, see Codex Alimentarius, *International Food Standard*, available at www.fao.org/fao-who-codexalimentarius/standards/list-of-standards/en/ (last visited 29 August 2017).

still be subject to the TBT rules, allowing the parties wider discretion in the formulation and adoption of regulatory measures.

As explained above, the SPS Agreement's definition of SPS measures is incorporated in the TPP's SPS Chapter. It provides, in part, that '[s] anitary or phytosanitary measures include . . . packaging and labelling requirements directly related to food safety'. Apparently, it is not likely to exclude 'all' package/packaging-related food safety measures from the application of the provisions and requirements in the SPS Chapter. If TPP parties seek to have reasonably wider discretion in the adoption of PRMs for food safety purposes, a related issue is whether the definition of SPS measures, including 'packaging . . . requirements directly related to food safety', could be interpreted so as not to cover all package/packaging-related requirements related to food safety.

The author is of the view that it is desirable for the TPP parties to have wider discretion in the adoption of PRMs for food safety purposes, and that it is reasonably possible to allow for wider discretion of the parties through the interpretation of the definitional provision.

Concerning desirability, as mentioned above, the negotiators strove to balance the need for trade liberalization, on the one hand, and the need for protecting human health, on the other. However, the balance struck under the SPS rules and that struck under the TBT rules is somewhat different. For SPS matters, the balance more heavily favors ensuring the removal of obstacles to international trade, and as a result, the requirements for adopting an SPS measure are stricter. For TBT matters, the balance more heavily favors the allowing of wider discretion to importing countries. The unevenness of the balance does not make much sense from the perspective of ensuring the removal of unnecessary obstacles to international trade and protecting human health and life. Also, from the perspective of the relatively higher importance of human health protection, allowing certain flexibilities for the regulating countries would greatly aid in the enhancement of food safety but would not give rise to great concerns regarding trade barriers.

Concerning the possibility of interpreting certain PRMs as subject to the TPP TBT provisions, it is suggested in this chapter that the definition of SPS measures to include 'packaging and labelling requirements directly related to food safety' should be re-examined to consider the wording 'packaging . . . requirements directly related to food safety' as limited to safety issues arising from food packaging processes. It should not include safety issues arising from the packages themselves. This is because before the materials are actually used as food packages, countries should be able to regulate the production and transaction of such packaging materials if they can emit hazardous chemicals or can give rise to biological or physical hazard. When such packaging materials have not been used for packaging of foods, a reasonable interpretation should be that they cannot be considered as 'packaging directly related to food safety'. Hence, the regulation of such materials (which can be, but have not been, used to package foods) should be subject to the TBT rules. It would obviously be absurd to stipulate that prior to applying the materials for the actual packaging of foods, the materials are subject to the TBT rules. However, after the exact same materials are actually used to package foods, they will in turn be subject to the SPS rules.

The Vienna Convention on the Law of Treaties actually has a provision to support the avoidance of absurdity arising from the interpretation of treaty text based on the ordinary meaning of the textual wording and its context, as well as the object and purpose of the interpreted treaty. It provides in Article 32(b) that:

> Recourse may be had to supplementary means of interpretation . . . in order . . . to determine the meaning when the interpretation according to article 31: . . . (b) Leads to a result which is manifestly absurd or unreasonable.

If this interpretation of avoiding absurdity is reasonable, it would mean that all food packages used in any stage of production and processing which cause physical, chemical, or biological hazards should be subject to the TBT rules, and therefore the country which adopts PRMs for food safety purposes should not be required to have scientific evidence to support serious health implications, nor should it be required to conduct risk analysis under the SPS provisions. As long as the measure is not more trade restrictive than necessary to fulfil a legitimate objective, taking account of the risks non-fulfilment would create, then the measure can be justified.

The only packaging-related measures that are subject to the SPS provisions should be packaging procedures, which include packaging procedures during the manufacturing stage and those during the processing, storage, and transportation stages. For instance, food hygiene requirements (to require the packages to be clean or to require the packaging to be conducted in a vacuum or modified atmosphere) represent matters that should fall within the definition of 'packaging . . . requirements directly related to food safety'.

V. CONCLUDING REMARKS

The author is of the view that when comparing the TPP's SPS and TBT Chapters with the SPS and TBT Agreements under the WTO, the TPP does not offer much progress with respect to the protection of food safety (including the PRMs designed to protect food safety). This chapter offers an interpretative view to at least allow for PRMs developed for food safety purposes to be regulated under the TPP TBT provisions, and to provide its parties wider discretion in the formulation of PRMs to secure food safety. The primary goal is to avoid the result of interpretations of the SPS and TBT provisions becoming absurd.

According to this interpretation, all PRMs would be subject to TBT rules. Hence, scientific principles and risk analysis are not required for the purpose of adopting the PRMs. However, it must be said that although the TPP is considered to be a new generation of, or model for, free trade agreements, it is not particularly impressive in the handling of food safety issues, especially food safety-related package issues. The interpretative approach may offer some aid in this regard. Ultimately, a new balance must be struck between food safety protection and free trade so as to render the free trade agreement more favorable to the protection of food safety.

PART V

Intellectual property rights

13. TPP, RCEP, and the crossvergence of Asian intellectual property standards

Peter K. Yu*

I. INTRODUCTION

The debate on convergence and divergence has garnered considerable attention from policy-makers and commentators involved in regulatory developments in Asia. The developments surrounding the Trans-Pacific Partnership (TPP) and the Regional Comprehensive Economic Partnership (RCEP) have added fuel to this debate. Given the different leadership in these two megaregional agreements and the exclusion of many RCEP parties from the TPP negotiations,[1] it will be interesting to see how the agreements will affect the future efforts to set regional intellectual property standards. It will also be curious to see whether the draft and finalized standards could reveal policy preferences of the participating countries.

In January 2017, US President Donald Trump signed a memorandum directing the United States to withdraw from the TPP,[2] putting the megaregional pact on life support.[3] A year later, however, the eleven remaining TPP partners signed the Comprehensive and Progressive Agreement for Trans-Pacific Partnership (CPTPP). While this transition instrument suspended some provisions in the TPP Intellectual Property Chapter, many

---

* This chapter draws on research from the author's earlier article in the VANDERBILT JOURNAL OF TRANSNATIONAL LAW and book chapters published by the ANU Press, Edward Elgar Publishing, and Routledge.

1 Whether intentionally excluded or not, China, India, Indonesia, the Philippines, South Korea, and Thailand did not participate in the TPP negotiations.

2 Presidential Memorandum Regarding Withdrawal of the United States from the Trans-Pacific Partnership Negotiations and Agreement, 82 Fed. Reg. 8497 (23 January 2017).

3 Peter K. Yu, *Thinking About the Trans-Pacific Partnership (and a Mega-Regional Agreement on Life Support)*, 20 SMU SCI. & TECH. L. REV. 97 (2017).

original provisions remain. For illustrative purposes, this chapter focuses its analysis on the TPP Intellectual Property Chapter unless the suspended provisions would change the analysis.

This chapter begins by examining the regulatory convergence narrative, focusing on efforts to harmonize Asian intellectual property standards through the Agreement on Trade-Related Aspects of Intellectual Property Rights (TRIPS Agreement) and TRIPS-plus bilateral, regional, and plurilateral agreements. The chapter then turns to the regulatory divergence narrative, discussing the region's inherent nation-based differences, the development considerations involved in developing Asian intellectual property laws and policies, and the growing rivalry between the TPP/CPTPP and the RCEP. This chapter concludes by suggesting that neither the convergence narrative nor the divergence narrative presents a complete and convincing story for a region as large, complex, diverse, and internally inconsistent as Asia. Instead, the chapter contends that the region is likely to see 'regulatory crossvergence'—a simultaneous convergence and divergence of regulatory standards. Such crossvergence not only has resulted in the region's development of compromising standards but has also been highly indicative of the ongoing and future standard-setting efforts in Asia.

II. REGULATORY CONVERGENCE

The historical, political, cultural, economic, and technological conditions in Asia have been highly diverse. Yet, the regional intellectual property standards have converged to a great extent. Such convergence can be attributed to a number of factors, most notably the wide-ranging influences from the TRIPS Agreement and TRIPS-plus bilateral, regional, and plurilateral agreements.

1. TRIPS Agreement

The primary driver of convergence of intellectual property standards in Asia is the TRIPS Agreement of the World Trade Organization (WTO). Adopted in April 1994, this Agreement employed a one-size-fits-all—or, more precisely, super-size-fits-all—approach to set international minimum standards. Because virtually all Asian countries are WTO members,[4] they abide by the same TRIPS standards.

---

[4] Bhutan and Timor-Leste are the rare exceptions in East, South, and Southeast Asia.

Part II of the TRIPS Agreement stipulates the high minimum standards of intellectual property protection in a wide variety of areas. These areas include copyrights, patents, trademarks, geographical indications, industrial designs, plant variety protection, integrated circuit topographies, and protection of undisclosed information (such as trade secrets and clinical trial data). Part III further delineates the standards of intellectual property enforcement, including civil, administrative, and criminal procedures and remedies, as well as border control measures.

In addition, Article 64 of the TRIPS Agreement requires WTO members to settle all TRIPS-related disputes through the mandatory dispute settlement process. Since its inception, this process has been used by powerful developed countries as a major weapon to induce Asian trading partners to bring their laws into conformity with the high TRIPS standards.[5] In the past two decades, the European Union and the United States have filed TRIPS complaints against Japan, Pakistan, India, Indonesia, and China. By comparison, Asian countries did not file any TRIPS complaint until May 2010, with India and Indonesia being the only countries to have ever done so.

In the beginning, virtually all Asian developing countries struggled with TRIPS standards, due to unfamiliarity, inappropriateness, or both.[6] As Jagdish Bhagwati lamented, 'TRIPS does not involve mutual gain; rather, it positions the WTO primarily as a collector of intellectual property-related rents on behalf of multinational corporations'.[7] Likewise, the World Bank noted that a fully implemented TRIPS Agreement would transfer more than US$20 billion of rents from developing countries 'to major technology-creating countries—particularly the United States, Germany, and France—in the form of pharmaceutical patents, computer chip designs, and other intellectual property'.[8] According to Michael Finger, the total rent transfer from developed to developing countries could be as high as US$60 billion per year.[9]

---

[5] Peter K. Yu, *Are Developing Countries Playing a Better TRIPS Game?*, 16 UCLA J. Int'l L. & Foreign Aff. 311, 333–7 (2011).

[6] UN Development Programme, Human Development Report 1999, at 74 (1999).

[7] Jagdish Bhagwati, *What It Will Take to Get Developing Countries into a New Round of Multilateral Trade Negotiations*, *in* Trade Policy Research 2001, at 19, 21 (John Curtis ed., 2001).

[8] World Bank, Global Economic Prospects and the Developing Countries 2002, at xvii (2002).

[9] J. Michael Finger, *The Doha Agenda and Development: A View from the Uruguay Round* 13 (Asian Dev. Bank, ERD Working Paper Series No. 21, 2002); J. Michael Finger, *Introduction and Overview*, *in* Poor People's Knowledge:

Nevertheless, some large Asian developing countries, such as China and India, managed to carefully implement TRIPS standards in a way that benefited their overall development.[10] Such strategic implementation transformed these emerging economies in the end, making them globally competitive and technologically proficient.[11] In recent years, other Asian developing countries have also begun to appreciate the strategic benefits of stronger intellectual property protection and enforcement.[12] As a result, standards in this area have become more and more converged.

2. TRIPS-plus Agreements

Just when developing countries started to benefit from TRIPS standards, or at least appreciate the benefits of those standards, developed countries once again pushed for higher intellectual property standards.[13] These so-called TRIPS-plus standards exceed what the TRIPS Agreement requires and are now being developed through the negotiation of bilateral, regional, and plurilateral trade agreements.

Since the early 2000s, the European Union and the United States have pushed aggressively for the development of bilateral and regional free trade agreements (FTAs) or economic partnership agreements (EPAs). Consider the United States, for instance. The country entered into the Central America-Dominican Republic Free Trade Agreement with Costa Rica, Dominican Republic, El Salvador, Guatemala, Honduras, and Nicaragua. The United States also established standalone FTAs with Australia, Bahrain, Chile, Colombia, Israel, Jordan, Morocco, Oman, Panama, Peru, Singapore, and South Korea.

Taken together, these FTAs have transplanted high intellectual property standards from the United States to its less powerful neighbours,

---

PROMOTING INTELLECTUAL PROPERTY IN DEVELOPING COUNTRIES 1, 4 (J. Michael Finger and Philip Schuler eds., 2004).

[10] Amy Kapczynski, *Harmonization and Its Discontents: A Case Study of TRIPS Implementation in India's Pharmaceutical Sector*, 97 CALIF. L. REV. 1571 (2009); Peter K. Yu, *The Transplant and Transformation of Intellectual Property Laws in China*, *in* GOVERNANCE OF INTELLECTUAL PROPERTY RIGHTS IN CHINA AND EUROPE 20 (Nari Lee et al. eds., 2016).

[11] Peter K. Yu, *The Middle Intellectual Property Powers*, *in* LAW AND DEVELOPMENT IN MIDDLE-INCOME COUNTRIES: AVOIDING THE MIDDLE-INCOME TRAP 84 (Randall Peerenboom and Tom Ginsburg eds., 2014).

[12] Peter K. Yu, *The RCEP and Trans-Pacific Intellectual Property Norms*, 50 VAND. J. TRANSNAT'L L. 673, 722 (2017).

[13] Peter K. Yu, *TRIPS and Its Achilles' Heel*, 18 J. INTELL. PROP. L. 479, 505–14 (2011).

including those in Asia. A case in point is the Korea-United States Free Trade Agreement.[14] Its Intellectual Property Chapter includes distinct provisions on copyrights, trademarks, patents, and other forms of intellectual property rights. The Chapter also includes detailed intellectual property enforcement provisions. Article 18.10.30 specifically requires the parties to address issues concerning Internet Service Provider (ISP) liability. The Agreement further includes two related confirmation letters, one on limitations on such liability and the other on 'online piracy prevention'.

While the regulatory standards included in these early FTAs or EPAs are already quite high, developed countries went even further in the mid- to late 2000s to establish new plurilateral trade, investment, and intellectual property agreements. Using a highly controversial 'country club' approach,[15] these agreements sought to bring together developed and likeminded countries to set new international intellectual property standards that are higher than those found in the multilateral trading system. The widely cited examples are the Anti-Counterfeiting Trade Agreement (ACTA) and the TPP Agreement.

Proposed by Japan,[16] ACTA aimed to set a new and higher benchmark for international intellectual property protection and enforcement. Among the countries participating in the negotiations were Australia, Canada, the European Union, Japan, Morocco, Mexico, New Zealand, Singapore, South Korea, Switzerland, and the United States (along with Jordan and the United Arab Emirates, both of which participated in only the first round of the negotiations).[17] After three years and eleven rounds of formal negotiations, ACTA was finally adopted on 15 April 2011. Thus far, only Japan, the country of depositary, has ratified the Agreement. Because this Agreement will not take effect until six parties have deposited their instruments of ratification, it remains unclear if the Agreement will ever enter into force.

While the United States was busy negotiating ACTA, it also launched

---

[14] Peter K. Yu, *Trade Agreement Cats and the Digital Technology Mouse*, *in* SCIENCE AND TECHNOLOGY IN INTERNATIONAL ECONOMIC LAW: BALANCING COMPETING INTERESTS 185, 195–6 (Bryan Mercurio and Ni Kuei-Jung eds., 2014).

[15] Daniel Gervais, *Country Clubs, Empiricism, Blogs and Innovation: The Future of International Intellectual Property Norm Making in the Wake of ACTA*, *in* TRADE GOVERNANCE IN THE DIGITAL AGE: WORLD TRADE FORUM 323 (Mira Burri and Thomas Cottier eds., 2012); Peter K. Yu, *The ACTA/TPP Country Clubs*, *in* ACCESS TO INFORMATION AND KNOWLEDGE: 21ST CENTURY CHALLENGES IN INTELLECTUAL PROPERTY AND KNOWLEDGE GOVERNANCE 258 (Dana Beldiman ed., 2014).

[16] Peter K. Yu, *Six Secret (and Now Open) Fears of ACTA*, 64 SMU L. REV. 975, 980–3 (2011).

[17] *Id.* at 1075.

the negotiations on an equally controversial plurilateral agreement known as the TPP Agreement. This megaregional agreement began as a quadrilateral agreement between Chile, New Zealand, Singapore and, later, Brunei Darussalam, known as the Trans-Pacific Strategic Economic Partnership Agreement or, more commonly, the 'P4' or 'Pacific 4'.[18] In March 2010, shortly before the eighth round of the ACTA negotiations in Wellington, New Zealand, negotiations began among Australia, Peru, Vietnam, the United States, and the P4 members for an expanded agreement. Malaysia, Mexico, Canada, and Japan joined the negotiations afterwards.

From its inception, the TPP was negotiated as a highly ambitious and comprehensive trade agreement that sought to cover '40% of global [gross domestic product] and some 30% of worldwide trade in both goods and services'.[19] Targeted areas included market access, textiles and apparel, sanitary and phytosanitary measures, investment, financial services, telecommunications, electronic commerce, government procurement, competition, intellectual property, labour, the environment, and regulatory standards.

After nearly six years of formal negotiations, the TPP Agreement was finally signed in Auckland, New Zealand, on 4 February 2016. The final text contains thirty chapters. Chapter 18 is devoted specifically to intellectual property matters; it covers issues such as trademarks, country names, geographical indications, patents and undisclosed test data, industrial designs, copyright and related rights, enforcement, and ISPs.

Although the US Obama administration considered the TPP 'a cardinal priority and a cornerstone of [its] Pivot to Asia',[20] the new Trump administration reversed course by directing the US Trade Representative to withdraw from the TPP and related negotiations. At the time of writing, the TPP has been placed on life support.[21] Nevertheless, Japan and New Zealand already ratified the Agreement. The eleven remaining TPP partners also managed to establish the CPTPP. This transition instrument sought to "incorporate provisions of the TPP, with the exception of a limited set of provisions, which will be suspended."[22]

---

[18] Meredith Kolsky Lewis, *Expanding the P-4 Trade Agreement into a Broader Trans-Pacific Partnership: Implications, Risks and Opportunities*, 4 Asian J. WTO & Int'l Health L. & Pol'y 401, 403–4 (2009).

[19] David A. Gantz, *The TPP and RCEP: Mega-Trade Agreements for the Pacific Rim*, 33 Ariz. J. Int'l & Comp. L. 57, 59 (2016).

[20] Kurt M. Campbell, The Pivot: The Future of American Statecraft in Asia 268 (2016).

[21] Yu (n. 3 above).

[22] Global Affairs Canada, *Trans-Pacific Partnership Ministerial Statement*

3. RCEP

While the developed and likeminded countries were busy negotiating the TPP, the Association of Southeast Asian Nations (ASEAN), Australia, China, India, Japan, New Zealand, and South Korea began negotiating the RCEP. Launched in November 2012, these negotiations built on prior efforts to facilitate regional economic integration and cooperation under the frameworks of ASEAN+3 (ASEAN, China, Japan, and South Korea), ASEAN+6 (ASEAN+3, Australia, India, and New Zealand), and the Asia-Pacific Economic Cooperation Forum (APEC).[23]

In terms of coverage, the RCEP compares favourably with the TPP; the former will 'account for almost half of the world's population, almost 30 per cent of global [gross domestic product] and over a quarter of world exports'.[24] Once established, the RCEP will cover not only China and India but also two high-income Asian economies (Japan and South Korea) and six other TPP partners (Australia, Brunei Darussalam, Malaysia, New Zealand, Singapore, and Vietnam). The RCEP will also be larger in size than the CPTPP.

At the time of writing, ASEAN+6 members have already entered into twenty rounds of negotiations. Although it remains to be seen what standards the RCEP Agreement will eventually include, the final text is likely to contain an Intellectual Property Chapter.[25] Thus far, no draft negotiating text has been officially released. Nevertheless, Knowledge Ecology International has made available online the 15 October 2015 version of the draft RCEP Intellectual Property Chapter, along with the original proposed Intellectual Property Chapters from ASEAN, India, Japan, and South Korea.

At first glance, this leaked Chapter is as substantial as the TPP Intellectual Property Chapter. It includes thirteen sections, covering copyright; trademarks; geographical indications; patents; industrial designs; genetic resources, traditional knowledge and folklore; unfair competition; and enforcement of intellectual property rights. The included standards are

---

para. 3, http://www.international.gc.ca/trade-commerce/trade-agreements-accords-commerciaux/agr-acc/tpp-ptp/statement-declaration.aspx (last modified 11 November 2017).

[23] Yu (n. 12 above) 678–85.

[24] Dep't Foreign Aff. & Trade (Austl.), *Regional Comprehensive Economic Partnership*, http://dfat.gov.au/trade/agreements/rcep/pages/regional-comprehensive-economic-partnership.aspx (last visited 10 August 2017).

[25] Yu (n. 12 above) 720–31.

also quite similar to those found in the TPP Intellectual Property Chapter. As Jeremy Malcolm of the Electronic Frontier Foundation declared:

> We might . . . expect that [the] RCEP could be the 'anti-TPP'; a vehicle for countries to push back against the neo-colonial ambitions of the United States, by proposing alternative, home-grown standards on the TPP's thorniest issues such as copyright, patents, and investor protection . . . But based on [the] leaks, the promise of [the] RCEP pushing back against the TPP is being squandered. Instead, its [intellectual property] chapter is turning out as a carbon copy.[26]

Thus, even though the TPP has remained the controversial poster child of the developed countries' aggressive push for high intellectual property standards in Asia, both the TPP and the RCEP aim to raise the regional standards beyond what the TRIPS Agreement requires. From a standpoint of regulatory convergence, both megaregional agreements will serve a similar goal, though they may result in a somewhat different level of convergence.[27]

III. REGULATORY DIVERGENCE

While the TRIPS Agreement and TRIPS-plus bilateral, regional, and plurilateral trade agreements have pushed for greater convergence of Asian intellectual property standards, the region faces an equally strong impulse for regulatory divergence. This impulse can be attributed to the region's inherent nation-based differences, the development considerations involved in developing Asian intellectual property laws and policies, and the growing rivalry between the TPP/CPTPP and the RCEP.

1. Inherent Differences

Asia is large, complex, diverse, and often internally inconsistent. As I noted earlier in a chapter published in the *Routledge Handbook of Asian Law*, a wide range of historical, political, cultural, economic, and technological differences continue to militate against efforts to converge regulatory standards in the region.[28]

---

26 Jeremy Malcolm, *Meet RCEP, a Trade Agreement in Asia That's Even Worse than TPP or ACTA*, ELECTRONIC FRONTIER FOUND. (4 June 2015), https://www.eff.org/deeplinks/2015/06/just-when-you-thought-no-trade-agreement-could-be-worse-tpp-meet-rcep.

27 Yu (n. 12 above) 729–31.

28 Peter K. Yu, *Clusters and Links in Asian Intellectual Property Law and*

Historically, the colonization efforts of European imperialist powers have deeply affected Asian countries. For instance, the Opium War (1839–42) led to an influx of foreign ideas and institutions that shook the foundation of traditional Chinese culture. The arrival of the British East India Company and its counterparts in continental Europe resulted in the transplant of laws, policies, practices, and institutions that were different from those in other parts of Asia. Yet, not all Asian countries have been colonized. Nor were those colonized always subject to the same influence or controlled to the same extent.

For example, India, Malaysia, and Singapore were British colonies, and the Dutch East Indies and French Indochina belonged to the Netherlands and France, respectively. The Philippines was once a Spanish colony but was later ceded to the United States. China was merely a semi-colony, with foreigners having control and special rights in different parts of the country. Meanwhile, Thailand remained an independent country throughout the colonial era, acting only as a buffer state. In the first half of the twentieth century, Korea and Taiwan became colonies of another Asian country, Japan. Given these developments, it is small wonder that Simon Tay has noted that any discussion of homogenous values in Asia 'underestimates . . . the historical ruptures of colonization'.[29]

The political landscape in Asia is equally complicated. Since the Second World War, the geopolitical rivalries, tensions, and conflicts within Asia have deeply affected regulatory developments in the region, including developments in the areas of intellectual property and international trade. Lacking a regional hegemon, Asia is filled with developments spearheaded by three different leaders: China, India, and Japan. If one includes the important role that the United States has played for decades in the region, one will find the picture even more complicated. Certainly, similarities can be found between China and India, and between Japan and the United States, in light of their similar stages of development. Nevertheless, these similarities do not undercut the impact of geographical rivalries and the regional leaders' continued disagreement over how intellectual property standards are to be harmonized.

As if these historical and political backgrounds were not complicated enough, there is as much cultural diversity as one could find in Asia. Although commentators have widely noted how Confucianism has

Policy, *in* ROUTLEDGE HANDBOOK OF ASIAN LAW 147, 148–50 (Christoph Antons ed., 2017).

[29] Simon S.C. Tay, *Human Rights, Culture, and the Singapore Example*, 41 MCGILL L.J. 743, 747 (1996).

militated against intellectual property reforms in Asia,[30] Confucianism forms the cultural basis of only a small number of countries in East Asia. Islam, for instance, is important to countries such as Indonesia, Malaysia, and Pakistan. Hinduism is very important to South Asia, covering places such as Bangladesh, India, and Nepal. Buddhism is also very important to countries in Southeast Asia, such as Cambodia, Laos, Myanmar, Thailand, and Sri Lanka. In the words of David Kang, 'the states of Southeast Asia experienced twin cultural influences, from India and from China'.[31] George Coedès also emphasized India's influence on Southeast Asian culture in his book *The Indianized States of Southeast Asia*.[32]

Even in China, Confucianism is only one among the three dominant philosophies in traditional Chinese society.[33] Buddhism and Daoism (which drew on the teachings of Laozi and Zhuangzi) had, and continue to have, a very significant influence.[34] Other philosophies, such as the Yin-Yang school, could also be useful for understanding the ongoing and future intellectual property challenges in China.[35] In addition, China is home to many minority cultures and beliefs, including those of the Zhuang, Hui, Uygur, Yi, Tibetan, Miao, Manchu, Mongol, and Buyei.[36] These cultures and beliefs will be particularly important in the debate on the protection of traditional knowledge and traditional cultural expressions.

Finally, the economic developments in Asia have been highly diverse and uneven.[37] As shown in the data provided by the World Bank and the

---

[30] William P. Alford, To Steal a Book Is an Elegant Offense: Intellectual Property Law in Chinese Civilization 19–29 (1995); R. Michael Gadbaw, *Republic of Korea*, *in* Intellectual Property Rights: Global Consensus, Global Conflict? 272, 275 (R. Michael Gadbaw and Timothy J. Richards eds., 1988); Peter K. Yu, *Piracy, Prejudice, and Perspectives: An Attempt to Use Shakespeare to Reconfigure the U.S.-China Intellectual Property Debate*, 19 B.U. Int'l L.J. 1, 16–21 (2001).

[31] David C. Kang, East Asia Before the West: Five Centuries of Trade and Tribute 52 (2010).

[32] George Coedès, The Indianized States of Southeast Asia (Walter F. Vella ed. and Sue Brown Cowing trans., 1996) (1968).

[33] Peter K. Yu, *Intellectual Property and Confucianism*, *in* Diversity in Intellectual Property: Identities, Interests, and Intersections (Irene Calboli and Srividhya Ragavan eds., 2015).

[34] Peter K. Yu, *The Confucian Challenge to Intellectual Property Reforms*, 4 WIPO J. 1, 6 (2012).

[35] Peter K. Yu, *Intellectual Property, Asian Philosophy and the Yin-Yang School*, 7 WIPO J. 1 (2015).

[36] James C.F. Wang, Contemporary Chinese Politics: An Introduction 176 (6th ed. 1999).

[37] Assafa Endeshaw, Intellectual Property in Asian Emerging Economies 3 (2010); Mark Beeson, Institutions of the Asia-Pacific: ASEAN, APEC and

World Intellectual Property Organization (WIPO), as well as the Global Competitiveness Index and the Global Innovation Index, considerable variations have existed in technological developments and innovation capabilities in Asian countries.[38] Because economic and technological developments heavily influence the standards for intellectual property protection and enforcement, the wide diversity of regional developments virtually guarantees the non-existence of any established consensus on intellectual property standards in Asia.

2. Development Considerations

Thus far, development considerations have played a salient and crucial role in intellectual property laws and policies in Asia. These considerations affect not only the poorest countries in the region, such as those that the United Nations have deemed to be least developed countries.[39] Development is also a major concern in large Asian economies, such as China and India. Although these countries have powerful aggregated economies and are keenly aware of the myriad benefits provided by stronger intellectual property protection and enforcement, they remain middle-income countries on a per capita basis and continue to struggle with problems relating to their highly uneven internal developments.[40]

A case in point is China. Some of the recent intellectual property discussions have focused on the country's emergence as an intellectual property power.[41] Based on the 2017 WIPO statistics, China had the world's second largest number of international applications filed through the Patent Cooperation Treaty (PCT) and third largest number of international trademark applications under the Madrid System.[42] Among all corporate applicants, two

---

BEYOND 4 (2009); Yash Ghai, *Asian Perspectives on Human Rights, in* HUMAN RIGHTS AND INTERNATIONAL RELATIONS IN THE ASIA-PACIFIC REGION 54, 54–5 (James T.H. Tang ed., 1995).

[38] Peter K. Yu, *Intellectual Property and Asian Values*, 16 MARQ. INTELL. PROP. L. REV. 329, 364 (2012); Yu (n. 11 above) 92–5.

[39] Least developed countries in East, South, and Southeast Asia include Afghanistan, Bangladesh, Bhutan, Cambodia, Laos, Myanmar, Nepal, and Timor-Leste.

[40] Peter K. Yu, *Intellectual Property, Economic Development, and the China Puzzle, in* INTELLECTUAL PROPERTY, TRADE AND DEVELOPMENT: STRATEGIES TO OPTIMIZE ECONOMIC DEVELOPMENT IN A TRIPS PLUS ERA 173, 203 (Daniel J. Gervais ed., 1st ed. 2007); FAREED ZAKARIA, THE POST-AMERICAN WORLD 133 (2008).

[41] Peter K. Yu, *The Rise and Decline of the Intellectual Property Powers*, 34 CAMPBELL L. REV. 525, 529–32 (2012).

[42] WIPO, *Who Filed the Most Madrid Trademark Applications in 2017?*, http://

Chinese firms, Huawei Technologies and ZTE Corporation, also had the first and second largest number of PCT applications, respectively.

When one focuses on developments at the provincial level, however, the distribution of innovation in the country has been disturbingly uneven. Based on the 2016 figures on invention patents provided by the State Intellectual Property Office of China, Jiangsu, Guangdong, and Anhui provinces had a total of 184,632, 155,581, and 95,963, respectively.[43] By contrast, Yunnan, Jilin, and Gansu provinces had a total of only 7,907, 7,537, and 6,114, respectively, not to mention that six other provinces or autonomous regions received fewer than 4,000 patent applications. Given the enormous gap between the highly innovative provinces and their less innovative counterparts, it is understandable why a country like China would be concerned about the potential problems generated by high intellectual property standards, especially in areas that are largely underdeveloped.

To make matters even more complicated, most Asian developing countries simply do not have as large an aggregated economy as China or India. As developing or least developed countries of much smaller sizes, they fear that the introduction of high intellectual property standards, as required by TRIPS-plus bilateral, regional, and plurilateral agreements, would stifle their already limited access to essential medicines, knowledge, information and communication technologies, and other key development resources. They also remain concerned about the mismatch between those high, and arguably inappropriate, standards and their local needs, national interests, technological capabilities, institutional capacities, and public health conditions.[44]

After all, an innovative model that works well in the developed world is unlikely to have the same beneficial impact in the developing world. Moreover, because of variations in economic conditions, imitative or innovative capacities, research and development productivities, and availability of human capital,[45] stronger protection is not always optimal. As

---

www.wipo.int/export/sites/www/ipstats/en/docs/infographic_madrid_2017.pdf (last visited 28 March 2018); WIPO, *Who Filed the Most PCT Patent Applications in 2017?*, http://www.wipo.int/export/sites/www/ipstats/en/docs/infographic_pct_2017.pdf (last visited 28 March 2018).

[43] State Intellectual Property Office (China), *Table 2 Distribution of [Applications for] Inventions Received from Home 2016*, http://english.sipo.gov.cn/statistics/2016/12/201704/t20170407_1309326.html (last visited 10 August 2017).

[44] Peter K. Yu, *The International Enclosure Movement*, 82 Ind. L.J. 827, 866–70 (2007).

[45] *Id.* at 889; Claudio R. Frischtak, *Harmonization Versus Differentiation in Intellectual Property Rights Regime*, *in* Global Dimensions of Intellectual Property Rights in Science and Technology 89, 97 (Mitchel B. Wallerstein et al. eds., 1993).

Josh Lerner rightly reminded us, 'Almost all economists would agree that some intellectual property protection is better than no intellectual property protection at all. But this does not mean that very strong protection is better than a more moderate level of protection'.[46]

To a large extent, the TRIPS-plus bilateral, regional, and plurilateral agreements have brought with them the widely documented problems of legal transplants. Not only may the unquestioned adoption of high TRIPS-plus intellectual property standards from abroad fail to result in greater innovative efforts, industrial progress, and technology transfer, such adoption may drain away the resources needed for dealing with the socio-economic and public health problems created by new intellectual property laws and policies. Such adoption may also exacerbate the dire economic plight of many developing countries by enabling foreign rights holders in developed and emerging countries to crush local industries through litigation threats or actual lawsuits.[47] Even if these new intellectual property standards could be beneficial *in the long run*, many of these countries might not have the wealth, infrastructure, and technological base to take advantage of the opportunities created by the system *in the short run*.[48] For countries with urgent public policy needs and a population dying due to a lack of access to essential medicines, the realization of the hope for a brighter long-term future seems far away, if not unrealistic.

Worse still, greater harmonization of intellectual property standards can take away valuable opportunities for experimentation with new regulatory and economic policies.[49] The lack of diversified standards can also reduce competition among jurisdictions while preventing each jurisdiction from deciding for itself what rules and systems it should adopt.[50] Greater harmonization could therefore render the law-making process less accountable to the local populations.[51] In the digital age, when laws are hastily introduced and often without convincing empirical evidence, greater experimentation and competition are indeed badly needed.[52]

Finally, many Asian developing countries have remained far behind

---

46 Josh Lerner, *The Patent System in a Time of Turmoil*, 2 WIPO J. 28, 32 (2010).

47 Ellen 't Hoen, *TRIPS, Pharmaceutical Patents, and Access to Essential Medicines: A Long Way from Seattle to Doha*, 3 CHI. J. INT'L L. 27, 30–1 (2002).

48 KEITH E. MASKUS, INTELLECTUAL PROPERTY RIGHTS IN THE GLOBAL ECONOMY 237 (2000).

49 John F. Duffy, *Harmony and Diversity in Global Patent Law*, 17 BERKELEY TECH. L.J. 685, 707–8 (2002).

50 *Id.* at 703–6.

51 *Id.* at 706–7.

52 Peter K. Yu, *Anticircumvention and Anti-Anticircumvention*, 84 DENV. U. L. REV. 13, 40–58 (2006).

their neighbours in their enforcement of intellectual property rights. As a result, they continue to struggle with massive piracy and counterfeiting problems. Such problems have not only slowed down the development of their domestic intellectual property industries but have also created considerable demands on enforcement resources—resources that these countries either do not have or are reluctant to provide at the expense of other equally, or more, pressing public needs.[53] Because piracy and counterfeiting activities remain pervasive, the entrenched beneficiaries may also have enough political clout to block intellectual property reforms, including those that will benefit the country as a whole.[54]

3. Rivalry Between Megaregionals

The previous section has discussed how the TPP and the RCEP have both pushed for higher intellectual property standards in Asia. Nevertheless, the existence of demands for such higher standards does not necessarily result in greater convergence of the covered standards. Indeed, if the standards required by the two megaregional agreements differ significantly from each other, inconsistencies, tensions, or conflicts will arise. Such inconsistencies could pave the way for what I have described as the 'battle of the FTAs',[55] which in turn might make Asia 'a vital battleground in setting the rules of the global economic order'.[56]

Until recently, the TPP negotiations have been driven by the United States. Meanwhile, the RCEP negotiations have heavily involved China, India, and other large Asian developing countries, many of which have been excluded from the TPP negotiations. Given the different leadership, participants, and preferences, one cannot help but notice the significant differences in the TPP Intellectual Property Chapter and the draft RCEP Intellectual Property Chapter.

For example, although the TPP Chapter extends the copyright term beyond the life of the author plus fifty years—the international minimum

---

53 Peter K. Yu, *Enforcement, Economics and Estimates*, 2 WIPO J. 1, 3–4 (2010).

54 Edmund W. Kitch, *The Patent Policy of Developing Countries*, 13 UCLA Pac. Basin L.J. 166, 178 (1994); Robert P. Merges, *Battle of the Lateralisms: Intellectual Property and Trade*, 8 B.U. Int'l L.J. 239, 243–4 (1990).

55 Peter K. Yu, *Sinic Trade Agreements*, 44 U.C. Davis L. Rev. 953, 1018–27 (2011); Peter K. Yu, *TPP, RCEP and the Future of Copyright Normsetting in the Asia-Pacific*, *in* Making Copyright Work for the Asian Pacific? Juxtaposing Harmonisation with Flexibility (Susan Corbett and Jessica Lai eds., forthcoming 2018).

56 Campbell (n. 20 above) 267.

standard required by the Berne Convention for the Protection of Literary and Artistic Works—the RCEP Chapter retains this international standard. Likewise, the TPP Chapter includes a highly controversial provision introducing a data exclusivity regime in relation to the clinical trial data submitted for the marketing approval of biological medicines.[57] Yet, the draft RCEP Chapter does not include such a provision. That Chapter also declines to extend criminal procedures and penalties to trade secret infringement and the circumvention of technological protection measures, both of which will be criminalized under the new TPP standards.

To be sure, the CPTPP suspended a number of provisions in the TPP Intellectual Property Chapter, such as those covering copyright and patent terms, undisclosed test or other data, biologics, technological protection measures, and legal remedies and safe harbours.[58] Such suspension has undoubtedly reduced the differences between the TPP/CPTPP and the RCEP. Nevertheless, because many provisions in the TPP Intellectual Property Chapter remain intact in the CPTPP, significant differences between the two megaregional agreements continue. Should the United States rejoin the TPP, these differences will be enlarged again.

IV. REGULATORY CROSSVERGENCE

The two previous sections have revisited the two usual narratives about regulatory developments in Asia, focusing on intellectual property standards. While policy-makers and commentators have embraced either the convergence narrative or the divergence narrative, depending on their worldviews and assessments, neither narrative is complete and satisfactory. In fact, both of them have presented too simple a story for a region as large, complex, diverse, and internally inconsistent as Asia.

To fully capture the regulatory developments in Asia, whether in the intellectual property area or elsewhere, this section advances the concept of crossvergence, which has already been advanced in literature in other

---

57 Burcu Kilic and Courtney Pine, *Decision Time on Biologics Exclusivity: Eight Years Is No Compromise*, INTELL. PROP. WATCH (27 July 2015), https://www.ip-watch.org/2015/07/27/decision-time-on-biologics-exclusivity-eight-years-is-no-compromise/ (last visited 10 August 2017).

58 *Trans-Pacific Partnership Ministerial Statement*, Annex II, GLOBAL AFFAIRS CANADA, http://www.international.gc.ca/trade-commerce/trade-agreements-accords-commerciaux/agr-acc/tpp-ptp/annex2-annexe2.aspx (last modified 11 November, 2017).

disciplines.[59] The section contends that a crossvergence of intellectual property standards is slowly emerging in Asia. Instead of either convergence or divergence, the ongoing development reflects a simultaneous convergence and divergence of regulatory standards, which is the result of the continuous and dynamic interactions between convergence and divergence forces.

1. RCEP as an Illustration

The leaked RCEP Intellectual Property Chapter provides a highly instructive illustration of the crossvergence narrative. Specifically, the Chapter includes three types of provisions: (1) those that are the same as the TPP standards ('TPP-like'); (2) those that are lower ('TPP-minus'); and (3) those that are higher ('TPP-plus'). Whether one sees convergence, divergence, or crossvergence will largely depend on the provisions on which they focus their analysis.

As shown in the leaked version, the draft RCEP Intellectual Property Chapter calls for standards that go beyond the TRIPS requirements, similar to those required by the TPP Intellectual Property Chapter. A case in point is the similar protection the two megaregional agreements offer to copyrighted works. Both Chapters include provisions on technological protection measures, electronic rights management information, and ISPs, although the draft RCEP provisions are admittedly shorter and more flexible than those found in the TPP Agreement. In addition, both Chapters target online streaming and other new means of digital communication. They also outlaw the government use of infringing computer software while criminalizing unauthorized camcording in cinemas.

Notwithstanding these similarities, the draft RCEP Intellectual Property Chapter includes a section on the protection of genetic resources, traditional knowledge, and folklore. Drawing heavily on India's ten-paragraph original proposal, that section is more lengthy and detailed than the one found in the TPP Agreement.[60] The TPP's unenthusiastic treatment in this section is understandable given the continued resistance of Japan, South Korea, and the United States to setting new international minimum standards in this area.[61] The RCEP's welcome inclusion of this section is equally unsurprising considering that the United States did not participate in the RCEP negotiations and that the laws in China, India, the Philippines, and Vietnam have

---

59 A widely cited example in the international management literature is David A. Ralston, *The Crossvergence Perspective: Reflections and Projections*, 39 J. INT'L BUS. STUD. 27 (2007).

60 Yu (n. 12 above) 716–17.

61 Yu (n. 44 above) 900.

already required patent applicants to disclose the traditional knowledge and genetic resources used in their inventions.[62] Of the sixteen participants in the RCEP negotiations, China, India, and Thailand have also co-sponsored the proposal for a new Article 29*bis* of the TRIPS Agreement, which aimed to create a similar disclosure obligation under the WTO rules.[63]

Finally, the draft RCEP Intellectual Property Chapter includes some rare provisions calling for standards that are even higher than those found in the TPP Agreement. The best illustration concerns the provision targeting the unauthorized retransmission of television signals over the Internet. As Jeremy Malcolm observed:

> Based on the current text proposals, [the] RCEP may actually impose more stringent protections for broadcasters than the TPP does. The TPP allows authors, performers and producers to control the broadcast of their work, but it does not bestow any independent powers over those works upon broadcasters. [The] RCEP, in contrast, could create such new powers; potentially providing broadcasters with a 50 year monopoly over the retransmission of broadcast signals, including retransmission of those signals over the Internet.[64]

In sum, the RCEP negotiations are likely to result in greater crossvergence of intellectual property standards, which includes convergence as a result of the growing harmonization of regional standards and divergence as a result of the inconsistencies between the TPP/CPTPP and RCEP obligations. Such crossvergence has also been memorialized by the simultaneous inclusion of TPP-like, TPP-minus, and TPP-plus provisions in the draft RCEP Intellectual Property Chapter.

2. Why Crossvergence?

In view of the ongoing crossvergence in the region, one may wonder why regulatory developments have been moving in this direction. There are at least three reasons.

---

62 WIPO, *Disclosure Requirements Table* (April 2016), http://www.wipo.int/export/sites/www/tk/en/documents/pdf/genetic_resources_disclosure.pdf.

63 WTO, General Council, Doha Work Programme—The Outstanding Implementation Issue on the Relationship Between the TRIPS Agreement and the Convention on Biological Diversity: Communication from Brazil, China, Colombia, Cuba, India, Pakistan, Peru, Thailand and Tanzania—Revision, WTO Doc. WT/GC/W/564/Rev.2 (5 July 2006).

64 Jeremy Malcolm, *RCEP: The Other Closed-Door Agreement to Compromise Users' Rights*, Electronic Frontier Found. (20 April 2016), https://www.eff.org/deeplinks/2016/04/rcep-other-closed-door-agreement-compromise-users-rights.

First, in determining what standards to adopt, countries in the region are highly reluctant to side with either China or the United States.[65] As David Shambaugh rightly observed, '[h]aving to choose between Beijing and Washington . . . is the nightmare scenario for the vast majority of Asian states'.[66] Thus, the RCEP negotiations have been filled with compromises reflecting the different standards, models, and approaches preferred by both dominant players. Indeed, because seven of the sixteen RCEP negotiating parties are also TPP members, many policy-makers and commentators anticipate the eventual merger of the two megaregional agreements.[67] As Kurt Campbell, former Assistant US Secretary of State for East Asian and Pacific Affairs, observed, 'For many in Asia, both the TPP and the RCEP are way stations on the path to the ultimate destination'.[68]

Second, megaregional agreements are so-called minimum standards agreement. As a result, the participating countries have discretion to determine what standards they want to adopt as long as those standards do not go below the minima required by the agreement or interfere with the most-favoured-nation (MFN) or other obligations under pre-existing trade agreements. While countries with limited economic and technological developments may stick to the bare minima, those with higher level of development or those aspiring to achieve such a level will certainly opt for higher standards. These different preferences and choices, in turn, will create greater divergence even though the minimum standards were initially introduced to foster convergence.

Third, megaregional agreements are being developed in parallel with the pre-existing agreements in the multilateral forum.[69] Such development is

---

65 Peter K. Yu, *TPP and Trans-Pacific Perplexities*, 37 FORDHAM INT'L L.J. 1129, 1151 (2014).

66 David Shambaugh, *Introduction: The Rise of China and Asia's New Dynamics*, *in* POWER SHIFT: CHINA AND ASIA'S NEW DYNAMICS 1, 17 (David Shambaugh ed., 2006).

67 Matthew P. Goodman, *US Economic Strategy in the Asia-Pacific Region: Promoting Growth, Rules, and Presence*, *in* NEW DIRECTIONS IN ASIA-PACIFIC ECONOMIC INTEGRATION 169, 174–5 (Tang Guoqiang and Peter A. Petri eds., 2014); Meredith Kolsky Lewis, *Achieving a Free Trade Area of the Asia-Pacific: Does the TPP Present the Most Attractive Path?*, *in* THE TRANS-PACIFIC PARTNERSHIP: A QUEST FOR A TWENTY-FIRST CENTURY TRADE AGREEMENT 223, 235 (C.L. Lim et al. eds., 2012); Robert Scollay, *The TPP and RCEP: Prospects for Convergence*, *in* NEW DIRECTIONS IN ASIA-PACIFIC ECONOMIC INTEGRATION 235, 235 (Tang Guoqiang and Peter A. Petri eds., 2014).

68 CAMPBELL (n. 20 above) 193.

69 Peter K. Yu, *The Non-Multilateral Approach to International Intellectual Property Normsetting*, *in* INTERNATIONAL INTELLECTUAL PROPERTY: A HANDBOOK OF CONTEMPORARY RESEARCH 83, 118–20 (Daniel J. Gervais ed., 2015); Peter K.

understandable considering that the *demandeur* countries wanted to raise international standards without reopening the negotiations at either the WTO or WIPO.[70] More recently, Rochelle Dreyfuss also noted that the plurilateral negotiations have caused the harmonization effort to go 'sideways', as opposed to following the traditional top-down or bottom-up approach.[71] Because Asian countries are now taking on new obligations under megaregional agreements even though they remain subject to obligations arising from the multilateral system, the parallel arrangements have produced incoherence, fragmentation, and crossvergence.[72]

3. Studying Crossvergence

It is important to explore why we should devote more time and effort to studying the emergent crossvergence of Asian regulatory standards. It will also be useful to understand why studying the convergence or divergence narrative alone would not enable us to see the full picture of regulatory developments in Asia.

First, as far as standard setting in Asia is concerned, what appears in the RCEP negotiations is likely to stay. Those negotiations are important because they will have a major impact on the future development of the Free Trade Area of the Asia-Pacific (FTAAP). This impact is already bigger after the United States withdrew from the TPP. It will become even bigger if the CPTPP fails to enter into force. APEC started studying the FTAAP concept in November 2006 and pledged to create an agreement to realise its conceptual vision three years later.[73] Since then, APEC leaders have endorsed various declarations laying down the incremental steps needed to realize the FTAAP. As stated in the 'Pathways to FTAAP', 'an FTAAP should be pursued . . . by developing and building on ongoing regional undertakings, such as ASEAN+3, ASEAN+6, and the Trans-Pacific Partnership, among others'.[74] Based on this document,

---

Yu, *The Strategic and Discursive Contributions of the Max Planck Principles for Intellectual Property Provisions in Bilateral and Regional Agreements*, 62 DRAKE L. REV. DISCOURSE 20, 32 (2014).

[70] Yu, *Non-multilateral Approach* (n. 69 above) 88.

[71] Rochelle C. Dreyfuss, *Harmonization: Top Down, Bottom Up—and Now Sideways? The Impact of the IP Provisions of Megaregional Agreements on Third Party States*, *in* MEGAREGULATION CONTESTED: GLOBAL ECONOMIC ORDERING AFTER TPP (Benedict Kingsbury et al. eds., forthcoming 2018).

[72] Yu (n. 12 above) 734–6.

[73] Lewis (n. 67 above) 223.

[74] APEC, *Pathways to FTAAP*, 14 November 2010, https://www.apec.org/meeting-papers/leaders-declarations/2010/2010_aelm/pathways-to-ftaap.aspx.

the RCEP is clearly one of the agreed and anticipated routes to develop the FTAAP.

Second, the crossvergence narrative fits naturally with the wide range of inconsistencies, tensions, and contradictions commonly found in Asia. To be sure, many policy-makers and commentators, especially those subscribing to the Western analytical tradition, will remain uncomfortable with the non-linear development of regulatory standards in the crossvergence narrative. Nevertheless, we should take the region as it is, even with all the undesirable messiness. As I noted in an earlier work, because duality, or yin and yang, is inherent in Asian societies, 'there is no easy way to discuss intellectual property developments in Asia without also mentioning their complexities'.[75] Indeed, many commentators who are familiar with Asian developments have already remarked on the seemingly schizophrenic positions taken by Asian policy-makers.[76]

Third, the crossvergence narrative requires policy-makers and commentators to pinpoint what has converged and diverged in their respective areas, as noted in the two earlier sections. While a more precise analysis is inevitably more complicated, challenging, and time-consuming, greater precision could be highly beneficial to those policy-makers and commentators seeking solutions to address specific regulatory challenges in Asia. After all, even with the establishment of all these megaregional agreements, the highly uneven developments in the region are unlikely to disappear any time soon.

V. CONCLUSION

Asia is large, complex, diverse, and often internally inconsistent. Although literature in the areas of intellectual property, trade, and investment often lumps Asian countries together, these countries are more different than similar. As Simon Tay declared, 'The region has no single, strong, and enduring history of unity and accepted commonality, whether in polity, culture, language, or religion'.[77] Likewise, David Llewellyn observed:

---

[75] Yu (n. 28 above) 148.

[76] Vinay Rai and William L Simon, Think India: The Rise of the World's Next Superpower and What It Means for Every American 211 (2007); Dwijen Rangnekar, *Context and Ambiguity in the Making of Law: A Comment on Amending India's Patent Act*, 10 J. World Intell. Prop. 365, 380 (2007); Peter K. Yu, *International Enclosure, the Regime Complex, and Intellectual Property Schizophrenia*, 2007 Mich. St. L. Rev. 1, 25–6.

[77] Simon S.C. Tay, Asia Alone: The Dangerous Post-Crisis Divide from America 19 (2010).

> The term 'Asia' . . . incorporates a number of regions and peoples from vastly varied civilisations. It is likely that the peoples of ancient Asia themselves, such as the Chinese, Indians, Japanese, Persians and Arabs, did not conceive the idea of Asia because they did not view themselves collectively in the way Europeans did.[78]

In the past decade, Asian countries have actively engaged in the development of megaregional agreements, including both the TPP and the RCEP. Through these negotiations and other discussions within ASEAN+6 and APEC, Asian countries have also actively explored the incremental steps needed to develop the FTAAP. Although it is tempting to utilize either the convergence narrative or the divergence narrative to describe ongoing regulatory developments in the region, the crossvergence narrative advanced in this chapter is likely to better capture these developments. Such a narrative will also provide a more complete explanation for both ongoing and future developments.

[78] David Llewellyn, Invisible Gold in Asia: Creating Wealth Through Intellectual Property, at xiv–xv (2010).

14. International harmonization with regulatory competition: A case of intellectual property law

Branislav Hazucha

I. INTRODUCTION

Although the trend in negotiating and concluding regional free trade agreements was welcomed, with hopes of achieving further growth in international trade and economic development in its early days,[1] views on the actual role of trade agreements have recently changed considerably. Many critics question whether bilateral and regional free trade agreements have any benefits. They often point out the agreements' hidden drawbacks and possible negative economic and social impacts.[2]

As intellectual property plays an important role in contemporary post-industrial economies, it is not so surprising that its protection nowadays forms an integral part of free trade agreements (FTAs), be they bilateral,[3]

---

[1] See e.g., Paul Bowles and Brian MacLean, *Regional Trading Blocs: Will East Asia Be Next?*, 20 Cambridge J. Econ. 393 (1996); James Thuo Gathii, *The Neoliberal Turn in Regional Trade Agreements*, 86 Wash. L. Rev. 421 (2011).

[2] See e.g., Jana Kasperkevic, *You Down with TPP? An Explainer on Obama's 'Secret' Trade Pact*, The Guardian (12 May 2015), available at www.theguardian.com/us-news/2015/may/12/trans-pacific-partnership-explainer (last visited 5 July 2017); Editorial, *Trade, At What Price?*, The Economist (2 April 2016), available at www.economist.com/news/united-states/21695855-americas-economy-benefits-hugely-trade-its-costs-have-been-amplified-policy (last visited 5 July 2017); Stan Sorscher, *How to Tell TPP is a Bad Deal*, The Huffington Post (1 May 2016), available at www.huffingtonpost.com/stan-sorscher/how-to-tell-tpp-is-a-bad_b_8914388.html (last visited 5 July 2017); Editorial, *TPP: What is It and Why Does it Matter?*, BBC News (27 July 2016), available at www.bbc.com/news/business-32498715 (last visited 5 July 2017).

[3] See e.g., United States-Chile Free Trade Agreement (FTA), Ch. 17 (6 June 2003), 42 ILM 1026; United States-Australia FTA, Ch. 17 (18 May 2004), 43 ILM 1248; United States-Dominican Republic-Central America FTA, Ch. 15 (28 May 2004), 43 ILM 514.

regional,[4] or multilateral.[5] With the change in the views on the role of trade agreements over the last two decades, bilateral and regional FTAs are frequently criticized for imposing too-high standards of intellectual property protection on developing countries by powerful economies, such as the United States and the European Union.[6] As those standards tend to be higher than the ones recognized and required on the international level, it is usually argued that such an approach can hinder developing countries in designing their national policies in a way that allows them to catch up with advanced countries in terms of economic development and technological progress.[7]

This chapter shows that although bilateral and regional FTAs lead to international harmonization on ever-higher levels of intellectual property protection, they still provide room for regulatory competition[8] between individual countries so that they can further their national policies in the field of innovation and technological progress. At the same time, it is recommended that trade negotiators cultivate better awareness of the

---

[4] See e.g., North American Free Trade Agreement, art. 1102 (17 December 1992), 32 ILM 296, 639 (NAFTA); Trans-Pacific Partnership Agreement, Ch. 18 (4 February 2016), available at https://ustr.gov/trade-agreements/free-trade-agreements/trans-pacific-partnership/tpp-full-text (TPP).

[5] See e.g., Agreement on Trade Related Aspects of Intellectual Property Rights (15 April 1994), Marrakesh Agreement Establishing the World Trade Organization, Annex 1C, Legal Instruments-Results of the Uruguay Round, 1869 UNTS 299, 33 ILM 1197 ('TRIPS Agreement').

[6] See e.g., Christopher Heath and Anselm Kamperman Sanders (eds.), Intellectual Property and Free Trade Agreements (2007); Henning Grosse Ruse-Khan, *The International Law Relation Between TRIPS and Subsequent TRIPS-Plus Free Trade Agreements: Towards Safeguarding TRIPS Flexibilities?*, 18 J. Intell. Prop. L. 325 (2011); Susan K. Sell, *TRIPS Was Never Enough: Vertical Forum Shifting, FTAS, ACTA, and TPP*, 18 J. Intell. Prop. L. 447, 453–5 (2011); Johanna von Braun, The Domestic Politics of Negotiating International Trade: Intellectual Property Rights in US-Colombia and US-Peru Free Trade Agreements (2012); EU Bilateral Trade Agreements and Intellectual Property: For Better or Worse (Josef Drexl et al. eds., 2014); Christoph Antons and Reto M. Hilty (eds.), Intellectual Property and Free Trade Agreements in the Asia-Pacific Region (2014).

[7] See e.g., Christine Haight Farley, *TRIPS-Plus Trade and Investment Agreements: Why More May be Less for Economic Development*, 35 U. Pa. J. Int'l L. 1061 (2014).

[8] See e.g., Daniel C. Esty and Damien Geradin (eds.), Regulatory Competition and Economic Integration: Comparative Perspectives (2001); Dale D. Murphy, The Structure of Regulatory Competition: Corporations and Public Policies in a Global Economy (2007); Erin A. O'Hara and Larry E. Ribstein, The Law Market (2009).

limits in strengthening intellectual property protection. Strong intellectual property protection does not necessarily lead to an increase in innovation and technological progress. Any protection, if too restrictive, can present a significant obstacle to development and dissemination of new technologies.

This chapter is divided into three sections. Section II outlines the relationship between FTAs and the level of intellectual property protection. It demonstrates how bilateral and regional FTAs are used to circumvent opposition towards the strengthening of intellectual property protection on both national and international levels. It also examines the pros and cons of strengthening the level of intellectual property protection with a focus on developing countries.

Sections III and IV then scrutinize whether strengthening intellectual property protection actually leads to international harmonization or whether there is still enough room left for regulatory competition between individual countries to design their national policies in a way that allows them to promote their indigenous creativity and innovation. As creativity and innovation is closely related to copyright and patent protection, both sections mainly focus on these two branches of intellectual property law, but similar issues can also be found in other branches of intellectual property. Section III thus enquires into copyright protection and development of new technologies that can be employed in the consumption or dissemination of copyrighted works. Section IV analyses the impact of patent protection on innovation in the field of computer-related inventions and biotechnology.

One might argue that the examples provided, of the divergences in intellectual property protection presented in sections III and IV, are taken from developed countries and therefore may not be very applicable to developing countries. However, the main point of this chapter is to show that there is insufficient harmonization even between major developed countries on several crucial points concerning intellectual property protection. In addition, the chapter attempts to demonstrate that trade negotiators from developed countries should be more cautious in pushing for strengthened intellectual property protection, based upon a model of intellectual property protection adopted by only one of the major developed countries. At the same time, knowledge of the divergences, even between major developed countries, can allow trade negotiators from developing countries to object to such efforts to strengthen intellectual property protection for any cost by pointing to approaches that can be found in other developed countries.

II. TRADE AGREEMENTS AND INTERNATIONAL HARMONIZATION

Intellectual property protection is already harmonized to a certain degree at an international level through international treaties administered by the World Intellectual Property Organization (WIPO).[9] It has been harmonized further by incorporating it into the framework of the World Trade Organization (WTO) regime.[10] Nevertheless, due to problems faced by more recent proposals for strengthening intellectual property protection at both these international organizations, the current strengthening attempts concentrate on bilateral and regional trade negotiations. This raises several issues related to the legitimacy of harmonizing the standards of intellectual property protection in such a way.

1. Trade Negotiations and their Legitimacy

Bilateral and regional trade negotiations are frequently seen as a way of circumventing deadlocks encountered by attempts to increase the level of intellectual property protection on a national or international level. In the case of the WIPO, a specialized United Nations organization for intellectual property protection, developing countries hold the majority of votes and can thus effectively oppose any proposal on strengthening intellectual property protection under its auspices, when the proposal does not adequately take into consideration the interests of developing countries.[11] Similarly, since the WTO was established, it has become quite difficult to agree any proposed changes in intellectual property protection on an international level through worldwide trade negotiations.[12]

---

[9] For treaties administered by the World Intellectual Property Organization (WIPO), see www.wipo.int/treaties/en/ (last visited 5 July 2017).

[10] TRIPS Agreement (n. 5 above).

[11] See e.g., DANIEL GERVAIS, THE TRIPS AGREEMENT: DRAFTING HISTORY AND ANALYSIS 8–10 (3rd ed., 2008); Charles Clift, *Why IPR Issues Were Brought to GATT: A Historical Perspective on the Origins of TRIPS*, *in* I RESEARCH HANDBOOK ON THE PROTECTION OF INTELLECTUAL PROPERTY UNDER WTO RULES: INTELLECTUAL PROPERTY IN THE WTO 3, 6–7 (Carlos M. Correa ed., 2010); Carolyn Deere-Birkbeck, *Developing Countries in the Global IP System Before TRIPS: The Political Context for the TRIPS Negotiations*, *in* I RESEARCH HANDBOOK ON THE PROTECTION OF INTELLECTUAL PROPERTY UNDER WTO RULES: INTELLECTUAL PROPERTY IN THE WTO 22, 30–38 (Carlos M. Correa ed., 2010).

[12] See e.g., Huaiwen He, *The Development of Free Trade Agreements and International Protection of Intellectual Property Rights in the WTO Era: New Bilateralism and Its Future*, 41 INT'L REV. INTELL. PROP. & COMPETITION L. 253

Major global players, such as the United States and the European Union, have thus focused their efforts on strengthening the level of intellectual property protection in developing or transition countries via bilateral and regional trade agreements. These developments—concerning how harmonization of national intellectual property laws can be achieved—are frequently criticized by commentators.[13] The critics stress that a strong level of intellectual property protection is not particularly appropriate for developing economies. They argue that it can even hamper developing countries' economic development and ability to catch up with developed countries.

Trade negotiations are also used by some national governments to overcome domestic opposition towards controversial measures. This does not need to be the case in a developing country. For instance, the extension of copyright protection term from fifty to seventy years *post mortem auctoris* was rejected in Japan a few years ago.[14] Although the European Union, followed by the United States, adopted such an extension, several empirical studies show that the copyright term extension lacks any economic justification[15] and can even have a negative impact on the availability of and accessibility to old copyrighted works on the market.[16]

As the Trans-Pacific Partnership (TPP) requires a copyright term to extend at least seventy years *post mortem auctoris*, Japan, together with New Zealand, Canada and several other participating countries, would be obliged to prolong the term of copyright, were the TPP ratified and entered into force even after the withdrawal from the TPP by the United States. The TPP's adoption would therefore allow the Japanese government to overcome any domestic opposition towards copyright term extension.

(2010); World Trade Organization (WTO), *WTO IP Rules Amended to Ease Poor Countries' Access to Affordable Medicines*, available at www.wto.org/english/news_e/news17_e/trip_23jan17_e.htm (last visited 5 July 2017).

[13] See nn. 6 and 7 above.

[14] See e.g., ThinkC, http://thinkcopyright.org/ (last visited 28 January 2017).

[15] See e.g., William M. Landes and Richard A. Posner, *Indefinitely Renewable Copyright*, 70 U. Chi. L. Rev. 471 (2003); Edward Rappaport, *Copyright Term Extension: Estimating the Economic Values* (Congressional Research Service Report No. 98-144E, 1998).

[16] See e.g., Paul J. Heald, *Property Rights and the Efficient Exploitation of Copyrighted Works: An Empirical Analysis of Public Domain and Copyrighted Fiction Bestsellers*, 92 Minn. L. Rev. 1031 (2008); Paul J. Heald, *Does the Song Remain the Same? An Empirical Study of Bestselling Musical Compositions (1913–32) and Their Use in Cinema (1968–2007)*, 60 Case. W. Res. L. Rev. 1 (2009); Christopher Buccafusco and Paul J. Heald, *Do Bad Things Happen When Works Enter the Public Domain?: Empirical Tests of Copyright Term Extension*, 28 Berkeley Tech. L.J. 1 (2013).

Accordingly, it was not surprising that although Japan achieved several concessions concerning intellectual property protection during the TPP negotiations, the length of copyright term was not the major issue for Japanese negotiators.

The use of international treaties to avoid domestic objections towards unpopular regulatory measures raises the issue of circumventing the democratic methods of adopting national policies. Criticism of this approach to international harmonization is boosted by the fact that trade negotiations are regularly conducted in high secrecy. Good examples are cases of leaked documents from the Anti-Counterfeiting Trade Agreement (ACTA), as well as TPP negotiations. In response to the leaks, requests were made by citizens of several negotiating countries to obtain access to information under negotiation via their public information access laws, but these requests were rejected. The reason for the rejection was that information on trade negotiation was classified as state secret.[17] Some officials even publicly denied any participation by their country in the negotiations, despite the country's actual involvement. Moreover, in some countries, the leaks have been investigated as serious criminal offences due to the high secrecy classification of trade negotiations.[18]

The doubts about the ways of conducting international harmonization through trade negotiations are even clearer after considering the fact that while citizens are habitually refused access to information on trade negotiations, major corporations and associations representing the interests of intellectual property right holders are usually able to lobby their national governments in order to include certain topics in trade negotiations.[19]

---

[17] See e.g., Letter from the General Secretariat of the Council of the European Union to Mr. Wessels (5 November 2008), available at http://action.ffii.org/acta/Analysis?action=AttachFile&do=get&target=08-1835en.wes.ws-jj.doc (last visited 5 July 2017); Maira Sutton, *The Secrecy Must be Stopped: Congress Members Probe USTR on the Confidential TPP Negotiations*, Electronic Frontiers Foundation (27 September 2012), available at www.eff.org/ja/deeplinks/2012/09/TPP-secrecy-must-be-stopped (last visited 5 July 2017); Michelle Limenta, *Open Trade Negotiations as Opposed to Secret Trade Negotiations: From Transparency to Public Participation*, 10 NZ Y.B. Int'l L. 73 (2012).

[18] See e.g., Ed Pilkington, *US Government Still Hunting WikiLeaks as Obama Targets Whistleblowers*, The Guardian (5 March 2015), available at www.theguardian.com/media/2015/mar/05/us-government-still-hunting-wikileaks-obama-targets-whistleblowers (last visited 5 July 2017).

[19] See e.g., Peter Drahos and John Braithwaite, Information Feudalism: Who Owns the Knowledge Economy (2002); Susan K. Sell, Private Power, Public Law: The Globalization of Intellectual Property Rights (2003).

2. Trade Agreements and Intellectual Property Protection

There are several ways in which trade agreements regulate intellectual property issues. Earlier agreements customarily required their contracting countries to accede to existing international treaties on intellectual property protection, which are administered by the WIPO.[20]

More recent agreements tend either to incorporate aspects of such treaties[21] or to restate their rules.[22] This repeatedly raises questions and criticism.[23] Although incorporating certain parts of other international treaties into trade agreements might seem to be wasteful duplication, the reason is often that trade agreements contain several mechanisms for settling disputes between the contracting parties, which can range from informal negotiation to international arbitration.[24] Consequently, the incorporation of rules administered by the WIPO allows the contracting parties to enforce them through dispute settlement mechanisms provided by trade agreements.

On the other hand, restatements of rules taken from other existing international treaties can bring problems with their interpretation, specifically whether the contracting parties intended to broaden or narrow a particular rule by its restatement. Restatements in trade agreements habitually occur without any intention to modify the original rules. They are frequently used as a result of the trade negotiators' tendency to rely on the text of their domestic laws, which are deemed to be in compliance with international standards. However, many examples of legal transplants show that taking one legal rule from one legal system to another can lead to completely different legal consequences.[25] Accordingly, some of most recent trade agreements explicitly stipulate that the contracting parties' intention behind the restatement was neither to broaden nor to narrow the scope of rules taken from other international treaties.[26]

---

[20] See e.g., United States-Australia FTA, Art. 17.1(4); United States-Jordan FTA, Art. 4.1(2) (24 October 2000), 41 ILM 63 (2002); TPP, Art. 18.7(2), available at https://ustr.gov/sites/default/files/TPP-Final-Text-Intellectual-Property.pdf (last visited 5 July 2017).

[21] See e.g., TRIPS Agreement, Arts. 2.1 and 9(1).

[22] See e.g., TPP, Art. 18.65(1).

[23] See e.g., Henning Grosse Ruse-Khan (n. 6 above).

[24] See e.g., TRIPS Agreement, Part V; United States-Australia FTA, Ch. 21, s.B; TPP, Ch. 28.

[25] See e.g., Paul Edward Geller, *Legal Transplants in International Copyright: Some Problems of Method*, 13 UCLA Pac. Basin L.J. 199 (1994); Wei Shi, *Globalization and Indigenization: Legal Transplant of a Universal TRIPS Regime in a Multicultural World*, 47 Am. Bus. L.J. 455 (2010).

[26] See e.g., TPP, Art. 18.65(2).

Finally, trade agreements also create new rules of intellectual property protection. Although they tend to increase the level of intellectual property protection,[27] there are also a few cases of introducing exceptions to existing intellectual property protection rules.[28]

3. Intellectual Property, Innovation, and Economic Development

Despite worries concerning how the level of intellectual property protection is strengthened through trade negotiations, and the legitimacy thereof, intellectual property protection can in fact be beneficial to developing countries. It can facilitate the transfer of advanced proprietary technologies, which are necessary for the countries' economic development and technological progress.[29] The existence of a sufficient and efficient protection of intellectual property rights on a national level can assuage foreign investors' concerns that their state-of-the-art technologies, protected by intellectual property rights, might be easily copied by local manufacturers, when manufacturing of those technologies begins in a particular developing country.

Moreover, the technology transfers usually have spill-over effects on local indigenous creativity and innovation. A good example is the technology transfer that occurred in relation to the second generation of mobile telephony in South Korea and China.[30] In that case, both countries opted for the adoption of foreign state-of-the-art technologies. This technology transfer allowed South Korean and Chinese manufacturers to catch up with leading technology developers from the United States, the European Union, and Japan. The spill-over effects were so strong that have enabled South Korean and Chinese manufacturers to become leaders in the field of wireless communication technology.[31]

At the same time, the failure to adopt strong intellectual property protection standards is not always detrimental to direct foreign investment and transfer of technologies from developed countries to developing and

---

[27] See e.g., TPP, Ch. 18, s.F, ss.C (measures relating to pharmaceutical products).

[28] See e.g., TPP, Ch. 18, s.J (safe harbours for ISPs).

[29] See e.g., Santos Vargas, *NAFTA: How it has Affected Technology Transfer Between the United States, Canada, and Mexico*, 2003 SYRACUSE L. & TECH. J. 7; Sunil Kanwar, *Intellectual Property Protection and Technology Licensing: The Case of Developing Countries*, 55 J. LAW & ECON. 539 (2012).

[30] See e.g., Jaesun Wang and Seoyong Kim, *Time to Get In: The Contrasting Stories about Government Interventions in Information Technology Standards (the Case of CDMA and IMT-2000 in Korea)*, 24 GOV'T INFO. Q. 115 (2007).

[31] See, e.g., Rudi Bekkers and Joel West, *The Limits to IPR Standardization Policies as Evidenced by Strategic Patenting in UMTS*, 33 TELECOM. POL'Y 80 (2009).

transition countries. One of the reasons is that the main markets for foreign investors from developed countries are commonly located in developed countries and therefore the right-holders are primarily concerned with preventing any importation of cheap knock-offs into their key markets.

Sometimes foreign investors even hope that local manufacturers make sufficient efforts to copy their advanced technologies. This can bring new indigenous ways of producing the technologies in question in a more cost-efficient way. The reduction in production costs can then make their products more competitive on the market.

There are even cases where technology leaders have decided to make their proprietary technologies free and open to their competitors in order to encourage other manufacturers to invest in those emerging technologies.[32] Massive and broad adoption of a technology can mean that, because of direct or indirect network effects,[33] the technology becomes the dominant standard on the market.[34] This can lead to the creation of a market for that technology and to a switch from incumbent technological solutions to the ones advocated by the technology leaders.

With regard to governing new technologies in the era of megaregional trade agreements, such as the TPP and the Transatlantic Trade and Investment Partnership (TTIP), the question arises whether the regulatory convergence that they attempt to bring about is really beneficial to technological progress and whether such convergence is even achievable. Hence, the following analysis examines the impact of increasing international harmonization in the fields of copyright and patent protection brought about by bilateral and regional trade agreements on regulatory competition amongst countries with different competitive advantages.

In the case of copyright protection, it scrutinizes the role of copyright law as a way of regulating the development of new information and communication technologies that can be used for exploiting and disseminating copyrighted works. It also examines the role of patent protection in regulating the development of new technologies in the fields of software and biotechnology.

---

[32] See, e.g., Elon Musk, ALL OUR PATENT ARE BELONG TO YOU, https://www.tesla.com/blog/all-our-patent-are-belong-you (last visited 5 July 2017).

[33] For an outline of network effects, *see, e.g.*, Joseph Farrell and Paul Klemperer, *Coordination and Lock-In: Competition with Switching Costs and Networks Effects*, *in* HANDBOOK OF INDUSTRIAL ORGANIZATION Vol. 3 1967 (Mark Armstrong and Robert H. Porter eds., 2007).

[34] See, e.g., Neil Gandal, Shane Greenstein and David Salant, *Adoptions and Orphans in the Early Microcomputer Market*, 47 J. IND. ECON. 87 (1999); JEFFREY H. ROHLFS, BANDWAGON EFFECTS IN HIGH-TECHNOLOGY INDUSTRIES (2001).

III. COPYRIGHT AND NEW REPRODUCTION AND COMMUNICATION TECHNOLOGIES

Although copyright protection is deemed to be harmonized to a high degree on an international level, there are still considerable divergences between individual countries. This allows a certain degree of regulatory competition between countries when designing their domestic innovation policies so that they are suitable for the countries' particular needs. Though copyright protection might not initially seem to be especially related to technology regulation, the reverse is the case.

In the past, courts in many countries expressed their concerns about the need to guarantee breathing space for technology developers, especially in the case of dual-use technologies, i.e. technologies that can be used for copyright-infringing as well as non-infringing purposes. This was the case with the US staple article of commerce,[35] UK authorization,[36] and German adequate causation doctrines.[37] By developing and applying those doctrines, courts attempted to balance contravening and competing legitimate interests of copyright holders, technology developers, and consumers. Despite the courts in individual countries advancing different assessment tests, they came to very similar results. When there is no close link between a technology provider and a user of its technology, the technology provider cannot be held liable for employment of its dual-use analogue technology for copyright-infringing purposes by the technology user.

Nonetheless, the introduction of new digital reproduction and communication technologies has disturbed the balance struck between legitimate interests of concerned stakeholders and the convergence in approaches towards regulating dual-use technologies in the field of copyright law.

1. Challenges Brought by Digital Technologies

The convergence in copyright approaches towards regulating dual-use technologies, which was achieved with regard to analogue reproduction

---

[35] See, e.g., Sony Corp. of Am. v. Universal City Studios Inc. 464 U.S. 417, 104 S.Ct. 774 (Sup. Ct. 1984) (U.S.).

[36] See, e.g., CBS Songs Ltd. v. Amstrad Consumer Electronics Plc., [1988] UKHL 15, [1988] A.C. 1013 (HL) (U.K.).

[37] See, e.g., Bundesgerichtshof (BGH) [Fed. Ct. of Just.], Grundig Reporter, I ZR 8/54, 1955 G.R.U.R. 492 (Ger.); Bundesgerichtshof, GEMA-Hinweis, I ZR 41/58, 1960 G.R.U.R. 340 (Ger.); Bundesgerichtshof, Personalausweise, Ib ZR 4/63, 1965 G.R.U.R. 104 (Ger.).

and communication technologies, was disrupted by the application of established national doctrines to new digital technologies, which resulted in diverse implications for technology providers around the world. For instance, in the United States, a new line of indirect copyright liability (inducement doctrine) has been developed.[38] The authorization doctrine, developed in the United Kingdom and other Commonwealth countries, has been extensively adjusted in Australia so as to cover activities of the entities organizing peer-to-peer file sharing networks.[39] Similarly, the German courts have interpreted quite narrowly the technology providers' defence of the unavailability of economically and technologically feasible precaution measures.[40]

On the other hand, the Dutch courts had no problem in applying the concepts stemming from the US staple article of commerce doctrine on technology providers and thus finding that a provider of decentralized peer-to-peer file sharing technology is not liable for using such technology for copyright-infringing purposes by its users.[41] This finding has raised considerable criticism of the Netherlands as a pirate country amongst supporters of strong copyright protection.

A similar divergence in national solutions adopted within the scope of internationally harmonized copyright standards can be found with regard to the application of national copyright laws to new services that allow remote recording and streaming of television broadcasting by individual TV viewers through digital communication networks.[42] Courts in some countries stress the need to strongly protect the rights of TV broadcasters and to create an environment for establishing a market for licensing TV recording and streaming by broadcasters.[43] They thus tend to find that

---

[38] See MGM Studios v. Grokster, Ltd., 545 U.S. 913 (Sup. Ct 2005) (U.S.).

[39] See Universal Music Australia Pty. Ltd. v. Shaman License Holdings Ltd., [2005] F.C.A. 1242 (Fed. Ct. Austl.) (Austl.).

[40] See, e.g., Matthias Leistner, *Structural Aspects of Secondary (Provider) Liability in Europe*, 9 J. Intell. Prop. L. & Prac. 75, 78–81 (2014).

[41] See Hoge Raad der Nederlanden (HR) [Sup. Ct. Neth.], Vereniging Buma & Stichting Stemra v. KaZaA B.V., December 19, 2003, No. C02/186HR (Neth.).

[42] See, e.g., Rebecca Giblin and Jane C. Ginsburg, *We (Still) Need to Talk About Aereo: New Controversies and Unresolved Questions After the Supreme Court's Decision*, 38 Colum. J.L. & Arts 109 (2015); Katarzyna Klafkowska-Waśniowska, *Under One Umbrella: Problems of Internet Retransmissions of Broadcasts and Implications for New Audiovisual Content Services*, 6 J. Intell. Prop. Info. Tech. & E-Com. 86 (2015).

[43] See, e.g., Case C-607/11, ITV Broadcasting Ltd. and Others v. TV Catch Up Ltd., EU:C:2013:147 (Ct. J. Mar. 7, 2013) (E.U.); ABC, Inc. v. Aereo, Inc., 134 S. Ct. 2498 (Sup. Ct. 2014) (U.S.).

permitting such activities would undermine the emergence and development of a market for licensing TV broadcasting for online streaming.

Conversely, courts in other countries emphasize the need for freedom, competition, and technological progress. They point out that strong copyright protection can stifle technological progress and development of new technologies.[44]

2. Possible Ways of Regulating New Technology

The question then arises how a fair and reasonable balance should be struck between the interests of copyright holders, on the one side, and those of entities developing and providing technologies, which are used for new ways of consuming and disseminating copyrighted content, on the other.[45] There might be two extremes in striking such a balance. While the pro-copyright approach is built on the idea that copyright holders should be guardians or stewards of new technologies,[46] the pro-technology approach stems from the importance of the free development of new technologies.[47] Nonetheless, both approaches have their pros and cons.

Understanding the advantages and disadvantages is essential for designing an appropriate and adequate way of regulating new reproduction and communication technologies. This is especially so, when the current trend in regulating copyright protection through free trade agreements is to require the participating countries to provide copyright holders with expeditious remedies against any act of copyright infringement with a deterrent effect upon further infringements.[48] Moreover, those remedies also need to be available for use against intermediaries who can police or disturb copyright-infringing practices of technology users.

The problem with the stewardship approach, which allows copyright holders to be stewards of new technologies, is that as experience

---

44 See, e.g., Chiteki Zaisan Kōtō Saibansho [Japan Intell. Prop. H. Ct.] Jan. 27, 2009, Rokuraku case, H20-NE-10055 (Japan); RecordTV Pte Ltd. v. MediaCorp TV Singapore Pte Ltd. & others, [2010] 2 SLR 152 (C.A. Dec. 1, 2010) (Sing.).

45 See, e.g., Timothy Wu, *Copyright's Communications Policy*, 103 MICH. L. REV. 278 (2004); Randal C. Picker, *Rewinding Sony: The Evolving Product, Phoning Home and the Duty of Ongoing Design*, 55 CASE W. RES. L. REV. 749 (2005); Jane C. Ginsburg, *Separating the Sony Sheep From the Grokster Goats: Reckoning the Future Business Plans of Copyright-Dependent Technology Entrepreneurs*, 50 ARIZ. L. REV. 577 (2008).

46 See, e.g., Timothy Wu, *supra* note 45, 329–31 (2004).

47 See *id.*, at 331–2.

48 See, e.g., NAFTA, *supra* note 4, art. 1714(1); TRIPS Agreement, *supra* note 5, art. 41(1).

demonstrates, the incumbents frequently lose their innovative edge, which loss can be detrimental to technological progress and consumers. A good example is the attempt by the major corporate copyright holders to introduce then new business models for online music distribution in the early 2000s.[49] Their major problem was that they were not commercially viable on the market. Accordingly, there was no significant, authorized method of online music distribution until the entrance of a then newcomer into the market (Apple) with its iTunes service.[50] Since that time, the volume of authorized online music distribution has been constantly growing. In several major markets, authorized online music distribution even overtook the traditional method of music distribution on tangible media, such as LPs, cassettes, and CDs, a few years ago.[51]

The reason for the failure encountered by the business models advocated by major corporate copyright holders in the early 2000s was that the structure of the services they provided to customers was too complicated. In addition, they tried to significantly restrict the use of music by their customers and therefore were not very attractive. In contrast, the iTunes service was much simpler and less restrictive. This induced millions of music consumers to use it. Hence, the stewardship model in relation to new technologies can lead to the hampering of technological progress as a result of diverse restrictions being imposed on the development of new technologies in order to gain the support of incumbent, dominant corporate copyright holders.

Another example of negative impact caused by strong copyright protection on technology development is the situation in Japan prior to the copyright law amendments in 2009 and 2012,[52] which introduced several exemptions for copyright uses in the digital environment regardless of whether they were conducted for private or commercial use. Prior to the amendments, several major Japanese companies moved some of their research activities onto online search engines overseas in order to avoid potential copyright liability under then inflexible limitations of Japanese copyright law, which considered many types of copies normally made in the digital environment as copyright infringing.

---

49 See, e.g., Joel Waldfogel, *Music File Sharing and Sales Displacement in the iTunes Era*, 22 INFO. ECON. & POL'Y 306, 308 (2010).

50 See *id.*

51 See, e.g., International Federation of the Phonographic Industry ('IFPI'), IFPI DIGITAL MUSIC REPORT 2015 6 (2015); James Vincent, *Digital Music Revenue Overtakes CD Sales for the First Time Globally*, THE VERGE, Apr. 15, 2015, http://www.theverge.com/2015/4/15/8419567/digital-physical-music-sales-overtake-globally (last visited 5 July 2017).

52 Law No.53 (2009) and Law No.43 (2012).

The abovementioned pro-technology approach to regulation of new technologies by copyright law is based on free innovation, which can lead to further technological progress. Empirical studies on the impact of copyright protection on technological innovation show that a weaker copyright protection creates a good environment for the development of new technologies which can be employed for the exploitation and dissemination of copyrighted works.[53]

The drawback of those studies is that they did not measure the extent that technological innovation can be offset against the production of content for such technologies. In some cases, the limited scope of copyright protection can destroy new sources of revenue for content-producing industries. For instance, in the early days of cable television the courts in several jurisdictions were reluctant to broaden the scope of copyright protection to cover cable retransmission of a television broadcasting signal.[54] This broadcasting was justified in the way that cable retransmission of free-to-air television broadcasting is mainly beneficial to the interests of television broadcasting companies, since the size of their audience is only increased by such retransmission and therefore broadcasters can collect more revenues from advertisements incorporated into their broadcast. Later, legislators stepped in and broadened the scope of copyright protection to also cover cable retransmission as a way of exploiting copyrighted works, which is regulated by copyright law.[55] This created a new source of revenue for copyright holders.

Similar arguments have been made before courts in several jurisdictions, while ruling on services allowing remote recording of television broadcasts by the public in order to view it later through digital networks.[56] One of

---

[53] See Josh Lerner, *The Impact of Copyright Policy Changes on Venture Capital Investment in Cloud Computing Companies* (2011), http://www.analysisgroup.com/uploadedfiles/publishing/articles/lerner_fall2011_copyright_policy_vc_investments.pdf (last visited 5 July 2017); Josh Lerner, *The Impact of Copyright Policy Changes in France and Germany on Venture Capital Investment in Cloud Computing Companies* (2012), http://www.analysisgroup.com/uploadedfiles/news_and_events/news/2012_eu_cloudcomputing_lerner.pdf (last visited 5 July 2017); Chris Borek et al., *Lost in the Clouds: The Impact of Copyright Scope on Investment in Cloud Computing Ventures* (2012), http://www.analysisgroup.com/uploadedFiles/Publishing/Articles/2012_ChristensenLerner_Lost_In_the_Clouds.pdf (last visited 5 July 2017).

[54] See, e.g., Makeen Fouad Makeen, Copyright in a Global Information Society 263–5 (2000).

[55] See *id.*, at 265–6.

[56] See, e.g., Rebecca Giblin and Jane C. Ginsburg, *Asking the Right Questions in Copyright Cases: Lessons from Aereo and its International Brethren* (2014), https://papers.ssrn.com/sol3/papers.cfm?abstract_id=2539142 (last visited 5 July 2017).

the arguments put forward by copyright holders was that allowing such activity would harm the development of a market for licensing online streaming services. On the other hand, the arguments used against the broadening of copyright protection emphasized the need to leave room for innovation. In addition, it was argued that it is not within the remit of the courts to broaden the scope of copyright protection.

The problem with the courts' role in regulating new technologies by widening the scope of copyright protection on a case-by-case basis is that courts do not possess enough information on the implications of such regulation for the development of new technologies and for the production of copyrighted works. Conversely, legislators are in a better position to collect such information and data necessary for informed decision-making.

Nevertheless, the main problem with regulating technologies by way of intellectual property laws is that an actual cost-benefit analysis of such regulation has seldom been conducted. The decision-making process is usually based on the views of the main stakeholders and anecdotal evidence. Strengthening of copyright protection has rarely been adopted based upon any solid empirical evidence to support it. Moreover, the studies, which showed that extension of copyright protection is not necessary, have been expressly disregarded by instead emphasizing other social values, such as equal treatment.[57] On the other hand, when proposals to limit the scope of copyright protection are made, hard empirical evidence is habitually requested to prove the necessity of limiting copyright protection.[58]

IV. PATENTS, INNOVATION, AND REGULATORY COMPETITION

In contrast to copyright law, patent law is characterized by close cooperation between the main patent offices in adopting standardized practices for examining patent applications.[59] Furthermore, diverse

---

[57] See, e.g., Michael Geist, *The Great Canadian Copyright Giveaway: Why Copyright Term Extension for Sound Recordings Could Cost Consumers Millions*, Apr. 22, 2015, http://www.michaelgeist.ca/2015/04/the-great-canadian-copyright-giveaway-why-copyright-term-extension-for-sound-recordings-could-cost-consumers-millions/ (last visited 5 July 2017).

[58] See, e.g., R. (on the application of British Academy of Songwriters, Composers and Authors) v. Secretary of State for Business, Innovation and Skills, [2015] EWHC 1723 (Admin.), [2015] WLR(D) 268 (High Ct. June 19, 2015) (U.K.).

[59] See, e.g., Peter Drahos, The Global Governance of Knowledge (2010).

drafting practices allow patent applicants to secure patents in several jurisdictions with the same, similar, or comparable claims. Their success is evidenced by so-called triadic patent families, i.e. patents granted in three major economics, namely, the United States, the European Union, and Japan.[60] While in some cases there might be minor differences between claims granted in individual jurisdictions, or applications can be divided into separate applications, depending upon the jurisdictions concerned, this does not prevent the patent holders enjoying the protection of their proprietary technologies within major markets.

The described harmonious practice amongst the main patent offices is sometimes disrupted by domestic courts, which may modify patentability requirements and vary interpretation of claims on a case-by-case basis. Many developed countries have, over time, established specialized intellectual property courts,[61] which also monitor the developments in other major jurisdictions. Nevertheless, their rulings are regularly exposed to appeals to national supreme courts, which are rarely specialized intellectual property courts. As general courts, the supreme courts tend to focus on preserving consistencies within their own jurisdictions and rarely attempt to achieve unity with foreign courts.

Recently, the validity of patents to certain types of subject matters, such as deoxyribonucleic acid (DNA) sequences and software, has been challenged in several jurisdictions. Their outcomes vary quite substantially.

1. Genetic Information

With regard to patenting of DNA sequences, the US Supreme Court came to the conclusion that sequences of naturally occurring DNAs are not patentable.[62] On the other hand, their complementary DNAs ('cDNAs') cleared of sequences, which do not carry necessary information, are a patentable subject matter, since such substances are not naturally

---

[60] See, e.g., Organisation for Economic Co-operation and Development ('OECD'), Triadic Patent Families, https://data.oecd.org/rd/triadic-patent-families.htm (last visited July 5 2017).

[61] See, e.g., Bruce D. Abramson, The Secret Circuit: The Little-Known Court Where the Rules of the Information Age Unfold (2007); Rohazar Wati Zuallcobley et al., *Study on Specialized Intellectual Property Courts*, Jan. 25, 2012, http://iipi.org/wp-content/uploads/2012/05/Study-on-Specialized-IPR-Courts.pdf (last visited 5 July 2017); Specialised Intellectual Property Courts: Issues and Challenges (Jacques de Werra ed., 2016).

[62] Ass'n for Molecular Pathology v. Myriad Genetics, Inc., 133 S. Ct. 2107, 2116 (Sup. Ct. 2013) (U.S.).

occurring and are created by man.[63] Although patents for purified cDNAs can pass the test set up by the Supreme Court, they can still be challenged on other patentability requirements, especially the non-obviousness test.

Contrary to the recent US approach, the Australian courts have opted for their indigenous way in this regard. The Federal Court of Australia adopted a higher standard of patentability by requiring that a patentable invention must contain more than information carried by the DNA sequence in question. In the case decided by the Federal Court, it was information on a person's predisposition because of a particular genetic mutation to developing a specific disease during her life.[64] Patentable invention is therefore required to be about the practical application of such information, for example, in the form of manufacturing a drug for curing a specific disease.[65] Accordingly, neither sequences of naturally occurring DNAs nor purified versions of complementary DNAs are patentable subject matters under this approach, unless the invention discloses more than information carried by the genetic material concerned.

In principle, the latter approach can be viewed as more open to research activities, since the discoveries of information carried by DNA sequences are not patentable. This might prevent an occurrence of the current situation in the United States, where a holder of patents disclosing DNA sequence information has been able to dominate breast cancer research via a combination of patents and contractual arrangements. The outcome of that practice is that other researchers are in a worse position in terms of having access to materials necessary for conducting research in breast cancer due to patents covering sequences of purified complementary DNAs. Accordingly, at least in theory, the Australian approach seems to be more beneficial to conducting research.

However, in practice the actual situation might be completely reversed. There is no doubt that the Australian approach is beneficial for diagnosing patients prone to developing breast cancer. Cost of diagnosis can be considerably reduced, since there is no need to pay licence fees to patent holders or to use laboratories specified by them.

Nonetheless, this does not automatically mean that Australian cancer research is in a better position in comparison to a patent holder in the United States. In order to be able to conduct efficient cancer research, there is a need to access a large population with a sufficient number of samples and patient medical records. Through the use of its patents and

---

63 See *id.* at 2117.

64 D'Arcy v. Myriad Genetics Inc., [2015] HCA 35 (High Ct. Austl.) (Austl.).

65 See *id.*

agreements with medical centres, the US patent holder has been able to secure a large number of samples and access to the patient medical reports. This can be a significant advantage, in contrast to breast cancer research by other researchers and research centres. The new discoveries stemming from such research can then enable the patent holder to dominate breast cancer research in the United States for quite a long time by securing the respective patents.

Furthermore, in the regimes without patents to DNA sequences the companies might not have sufficient incentives to invest in costly research and development ('R&D') activities, if they are not able to secure proprietary interests in the results of their research into information carried by individual sequences of DNA. A counter-argument to possible objections against patenting DNA sequences is often that patent holders will attempt to monetize the value of their assets by licensing them to other entities. The problem with this licensing argument is that actual practice shows that many patents are not commonly licensed, with the exception of patents in some fields of industries, such as consumer electronics and software industries.

2. Computer-related Inventions

Similarly, approaches to patenting computer-related invention vary in time as well as between countries. For instance, the early US decisions rejected patenting of algorithms when the invention was not about their practical application through a particular device.[66] Later decisions became more open to software patents, until the US courts reached the conclusion that 'anything under the sun that is made by man' could be patentable.[67] In practice, it led to the situation that any combination of algorithm with a computer was a patentable subject matter.[68] However, the US Supreme Court has recently rejected that practice and has stipulated that there needs to be some inventive concept in a software invention in order to allow its patenting.[69]

The European approach to patentability of computer programs has been a little different. First, the exclusion of software from

---

[66] See, e.g., Gottschalk v. Benson, 409 U.S. 63 (Sup. Ct. 1972) (U.S.); Parker v. Flook, 437 U.S. 584 (Sup. Ct. 1978) (U.S.).

[67] Diamond v. Chakrabarty, 447 U.S. 303, 309 (Sup. Ct. 1980) (U.S.).

[68] See, e.g., In re Alappat, 33 F.3d 1526, 31 U.S.P.Q.2d (BNA) 1545 (Fed. Cir. 1994) (en banc) (U.S.).

[69] See Alice Corp. Pty. Ltd. v. CLS Bank Int'l, 134 S. Ct. 2347 (Sup. Ct. 2014) (U.S.).

patentability, which was included in the 1973 Convention on the Grant of European Patents ('European Patent Convention'), had to be narrowed down.[70] Although this was achieved over time, the exclusion presented a hurdle for granting patents to pure software. In the early days, it was required that the contribution of a patentable invention had to be technical.[71] Nevertheless, recent developments have allowed patenting of any software, when it is linked to a device.[72] As shown above, this approach has lately been rejected by the US Supreme Court.[73]

3. Implications

Consequently, despite patent law being internationally harmonized to a certain degree, and the steadily increasing level of harmonization through FTAs, the above-described cases show that there is still room for national policy-makers to design their policies in such a way that the adopted policies fit the needs of their economies.

At the same time, it should be acknowledged that although there are differences between individual countries in patenting biotechnology and computer-related inventions, this does not prevent the concerned stakeholders drafting their patent applications so that they are able to secure proprietary interests to their inventions in major economies. Skilful drafting techniques can thus circumvent restrictions and limitations imposed on patentability of certain subject matters.

Here, it should also be noted that strengthening of patent protection is not always socially beneficial, which is often disregarded by trade negotiators. Several recent empirical studies show that patents work quite well in some types of industries (e.g., pharmaceutical and chemical industries) and not so well in others (e.g., automotive, consumer electronics, and software industries).[74] Some studies even suggest that the costs incurred by the operation of a patent regime are greater than

---

[70] See Convention on the Grant of European Patents, art. 52(2)(c), Oct. 5, 1973, 1065 U.N.T.S. 199.

[71] See, e.g., Pattersson/Queueing System, T 1002/92, [1995] OJ EPO 605 (T.B.A. July 6, 1997); IBM/Computer Program Product II, T 935/97 (T.B.A. Feb. 4, 1999); and IBM/Computer Program Product, T 1173/97 (T.B.A. July 1, 1998).

[72] See, e.g., Pension Benefit Systems, T 931/95, [2001] OJ EPO 441 (T.B.A. Sept. 8, 2000); Hitachi/Auction method, T 258/03, [2004] OJ EPO 575 (T.B.A. Apr. 21, 2004); Microsoft/Clipboard formats I, T 424/03 (T.B.A. Feb. 23, 2006).

[73] See *supra* note 69, at 2357–9.

[74] See, e.g., Richard C. Levin et al., *Appropriating the Returns from Industrial Research and Development*, 3 Brkgs. Papers on Econ. Activity 783 (1987).

its benefits in most industries except for pharmaceutical and chemical industries.[75]

V. CONCLUSION

This chapter has shown that despite significant harmonization of intellectual property law at international and regional levels, there are still considerable differences between individual jurisdictions, even those with high standards of intellectual property protection. The presented divergence between approaches adopted in developed countries can be harnessed by developing countries in designing their intellectual property policies so that they properly and adequately achieve the development goals pursued by individual countries.

Moreover, this chapter demonstrated that allowing a single person or a small group of entities to control the development of new technologies frequently presents an obstacle to such development, since technology developers are notably restricted in their technological choices to solving a particular technical problem. The outcomes of such technological development tend to be consumer unfriendly and rather expensive. The fact that strong intellectual property protection does not automatically equate to technological progress and development is commonly overlooked by trade negotiators, who tend to push for strengthening intellectual property protection on the international and regional levels at any cost.

---

[75] *See, e.g.*, JAMES BESSEN AND MICHAEL J. MEURER, PATENT FAILURE: HOW JUDGES, BUREAUCRATS, AND LAWYERS PUT INNOVATORS AT RISK 120–46 (2008).

15. Harmonization without localization: Trendspotting pharmaceutical patent law in recent FTAs

Bryan Mercurio*

I. INTRODUCTION

The trend of regulatory convergence is present in almost all Chapters of the modern day megaregional free trade agreement (FTA), but perhaps none is more controversial than in the intellectual property (IP) Chapter. In almost all agreements, at least one party will seek to have the FTA 'harmonize' both substantive and procedural IP standards among the parties. Of course, by harmonize what is really meant is that the *demandeur* will seek to have the other party or parties meet its domestic standard. This occurs in every form of IP but is most obvious, and again controversial, in the case of patents—and more specifically, patents and related rights in regards to pharmaceutical products.

Traditionally, countries maintained and operated quite divergent standards and systems for the protection of pharmaceutical patents. For instance, some countries protected both products and processes while others protected only products, some limited or prohibited patents on pharmaceuticals and others provided only a short period of protection. Since 1995, IP rights (IPRs) have been directly incorporated into the international trade system through the World Trade Organization (WTO) Agreement on Trade-Related Aspects of Intellectual Property Rights ('TRIPS Agreement'), which now provides standards on a range of IPRs (including most notably copyright, patents, and trademarks). With membership almost universal and covering over 96 percent of world trade, the

* The author acknowledges the support of Hong Kong General Research Fund No. CUHK450012 and a Direct Grant awarded by the Faculty of Law in 2017. This chapter draws on other works by the author, in particular DRUGS, PATENTS AND POLICY: A CONTEXTUAL STUDY OF HONG KONG (Cambridge University Press, forthcoming 2018).

obligations contained in the TRIPS Agreement have become the minimum 'adequate' world standard. These minimum standards have gone some way in harmonizing protection and enforcement among the over 164 members of the WTO. That being said, the TRIPS Agreement does not completely harmonize protection or enforcement, instead leaving ample scope for differing interpretations which could have serious impact on stakeholders.

Certain countries have used trade agreements to raise standards of protection and enforcement above the level established in the TRIPS Agreement, thereby reducing divergence and increasing convergence. The trend is clearly towards maximalist standards and of regulatory harmonization. Likewise, the trend of adding coherence between regulations in differing countries encompasses and necessarily impacts health policy, including access to medicines. Of course, it is entirely reasonable for the branded pharmaceutical industry and sympathetic governments to seek enhanced protection. Unlike almost every other product, the effective patent term of a pharmaceutical is not the minimum period of twenty years set by the TRIPS Agreement, but rather eight to twelve years as patents are applied for long before the conclusion of clinical trials which demonstrate the safety and efficacy of the product.[1] Thus, a significant portion of the patent period elapses prior to the product being allowed to be placed on the market. In some respects, the branded industry is simply seeking a minimum period of marketing exclusivity.

This chapter argues that the trend of 'blind convergence' is dangerous in that it is harmonizing standards without taking into account context and different levels of appropriateness, development, or preparedness. More specifically, the chapter makes a nuanced argument that while harmonization can potentially yield benefits there are dangers to harmonization/regulatory coherence in the area of pharmaceutical patents. In some cases, harmonization will help efficiency and effectiveness but in the majority of cases such standards tend to ignore context and result in inappropriate and misplaced obligations. The chapter concludes that regulations which increase normative standards should be carefully tailored to the specific context of the country at issue, while harmonization of practical standards could reduce costs and increase efficiencies in the public health system.

The chapter proceeds as follows: Section II forms the main basis of the chapter and provides several examples of recent attempts to harmonize

---

1 For instance, the Therapeutic Goods Administration (TGA) in Australia—part of the Department of Health and Ageing—is the regulatory agency responsible for approving the marketing of therapeutic goods, including prescription medicines, vaccines, sunscreens, vitamins and minerals, medical devices, blood and blood products. See www.tga.gov.au/ (last visited 20 August 2017).

standards without localization. Section III discusses more appropriate, but less utilized, forms of convergence which would reduce burdens and increase efficiencies in both the *demandeur* and recipient countries. Section IV concludes.

II. TRENDS TOWARDS CONVERGENCE IN PHARMACEUTICALS: BLIND CONVERGENCE

This section highlights the current trend to convergence—that is, where all parties of the agreement adopt what is essentially the domestic regime of the *demandeur* country in what can be called 'blind convergence'. In many cases, these obligations serve to elongate the period of marketing exclusivity of the patented pharmaceutical such that generic competition is delayed. The result is, of course, that consumers in these nations (which may in large part be the government) will end up paying the higher monopoly price for the pharmaceutical product for a longer period of time. In the vast majority of cases, the obligations are taken on the basis of no empirical studies or widespread stakeholder consultations. The potential effect of the obligations on the health budget or on access to medicines for the populace does not seem to figure into the equation of most governments when agreeing to these standards. This is a dangerous and reckless trend which does not seem to be in the best interest of the recipient country. It is not of course possible to provide every example of maximalist TRIPS-plus provision relating to pharmaceuticals included in FTAs.[2] Instead, the remainder of this section will provide four examples of the trend in order to make obvious the broader point.

1. Patent Term Extension

As mentioned above, Article 33 of the TRIPS Agreement provides that patent protection be granted for a minimum period of twenty years from the date of filing. While this is broadly in line with the practice of the developed world prior to the agreement coming into force, it did extend the length of patent protection in many countries.

The innovation of FTAs is to extend patent protection beyond that twenty-year period. This occurs in two ways, when there is an 'unrea-

[2] For further examples, see Michael Handler and Bryan Mercurio, *Intellectual Property*, *in* Bilateral and Regional Trade Agreements: Commentary and Analysis 324–63 (Simon Lester, Bryan Mercurio, and Lorand Bartels eds., 2016).

sonable' delay in either the granting of the patent or in the granting of marketing approval. The country which most ardently seeks this enhanced protection is the United States, with almost all of its FTAs specifically calling for these extensions in order to 'compensate' the patent owner. Both of these provisions reflect domestic American law and have their origins in the Drug Price Competition and Patent Term Restoration Act of 1984 ('Hatch-Waxman Act').

With regard to marketing approval, FTAs offer compensation to patent owners for delays caused by the drug regulatory authority in examining an application for registration. Article 18.48 of the signed but not ratified (but nevertheless important) Trans-Pacific Partnership (TPP) provides a typical (if slightly more complicated) example of such provision:

> 1. Each Party shall make best efforts to process applications for marketing approval of pharmaceutical products in an efficient and timely manner, with a view to avoiding unreasonable or unnecessary delays.
> 2. With respect to a pharmaceutical product that is subject to a patent, each Party shall make available an adjustment of the patent term to compensate the patent owner for *unreasonable curtailment* of the effective patent term as a result of the marketing approval process.
> 3. For greater certainty, in implementing the obligations of this Article, each Party may provide for conditions and limitations, provided that the Party continues to give effect to this Article.
> 4. With the objective of avoiding unreasonable curtailment of the effective patent term, a Party may adopt or maintain procedures that expedite the processing of marketing approval applications.[3] (Emphasis added)

Worth noting here is that the term 'unreasonable' is left undefined as is the period of term extension. This is in contrast to the European Union (EU) and European Free Trade Association (EFTA), which both generally provide for an additional protection period of up to five year years in order to 'compensate the patent owner for the reduction in the effective patent life as a result of the first authorization to place the product on their respective markets'.[4] The EFTA FTAs most often provide a compensatory term

---

[3] See also United States-Chile FTA, Art. 17.10.2 (6 June 2003), 42 ILM 1026; United States-Singapore FTA, Art. 18.8.4(a) (6 May 2003), 42 ILM 1026; United States-Australia FTA, Art. 17.10.4 (18 May 2004), 43 ILM 1248; United States-Morocco FTA, Art. 15.10.3 (15 June 2004), 44 ILM 544; Dominican Republic-Central America-United States FTA, Art. 15.10.2 (5 August 2004), 43 ILM 514; United States-Bahrain FTA, Art. 14.8.6 (14 September 2004), 44 ILM 544; United States-Oman FTA, Art. 15.8.6(a) (19 January 2006), KAV No. 8673; United States-Korea FTA, Art. 18.8.6(b) (30 June 2007), 46 ILM 642.

[4] EU-Korea FTA, Art. 10.35.2 (15 October 2009) [2011] OJ L127. See also EU-Singapore FTA, Art. 11.31, authentic text as of May 2015, available at http://

of protection for pharmaceuticals (and plant protection products) if more than five years has elapsed between the filing date of the patent application and the date of market authorization, subject to certain conditions.[5]

With regard to patent office delays in assessing the application for a patent, the standard US FTA is slightly more prescriptive. The US FTAs generally provide for a mandatory additional period of patent protection as compensation for 'unreasonable' delays in the issuance of the patent, with 'unreasonable' being defined in the relevant agreement.[6] For example, Article 18.46 paragraph 3 and 4 of the TPP states:

> 3. If there are unreasonable delays in a Party's issuance of patents, that Party *shall* provide the means to, and at the request of the patent owner shall, adjust the term of the patent to *compensate* for such delays.
> 4. For the purposes of this Article, an unreasonable delay at least shall include a delay in the issuance of a patent of more than *five years from the date of filing* of the application in the territory of the Party, or *three years after a request for examination* of the application has been made, whichever is later. A Party may exclude, from the determination of such delays, periods of time that do not occur during the processing of, or the examination of, the patent application by the granting authority; periods of time that are not directly attributable to the granting authority; as

---

trade.ec.europa.eu/doclib/docs/2013/september/tradoc_151742.pdf (last visited 21 August 2017). It should be noted that EFTA has at times shifted the nature of the extension from mandatory to optional with 'shall' being replaced by 'may'. See e.g. EFTA-Colombia FTA, Art. 6.9(5) (25 November 2008), available at www.efta.int/media/documents/legal-texts/free-trade-relations/colombia/EFTA-Colombia%20Free%20Trade%20Agreement%20EN.pdf (last visited 21 August 2017).

[5] See e.g., EFTA-Albania FTA, Annex V, Art. 4 (17 December 2009), available at www.efta.int/free-trade/free-trade-agreements/media/documents/legal-texts/free-trade-relations/albania/EFTA-Albania%20Free%20Trade%20Agreement.pdf (last visited 21 August 2017); EFTA-Montenegro FTA, Annex VI, Art. 5 (14 November 2011), available at www.efta.int/media/documents/legal-texts/free-trade-relations/montenegro/montenegro-main-agreement.pdf (last visited 21 August 2017); EFTA-Ukraine FTA, Annex XIII, Art. 4 (24 June 2010), available at www.efta.int/sites/default/files/documents/legal-texts/free-trade-relations/ukraine/EFTA-Ukraine%20Free%20Trade%20Agreement.pdf (last visited 21 August 2017). Curiously, Art. 117.6(c) of the Japan-Switzerland FTA provides differing levels of protection for each of the parties, with additional protection being a maximum of five years for Japan and a maximum of 'at least five years' for Switzerland; Japan-Switzerland Economic Partnership Agreement (EPA), Art. 117.6(c) (19 February 2009), 2642 UNTS 3.

[6] It should be noted that United States-Peru Trade Promotion Agreement (TPA), Art. 16.9.6 (12 April 2006); United States-Colombia TPA, Art. 16.9.6 (22 November 2006); United States-Panama TPA, Art. 15.9.6 (28 June 2007), are less onerous in that they substitute the word 'may' for 'shall' and call upon those parties to use 'best efforts' to process applications expeditiously with a view to avoiding unnecessary delays.

well as periods of time that are attributable to the patent applicant.[7] (Footnote deleted, emphasis added)

Neither the EU nor EFTA has sought in its FTAs to provide for an additional period of patent protection due to delays in the issuance of the patent.

The extension of the effective period of market exclusivity may have serious consequences for public health in developing countries which rely on competition from generics to supply essential medicines. Due to the unique nature of pharmaceuticals, however, it is sensible to extend patents when 'unreasonable' delay prevents the patent holder from exploiting their invention. It is likewise not difficult to imagine a patent office or drug regulatory authority abusing the system so as to unnecessarily delay the issuance of the patent or marketing approval. What is disconcerting, however, is the undefined nature of what is an 'unreasonable curtailment' or compensable delay in the regulatory process and the strict timeline of 'unreasonable delays' caused by the patent office.

What is surprising, and again worrying, is that most countries simply agree to the demands without negotiating any safeguards. Three safeguards which developing countries should attempt to include in any negotiation are language (1) indicating that patent term extension is hortatory rather than mandatory through the use of 'may' rather than 'shall'; (2) specifying a time period based on the particular context of the country at issue for what may constitute an unreasonable curtailment or compensable delay in the granting of marketing approval; and (3) limiting the patent term extension to products which contain a new chemical entity that has not been previously approved as a pharmaceutical product in the territory of the party.[8] Such limitations are rarely included in FTAs

[7] Other US FTAs vary only in the number of years considered 'unreasonable'. For example, the United States-Singapore FTA, Art. 16.7.7; United States-Australia FTA, Art. 17.9.8; United States-Morocco FTA, Art. 15.9.7; United States-Bahrain FTA, Art. 14.8.6; and United States-Oman FTA, Art. 15.8.6(a) refer to four and two years, respectively, while the United States-Chile FTA, Art. 17.9.6; United States-Colombia FTA, Art. 16.9.6 (b); United States-Peru TPA, Art. 16.9.6(b); United States-Panama TPA, Art. 15.9.6(b) refer to five and three years, respectively. The United States-Korea FTA, Art. 18.8.6(a) refers to four and three years, respectively. In some US FTAs, including the United States-Singapore FTA, Art. 16.7.8, where the patent is granted on the basis of examination conducted in another nation, a five-year extension of the patent term will be granted when it has also been awarded in the other country.

[8] The author is aware of only one agreement, the United States-Korea FTA, Art. 18.8.6 (b) n. 21, which limits the patent term extension to new pharmaceutical

but would go some way in guarding against abuse of term extensions and safeguarding public health systems.

2. Patent Linkage

Patent linkage is the practice of national pharmaceutical registration authorities 'linking' the granting of marketing approval. In so doing, patent linkage often prevents the relevant regulatory authority from granting marketing approval (i.e., registration of a generic drug for sale on the market) for so long as a patent remains in force on the originator drug. The 'link' is thus between the right to market the drug with the patent status of the originator drug.

Such a practice is in contradistinction to the traditional approach to drug regulation and marketing and that of the patent process. Historically, registration authorities (i.e., governmental health agencies) merely assess whether the pharmaceutical under investigation is safe and effective, while the Patents Act governs protection granted by the IPR. The patent status of the pharmaceutical or any ingredient therein was irrelevant to the registration process. Likewise, should a patent owner believe that a product has been brought onto the market despite the existence of a valid patent it could bring an infringement claim to halt sales and claim damages. Patents, therefore, are a matter of private enforcement. The Canadian Supreme Court recognized the tension between these two processes in the 2006 case of *AstraZeneca* when it stated that patent linkage regulations 'lie at the intersection of two regulatory systems with sometimes conflicting objectives'.[9]

The TRIPS Agreement does not mention patent linkage, such that it is not prohibited or mandated by the WTO. Patent linkage is therefore clearly a 'TRIPS-plus' provision. Existing in several countries, including those as diverse as Cambodia, Canada, China, Japan, Mexico, Singapore, South Korea, and the United States, patent linkage continues to spread. Most often patent linkage is included in FTAs with the United States, but several countries have included patent linkage as part of their WTO Accession Protocol (i.e., Cambodia and China) or independently (i.e., Taiwan). Patent linkage is technically unlawful in the EU, although this is somewhat of a fiction as several Member States have some form of patent linkage in their domestic legislation.[10]

---

products that 'at least contains a new chemical entity that has not been previously approved as a pharmaceutical product in the territory of the Party'.

[9] *AstraZeneca Canada Inc. v. Canada (Minister of Health)* [2006] 2 SCR 560, 2006 SCC 49, para. 12.

[10] See Regulation 726/2004 [2004] OJ L136/81 (EC), setting out Community

Unsurprisingly, patent linkage is controversial and opinions on it starkly contrast. Advocates of patent linkage view it as merely part of the bargain whereby monopoly rights on the market are granted in exchange for the continued invention of new and innovative drugs (and, at least in the United States, for the facilitation of the timely entry of generic drugs). In this regard, advocates see patent linkage as an incentive to the industry to ensure the creation of new pharmaceuticals and thus better health outcomes. On the other hand, critics view patent linkage simply as a means for extending monopoly pricing and delaying access to more affordable medicines.

The genesis is in the United States with the adoption of the Hatch-Waxman Act (1984),[11] which was introduced to better balance incentives to stimulate innovation and the development of new medicines with increasing access and availability of generic competition into the market. Prior to the Hatch-Waxman Act, undisclosed clinical trial and other data submitted by a pharmaceutical company/originator in an application for marketing approval was treated as a trade secret.[12] Thus, competitors could not access or rely upon this data when seeking to obtain marketing approval for generic versions of the patented pharmaceutical. The practical reality of such treatment meant that originators received not only the monopoly offered by and during the patent term but also an extended exclusive selling period for a period of time thereafter as generic competitors had to prepare and apply for marketing approval.[13]

---

procedures for the authorization and supervision of medicinal products for human and veterinary use and establishing a European Medicines Agency. See also Council Directive 2001/83 [2001] OJ L311, arts. 10.6 and 126 (EC), on the Community code relating to medicinal products for human use. Patent linkage is in fact in the laws and regulations of several Member States. See European Commission, *Pharmaceutical Sector Inquiry: Preliminary Report* 14, 113, Table 22 (DG Competition Staff Working Paper, 28 November 2008), available at http://ec.europa.eu/competition/sectors/pharmaceuticals/inquiry/preliminary_report.pdf (last visited 21 August 2017).

[11] See Drug Price Competition and Patent Term Restoration Act of 1984, 98 P.L. 417 (24 September 1984); 21 U.S.C. §§ 355(c)(3)(D), *reprinted in* 21 C.F.R. § 314.108 (1993).

[12] See 21 U.S.C. § 355(b)(1)(A). For background and a modern critique, see Robert A. Armitage, *The Hatch-Waxman Act: A Path Forward for Making It More Modern*, 40 Wm. Mitchell L. Rev. 1200 (2014).

[13] Generic applicants could conduct their own clinical trials and apply for marketing approval during the patent term, but the time and expense of conducting the duplicative trials, the unlikelihood of recouping R&D costs, and ethical concerns of repeating trials to achieve an already established result meant in reality that competitors would not apply for marketing approval during the term of the patent.

The Hatch-Waxman Act undoubtedly increased the availability of generic pharmaceuticals on the US market and it gave generic companies the right to 'use' a patented process or product for the purposes of seeking marketing approval from the Food and Drug Agency (FDA), the US regulator.[14] More specifically, a generic applicant can use the data to prove the bioequivalence—that is, potency and availability in the body—of its version of the pharmaceutical with the originator product.[15]

In return, however, the Hatch-Waxman Act also 'linked' the patent status of a pharmaceutical (under the Patent Act) to marketing approval (under the Food, Drug, and Cosmetic Act) in such a way so as to prevent the FDA from granting marketing approval to a generic product so long as the originator company which filed a New Drug Application (NDA) 'listed' or 'registered' at least one patent contained in the approved drug (which can relate to a variety of drug-related factors, including active ingredient, formulation, dosage, type of use, and new use) in the 'Approved Drug Products with Therapeutic Equivalence' (commonly referred to as the 'Orange Book').[16] Generic applicants must then file an Abbreviated New Drug Application (ANDA) to enter the market and certify that (1) the drug has not been patented; (2) the patent has expired; (3) that the generic drug will not be placed on the market until the patent expires; or (4) that the patent is not infringed or is invalid. It is the paragraph IV certification that is most relevant: It requires the generic applicant to notify the innovator company of its filing and describe the reasons why it believes the patent will not be infringed or is invalid or unenforceable. Following receipt of the notice, the originator is given forty-five days to file a lawsuit for infringement (submission of a paragraph IV certificate to the FDA triggers an infringement for purposes of the Federal Court). The proceedings (that is the claim of a valid patent by the originator) trigger an 'automatic' thirty-month injunction. Upon the expiration of the stay, the FDA can issue tentative marketing approval allowing an ANDA applicant to enter the market. While the Hatch-Waxman Act provides a financial incentive to facilitate early entry of generics into the market by granting the first generic that successfully challenges the validity of a

---

[14] 35 U.S.C. § 271(e)(1) (2000 & Supp. 2005). It should also be noted that the US Supreme Court has expanded the boundaries of activities that qualify under the exemption. See e.g., *Eli Lilly & Co. v. Medtronic*, 496 U.S. 661 (1990); *Merck KgaA v. Integra Lifesciences I, Ltd.*, 545 U.S. 193 (2005); *Momenta Pharm. v. Amphastar Pharm*, 686 F.3d 1348 (2012).

[15] 21 C.F.R. Pt 211 (2007).

[16] 35 U.S.C. §§ 1-376 (2006); Federal Food, Drug and Cosmetic Act, 21 U.S.C. §§ 301-97 (2006).

patent with its own six-month period of market exclusivity,[17] most generic applicants do not actually market the product until resolution of the litigation in order to avoid what could be significant liability for damages if the court ultimately finds a patent infringement.

In sum, the Hatch-Waxman Act includes four elements: a notification requirement; an obligation to prevent or delay a generic drug applicant from gaining marketing approval for a product covered by an originator during the patent term; a register of patents and to verify the patent status of any drug during the registration process; and an automatic injunction against the generic once the originator triggers an infringement claim. In addition, the US scheme provides an incentive for generics to challenge the validity of the patent.

In contrast to the US experience, prior to the introduction of patent linkage as part of the implementation legislation following the North American Free Trade Agreement (NAFTA), Canada operated a system of compulsory licence for pharmaceuticals and generics flourished in the country. More specifically, prior to 1987 medicines were almost automatically compulsory licenced at 4 percent royalty rate after a waiting period of ten years when the medicine was imported and seven years if the product was manufactured in Canada. After a slight pullback, the system fundamentally changed in 1993 to take account of NAFTA and upcoming TRIPS Agreement. The result of the changes in Canada was to virtually kill the local generic industry and delay competition on the market in the pharmaceutical sector. The point here is again to illustrate that the virtually identical legislation produced totally opposite results due to context— in the United States, patent linkage sped up the entry of generics into the market while in Canada it raised the price of medicines and delayed the entry of generic competition in the marketplace. Moreover, there is no evidence that Canada's rather dramatic change in legal landscape ensured continued innovation or in any way led to increased research and development (R&D) in the pharmaceutical sector.

Most jurisdictions follow Canada in combining some or all of the US factors when legislating for and implementing patent linkage. An example in this regard is Singapore, which agreed to adopt patent linkage in the United States-Singapore FTA. Like the United States, Singapore divides generic applications for marketing approval into four categories, with section 12A of the Medicines Act (1975) requiring applicants to provide a declaration to the Health Sciences Authority (HSA) stating whether there are any relevant patents in Singapore. Under what is referred to

---

17 21 U.S.C. § 355(j)(5)(B)(iv) (2000 & Supp. V 2005).

as Category B, the applicant can contest the validity of the patent by providing the patent holder with a notice of the application setting out the reasons why the applicant believes the application does not infringe the patent ('Notice to Proprietor of Patent'). The originator has forty-five days to commence an infringement claim against the generic, which triggers an 'automatic' thirty-month injunction against the granting of marketing approval. If the patent holder takes no action, the HSA may proceed to grant the marketing approval. This process of notification and the triggering of an automatic injunction is taken from the paragraph IV certification process in the United States. Unlike the United States, Singapore does not maintain a patent register nor does it provide the incentive of a period of exclusivity to the first successful generic challenger. Moreover, since Singapore simply added section 12A to the Medicines Act as opposed to introducing an amendment to the Singapore Patents Act to add a new cause of action—in contract to the US Patent Code, which statutorily provides the submission of an application for a patented drug is an infringement—there was a question of cause of action which required the court in *AstraZeneca v. Sanofi-Aventis* to hold that section 12A, read together with the accompanying regulations, constituted a cause of action separate and independent from a patent infringement action under the Patents Act.[18]

Taiwan is the most recent adherent to patent linkage, having adopted it in 2016 after considerable consultation. In the end, however, Taiwan drafted a law which is almost identical to the US model, with articles 48-2 to 48-21 of the Pharmaceutical Affairs Act providing for all four elements included in the US model and the incentive for generic challenge. One added safeguard, however, is that the originator only has a forty-five-day window from the issuance of marketing approval to list patents and specified claims that cover the pharmaceutical product. While the guidelines addressing the particulars and scope of the listings had not been drafted as of the time of this writing, it will certainly include drug substance patents, composition patents, formulation patents, and medical use patents. A connected safeguard is that the law allows any third party to challenge the veracity of the listed patent information by notifying the Taiwan Food and Drug Agency (TFDA) with written explanation and evidence, who will then investigate the matter.

Like in the United States, a generic ANDA applicant must select one of the following options: (i) no patent information has been listed for the new drug; (ii) the patent corresponding to the new drug has extinguished;

---

[18] *AstraZeneca AB (SE) v. Sanofi-Aventis Singapore Pte Ltd.* [2012] SGHC 16.

(iii) the TFDA will issue the generic market approval after the extinguishment of the patent(s) corresponding to the new drug; or (iv) the patent corresponding to the new drugs should be revoked or will not be infringed by the generic drugs for which market approval is sought. If paragraph IV is selected, the applicant has twenty days to notify the originator, who then has a forty-five-day period to file an infringement suit. The filing of the infringement suit will trigger an automatic injunction of fifteen months during which time the TFDA cannot grant marketing approval to the ANDA applicant (unless the ANDA applicant obtains a judgment that the patent has not been infringed within that time period). Once again similarly to the United States, a twelve-month period of exclusivity is granted to the first generic who successfully challenges the patent. One final noteworthy aspect of the Taiwanese law is that it also obliges any pay-for-delay or reverse payment agreement between the originator and a generic manufacturer to be notified to the Taiwan Fair Trade Commission (TFTC), and presumably such agreement will have to comply with yet-to-be drafted guidelines.

For all intents and purposes, the Taiwanese law is virtually identical to the US model. This is the case with most new adherents to patent linkage. In fact, only Australia and South Korea have deviated from the US model with the inclusion of several additional safeguards and protections. For example, in Australia (where there is no register) the patent owner must apply to court for injunction as opposed to it being granted automatically, with penalties for not acting in good faith.[19] South Korea goes even further in that injunctions apply to generic 'sales', not to the granting of marketing approval, are only granted if there is a 'need to prevent significant damage' and limited to a nine-month period from the date of notice.[20] Moreover, in Korea the originator must apply for and place all relevant patents on the register before marketing approval is granted—the originator cannot later claim or add patents to the register.[21] Another important safeguard is that the Korean regulatory authority does not simply list all patents claimed by the originator on its register but instead reviews the substance of the 'Patent Listing Applications' to ensure the legitimacy between the patent claims and approved product. Importantly, the regulator has the authority to change, narrow, edit, and delist patent claims for failing to

---

[19] Therapeutic Goods Act 1989 (Cth), s. 26C (Austl.).

[20] Korean Pharmaceutical Affairs Act, art. 50-5, Act No. 13655 (29 December 2015), available at https://elaw.klri.re.kr/eng_mobile/viewer.do?hseq=37255&type=part&key=37 (last visited 24 August 2017).

[21] Enforcement Decree of Korea Pharmaceutical Affairs Act, art. 30*ter*, Decree No. 162 (18 October 2012).

meet the requisite standard.[22] Thus, while both Australia and Korea based their patent linkage regimes on that of the United States, they added safeguards to better safeguard the health system and guard against abuse by the originator.

It is worth highlighting yet again that while the US model of patent linkage was introduced as part of a larger 'grand bargain' and suitable perhaps in the local situation, patent linkage models based on and closely resembling the US system are being introduced in totally different contexts and as stand-alone provisions without any countering balancing regulations. Moreover, despite patent linkage existing in the United States, Canada and elsewhere for over twenty years, such provisions are being introduced with little to no empirical evidence assessing the potential monetary and health effects.

Even the US attempt at balance through a six-month period of exclusivity for the first generic to successfully challenge the validity of the originator's patent is jurisdiction specific—while the value to a generic in the US market, with 50 percent of worldwide pharmaceutical market, is obviously substantial. However, the cost of challenging the validity of a patent through litigation is high in most jurisdictions, but the benefits of a period of exclusivity significantly differ with the size of the market. Simply stated, in most jurisdictions the cost of litigation will infringe upon and overtake the benefits of the exclusivity period and it may not make economic sense for a generic to challenge the validity of the patent.[23]

The simple fact is that the net result of patent linkage is to delay generic entry into the market, and thus adds to the costs of health spending. Despite this, many jurisdictions are considering the adoption of patent linkage. Again, most will likely copy the US model of patent linkage. This is unfortunate, as it is abundantly clear that differences in design and implementation can have a large impact on availability of generic medicines and price of pharmaceuticals in the marketplace. With the US dropping out of the TPP, the remaining signatories have suspended the obligations relating to pharmaceutical patents (among other things), but should these provisions be reinstated, Brunei, Malaysia, New Zealand, and Vietnam (and all aspirants) will have to amend legislation to provide

---

22 *Ibid.* art. 24, para. 10; art. 30*ter*, para. 5. The Korean scheme also applies to biologic medicines, whereas in the United States biologics are separately regulated.

23 Here again, Korea differs from the United States in that while it provides for a period of exclusivity to the first generic company to successfully challenge the validity of a pharmaceutical patent, it doubles the period of exclusivity to a twelve-month period to the first generic covering the same type and amount of active ingredient, dosage form, usage, dosage, and indication.

for patent linkage. Moreover, an early leaked draft of the Regional Comprehensive Economic Partnership (RCEP) even included patent linkage; and while it was removed in the latest leaked draft, if it returns to the text a host of additional countries would need to design and implement a patent linkage regime.

3. Test Data and Biologics Protection

Test data protection prohibits a regulatory authority from 'using' originator test data to approve an application for a generic for a set period of years, most commonly ranging from five to eleven in FTAs. Separate to patents, test data protection grants a *sui generis* right to the originator which rewards the creation of data through rigorous and standardized tests. In this regard, test data protection is granted irrespective of the patent status of the originator drug. Thus, while test data protection most often runs concurrently with patent rights and ends prior to the expiration of the patent rights, this is not always the case. When there is no patent or the patent rights expire while the test data protection remains in force, there could be a delay in the granting of marketing approval to the generic and an extension in the period of monopoly sales to the originator. To some degree, this is exactly the point of test data protection; it is a way to protect significant investment in the R&D of pharmaceutical products by ensuring a minimum period of monopoly sales, irrespective of patent status.

The international standard, embodied in Article 39.3 of the TRIPS Agreement, is vague and subject to much debate. Article 39(3) of the TRIPS Agreement states:

> Members, when requiring, as a condition of approving the marketing of pharmaceutical or of agricultural chemical products which utilize new chemical entities, the submission of undisclosed test or other data, the origination of which involves a considerable effort, shall protect such data against unfair commercial use. In addition, Members shall protect such data against disclosure, except where necessary to protect the public, or unless steps are taken to ensure that the data are protected against unfair commercial use.[24]

Although still debated, the consensus opinion among governments and commentators is that the TRIPS Agreement does not require

---

[24] Protected data includes health and safety testing with regard to humans, animals, and plants, as well as environmental impact tests and other information the relevant authorities may require, which includes manufacturing, storage, and packaging tests. See Carlos M. Correa, *Unfair Competition Under the TRIPS Agreement: Protection of Data Submitted for the Registration of Pharmaceuticals*, 3(1) CHI. J. IN'T L. 69, 73 (2002).

test data protection. In this regard, an UNCTAD publication states: 'authorities are not prevented . . . from using knowledge of such data, for instance, to assess subsequent applications by third parties for the registration of similar products'.[25] Instead, Article 39.3 of the TRIPS Agreement merely protects against 'against unfair commercial use' and against disclosure, unless it is necessary to protect the public or unless steps are taken to protect against unfair commercial use. In such a circumstance, it is not 'unfair' for a generic applicant to use and benefit from pre-existing test data; indeed, such use is a 'legitimate exploitation of an externality created during legitimate competition in the market'.[26] Likewise, if the purpose of Article 39.3 is to prevent the unfair use of data it must be that the intended beneficiary would be competitors (through, for instance, dishonest practices) not to restrain governmental use in assessing an application for marketing approval of a pharmaceutical.[27]

On the other hand, the United States and EU assert that Article 39.3 mandates a period of test data exclusivity, that is, that the governmental regulatory authority cannot use, rely on otherwise review an application for marketing approval from a generic which seeks to rely upon the test data of the originator.[28] To substantiate the position, these jurisdictions argue that Article 39.3 does not refer to behaviour between competitors (as is the case in Article 39.1) but to the governmental function of protecting data so as not to provide unfair competitive advantages to generic manufacturers seeking marketing approval for their products. Of course, if this view is correct a country could provide for an indefinite period of test data exclusivity—in fact they would be required to do

---

[25] See UNCTAD, *The TRIPS Agreement and Developing Countries*, UN Doc. UNCTAD/ITE/1, 48 (1996), available at http://unctad.org/en/docs/ite1_en.pdf (last visited 21 August 2017).

[26] Correa (n. 24 above) 77.

[27] See Carlos M. Correa, Trade Related Aspects of Intellectual Property Rights 391 (2007); World Health Organization, Report of the Commission on Intellectual Property Rights, Innovation and Public Health 124 (2006), available at www.who.int/intellectualproperty/documents/thereport/ENPublicHealth Report.pdf?ua=1 (last visited 21 August 2017); Food and Agriculture Organization, Panel of Eminent Experts on Ethics in Food and Agriculture, *Report of Eminent Experts on Ethics in Food and Agriculture, Third Session* 23 (14 September 2005), available at www.fao.org/docrep/010/a0697e/a0697e00.HTM (last visited 21 August 2017).

[28] See US Trade Representative Office of the General Counsel, *The Protection of Undisclosed Test Data in Accordance with TRIPS Article 39.3* (unattributed paper for submission in bilateral discussions with Australia, May 1995); European Commission, *Questions on TRIPs and Data Exclusivity, An EU Contribution* (Brussels, 2001).

so—as the TRIPS Agreement fails to set any time limit to the period of exclusivity.

The better positions seem to be the view that Article 39.3 does not restrain governments from using test data for marketing approval purposes. This view is substantiated by the fact that during the negotiations for the TRIPS Agreement, test data exclusivity was discussed, debated, and rejected by the negotiating parties. More specifically, a US proposal and subsequent bracketed text in the Brussels Draft tabled at the Brussels Ministerial Meeting 1990 which would have required test data protection for a period of not less than five years (the US proposal also allowed for payment of reasonable compensation in lieu of the time period) was rejected and ultimately deleted from the final version of the clause—instead, the final version of the provision offers more limited protection to that of 'unfair commercial practices'. According to Jerome Reichman:

> the rejection of the [Brussels Draft] negated any inference that the TRIPS drafters had imposed an exclusive intellectual property right on this subject matter and indirectly confirmed the implications to be drawn from the deletion of the U.S.-EU bracketed proposal between 1990 and 1991.[29]

In the domestic context, jurisdictions adopt test data protection in order to 'strike a balance between the economic interests of the R&D based pharmaceutical industry on the one hand, and ethical considerations and the interests of the generic producers on the other hand', but balance these interests differently.[30] For example, test data protection varies in time from between five to eleven years (with the United States offering five and the EU eleven), on how much protection or exclusivity is offered and on the scope of exceptions.

The incorporation of test data protection in trade agreements varies depending upon the *demandeur* country, and has evolved since first being included in the NAFTA in 1993.[31] In all cases, the obligation extends far beyond that which is required in the TRIPS Agreement. For example, US FTAs include a five-year period of exclusivity for a new pharmaceutical product and expand coverage from a product 'which involves

---

[29] Jerome H. Reichman, *Rethinking the Role of Clinical Trial Data in International Intellectual Property Law: The Case for a Public Goods Approach* (2002) 13(1) Marq. Intell. Prop. L. Rev. 1, 18–19 (2002).

[30] See Bryan Mercurio, Drugs, Patents and Policy: A Contextual Study of Hong Kong ch. 6 (2018).

[31] North American Free Trade Agreement (NAFTA), Art. 1711 (17 December 1992), 32 ILM 289.

a considerable effort [and contains a] new chemical entity' to any 'new pharmaceutical product'. Article 17.10.1(a) of the Australia-United States FTA is an illustrative example:

> If a Party requires, as a condition of approving the marketing of a new pharmaceutical product, the submission of undisclosed test or other data concerning safety or efficacy of the product, the Party shall not permit third persons, without the consent of the person who provided such information, to market a same or similar product on the basis of (1) such information or (2) the approval granted to the person who submitted such information for at least five years from the date of marketing approval in the Party.

Importantly, US test data protection clauses also explicitly provide that the exclusivity period will remain intact even after the expiration or invalidation of the patent.[32]

The test data protection clauses of EU and EFTA FTAs are, for the most part, closer in line with Article 39.3 of the TRIPS Agreement but provide for a longer term of protection. For example, Article 20.29 of the EU-Canada Comprehensive Economic and Trade Agreement (CETA) provides for a six-year period of exclusivity and an eight-year period of protection from the date of the granting of the originators marketing approval against disclosure for 'new chemical entities . . . if the origination of such data involves considerable effort, except where the disclosure is necessary to protect the public or unless steps are taken to ensure that the data are protected against unfair commercial use'.

Hong Kong's experience with test data protection can be used as an illustrative case study of a jurisdiction taking the law of another, without any discussion, evaluation, or consultation. Hong Kong adopted test data protection of eight years as part of its obligations under the EFTA-FTA, with Article 4 ('Undisclosed Information') of Annex XII stating:

> 1. The Parties shall protect undisclosed information in accordance with Article 39 of the TRIPS Agreement.
> 2. For pharmaceuticals, including chemical entities and biologics, and agricultural chemical products that require marketing approval by a competent authority, the Parties shall prevent applicants for marketing approval for such products from relying on, or referring to, undisclosed test data or other data submitted to the competent authority by the first applicant for a period, counted from the date of marketing approval, of at least eight years for pharmaceuticals and at least 10 years for agrochemical products.
> 3. Reliance on or reference to such data may be permitted:

32 See e.g., United States-Australia FTA, Art. 17.10.3.

(a) in order to avoid unnecessary duplication of tests of agrochemical products involving vertebrate animals, provided that the first applicant is adequately compensated; or
(b) where a written consent from the first applicant is presented.[33]

Interestingly, such language shifts the TRIPS wording of the protection applying to 'new chemical entities' to the broader 'pharmaceuticals'—whether 'new' or otherwise. What is more curious is the fact that a number of prior EFTA FTAs simply repeat the TRIPS language; thus, the EFTA-Hong Kong FTA is more restrictive than most EFTA FTAs. Hong Kong's FTA with EFTA is also missing safeguards commonly found in other agreements, such as requiring originators to file for marketing approval within a set time period following first registration in order to benefit from exclusivity, allowing for compensation in lieu of exclusivity (a common feature of EFTA FTAs), or directly linking the provision to the flexibilities of the TRIPS Agreement or to the Doha Declaration on TRIPS and Public Health.

Even where safeguards exist in the text of FTAs, in order for the safeguards to apply they must be part of the local legislation. In Hong Kong it appears safeguards negotiated into FTAs do not find their way into local legislation. Using the elaborately designed IDEAS Index, Hong Kong's FTAs is ranked as twenty-third out of thirty-five jurisdictions with regard to appropriateness, flexibility, and safeguards but twenty-third out of twenty-three with regard to legislative safeguards.[34] In other words, even where Hong Kong's FTAs provide for safeguards they are not included in domestic legislation and thus are unavailable for use.

Understanding the local context of Hong Kong is also important. Unlike major pharmaceutical markets, it is rare for a generic to apply for marking approval during the life of the patent term. On average, a generic will apply for marketing approval eighteen months after the expiration of the patent. Given the reasoning behind test data protection, it would not appear there is a need for such protection in Hong Kong. It would seem odd that Hong Kong agreed to test data protection of eight years, and do so at the same time as the government is seeking to reduce the

---

33 See Hong Kong-EFTA FTA, Annex XII, para. 4 (21 June 2011), available at www.efta.int/media/documents/legal-texts/free-trade-relations/hong-kong-china/EFTA-Hong%20Kong%20China%20Free%20Trade%20Agreement.pdf (last visited 21 August 2017).

34 Owais H. Shaikh, *Index of Data Exclusivity and Access (IDEAS): An Analysis of Test Data Exclusivity in Free Trade Agreements and National Laws*, *in* CONTEMPORARY ISSUES IN PHARMACEUTICAL PATENT LAW: SETTING THE FRAMEWORK AND EXPLORING POLICY OPTIONS 89 (Bryan Mercurio and Daria Kim eds., 2016).

rising financial burden of healthcare as the health budget is rising at a rate far exceeding GDP growth. Perhaps most anomalous of all is that the government took this decision without public consultations, empirical studies, or data on effects of test data protection to health or the budget.

More broadly, it must be questioned whether the justification used to promote and expand test data protection—that it is a means for originators to recoup R&D costs—is applicable to small markets, developing and least-developed countries. The vast majority of pharmaceutical revenue comes from large developed country markets, namely, the United States and EU. Whether a smaller country adopts test data protection will, quite frankly, have no effect on the decision of an originator to devote resources to and conduct R&D.

Again, the point here is that what is appropriate in one jurisdiction may not be for another and the justification used for the adoption of test data protection in one jurisdiction may not be transferable or applicable to another jurisdiction. Yet as we have seen with regard to patent linkage, jurisdictions continue to adopt test data protection without any empirical basis and without contextualizing the justification or implementation.

III. CONVERGENCE FOR THE GREATER GOOD

The preceding section provided examples where the trend of convergence is perhaps inappropriate or done without the 'taking' considering local context. This has been the norm, and it is unfortunate that areas where convergence or even harmonization could actually be beneficial have been virtually ignored by trade negotiations.

The possibilities for convergence for the greater good are numerous. For instance, treaty drafters and governments could ensure that FTAs include a direct link to and build upon the flexibilities existing in the TRIPS Agreement. Correspondingly, agreements could explicitly state that nothing in the FTA shall be read as preventing any TRIPS-compatible flexibility—for example, that test data protection will not hamper or prevent the issuance of a compulsory license in accordance with Article 31 of the TRIPS Agreement.

Moving beyond standard treaty terms, the area of potential convergence which could perhaps bring about the greatest impact is with regard to regulatory cooperation. The savings in terms of human capital and costs of not having to duplicate clinical trials, submissions to regulatory agencies, and the like could potentially bring about significant monetary savings and human capital.

Likewise, enhanced cooperation and regulatory convergence with respect to both the standardization of the presentation of medicines (for example, pill color, shape, size, etc.) greatly reduces opportunities for trade diversion and allows for a more effective and efficient customs operation. Similarly, regulatory convergence with regard to customs laws would enhance efficiencies, facilitate more meaningful cooperation in customs, and lead to additional seizures of counterfeit pharmaceuticals.

IV. CONCLUSION

Regulatory convergence, or even harmonization of regulations, is not in itself an evil, but blindly accepting the laws and regulations of a treaty partner does not make for good law. In the area of pharmaceutical patents, the pattern of a *demandeur* country exporting its laws to its treaty partner is all too familiar. As demonstrated in section II, this is done without considering that the background or justification for the law in the *demandeur* country may be vastly different to that of the taking country. The pattern repeats in almost every case, and too few taking countries even attempt to contextualize the transplanted law and make it more appropriate for its legal, economic, social, and cultural framework. Likewise, it is rare for a taking country to even attempt to provide empirical data or otherwise justify the transplantation of the law of the partner country. This is truly unfortunate, as not all convergence has to result in economically inefficient and negative health outcomes. Moreover, as briefly detailed in section III, there are several areas of potential convergence which could reduce costs and result in positive health outcomes which are being ignored by governments and trade negotiators.

The trend of transplanting the law of a treaty partner (harmonization) without adequate consideration and due consideration of the local context (localization) must cease. Countries must be able to provide justification not only for why it has accepted the law of a treaty partner but also why it has chosen to implement that law. There is still an opportunity for some countries to learn from the mistakes of others, but with each new mega-regional agreement being negotiated, the time to correct these mistakes is getting shorter.

16. Internet-related unfair competition: The impact of treaties and challenges for mainland Chinese law and jurisprudence

Shujie Feng

The international harmonization of intellectual property ('IP') laws has been ongoing since the nineteenth century, stemming from the conclusion of the Paris Convention for the Protection of Industrial Property in 1883 ('Paris Convention'), and the Berne Convention for the Protection of Literary and Artistic Works in 1886. This movement has continued until today, and has given rise to enhanced protection for IP that has become indispensable for the globalized economy. IP issues are always part of multilateral and bilateral trade-related treaties: the Trans-Pacific Partnership (TPP)[1] and China-Australia Free-Trade Agreement (FTA)[2] are very fresh examples in point. Furthermore, there has been a remarkable convergence between national laws in the areas of patent, trademark, and copyright, as other contributors have addressed elsewhere in this collection. On the other hand, as a contrast, relatively little harmonization has been achieved since the nineteenth century regarding unfair competition laws. However, the development of global markets has made necessary the harmonization of anti-unfair competition laws amongst countries and regions.[3] This is a task as important as the harmonization of IP laws, since the objective and purpose are the same: IP protection and the prohibition of unfair competition both aim

[1] The TPP is a trade agreement among twelve Pacific Rim countries, notably not including China. The final proposal was signed on 4 February 2016 in Auckland, New Zealand, and is awaiting ratification to enter into force.

[2] Australia-China, 17 June 2015, [2015] ATS 15.

[3] See e.g., Asia Pacific Economic Cooperation (APEC), APEC Principles to Enhance Competition and Regulatory Reform (13 September 1999), available at www.apec.org/Meeting-Papers/Leaders-Declarations/1999/1999_aelm/attachment_apec.aspx (last visited 10 July 2017).

to facilitate fair market conditions and protect differentiation amongst undertakings.[4]

Divergence amongst national laws distorts the global market by affecting the behavior of enterprises in different markets. This is especially important for Internet-related companies because the Internet has pushed forward globalization beyond the concept of territory in a revolutionary manner.[5] New business models and various types of competition behaviors have created emerging challenges for classical unfair competition laws.[6] The European Commission, in its Guidance on the Implementation/Application of Directive 2005/29/EC on Unfair Commercial Practices ('EU UCPD'), for instance, emphasized the importance of the regulation of online sectors.[7] Likely, in 2015, courts in the People's Republic of China (PRC) received 2,025 unfair competition cases.[8] The Haidian District Court of Beijing, the most important district court located in the Chinese Silicon Valley with competence for IP and unfair competition cases, received 238 cases of unfair competition, among which 160 were related to the Internet, accounting for 67 percent. From 2012 to 2015, the Haidian District Court has treated about 10 percent of unfair competition cases in China, among which about 66 percent are related to the Internet.[9] In the first five months of 2016, this court

---

[4] Nuno Pires de Carvalho, *Current Trends in the Multilateral Evolution of Unfair Competition Law*, *in* DÉFIS DU DROIT DE LA CONCURRENCE DÉLOYALE [CHALLENGES OF UNFAIR COMPETITION LAW] 1–29 (Jacques de Werra ed., 2014).

[5] See, e.g., Statista, *Total and E-commerce Value of U.S. Retail Trade Sales from 2000 to 2015 (in Billion U.S. Dollars)*, available at www.statista.com/statistics/185283/total-and-e-commerce-us-retail-trade-sales-since-2000/ (last visited 10 July 2017). It is indicated that the amount of e-commerce sales between 2000–2014 increased by a factor of more than 10 in the US market.

[6] Cin-kun Jhang, *Jhongguo Hulianwang Bujhengdang Jingjheng Anjian Fajhan Shihjheng Fensi* [*An Empirical Study on Internet Related Unfair Competition Disputes in China*], 2014(10) DIANZIH JHIHSHIH CHANCYUAN [ELECTRONICS INTELLECTUAL PROPERTY] 26, 26–37 (2014).

[7] European Commission, *Guidance on the Implementation/Application of Directive 2005/29/EC on Unfair Commercial Practices, accompanying the Communication from the Commission to the European Parliament, the Council, the European Economic and Social Committee and the Committee of the Regions* 121–51, COM (2016) 320 final (25 May 2016) (s. 5.2, titled 'Online Sector').

[8] ZUIGAO RENMIN FAYUAN [SUPREME PEOPLE'S COURT], ZUEIGAO RENMIN FAYUAN JHIHSHIH CHANCYUAN ANJIAN NIANDU BAOGAO [SUPREME PEOPLE'S COURT ANNUAL REPORT ON INTELLECTUAL PROPERTY CASES] (2015), available at www.court.gov.cn/zixun-xiangqing-42362.html.

[9] BEIJING SHIH HAIDIAN CYU RENMIN FAYUAN KETI ZU, BEIJING SHIH HAIDIAN CYU RENMIN FAYUAN GUANYU WANGLUO BUJHENGDANG JINGJHENG JIOUFEN ANJIAN DE TIAOYAN BAOGAO [INVESTIGATION AND RESEARCH REPORT BY THE HAIDIAN DISTRICT, BEIJING CITY PEOPLE'S COURT ON INTERNET-RELATED

has received a further 163 Internet-related unfair competition cases, demonstrating the remarkable increase in interest in this field from market forces, and thus the need for regulated market order. The cases concern AdWords services, search engines, social media software (chatting software), tool software, incompatibility between software, interfering in business methods, online games, etc. The PRC Anti-unfair Competition Law ('PRC AUCL') of 1993 provides for eleven types of concrete unfair competition behavior[10] and a general rule based on the *bona fide* principle of prohibiting any unfair competition practice.[11] Many new types of behavior amongst competitors in the market cannot be qualified as any of the eleven types and therefore the general rule will be applied. This presents a big challenge for the courts in the application of the abstract principle in concrete cases. But, in dealing with this tough mission, neither the Chinese courts nor academics have taken due consideration of treaties to which China is a contracting party. In 2015, the Haidian District Court received ninety-three Internet-related unfair competition cases in which the general rule was applied. Such cases account for 58 percent of all unfair competition cases of this court. IP treaties have no impact on the interpretation and application of Chinese laws in this regard, even though the Paris Convention provisions are self-executing in China because the utility of Article 10*bis* of the Paris Convention has not been noted. On the other hand, it is also true that though relevant treaty provisions are useful for the interpretation and application of Chinese laws, further international harmonization is still needed.

Until now, the most pertinent effective treaty provision on unfair competition has been Article 10*bis* of the Paris Convention, which provides for a definition of unfair practice and three typical unfair commercial practices: confusion, defamation, and deception. The imprecision of this definition renders it ill-suited to cope with the enormous variety of anti-unfair competition cases that domestic courts adjudicate upon. In this chapter, I will first review the anti-unfair competition rules in treaties. Secondly, the difficulties in comparative laws regarding the qualification of uncategorized unfair com-

---

UNFAIR COMPETITION] (2012–2016), available at www.netmvp.cn/uploadfile/file/20161202/20161202_24aabdd5.pdf (last visited 10 July 2017).

[10] They are: passing off; abuse of dominant position; government interference; commercial bribery; misrepresentation; infringement of trade secret; dumping; tie-in sale; certain prize-giving sales; commercial detriment; and cahoots bids. See PRC AUCL, arts. 5–15.

[11] In China, art. 2 of the PRC AUCL provides that business operators shall abide by voluntariness, equality, fairness, and *bona fides* principles and commonly recognized commercial morality, and unfair competition practices are those which are contrary to the law and harm the legal rights and interests of other competitors and which disrupt economic order of the society.

petition practice will be examined. Thirdly, the principle of 'no interference except for public interest'[12] that has recently been developed by the Chinese court in Internet-related cases will be analyzed. Finally, the possibility for new types of unfair practice to be included in treaties will be evaluated. The objective of this chapter is to assess the impact of the current treaty provisions on national laws and practice and to evaluate the possibility of achieving further international harmonization of anti-unfair competition laws.

I. TREATY REGIMES REGARDING ANTI-UNFAIR COMPETITION LAW

The Paris Convention established the first comprehensive international harmonization of unfair competition laws which focuses more on competitors' interests. Recent evolution in Europe and the Asia-Pacific has demonstrated the importance of the consumer protection dimension in the evolution of anti-unfair competition law.

1. Paris Convention: A Milestone for International Harmonization

Protection against unfair competition was introduced into the Paris Convention as an issue affecting IP in 1900, and then a definition and three examples of unfair competition were added in the subsequent revision conferences in 1911 and 1958, which formed the current iteration of Article 10*bis* of the Paris Convention.[13] Article 10*bis* has brought three contributions to the harmonization of anti-unfair competition laws.[14] First, it creates a general obligation for contracting parties to assure effective protection against unfair competition. Secondly, it provides a definition of unfair competition acts: any act of competition contrary to honest practices in industrial or commercial matters constitutes an act of unfair competition. This definition serves as the basic rule for the qualification of unfair competition acts at an international level. Though anti-unfair competition law has deep moralistic roots,[15] honest practices,

---

[12] This principle will herein be referred to as 'no interference' principle.

[13] For more details on negotiation of Paris Convention in this respect, see Pires de Carvalho (n. 4 above) 1–29.

[14] For more details on interpretation of Art. 10*bis* of the Paris Convention, see G.H.C. Bodenhausen, Guide to the Application of the Paris Convention for the Protection of Industrial Property as Revised at Stockholm in 1967 142–6 (1968).

[15] Pires de Carvalho (n. 4 above) 1–29.

as a criterion of evaluation in the Paris Convention, should be determined according to moral principles within the relevant business field which may be different from general moral principles which apply to daily life. In particular, the freedom of competition should be duly respected so that anti-unfair competition measures do not create unjustified barriers to freedom of competition. Thirdly, the Convention specifies three types of unfair competition acts. It concerns (i) all acts of such a nature as to create confusion by any means whatever with the establishment, the goods, or the industrial or commercial activities, of a competitor; (ii) false allegations in the course of trade of such a nature as to discredit the establishment, the goods, or the industrial or commercial activities, of a competitor; (iii) indications or allegations the use of which in the course of trade is liable to mislead the public as to the nature, the manufacturing process, the characteristics, the suitability for their purpose, or the quantity, of the goods.[16]

Notably, whilst legal practice differs amongst civil law countries and common law countries, the three examples of unfair practice listed under Article 10*bis* are all identified as prohibited practices by contracting parties, even if their scope and conditions of application vary among countries. However, a general concept of unfair competition only exists in civil countries and not in common law countries. Therefore, at the time, inclusion of a general definition of unfair competition into the Paris Convention was the most remarkable fruit.[17] Since the revision of the Paris Convention in 1958, however, little progress has been achieved in respect of further international harmonization of unfair competition laws.[18] The Agreement on Trade-Related Aspects of Intellectual Property Rights of 1994 ('TRIPS'),[19] the most comprehensive and influential IP treaty, does not mention unfair competition, but instead provides a definition for the term 'trade secret'—giving birth to the fourth type of unfair practice recognized by treaties.[20] But the provisions of the Paris Convention have been an important reference point for several regional treaties, such as the Cartagena Agreement ('CAN') and MERCOSUR treaties.[21] But all these

---

[16] Article Paris Convention, art. 10 *bis*.

[17] Frauke Henning-Bodewig, *International Unfair Competition Law*, *in* LAW AGAINST UNFAIR COMPETITION: TOWARDS A NEW PARADIGM IN EUROPE? 55 (Reto M. Hilty and Frauke Henning-Bodewig eds., 2007).

[18] Pires de Carvalho (n. 4 above) 1–29.

[19] 33 ILM 1197 (1994).

[20] TRIPS Agreement, Art. 39.

[21] See FRAUKE HENNING-BODEWIG, INTERNATIONAL HANDBOOK ON UNFAIR COMPETITION 77–9 (2013).

developments have not gone further than the Paris Convention regarding the issue of harmonization.

The limits of the Paris Convention lie in the fact that its primary focus is on the conduct between competitors in the market. The insertion of the consumer misleading provision into the Paris Convention in the 1958 Lisbon Conference 'testifies a departure from the confinement to the interests of competitors' and 'offers a gateway for lending weight to protection of consumers'.[22] Since the 1960s, consumer rights movements have brought about national and international consumer rights protection laws.[23] Such laws are designed to prevent the businesses that engage in fraud or specified unfair practices from gaining an advantage over competitors. This inherent link between consumer protection and market competition shows that consumer protection has become an important dimension of unfair competition laws.

2. EU UCPD and TPP: A Further Development of the Consumer Protection Dimension

The EU UCPD of 2005 and the TPP of 2016 have made progress towards further harmonization by emphasizing the consumer protection dimension of anti-unfair competition law. It marks a new development direction for unfair competition laws at both a national and international level.

The EU UCPD aims to achieve a maximum harmonization of consumer protection laws among EU Member States[24] by requiring that the Directive be transposed into national laws without modification. The

---

[22] Marcus Höpperger and Martin Senftleben, *Protection Against Unfair Competition at the International Level: The Paris Convention, the 1996 Model Provisions and the Current Work of the World Intellectual Property Organisation, in* LAW AGAINST UNFAIR COMPETITION: TOWARDS A NEW PARADIGM IN EUROPE? (Reto M. Hilty and Frauke Henning-Bodewig eds., 2007) at 67.

[23] On 15 March 1962, President John F. Kennedy presented a speech to the United States Congress in which he extolled four basic consumer rights (the right to safety; the right to be informed; the right to choose; and the right to be heard), later called the Consumer Bill of Rights. The United Nations through the United Nations Guidelines for Consumer Protection expanded these into eight rights (by adding the right to satisfaction of basic needs; the right to redress; the right to consumer education; and the right to a healthy environment) and thereafter Consumers International adopted these rights as a Charter and started recognizing 15 March as World Consumer Rights Day.

[24] The Court of Justice of the European Communities played an important role in the development of the consumer protection dimension of unfair competition law before the birth of the EU UCPD. See FRAUKE HENNING-BODEWIG, UNFAIR COMPETITION LAW EUROPEAN UNION AND MEMBER STATES 26 (2006).

Directive is a milestone in consumer protection law and its implementation has produced vast and profound influence upon comparative laws. Bound by the competences conferred by the Treaty establishing the European Community (in particular Article 95), the EU Directive is only applicable to business-to-consumer ('B to C') commercial practices. But this definition includes any act, omission, course of conduct or representation, commercial communication including advertising and marketing, by a trader, directly connected with the promotion, sale, or supply of a product to consumers. Therefore, it has still a very large scope of application and covers all B to C commercial practices. According to article 5.2 of EU UCPD, two basic conditions must be met in order to define a commercial practice as unfair: it must flout the standard level of professional diligence expected of professionals involved in the relevant field of activity, and it must be able to distort the economic behavior of the average consumer, to the extent that it affects their ability to take an informed decision relating to a transaction that they would not otherwise make.[25] In particular, the Directive covers two types of unfair commercial practices: misleading practices and aggressive practices. Misleading practices constitute an evolution of the confusion and misleading practices as defined in the Paris Convention, while the definition of aggressive practices is an innovation for unfair competition laws both at a national and international level. The EU UCPD has a blacklist of thirty-one kinds of unfair practices which are illegal and unfair *ex lege*. The application of the EU UCPD involves a three-step test: if the act at issue falls within the scope of the blacklist, it is unfair *per se*; otherwise, it shall be evaluated according to the provisions defining misleading practices (articles 6 and 7) and provisions defining aggressive practices (articles 8 and 9); if the practice still does not fall within the ambit of the EU UCPD by virtue of these provisions, it shall be evaluated according to the general definition of unfair commercial practice. This requires one to answer the question of whether the relevant conduct infringes professional diligence and materially distorts the economic behavior of the average consumer (article 5(1)). It should be pointed out that the introduction of the blacklist and the definition of aggressive practices marked a new era of taking judicial action against unfair competition via use of the language of consumer protection. The first three years of

---

25 EU UCPD, art. 5.2, provides that: 'A commercial practice shall be unfair if: (a) it is contrary to the requirements of professional diligence, and (b) it materially distorts or is likely to materially distort the economic behaviour with regard to the product of the average consumer whom it reaches or to whom it is addressed, or of the average member of the group when a commercial practice is directed to a particular group of consumers'.

enforcement of the EU UCPD discipline in Italy has shown that aggressive practices are most common in the Telecommunication, Energy, Financial sectors, and that misleading practices are most frequent in the Foodstuffs, Services, Industry, and Tourism sectors.[26]

The TPP recognizes as the double objective of anti-unfair competition law the promotion of economic efficiency and consumer welfare, and it emphasizes the importance of consumer protection policy and enforcement for the creation of efficient and competitive markets in the free-trade area.[27] It gives three further examples of fraudulent and deceptive activities.[28] However, two of them do not concern competition interests and can be regulated by contract law,[29] while the third, which pertains to misleading practices, adds no more to the existing rules provided by the Paris Convention. Therefore, it can be said that the value of the contribution provided by the TPP lies in the explicit recognition of consumer protection as an objective of unfair competition law, rather than in its formulation of rules.

Though there has been limited development regarding unfair competition law and its competitor protection dimension since the 1958 revision of the Paris Convention,[30] developments via the dimension of consumer protection have been remarkable in concept, guiding spirit, and rule formulation. This should not only influence the interpretation of the treaty provisions under domestic laws, but also optimize the pace at which further harmonization of national laws is achieved.

---

[26] Antonio Mancini, 'Directive 2005/29/CE on Unfair Commercial Practices', paper delivered at Conference in Belgrade, 23 February 2011.

[27] TPP, Arts. 16.1.1, 16.6.1, available at https://ustr.gov/sites/default/files/TPP-Final-Text-Competition.pdf (last visited 10 July 2017).

[28] They are (a) a practice of making misrepresentations of material fact, including implied factual misrepresentations, that cause significant detriment to the economic interests of misled consumers; (b) a practice of failing to deliver products or provide services to consumers after the consumers are charged; (c) a practice of charging or debiting consumers' financial, telephone, or other accounts without authorization. TPP, Art. 16.6.2.

[29] Compared to the TPP, the EU UCPD sufficiently distinguishes the scope of application of contract nature laws from that of unfair competition law, insofar as it focuses rather on pre-contract and post-contract matters. See Mancini (n 26 above).

[30] For example, the evolution of unfair competition law has not clarified the concept and evaluation criteria on parasitism or free-riding, but has contributed to the creation of legal regimes for the protection of the phonogram, databases, and software. JÉRÔME PASSA, CONTREFAÇON ET CONCURRENCE DÉLOYALE 3–4 (1996).

II. METHODOLOGY AND DIFFICULTY IN THE APPLICATION OF THE GENERAL RULE PROHIBITING UNFAIR COMPETITION PRACTICE

For countries equipped with an anti-unfair competition regime identical or similar to the one prescribed by the Paris Convention, the common difficulty in the regulation of competition lies in the identification of unfair practices which do not fall into any of the three types of unfair practice as defined by Article 10*bis* of the Paris Convention. In other words, the difficulty rests upon the way to apply the general rule prohibiting unfair competition in concrete cases. The methodology varies amongst countries and the interpretations provided by national authorities in this regard are interesting.

1. Difficulty in Defining the Operational Criteria for Unfair Competition

As a contrast to IP law in a narrow sense, unfair competition laws are quite different among countries in terms of legal theories, legislation, and practice. First, unfair competition is an important concept in civil law countries, but it is still not embedded in common law countries. In civil law countries, the rules regulating practices amounting to unfair competition are all organized under this concept and a systematic theory and a specific jurisprudence has developed.[31] In common law countries like the United Kingdom, this concept is missing in legislation and the case law; in the United States, though the concept of unfair competition has emerged,[32] its application scope is confined to the limits of the passing off doctrine, and laws pertaining to commercial detriment and consumer protection. Secondly, civil law jurisdictions differ amongst themselves regarding the general method of comprehending unfair competition practices. For instance, it is notable that in France, it is the general tort law rule of article 1382 of the Civil Code which applies to unfair competition, whilst countries like Germany, Switzerland, Belgium, Luxembourg, and Italy have specific anti-unfair competition laws. In this regard, we need to celebrate the Paris Convention's achievement of spurring the adoption of a harmonized general rule and specific provisions for the three typical

[31] Jennifer Davis, *Unfair Competition Law in the United Kingdom*, *in* LAW AGAINST UNFAIR COMPETITION: TOWARDS A NEW PARADIGM IN EUROPE? (Reto M. Hilty and Frauke Henning-Bodewig eds., 2007) at 183–98.

[32] See Restatement (Third) of Unfair Competition, § 1, 4–5 (Am. Law Inst. 1995, update 2016).

unfair competition practices across different legal regimes. However, these provisions of the Paris Convention still need to be interpreted and applied within the legal contexts of each country. This poses a challenge not only for national legal systems attempting to apply this rule in practice, but also to the further harmonization of international law in this field.

Despite the differences between national laws, there is one common point amongst countries: competition law serves to safeguard and restore fair competition order, and, in doing so, protects the freedom of competition in a market economy.[33] According to the principle of freedom of competition, all professionals are legally entitled to attract clients of their competitors. Such prejudice caused by competition is lawful. But the freedom of competition has its limit: it must not be abused and the abuse of this freedom constitutes an act of unfair competition. In the application of anti-unfair competition law, it should always be borne in mind that safeguarding the freedom of competition is equally important as the fight against unfair competition. Thus, an appropriate balance of these factors should be reached when determining the substantive content and relevant criteria of anti-competition laws.

It is interesting to compare the different methods employed by countries for defining of the general principles. The French law, for instance, applies the general constituting conditions of torts: fault, damage, and causality between them, among which the fault is the key element. Bad faith is not required. Professor Passa defines acts amounting to unfair competition as any behavior which deviates from the normal conduct of a prudent professional, distorts the balance in competition relations, and breaks the equality of chance which should exist among competitors.[34] The German law once defined unfair competition practices as those which are contrary to *bonos mores* in its 1909 Anti-unfair Competition Law, but replaced this morally charged definition in 2004 with unfair practices which are detrimental to competitors, consumers, and other market participants and which impairs the competition in a not insignificant way.[35] The EU UCPD defines unfair commercial practices as those which fall short of the professional diligence required in the relevant field of activity that the professional is involved

[33] In France, the principle of commercial and industrial liberty, proclaimed by Law Le Chapellier of 3 and 17 March 1791 and reiterated by art. 1 of Law Royer of 27 December 1973, recognizes the principle of free competition. See J. THOMAS MCCARTHY, MCCARTHY ON TRADEMARKS AND UNFAIR COMPETITION para. 1:1 (4th ed. 1996, update 2016).

[34] PASSA (n. 30 above) 16–17.

[35] Gesetz gegen den Unlauteren Wettbewerb [UWG] [Act Against Unfair Competition], 3 March 2010, BGBL. I at 254, art. 3.

in, and are capable of distorting the economic behavior of the average consumer, affecting their ability to make an informed decision relating to a transaction that they would not otherwise make.[36] 'Professional diligence' is defined as 'the standard of special skill and care which a trader may reasonably be expected to exercise towards consumers, commensurate with honest market practice and/or the general principle of good faith in the trader's field of activity'.[37] The Swiss Federal Act on Unfair Competition defines unfair competition practices as those which are deceptive or are contrary to *bone fide* rules in any manner and have influence on the relationship between competitors or between a supplier and client.[38] In China, article 2 of the PRC AUCL of 1993 provides that:

> business operators shall abide by voluntariness, equality, fairness and bona fides principles and commonly recognized commercial morality, and unfair competition practices are those which are contrary to the law and harm the legal rights and interests of other competitors and which disrupt economic order of the society.

The National Supreme People's Court (NSPC) similarly defines unfair competition practices as those contrary to *bona fide* principle and commonly recognized commercial moralities.[39]

The vastly inclusive notion of fault under French law, the notion of unfairness under German law, and the *bona fide* principle and conception of commercial morality in Chinese law are all very abstract and difficult to apply in judicial practice.[40] The professional diligence standard in EU law does not provide substantial aid for the application of the general rule. It is commonly recognized that it is neither possible nor helpful to give

---

[36] EU UCPD, art. 5.2.

[37] *Ibid.* art. 2(h).

[38] Loi fédérale contre la concurrence déloyale [Federal Act on Unfair Competition] (LCD), 1 March 1988, RO 1988 223, art. 2.

[39] 山东省食品进出口公司、山东山孚日水有限公司、山东山孚集团有限公司诉青岛圣克达诚贸易有限公司、马达庆不正当竞争纠纷申请再审案 *Shandong Food Import & Export and others v. Ma Qingda and Qingdao Shengkedacheng*, (2009) Min Shen Zi No. 1065, available at www.pkulaw.cn/case/pcas_1970324837399004.html?keywords=%E6%BB%A5%E7%94%A8%E5%85%AC%E5%8F%B8%E6%B3%95%E4%BA%BA%E7%8B%AC%E7%AB%8B%E5%9C%B0%E4%BD%8D&match=Fuzzy.

[40] 郑友德, 范长 军，《反不正当竞争法一般条款具体化研究 — 兼论《 中华人民共和 国反不 正 当竞争法 》的 完善》, 法 商 研 究2005年第5期(总第109期)，第124-134页。Y. Zheng and C. Fan, *Study on the Concrete Application of the General Rule Prohibiting Unfair Competition and the Improvement of the PRC AUCL*, 5 Law & Commerce Rev. (2005).

a sweeping definition or to find a uniform operational criterion for the determination of what constitutes unfair competition practice.[41] It is commonly agreed that the appropriate means of making this determination is to allow the courts to decide on a case-by-case basis with the guidance of the general principles.[42] By using this approach, the non-exhaustive list of unfair competition practices and prior jurisprudence always play an essential role in the interpretation and application of unfair competition law. The former is adopted by the legislator and the latter by judges. Therefore, the general rule prohibiting unfair competition and the typical unfair competition practices in the list or in the jurisprudence should be interpreted in concert with each other: the former is always the basis and spirit for the latter, while the latter is referred to as a useful guide for the embodiment and development of the former. This concerted method is valid for both the interpretation of treaties and national laws. Further, the interpretation and application of national laws can serve as a reference point for the interpretation and application of treaties, and vice versa.

2. Limited Progress in the Categorization of Unfair Competition Practices

Legal theories and jurisprudence developed under the above-mentioned principles can serve as useful guidance for courts in several respects. For example, competitors' interests, consumers' interests, and fair economic order are all perspectives useful for criteria setting, while due diligence of professionals and commercial moralities are further standards for the determination of the intentional fault of market operators. During the course of judicial practice and legal research, attempts have been made to establish new categories of unfair competition that are comparable to the three included in Article 10*bis* of the Paris Convention. These efforts have not provided satisfactory results.

The German courts' case law for the application of the general rule prohibiting unfair competition are classified into four groups: disrupting consumers' decisions, obstructing competitors, unfair imitation, and illegal appropriation.[43] But operational common conditions of application are absent for each group and the classifications only serve as guidance for legal interpretation and application. The French Professor Roubier

---

41 McCarthy (n. 33 above) para. 1:8; Passa (n. 30 above) 20.

42 McCarthy (n. 33 above) para. 1:9; Passa (n. 30 above) 20.

43 范长军. 德国反不正当竞争法研究[M].北京:法律出版社, 2010 C. Fan, Study on German Anti-Unfair Competition Law 116–18 (2010).

classified unfair competition acts into a list of four non-exhaustive categories: confusion; defamation; disorganization of rival companies; and disorganization of the market.[44] The last two categories are new but are too large to be applied with concrete criteria.

As an example of a more concrete categorization in comparative laws, 'parasitism' is often invoked by French courts as a type of unfair competition act parallel to the three types of acts in the Paris Convention. It prohibits the free exploitation of other competitor's creations and investments. But this mature judicial practice is considered as lacking justification if its conditions of application are not well defined, because imitation itself is legal. It is the risk of confusion that results from the imitation that is illegal. Therefore, a creation, which is not protected by IP laws, is in the public domain and accessible for imitation or exploitation by anyone. Professor Passa suggests that French parasitism should be defined by the criterion of confusion according to the provisions of Article 10*bis* of the Paris Convention and otherwise it has no reason to exist.[45] In German law, parasitism is referred to as 'unfair imitation'. But due to the principle of free imitation, the German law only prohibits imitations that create confusion regarding origin of products or services, or those which unfairly take advantage of or harm the goodwill of the competitor, or which cause an infringement of the trade secrets of a competitor.[46] However, it is submitted that the first and the second kinds of situations covered by this rule can be qualified as confusion in a broad sense or as trademark dilution, not necessarily a new category of unfair competition.

Until now, the most successful adoption of concrete categories of unfair competition practices has been the EU UCPD, which provides a blacklist of thirty-one unfair commercial practices. It also describes the conditions on aggressive commercial practices which are operational and constitutes a further development of the general rule prohibiting unfair competition. Of course, the scope of its application is limited to practice in business to consumer relationship.

The Chinese courts have adopted the 'no interference' principle. It is intended to be a further development of the general rule and applicable to a type of competition practice regarding relationship between competitors (directly).

---

44 Paul Roubier, Le Droit de la Propriété Industrielle 505 (1952).

45 Passa (n. 30 above) 274–95.

46 UWG, art. 4.9. See Fan (n. 43 above) 149–51.

III. PRINCIPLE OF NO INTERFERENCE EXCEPT FOR PUBLIC INTERESTS: A FAILED EXPERIMENT OF THE CHINESE COURTS?

The Beijing Supreme People's Court created the 'no interference' principle in its interpretation of the general rule prohibiting unfair competition in *Baidu v. Qihu*.[47] To a certain extent, this principle was endorsed by the NSPC in the retrial procedure. Therefore, it has been invoked and also applied by certain courts in other cases. On the one hand, this principle has been regarded by supporters of the decision as a useful interpretation of the general rule and a new development of anti-unfair competition theory; on the other, there are sharp critics who have commented on the principle's foundations.

1. Creation of the Principle in *Baidu v. Qihu*

On the facts of this case, when Internet users installed 360 anti-virus software in their computers, a warning label would appear on certain search results provided by Baidu's search engine. Clicking on the warning label, the Internet user would see two types of notices. One type of warning alerted Internet users that the relevant website is dangerous in the sense that it may transmit computer viruses, such as Trojans, which will attack their computers; the other type states that the website is risky in the sense that there is fraudulent or unverified information or advertising on the websites which may mislead Internet users into a trap. If Internet users click on the term 'secured Internet browser' which appears also in the warning notice, they are led to the website of Qihu company (which has developed a reputation in China for its anti-virus software) which proposes the installation of its 360 safe Internet browser.

The Court found that, according to the 'no interference' principle, Internet-related services or products should peacefully coexist and product or service providers should not interfere with their competitors' operations, or interfere with the choice of the end-users. Such interference is permitted only when it is necessary for the protection of public interest. In this case, the Court found that Qihu's warning labels had disrupted Baidu's search engine service, and that this amounted to a flouting of the

---

47 百度在线网络技术（北京）有限公司等与北京奇虎科技有限公司等不正当竞争纠纷上诉案（北京市高级人民法院（2013）高民终字第2352号民事判决书）Beijing Supreme People's Court, Judgment (2013) Gao Min Zhong Zi No. 2352, available at www.iphouse.cn.

'no interference' principle. The Court found that the warning labels were neither legitimate nor necessary. Also, the Court found that Qihu has put warning labels on Baidu's search result under the guise of public interest or Internet security, but that the ultimate objective was to promote its own Internet browser.

The NSPC further indicated in its retrial decision that Qihu (the appellant), as a civil entity with equal status to Baidu (the appellee), had no right to assess the operation of the appellee or to take action thereon. The appellant, as a market operator, cannot represent the interest of public consumers, and therefore cannot disrupt the business model of the appellee in the name of public interest.[48]

The 'no interference' principle was also applied to render as an act of unfair competition a separate AdWord-related act of the appellant. Qihu company included the search engine frame of Baidu on its portal website (hao.360.cn). Normally, if Internet users input a keyword for a search on the website of Baidu, the suggested relevant AdWords of Baidu appear below the frame of input and they drive Internet users to the websites related to the AdWords. However, when they use the search engine of Baidu in Qihu's web browser, the suggested AdWords of Qihu appear instead of those of Baidu and they drive users to the websites planned by Qihu. The Beijing Supreme Court found that the act of Qihu disrupted the normal functioning of Baidu's searching services and prevented Internet users from normal use of the search results provided by Baidu. This disruption is not justified by any public interest and its sole objective and consequence was deemed to be to obtain more visitors for Qihu's search engine. This act exceeded the limit of fair competition according to article 2 of the PRC AUCL.

2. Critics of the Principle

The 'no interference' principle has been hotly debated amongst practitioners and scholars.[49] From the perspective of unfair competition law, the

---

48 奇虎公司与被申请人百度网讯公司、百度在线公司及一审被告奇智公司不正当竞争纠纷案【（2014）民申字第873号】Chinese NSPC, Decision (2014) Min Shen Zi No. 873, available at www.iphouse.cn.

49 石必胜，互联网竞争的非公益必要不干扰原则 兼评百度诉360插标和修改搜索提示词不正当竞争纠纷案，《电子知识产权》B. Shi, *No Interference Except for Public Interest Principle in Internet Related Competition Disputes with Comments on Baidu v. Qihu Warning Labels and AdWords Case*, 4 Electronics Intellectual Property 30–37 (2014); 薛军，质疑'非公益必要不干扰原则'《电子知识产权》 J. Xue, *Questioning No Interference Except for Public Interest Principle*, 1 Electronics Intellectual Property 66–70 (2015).

legitimacy of the employment of this principle as a criterion for identification of acts amounting to unfair competition is quite doubtful. The serious consequence of the application of this principle is that it will limit the freedom of competition of market operators. That is a fundamental problem. The freedom of competition entails the ability of a market operator to take any competitive measure for its own interest even if it impairs competitors' interests, and even if it is not for public interest. This principle is fundamental in private law: all is permitted except what is prohibited by laws (*nulla poena sine lege*). It derives therefrom that market operators can even disrupt or interfere with competitors' business so long as it is not contrary to honest practice or the *bona fide* principle. This freedom includes the possibility to connect to the server of competitors or to modify the software or code of competitors. Such acts are not comparable to the entry into private property in the real world where the entry itself is illegal. In the virtual world, such limits may be imposed in accordance with the need to protect individual privacy, confidential information, property rights, etc. But, if these rights or interests are not harmed, such acts are not necessarily imputative. Therefore, the application of this principle has resulted in a change of the underlying logic of the law—from the logic of freedom to the logic of authorization. According to the logic of authorization, competing acts (which disrupt or interfere with competitors) are permitted only if they are necessary for the protection of public interest. Conversely, the logic of freedom is as follows: competing acts are all permitted, but can be prohibited once they are deemed to be unfair or an infringement of the rights of others. Notably, it is unclear how an act can first be qualified as a disruption or interference, words which have a negative connotation according to their ordinary meaning.

As the 'no interference' principle has to a certain extent been endorsed by the NSPC, it is also invoked by other courts as a criterion for determining unfair competition practice under the general rule. Also, the Project of Revision Act for PRC AUCL ('PRC AUCL Project') included a type of unfair practice similar to the said principle: one shall not influence consumer's choice or disrupt competitor's normal business by 'disrupting or destroying, without consent or authorization, normal functioning of competitor's Internet service'.[50] But this rule is very abstract and its improper broad application would affect the freedom of competition and thus be detrimental to the Internet related industry. Fortunately, at the revision of the PRC AUCL on the 4th November 2017, the final provision of the law regulating internet-related competition criterion keeps a distance from

---

50 PRC AUCL Project, art. 13.

the "no-interference" principle. According to Article 12 of the new law, market operators shall not disrupt or break normal functioning of other operators' Internet products or services by influencing consumers' choice or other methods via technical means; the following acts are prohibited: (1) forcing the redirection by inserting links into the legal internet products or services of other operators without their consent, (2) misleading, deceiving or forcing consumers to modify, close or uninstall legal internet products or services of other operators, (3) rending incompatible legal internet products or services of other operators in bad faith, (4) other disrupting or breaking acts.

It can be noticed that, instead of forbidding interference with other operators' internet related services in a general manner, the new law has chosen to limit the application of this principle to certain acts defined by concrete technical terms on the basis of judicial experience. Also, the new law has abandoned terms such *as public interests* or *authorization* which connote an anti-free competition idea. Therefore, the new law will surely not be interpreted or applied under the guidance of the *no interference* principle.

IV. CHINESE LAW AND PRACTICE TO BE GUIDED BY TREATIES

China has been a contracting party to the Paris Convention since 1985. The PRC AUCL of 1993 sets out a general rule prohibiting unfair competition and, *inter alia*, the three types of unfair practices enshrined under Article 10*bis* of the Paris Convention: confusion, defamation, and misleading. But the Chinese legislator has used the model of the German law by generally prohibiting unfair competition and setting forth a number of rules on concrete types of unfair competition. The Chinese legislator wanted clearly delimited rules in order to avoid arbitrary decisions by judicial and administrative organs. This resulted in two weak points which now pertain to the PRC AUCL: the scope of application of the confusion provision is too narrow, and the general rule prohibiting unfair competition is considered as inapplicable in concrete cases.[51] Therefore, the Chinese legislator should improve the confusion and misleading provisions in light of Article

[51] However, in the absence of applicable concrete rules to regulate various new unfair practices, Chinese courts have had to apply the general rule: 邵建东，我国反不正当竞争法中的一般条款及其在司法实践中的适用《南京大学法律评论》J. Shao, *On the General Rule Prohibiting Unfair Competition and Its Application in Judicial Practice*, 1 NANKING UNIVERSITY LAW REV. 196–205 (2003).

10*bis* of the Paris Convention and explicitly recognize the applicability of the general rule prohibiting unfair competition. Notably, the PRC AUCL had not been modified for more than ten years (1993–2017), during which the consumer protection dimension of unfair competition law has been recognized in comparative laws and international treaties. Not only should the legislator introduce this dimension into the Chinese law, but the Chinese courts should also recognize consumer protection as an operational criterion in the qualification of unfair competition practice.

1. Improvement of the Confusing Rule in the PRC AUCL

The initial provision causing confusion is provided for under article 5 of the PRC AUCL of 1993, which prohibits the counterfeiting of trademarks, and imitation of particular names, packaging or decoration of known products, trade names or personal names, if there is a likelihood of confusion. In practice, trademark infringement matters are nearly all covered by trademark law and the function of this article may be deemed equivalent to the passing off regime in common law countries.[52] But, the scope of application of this provision is much narrower than Article 10*bis* of the Paris Convention in that it only protects against confusion caused by commercial signs. The revision of the PRC AUCL in 2017 has enlarged the scope of application of the confusion rule. On one part, Article 6 of the new law has added other types of commercial signs under protection by the confusion prohibition rule (i.e. domain names, website name, webpages etc.) in order to cover all kinds of commercial signs. On the other part, in the same provision, the new law prohibit confusion causing acts in a general manner, which has brought the opportunity for a much larger scope of application of this rule. The Chinese courts must understand that, in the theory and practice of unfair competition law, likelihood of confusion may exist even in the absence of commercial signs and that is the idea of Article 10*bis* of the Paris Convention which does not mention the use of commercial signs but 'by any means whatever'. Multiple examples can also be found in the French parasitism[53] and the German unfair imitation regimes[54] mentioned above.

In *Baidu v. Qihu*, consumers were deemed to be familiar with the AdWords service of Baidu provided by its search engine webpage, and

---

[52] S. Feng, *How are Unregistered Trademarks Protected in China*, 7 IIC, 815–30 (2013).

[53] Passa (n. 30 above) 254–94.

[54] Fan (n. 43 above) 141–52.

accustomed to viewing said AdWords below the keyword-inputting bar. The replacement of the AdWords by Qihu necessarily creates confusion among consumers about the origin of the service in this circumstance. In *Baidu v. Jolmo Lungma*,[55] the respondent inserted navigating links into the search result webpages of the claimant. The court found that this act disrupted the normal functioning of and the service provided by the claimant and thus violated the *bona fide* principle. Indeed, the circumstances may well lead to the conclusion that consumers will believe that the content on the search result pages of Baidu is the service provided by Baidu. This creation of confusion is a sufficient and well-founded ground to qualify such practices as unfair. In *Baidu v. Sougou (AdWords)*,[56] a more recent case decided in 2015 and whose facts are similar to the *Baidu v. Qihu* case, the court correctly applied the confusion rule in the determination of unfair practice. But the court applied article 2 instead of article 5 of the PRC AUCL of 1993.

2. Consumer Protection Dimension to be Introduced in Law and Practice

While article 1 of the current PRC AUCL of 1993 makes clear its purpose—to protect rights and interests of both business operators and consumers—this provision cannot be applied in concrete cases because the general rule prohibiting unfair competition in article 2 does not include the dimension of consumer protection in its definition of unfair competition. The consequence of this is that the harm to consumers' interests had not been considered by legislators or the courts as an independent and sufficient criterion for the qualification of unfair practice, while it is in the domestic laws of other jurisdictions and in treaties, as is mentioned above.

In practice, Chinese courts sometimes take into account the harm to consumers' interests just as a complementary element.[57] In the case *Baidu*

[55] 北京百度网讯科技有限公司诉北京珠穆朗玛网络技术有限公司等不正当竞争和侵犯著作权纠纷案——（2005）一中民初字第5456号 Beijing No. 1 Intermediate People's Court, （2005）Yi Zhong Min Chu Zi No. 5456.

[56] 北京百度网讯科技有限公司诉北京搜狗信息服务有限公司不正当竞争纠纷案， 北京市海淀区人民法院民事判决书 (2015)海民(知)初字第4135号 Haidian Court (Beijing), (2015) Hai Min (Zhi) Chu Zi No. 4135.

[57] For example, in *Tencent v. Sougou (Disrupting Use of Competing Software)*, Sougou induced consumers to uninstall a competing Chinese character-inputting software provided by Tencent. The Court found that this harmed the freedom of consumers to make an independent choice.腾讯科技(深圳)有限公司诉北京搜狗科技发展有限公司等不正当竞争纠纷案，(2009)一中民初字第16849号判决书 Beijing No. 1 Intermediate People's Court, (2009) Yi Zhong Min Chu Zi No. 16849.

v. Qihu as cited above, the Court already pointed out that Internet users have the freedom to determine services to use or not and that Internet Service Providers should not force them to use their services or to disrupt use of their competitors' services. In *Qihu v. Baidu*,[58] Baidu provides on its website free 360 software of the claimant for Internet users to download. During the downloading process, Baidu's website repeatedly reminds Internet users that it is necessary (although it is not) to download, install, and use Baidu's mobile phone software to complete the process of downloading 360's software. The Court found that there was no misleading or deception or manipulation of Internet users regarding the installment of Baidu's software. Yet, it should not be denied that an average consumer who does not want the Baidu mobile phone software may accept to download it because of Baidu's persistent claims, creating pressure for consumers which may reasonably lead to the conclusion that to abandon Baidu's website as source of 360 software will cause them to have to search for another website as source, a time-consuming inconvenience. The practice of Baidu should be considered as harassment, in fact.

In the revision of the PRC AUCL in 2017, the Chinese legislator modified article 2 of the law so that acts which harm consumers' interests are also defined as unfair competition in parallel to those that harm market operators' interests. This is an important progress but with a limited effect in practice because, regarding the concrete types of unfair competitive practices, no new rules like those in EU UCPD have been adopted. However, in Article 12 of the new law concerning internet-related competition, it can be well noticed that *influencing consumers' choice* has been adopted as one criterion in evaluating unfair practice and a concrete example for the application of this criterion has been given: *misleading, deceiving or forcing consumers to modify, close or uninstall legal internet products or services of other operators*. But, compared to the blacklist and general definition of aggressive commercial practices under the EU UCPD, the scope of application of this provision in Chinese law is too narrow, and its aim is to protect the interests of competitors rather than those of consumers. That is quite different from what is provided for under the EU UCPD. Article 8 of the Directive provides that:

> A commercial practice shall be regarded as aggressive if, in its factual context, taking account of all its features and circumstances, by harassment, coercion, including the use of physical force, or undue influence, it significantly impairs

---

[58] 北京奇虎科技有限公司诉北京百度网讯科技有限公司等不正当竞争纠纷案，(2014)海民初字第6256号判决书。Haidian Court (Beijing) (2014) Hai Min Chu Zi No. 6256.

> or is likely to significantly impair the average consumer's freedom of choice or conduct with regard to the product and thereby causes him or is likely to cause him to take a transactional decision that he would not have taken.

According to Article 9, in determining whether a commercial practice uses harassment, coercion, including the use of physical force, or undue influence, account shall be taken of: (a) its timing, location, nature or persistence; (b) the use of threatening or abusive language or behavior; (c) the exploitation by the trader of any specific misfortune or circumstance of such gravity as to impair the consumer's judgement, of which the trader is aware, to influence the consumer's decision with regard to the product; (d) any onerous or disproportionate non-contractual barriers imposed by the trader where a consumer wishes to exercise rights under the contract, including rights to terminate a contract or to switch to another product or another trader; (e) any threat to take any action that cannot legally be taken.

These rules in EU law are sufficiently clear and complete to be operational. Further, in the blacklist of Annex I to the Directive, Point No. 26, the persistent making of unwanted solicitations by telephone, fax, e-mail, or other remote media except in circumstances and to the extent justified under national law to enforce a contractual obligation is clearly prohibited. The aim of this ban is to protect consumers against pestering by distance-marketing tools.

Nevertheless, regarding the Chinese unfair competition law and practice, we can still optimistically predict that, based on the experience acquired in the field of internet-related competition and guided by the new provision of Article 2 of the law, Chinese courts should be able to develop new case-laws regarding not only online competition, but also offline competition by taking consumers interests protection as a criterion of unfair practice in a general manner. In this regard, the Chinese legislator and courts can both learn from these EU laws regarding the definition of unfair practice and its application from the perspective of consumer protection.

V. CONCLUSION

The basic but fundamental rules on unfair competition adopted by the Paris Convention in the 1950s are still very important in the handling of unfair practice under national laws. Apart the Paris Convention, the most important development in international unfair competition law has been the recognition of consumer protection both as an objective of anti-unfair competition laws and as the basis for identifying whether a particular practice can be regarded as unfair. The EU UCPD and TPP mark this new trend in the harmonization of national laws.

The influence of foreign laws on the evolution of Chinese law takes place in three ways: legal theories introduced by scholars, legal rules referenced by legislators, and treaties adopted by the government. Among the three sources, treaties are the most important because legal theories help identify the direction and basis for the change and foreign legislations are just reference while treaties are binding. In light of the great variety of Internet-related competition practices that have emerged, Chinese legislators in the revision of the PRC AUCL and the Chinese courts in the related cases should, first, be guided by and make full use of the provisions in the Paris Convention in order to broaden the scope of application of the Chinese law; and secondly, introduce consumer protection as a new criterion for the determination of unfair practice. The adoption of mega-regional trade agreements such as the EU UCPD and TPP will surely push forward the harmonization of national laws on unfair competition. Soon, the legal research and practice regarding the new Chinese unfair competition law will surely bring about a better implementation of Article 10*bis* of the Paris Convention, which will, then later, contribute to a convergence among national laws for a further international harmonization at treaty level.

Index